The Impact
of
Physical Illness

THE IMPACT OF PHYSICAL ILLNESS

and Related Mental Health Concepts

Vickie A. Lambert, R.N., M.S.N.

Assistant Professor, Medical-Surgical Nursing
University of Pennsylvania, School of Nursing
Philadelphia, Pennsylvania

Clinton E. Lambert, Jr., R.N., M.S.N.

Lieutenant, Nurse Corps, U.S. Navy
Phase II Neuropsychiatric Instructor
Naval Regional Medical Center
Oakland, California

Prentice-Hall, Inc., Englewood Cliffs, N.J. 07632

Library of Congress Cataloging in Publication Data

LAMBERT, VICKIE A
The impact of physical illness and related
mental health concepts.

Includes bibliographies and index.
1. Nursing—Psychological aspects.   2. Sick—
Psychology.   I. Lambert, Clinton E., joint author.
II. Title.
RT86.L35   616'.001'9   78-14556
ISBN   0-13-451732-6 pbk.

Editorial/production supervision and interior design
        by Karen J. Clemments
Cover design by A Good Thing, Inc.
Manufacturing buyers: Harry Baisley and Cathie Lenard

Printed in the United States of America

10   9   8   7   6   5   4   3   2   1

PRENTICE-HALL INTERNATIONAL, INC., *London*
PRENTICE-HALL OF AUSTRALIA PTY. LIMITED, *Sydney*
PRENTICE-HALL OF CANADA, LTD., *Toronto*
PRENTICE-HALL OF INDIA PRIVATE LIMITED, *New Delhi*
PRENTICE-HALL OF JAPAN, INC., *Tokyo*
PRENTICE-HALL OF SOUTHEAST ASIA PTE. LTD., *Singapore*
WHITEHALL BOOKS LIMITED, *Wellington, New Zealand*

To our daughter,
Lexy

Alexandra Kristina Lambert

CONTENTS

PART II   Alterations in Body Structure

8 THE PATIENT WITH A BURN   *144*

PART III   *Alterations in Life-Sustaining Functions*

9 THE PATIENT WITH AN ALTERATION IN CARDIOVASCULAR FUNCTION   *170*

10 THE PATIENT WITH AN ALTERATION IN RESPIRATORY FUNCTION   *205*

11 THE PATIENT WITH AN ALTERATION IN METABOLIC FUNCTION   *228*

PREFACE

The need to look at a human as a biopsychosocial being, as a total entity, is becoming increasingly obvious to the members of the nursing profession. However, nursing literature has not always presented the holistic view, and, as a result, man's problems and needs tend to be treated in a compartmentalized manner. In contrast, this book demonstrates the incorporation of the principles of mental health care into aspects of the physical health care of an adult with a medical or surgical problem.

We have divided the book into three parts: Theoretical Concepts, Alterations in Body Structure, and Alterations in Life-Sustaining Functions. In the first part, three major theoretical concepts are discussed: sick role, body image, and loss. An understanding of these issues and their effects on the adult during the course of illness is vital because the concepts are applied to material in later chapters.

Parts II, Alterations in Body Structure, and III, Alterations in Life-Sustaining Functions, address themselves to certain health care situations encountered by adults. We have selected those situations which we feel are most often dealt with by the majority of the nursing population.

The text demonstrates how each of these situations can affect the afflicted person's total being in terms of the impact on the individual's emotional well-being, somatic identity, sexuality, occupational identity, and social role. Both the problems incurred as a result of the impacts and the methods of dealing with a given situation and its impacts are described. At the end of each chapter in Parts II and III, we have provided a hypothetical patient situation, with a corresponding nursing care plan and patient care cardex, to aid the reader in making a successful transition from the text to a real-life situation.

We hope that this book, with its integrated approach to health care, will serve as a helpful tool in assisting the student and the practitioner of nursing to identify illness-related impacts to understand why these impacts occur, and to plan, develop, and initiate appropriate and comprehensive health care interventions.

Vickie A. Lambert
Clinton E. Lambert, Jr.

ACKNOWLEDGEMENTS

We wish to express our appreciation to Jean Polen and to Mary Theresa McNamee for their assistance in the preparation of the manuscript.

NOTE

The opinions or assertations contained herein are the private views of the authors and are not to be construed as official or as reflecting the views of the Department of the Navy or the Department of Defense.

The Impact
of
Physical Illness

PART

I

Theoretical Concepts

1

SICK ROLE

INTRODUCTION

People are complex beings consisting of many parts. They are physiological, cultural, religious, and psychosocial. In order for them to be dealt with as holistic beings, nursing needs to become increasingly aware of how their many parts contribute to their optimal state of wellness. When individuals become ill or are undergoing diagnosis for altered states of health, their complex parts contribute to their reactions to illness. For example, how individuals react to their illnesses may depend upon their perceptions of themselves, their body images, and how they feel significant others and society view them and their illnesses. However, it must not be forgotten that various cultures and subcultures within our society place varying values on illness and wellness (Mead, 1955).

For some individuals, illness is more a way of life than wellness. The presence of illness often provides a vehicle for both primary and secondary gain. Recognition by the family that one is ill might represent a primary gain since the tension or conflict of thinking one is ill has been reduced (Freedman, Kaplan, and Sadock, 1975). The increased attention and deliverance of flowers and gifts might demonstrate a secondary gain (Luparello, 1974). Thus, illness often becomes a means toward an end for self-recognition.

In an attempt to achieve self-recognition in our complex and ever-changing society, one is constantly expected to assume a variety of roles. Role assumptions are necessary for survival in today's demanding world. Commonly accepted societal roles include breadwinner, family member, community leader, and spiritual advisor. One is even expected to take on a set role during the course of illness. In order for the professional nurse to provide in-depth care, the nurse needs to be cognizant of some of the fundamental concepts of this identified role of illness, the sick role. Individuals assume the sick role because they perceive themselves as helpless and identify the need for assistance in order to alleviate or modify their condition. The condition of illness on the health continuum is a deviation from the "normal" functioning state of the individual, which includes the physiological state, personal state, and social situation (Parsons, 1951). Consequently, illness is both physiological and psychosocial in nature.

SICK ROLE

Four aspects of the sick role have been described in the literature: (1) exemption from social responsibility; (2) inability to achieve wellness simply by decision or will; (3) obligation to seek wellness; and (4) responsibility to seek and cooperate with technically competent assistance.

The first component characterizes the individual as being exempt from his or her usual social responsibilities. The degree of exemption, however, is related to the nature and severity of the illness (Parsons, 1951). Examples of this might include the decrease or total release of accountability in carrying out family or job requirements. Illnesses that are familiar to the general public are more likely to be accepted as an exemption from responsibilities than are illnesses that are unfamiliar. This may be seen in the comparison of society's understanding of coronary disease versus diseases of the integumentary system. The advertising media has stressed the do's and don'ts of heart disease to such a degree that most individuals comprehend with little negative reaction some of the necessary restrictions of an individual who has coronary problems. An individual who has lesions on the skin, however, may not receive the same positive understanding about health care restrictions because society lacks knowledge about this particular problem. Before the exemption from social responsibility is complete, legitimization of the illness is necessary, and members of the health team serve as the major legitimatizing agents. Once a health team member has acknowledged the existence of a health problem, the existence of the illness is legitimatized for society. One of the most typical statements made concerning legitimization is, "Have you been to see a doctor?"

The second aspect of the sick role is the individual's incapability of achieving wellness by an act of decision or will. Illness then becomes a state of "no-fault" on the part of the individual. This second aspect of the sick role also implies an exemption from responsibility and the necessity of seeking assistance in order to alleviate or modify the condition. Identification of the fact that the individual has lost control of his or her situation is crucial in bridging the gap between the recognized illness and the acceptance of assistance (Parsons, 1951).

The third reaction of the individual toward the sick role is the obligation of wanting to be well. The state of illness is a negatively acquired role, and one is obliged to set such a deviated role into a positive state, the state of wellness (Parsons, 1951). Society tends to frown upon the individual who walks about in a state of illness and does not try to attain wellness. This is particularly true in the case of a communicable disease such as the common cold. The individual is obligated not to disseminate the illness to others and to seek a state of wellness.

The fourth and final phase of the sick role is closely related to the element of obligation to achieve wellness. This fourth aspect of the sick role requires the individual to obtain technically competent assistance and to cooperate with the administrator of that assistance in the process of achieving a state of wellness. It is at this point that the ill individual becomes a complementary component in the health team role structure (Parsons, 1951).

The definition of what constitutes a technically competent health care provider varies among cultures and subcultures within our society. Judgment of proper selection of assistance will be based upon these cultural definitions (Mead, 1955). The nurse must be competent in identifying these cultural differences in health care selection and must make available to the individual appropriate avenues of assistance.

In dealing with the individual in the state of illness, the seeking of assistance is simply one component of the fourth aspect of the sick role. In order for health care therapies to be successful, the patient must cooperate in the implementation of these therapies. It is most assuredly the role of the professional nurse to understand individual and cultural differences that may affect the patient's cooperation in the execution of optimal health care (Davitz, Sameshima, and Davitz, 1976). For example, a person of Italian ancestry has sought guidance in obtaining an appropriate diet for weight control. The person is given a diet that includes the necessary caloric restrictions. The patient notices that the diet greatly decreases the amount of pasta that can be consumed and finds this restriction difficult to accept because of the importance placed on pasta. Unless the person truly understands and accepts the necessity for this restriction, the person may fail to carry out the necessary decrease in caloric intake. Thus, the execution of optimal health care therapy is rendered unsuccessful.

The four aspects of the sick role (exemption from social responsibility; inability to achieve wellness, simply by decision or will; obligation to seek wellness; and responsibility to seek technically competent assistance and cooperation with this assistance) provide the patterns of behavior expected from the individual during the assimilation of the sick role. However, it must be understood that in achieving and accepting this role of illness, individuals often demonstrate a variety of coping behaviors. These protective coping behaviors serve the important function of relieving stress, protecting self-esteem, and assisting the individual in dealing with problems connected with the stress of illness (Evans, 1971). The manner and degree to which these coping behaviors are exercised may vary among individuals. Some individuals need few psychological mechanisms in dealing with illness, others require a host of mechanisms, and there are some who, even with the use of all of their adaptive mechanisms (Kolb, 1973), never come to accept the sick role.

As with all roles, the individual learns his or her individual sick role (Hall, 1975; Maxon, 1974). The nurse must determine where the individual stands in relation to his or her assimilation of the role of illness. Using this data, the nurse must decide the appropriate intervention. If the individual is having difficulty accepting the fact that health assistance is needed, the nurse may have to intervene and, with the patient, attempt to identify this fact. An individual may seek assistance, faithfully carry out health care instructions, and then suddenly stop all necessary health care therapies. In this case, the nurse may have to assist the patient in identifying the reason for the sudden cessation of therapy. The lack of desirable behavior may suggest that ambiguities exist in the health care situation, and these ambiguities are restricting the individual's awareness of what is expected (Vincent, 1975). Thus, it can be seen that individuals vary both in their ability to assume the sick role and in their ability to maintain the sick role.

The following discussion will deal with some of the behavioral manifestations that might be seen in individuals who are attempting to cope with their newly defined role of illness, the sick role.

BEHAVIORAL REACTIONS SEEN DURING DIAGNOSIS AND ILLNESS

Anxiety

Undoubtedly, the most commonly occurring behavioral reaction to illness and diagnosis is anxiety. Anxiety can be described as the uneasiness, apprehension, or dread that is associated with an unrecognizable source of anticipated danger. It differs from fear in that with fear an identifiable source of danger can be designated (Freedman, Kaplan, and Sadock, 1975). One can be afraid of dogs, crowds, elevators, or lightning; however, one may not be aware of why he fears illness. Anxiety is essentially a human experience that is ever present and has always been a part of our human existence. It is the result of conflicts and frustrations in our daily lives, and it is a lifelong partner that one can either use constructively or succumb to its destructive forces.

When assuming the sick role, individuals are not always capable of determining the source of danger in their lives; consequently, anxiety can occur. Illness is both physically and mentally taxing and unknowns are ever present. Questions that come to the mind of the ill individual may include: "Why do I feel this way?" "What is wrong with me?" "How do ill people act?" "Should I seek medical attention?"

The degree and duration of anxiety demonstrated by each individual vary. The nurse may identify the presence of an anxiety-provoking situation for the patient, such as an impending hospitalization, and notes that individuals of the same sex, age, and socioeconomic status will react entirely differently. Each individual's perception of the same anxiety-provoking situation produces entirely different individual responses. Each response depends upon past experiences, learning, and the degree of emotional maturation. The results of such unpleasant feelings can be manifested in a variety of both physical and mental states. The nurse may identify a quavering voice, increased perspiration, breathlessness, pacing, and hand wringing. The individual may note difficulty in concentrating and tend to lose track of the environment. These physiological and psychological manifestations are just a few of the human responses to anxiety (Maher, 1966).

The individual's level of anxiety must be identified before efficient and effective health care therapies can be successfully instituted. Mild to moderate degrees of anxiety can be an asset to successful adaptation in life. When one is moderately anxious, one is more aware of environmental surroundings and is more receptive to learning (Evans, 1971; Paplau, 1957). Such an aroused state can be conducive to patient learning (Mischel, 1971). The individual who is mildly anxious about learning the procedure of insulin injection is more likely to be attentive to details in aseptic technique than the individual who is apathetic or extremely anxious.

As the level of anxiety increases, however, one loses the capability to function efficiently over a period of time (Mischel, 1971). In most instances, one is unable to tolerate feelings of high anxiety for sustained periods of time and attempts are made to terminate the anxiety in any way possible. As anxiety increases, one's perceptual field is reduced. The overly anxious individual loses track of time, space, and the meaning of environmental events. Situations become distorted and simple happenings may be blown out of proportion (Sedgwick, 1975). For example, a patient may become verbally loud and abusive to the nurse because a drinking straw has been omitted from the dietary tray. Heightened anxiety may produce panic and the individual's attention is so scattered that goal-directed activity is impossible (Luckmann and Sorensen, 1974). At this time patient teaching may be totally ineffective. Both verbal and nonverbal communication is imperative. An attempt must be made to decrease the individual's anxiety and to avoid enhancing the anxiety-provoked state. During high degrees of anxiety individuals have difficulty comprehending the details of their environmental surroundings; therefore, communication should be brief and simple. When the nurse directs the spouse of the surgical patient to the family waiting room the morning of surgery, the nurse should give clear, concise, and uncomplicated directions. If the directions are too complex, most likely the spouse will not comprehend all of what is being said because of the level of anxiety caused by the fear of the unknown about the patient's surgery.

To summarize, anxiety is a universal reaction to illness that must be dealt with by both the patient and the nurse. The level of anxiety demonstrated is individualized and the manner in which it can be channeled varies from person to person. It must be realized that the existence of anxiety can be either an asset or a liability to the successful institution of health care therapies.

Denial

One of the ways in which an individual deals with a stress-producing situation, such as illness, is to deny the existence of the threat. Denial operates to allay anxiety by decreasing perception of the threat. The tendency of the individual to deny the existence or the seriousness of an illness is one example frequently seen by health care deliverers.

Denial is a behavior that indicates the failure to acknowledge either the existence of a known fact or its significance. Various steps are involved in the denying behavior. First, a reality situation exists and the individual either perceives or anticipates some component of the situation as a threat. Second, anxiety transpires in response to the perceived threat. Next, the individual either completely or partially disclaims the facts or their significance in the threat-producing situation. In the last step of the denying behavior, the individual ignores or rejects data connected with the threatening situation in an attempt to regain and maintain psychological equilibrium (Kiening, 1970a).

As one examines the behavior of denial, it can be seen that it merely minimizes the anxiety-producing components of reality that comprise the threat. The use of denial may act as a temporary protector of the ego by preventing the individual from becoming totally overcome by anxiety (Kiening, 1970a). However, an adult's frank denial of obvious reality over a long period of time may indicate a more serious mental health disturbance.

In dealing with the coping mechanism of denial, the nurse first must be capable of recognizing manifestations of this behavior. These manifestations may be either subtle or explicit. The individual may be the quiet "model" patient who never expresses doubt that his or her life-style has contributed to the recurrence of the ulcer. Or the individual may be obnoxiously verbal and refuse medications stating that there is nothing wrong.

After identifying the patient's usage of denial, the nurse determines the degree to which the denial hinders the individual's progress toward wellness. Is denial preventing the individual from seeking much needed health assistance or is it allowing the individual time to regain his or her composure in dealing with a shocking emotional experience? It is essential for the nurse to be aware that total realization and acceptance of an emotionally charged experience are never accomplished at once.

After the degree of denial is determined, the nurse attempts to understand the need that this behavioral reaction serves for the specific individual. Why is this individual using denial? Possibly the existence of the state of illness is threatening the feeling of security. Or the presence of illness may carry with it the anxiety of possible loss. (The reader is advised to consult Chapter 3.)

The nurse must make a professional decision on how to deal with an individual's behavior based upon the manifestations of denial, the degree to which denial is utilized, and the need that denial serves. It is essential for the nurse to keep in mind that ego support of the individual demands a high priority in nursing intervention. The mechanism of denial should not be attacked directly while it is providing ego support. The nurse should explore the means available to the individual that would serve to decrease the anxiety at this time and hence to decrease the need for denial. This may be typified by a new postoperative patient who blatantly refuses pain medication and verbally denies being in pain. However, the patient has just experienced very extensive surgery, has a markedly increased pulse rate, and is extremely restless. The nurse should not directly attack the patient's denial by abruptly saying, "Don't kid me, I know you are having pain!" An approach that will serve the patient in a more therapeutic manner is to point out that the patient appears restless and uncomfortable and the pain medication will relieve some of the discomfort. The nurse at this point has not supported the patient's denial of pain; yet the denial has not been directly attacked. In addition, the nurse needs to clarify further the situation by pointing out that discomfort after this type of surgery is common and that it is appropriate to request relief from discomfort. In most situations, additional data about health care therapies tend to alleviate anxiety because the data clarify the unknown. With a decrease in anxiety the need for the use of denial is also decreased.

Questioning

When illness occurs, individuals often review their lives in an attempt to find an answer to the reason or purpose for the illness. "Why me?" "What did I do to deserve this?" "Why am I so sick and you are so well?" Some individuals fail to find answers to these questions, while others find a variety of explanations. The individual may view the illness as punishment for a sin, the result of unhealthy living, or simply as part of life. Regardless of whether or not the individual finds answers to his or her questions, the occurrence of illness evokes anxiety. Since the individual has temporarily lost control of life, feelings of uneasiness and apprehension develop. These anxious feelings are often manifested by repeated questioning.

The nurse's responsibility is to supply reliable data to the patient about the illness and to provide support during periods of anxiety. Support can be furnished by allowing and encouraging the patient to do as much as possible. This demonstrates to the patient that he or she still has some control over life. In the hospital setting, if possible, the patient should be permitted to carry out personal hygiene and to take an active part in arranging the daily schedule. If the nurse works with the patient on the patient's daily plan of care, he or she identifies the nurse as an available means of support and an avenue by which to relieve anxiety. As such, the nurse serves as a sounding board and an information supplier. Although the nurse may be unable to supply answers to all questions, the fact that the patient is allowed to ask questions and seek answers allays some of the apprehension about the unknown. The patient feels that he or she has greater control of the surroundings and hence anxiety is decreased. In turn, the need for constant questioning usually diminishes.

Ambivalence

Another behavior that may occur during the course of sick role assimilation is ambivalence. Ambivalence can be described as the coexistence of opposing emotions, attitudes, and desires toward the same object or situation (Freedman, Kaplan, and Sadock, 1975). The individual often has opposing emotions and desires about whether or not seeking medical attention for the illness is in his or her best interest. Once health care assistance is sought, the individual may be ambivalent about whether or not medical advice should be followed. Both of these examples demonstrate that ambivalence can result from the frustration of making decisions about the newly imposed role of illness.

It is therapeutic for individuals to express both the negative and positive aspects of their feelings (Kemp, 1970). With the expression of such feelings, the individuals may need to be informed that the existence of ambivalent feelings about illness are not abnormal. Often just verbalizing opposing feelings enables individuals to find a more realistic approach to their problems. Some individuals may harbor ambivalent feelings about a health care situation, but they remain able to take appropriate action. The woman who after surgery feels reassured that her mastectomy may control her cancer but remains appalled by its mutilating effects demonstrates ambivalence. Thus, therapeutic nursing practice requires the realization that human existence takes into account the likelihood that where there is love there may also be some hate (Ginott, 1965).

Suspicion

Some individuals look upon their illness with suspicion and do not completely accept the possibility that their diagnosis may be true. Such individuals may be suspicious if their diagnosis is serious or if their diagnosis does not appear to be serious. Suspicion is imagining the existence of guilt, fault, or defect on the part of another with little or no evidence. Individuals demonstrating suspicion attempt to find possible reasons for mistrusting their diagnosis and question the motives of others over minute matters (Evans, 1971). The suspicious individual thinks that the health team members are incorrect or defective in their judgments about the illness. The nurse can detect the suspicious individual by such statements as: "What are you trying to do, kill me? This food isn't mine!" "You are lying to me. I'm not well. I'm a very sick man!" Some doubt concerning illness is reasonable, but suspicion can be blown out of proportion so that the individual mistrusts everything. When carried to extremes, suspicious behavior can develop into a neurotic or psychotic disorder (Arieti, 1974).

An individual who is suspicious is frightened and often feels the need to be constantly on guard or that he or she may be taken advantage of. Such an individual lacks a sense of trust in others. In some cases, the absence of trust makes the successful institution of health care therapies difficult, if not impossible. In dealing with the suspicious individual, it is imperative that the nurse answer the individual's questions truthfully because any attempt to give false information increases the degree and usage of suspicion in an attempt to alleviate anxiety.

Hostility

Perhaps one of the most difficult barriers for the nurse to deal with when working with others is hostility. All humans experience hostility at some time or another. This behavior may be but one way a patient reacts to the threatening and frustrating situation of illness. Hostility can be delineated as the feeling of antagonism accompanied by the desire to harm or disgrace others. These desires subsequently may produce feelings of inadequacy and self-rejection on the part of the individual and lead to the loss of self-esteem (Kiening, 1970b).

Hostility is exemplified in a variety of ways in which each individual's display of such behavior is affected by each one's unique background and the situation itself. The manifestations can range from *extreme* polite behavior to external forms of rage or homicide or internal forms of depression or suicide (Freedman, Kaplan, and Sadock, 1975). What is important is that the individual may be unaware of these hostile feelings and desires that control his or her actions. The world may be perceived as unfriendly, dangerous, and hostile. Terms that may be used to describe the behavior of hostile individuals are picky, argumentative, irritable, sarcastic, demanding, critical, and uncooperative. However, nurses must be careful not to label hastily an uncooperative patient as hostile. Some individuals may demonstrate uncooperative behavior because of healthy self-assertion which is part of the human process of experiencing individual rights. Individuals who assert themselves with justifiable reason may not conform to what the health team sees as expected patient behavior. These individuals are not necessarily hostile. Such an incident is demonstrated by the female patient who refuses to wear an open-back gown to X-ray because she feels that it overly exposes her body. She has not conformed to hospital regulation, but is not her noncompliance justifiable?

A patient who demonstrates hostility represents a barrier to the nurse's goal of assisting the patient. The patient poses a threat to the nurse's self-image as an authority figure since the nurse is unable to control the hostile behavior (Ujhely, 1976). Even though the patient's hostile behavior may be directed toward the nurse, such behavior ought not be taken as a personal threat. Immediate reactions of counterhostility toward the patient by the nurse may represent the nurse's own fear of impending threat. When the nurse is counterhostile, a vicious attack and counterattack cycle of hostility can develop between patient and nurse.

Awareness of personal hostile impulses and thoughts (and the mechanisms used in coping with them) is essential for the nurse. This awareness is necessary before the nurse can effectively intervene with the patient. When the nurse perceives behavior that appears to indicate impending hostility (e.g., increased motor activity, angry facial expressions, increased verbal abuse), it is essential to validate these observations with the patient. Leading validating statements may include: "You appear upset." "Something seems to be bothering you." These leading statements can guide the patient toward describing what is being experienced and the possible reasons for these feelings. Approval or disapproval of the patient's comments should not be shown by the nurse's personal reaction during the interview. It is imperative that the nurse avoid conveying value judgments while demonstrating concern about the patient's well-being. One of the major aspects of nursing intervention is to identify and possibly to alter the condition leading to the hostility while ensuring the maintenance of the patient's self-respect. The patient has to express anger, but limits have to be provided so that the patient realizes that destructive aggression, such as striking someone or throwing a drinking glass, is not acceptable. Socially acceptable outlets for feelings of hostility may have to be suggested or provided. Possible suggestions may include running, pounding a table with the fist, stomping the floor with the foot, hitting a punching bag, squeezing a rubber ball, playing the piano, or typing. If the patient is unable to carry out any of the above activities, vicarious participation in much-loved television sports such as boxing or wrestling may provide an alternate, yet effective, outlet.

To recapitulate, when dealing with the hostile individual the therapeutic tasks of the nurse include the following: validating the existence of the behavior; allowing verbalization of feelings; providing firm but supportive direction; supplying alternate means of hostile expression and, above all, assisting the patient in regaining and maintaining self-esteem.

Regression

It is anticipated that during illness individuals may regress and demonstrate behavior that is not so mature as that which they assume during times of wellness. Regression can be defined as a protective reaction involving a retreat to the use of behavioral patterns that were appropriate during earlier stages of development. During stressful situations, such as illness, behavior from earlier developmental stages may be reassuring. Such behavior is less complicated than the behavior developed to maintain security and self-esteem in adult living (Freedman, Kaplan, and Sadock, 1975). Regression is seen in a variety of forms, such as helplessness, nail biting, inability to wash or feed oneself, crying, withdrawing from responsibility, preoccupation with self, untidyness, total dependence, giddiness, stubborness, and an altered capacity for human relationships (Grosicki, 1972). When it is not extreme, regression during illness is a natural reaction and can facilitate recovery because it permits the patient to be more dependent than usual (Luckmann and Sorensen, 1974). For example, dependence in the form of bed rest can restore strength and hence assist in progress toward wellness. Therefore, patients must be allowed sufficient and appropriate regression and dependency upon others so that they may work toward recovery. Forms of regression and dependency that are encouraged by health personnel to facilitate the achievement of wellness are deemed legitimate. Legitimate forms of patient regression and dependency could include being fed during the acute phase following a myocardial infarction requiring assistance on the first day of ambulation after surgery, and requesting help in splinting an abdominal wound during coughing and deep breathing.

However, individuals demonstrating inappropriate degrees of regression, such as demanding assistance with hygiene and elimination needs when they are unnecessary, may need encouragement to achieve adaptation to stress by other means. Extreme degrees of regression are not conducive to the patient's achievement of optimal wellness and it is undesirable to foster such behavior.

Nurses have to recognize that regression is a function of the individual's relationship with his or her environment (Freedman, Kaplan, and Sadock, 1975). In other words, the nurse has to understand the purpose or use that the behavior serves the individual in dealing with the environment. Does the individual cause family members or members of the health team to respond to what he or she wants? Is the individual capable of controlling and manipulating others? Is the individual's behavior a means of obtaining "mothering" or "fathering" from family members or from the nurse?

Regardless of what nursing intervention is used, nursing actions are to be developed around the individual patient and the patient's need for the use of regression. For successful institution of health care therapy, it is imperative that a therapeutic nurse-patient relationship be established. Therefore, the patient is provided with the opportunity to contribute his or her thoughts, feelings, and desires into the planning of the treatment. To illustrate: Does Mr. Jones prefer IPPB (intermittent positive pressure breathing) before or after his morning hygiene needs are carried out? Does Miss Kay prefer her morning bath before breakfast or after physical therapy? The decision process involved in the above examples is assumed easily by the nurse, but the decision should *include* the individual patient. By the nurse's not "taking over" for the patient an atmosphere of custodial care is avoided; hence, the individual is encouraged to be more independent.

In the process of assisting the patient in developing a plan of care, the nurse should always begin at the patient's level of ability. The nurse should avoid loading the patient with responsibilities he or she is unable to accomplish, since this might increase frustration and lead to further regression. Such a case might involve expecting the patient to carry out the change of a colostomy bag after only one demonstration by the nurse. Once the patient has assumed more responsibility or has done something unusually well, the nurse should compliment the patient's achievements. Positive reinforcement for a job well done does a great deal of good for anyone's self-esteem.

It can be seen that some form of regression during illness is expected. But if the degree of regression hinders the achievement of optimal wellness, the nurse must intervene to assist the individual in coping with the stress of illness and to limit regression throughout the various phases of health therapy. Otherwise, successful achievement of wellness will be deterred.

Loneliness and Rejection

The presence of illness can bring with it the feelings of loneliness and rejection. Patients often feel entrapped by the illness and feel isolated in dealing with its problems. Individuals who have a communicable disease may sense that others reject them because of the nature of the illness, such as in the case of a socially unacceptable disease like syphilis. In the case of a long-term chronic illness, such as emphysema, friends and relatives may begin to take the illness for granted and proceed with their own lives. This state of affairs may be interpreted by the chronically ill individual as rejection by significant others. Once loneliness or rejection is felt, it is not uncommon to hear the patient say, "I know what will become of me and there is nothing I can do to change it!" Despondency sets in and the patient has a real need for attention and companionship during the illness.

If asked to describe inward feelings, the lonely and rejected individual may allude to a sensation of being cut off from others; a feeling that no one understands or cares; a feeling of being unloved; a feeling of being forgotten with no one to turn to; or a perception of being deserted by friends and relatives.

Feelings of loneliness and rejection are intensified at various times of the day. Patients often comment that night is the most lonely and unfriendly time. The nurse may note that complaints of pain are more frequent at night than during the day. This may be an unconscious attempt by the lonely individual to seek human contact (Robinson, 1968). Darkness automatically decreases human interaction because it is the expected time for the privacy of rest. Night also is the end of the day for everyone, except possibly for the ill individual who views it as a continuation of both the illness and the separation from family and friends. Hence, feelings of loneliness and rejection tend to increase. If feelings of loneliness and rejection are severe, alterations in sensory experiences may occur. (Further discussion on alterations in sensory experiences are covered in Chapter 15.)

Avoiding pretense is important when dealing with the patient's feelings of loneliness and rejection. If approached, the nurse should not hide the fact that he or she also has experienced fear, loneliness, pain, or feelings of rejection. These are all human emotions and everyone experiences them at one time or another. However, this does not mean that the nurse should proceed to unfold personal problems and life experiences to the patient. Instead, it is advisable to provide the patient with acknowledgment of the reality of these feelings. In other words, when the patient says that he or she feels lonely and rejected, these emotions need recognition. The nurse can achieve this by verbalizing that it is understandable that the patient experiences these feelings. As the patient progresses toward wellness these feelings will begin to subside.

Accepting the patient as he or she is is necessary if the nurse wishes to avoid a display of rejection. The affect utilized by the nurse can demonstrate acceptance or rejection of the patient. Facial expressions, voice intonations, and body language are means of conveying these feelings toward another individual (Fast, 1970). Facial expressions and loud voice intonations displaying disgust while standing at a distance of 2½ feet to 4 feet from the patient during a personal conversation can be interpreted as nonacceptance (Hall, 1966). Touch also plays an important part in displaying acceptance. A light touch on the arm, shoulder, or hand indicates the presence and the existence of actual human contact (Hein and Leavitt, 1977). To illustrate, human contact made during the patient's evening back rub provides a message of "caring" on the part of the nurse. Since patients verbalize that increased loneliness occurs at night, the human contact during the back rub prior to sleep may increase the patient's awareness of someone to turn to in time of need. The importance of touch should not be minimized. Nursing research has demonstrated that even certain physiological changes can be related to the act of therapeutic touch (Krieger, 1975).

In the hospital setting, frequent superficial trips past or into the patient's room should be avoided. Simply walking by the patient's room or stepping into the doorway does not necessarily display acceptance. The extended distance between patient and nurse and the brief superficial encounter do not lead themselves to increasing the patient's self-worth. It would be more therapeutic to spend three to five minutes twice a day at the bedside conversing with the patient about how the patient feels about the illness instead of checking on the patient from the doorway every hour. Until the patient can adapt to the stress of illness, the patient may continue to feel lonely and rejected. With personalized human contact on the part of the nurse, loneliness and rejection can be minimized.

Depression and Withdrawal

One commonly occurring reaction to illness is depression, a feeling of sadness and self-depreciation accompanied by difficulty in thinking, reduced vitality, and lowered functional activity. In depression there can be failure in the ability to carry out household tasks and job responsibilities. The individual's general mood is one of sorrow, and crying spells may occur without warning. Physically, the entire body appears to be slowed down or working improperly. Appetite is poor; sleep disturbances occur; constipation is not uncommon; libido decreases; and personal appearance fails to be maintained. A frequently occurring behavior of the depressed individual is preoccupation with his or her body (Evans, 1971). It is not unusual for the patient to be seen in the physician's office or at an outpatient clinic with the complaint that his or her body is malfunctioning in one way or another. Such preoccupations with body malfunction may be reflected in such a statement as, "I have these pains in my stomach. Lately my joints have been killing me and my bowels just aren't working right!" Our society has deemed social acceptability for one's concern of proper body function but little understanding to emotional instability. Thus, the feelings of depression are often vented through the physical functioning of the body.

In order to deal with depression, some individuals resort to withdrawal, the act of retreating or retiring away from someone or something. Manifestations of withdrawal might include sleeping a great deal, staying in one's room, avoiding people, sitting alone, and daydreaming. In the hospital setting, feigning sleep is an excellent way to withdraw in an attempt to avoid human contacts that may be stress producing (Long, 1974).

In dealing with depression and withdrawal, the nurse's first task is to recognize their existence. Since nurses spend more time with patients and family members than any other individual on the health care team, they are in an opportune position to note the presence of depression. The existence of depression is not always clear-cut, and sometimes professionals may mistake depression in older individuals for organic conditions, such as cerebral arteriosclerosis, since some manifestations are common to both conditions (Diebel, 1976). To facilitate recognizing depression and withdrawal, the nurse should note changes in the individual's usual behavior, for example, refusal to eat, neglecting body hygiene, and sudden cessation of normal daily activities. The depressed and withdrawn individual may need assistance in mobilization. Setting up a schedule with the patient for personal hygiene, grooming, and eating may be helpful in mobilizing the patient's energies.

Since body functions are generally decreased in depression, constipation can occur. To assist in the prevention of constipation, the individual should be offered foods such as fruits, which facilitate elimination. In addition, fluids between meals and a regular schedule of exercise are helpful. Exercise is also therapeutic for the depressed and withdrawn individual because it allows for the release of internalized hostility in a socially acceptable manner. Playing table tennis, hitting a punching bag, working on leather tooling, or simply taking a brisk walk are other ways of releasing internalized feelings.

The nurse's presence also plays a vital role in working with the depressed and withdrawn person. It is important for the nurse to encourage the individual to express verbally feelings both of anger and sadness. Since the depressed and withdrawn individual may not be extremely verbal, various techniques of interviewing may be required. To encourage the individual to start talking about these feelings, the use of open-ended statements may be necessary. The following statements may provide an opening for the depressed and withdrawn person to express his or her feelings: "You seem down today." "The day doesn't seem to be going well for you." "It must be upsetting to be here in the hospital with your family at home." The use of such open-ended statements also demonstrates that the nurse is sensitive to the individual's existing feelings.

Reflection is another interviewing technique that may be used. In reflection, the nurse restates in question form part of the patient's statement. The purpose of reflection is to clarify and initiate additional communication on the part of the patient. An example of reflection may be, *Patient:* "I'm really no good to the world." *Nurse:* "No good to the world?" Here the patient is provided with the cue to develop what he means by "no good." Additional feelings that the patient is experiencing may then be explored by both the patient and the nurse.

Summation, a third interviewing technique, may be used at the close of the nurse-patient interview. The nurse outlines or reiterates the basic issues that the patient has presented during the conversation. The nurse clarifies what has been said and seeks confirmation of what the patient believes has been expressed. Summation is important because it provides an opportunity to make sure that the patient and nurse are in agreement with what has occurred during their conversation. In addition, summation leaves the patient with the key points that have been verbalized and it plants a "seed" for further thought of what the patient is feeling.

The success of nursing interventions used in dealing with depressed and withdrawn individuals is best measured by the individual's ability to function in the individual's usual manner in carrying out daily activities. Examples of improvement may be a good night's sleep for the first time in months, carrying out some aspect of personal hygiene, or an increase in appetite. The nurse, however, must keep in mind that a patient going into or coming out of depression is more prone to attempt suicide (Beck, Resnick, and Letteri, 1974). Sudden changes in mood should be noted and the patient should be closely observed. This is not to say that all depressed patients attempt suicide, but the nurse must be aware of the possibility with severely depressed and withdrawn individuals. In some cases, psychotherapy may be available.

In summary, depression and withdrawal are not uncommon behavioral reactions to illness. The body's response to depression is one of general slowing down of all body processes with possible withdrawal from surroundings. The nurse's goal entails assisting the individual in examining his or her feelings and modifying how the individual perceives his or her relation to others.

SUMMARY

Assumption of the sick role is not a simple task and changes in usual patterns of daily living are required in order to take on fully the role of illness. Four such changes in usual patterns of daily living have been identified for the sick role: (1) exemption from social responsibility; (2) inability to achieve wellness simply by decision or will; (3) obligation to seek wellness; and (4) responsibility to seek and cooperate with technically competent assistance (Parsons, 1951).

Incorporating these changes into one's life does not always take place with ease, and often various behavioral reactions occur during the course of sick role assimilation. Some of the more common behavioral reactions occurring during diagnosis and illness include anxiety, denial, questioning, ambivalence, suspicion, hostility, regression, loneliness and rejection, and depression and withdrawal.

The nurse's role centers around identifying the existence of each behavioral reaction, assisting the individual in dealing with each behavior, and facilitating the individual's assimilation of the sick role. Without adequate sick role assimilation, successful health care therapies cannot be instituted and the individual will be unable to achieve an optimal state of wellness.

REFERENCES

Arieti, S. *Interpretation of schizophrenia*. New York: Basic Books, Inc., 1974.

Beck, A., Resnick, H., and Letteri, D. *The prediction of suicide*. Bowie, Maryland: The Charles Press Publishers, Inc., 1974.

Davitz, L., Sameshima, Y., and Davitz, J. Suffering as viewed in six different cultures, *American Journal of Nursing*, 1976, 76 (8), 1296-1297.

Diebel, A. Brief notes on brain syndrome in aging persons, *Journal of Psychiatric Nursing and Mental Health Services*, 1976, 14 (8), 51-52.

Evans, F. *Psychosocial nursing: theory and practice in hospital and community mental health*. New York; The Macmillan Co., 1971.

Fast, J. *Body language*. New York: Pocket Books, 1970.

Freedman, A., Kaplan, H., and Sadock, B. *Comprehensive textbook of psychiatry-II-Volume I*. Baltimore: The Williams & Wilkins Co., 1975.

Ginott, H. *Between parent and child*. New York: The Macmillan Co., 1965.

Grosicki, J. (Ed.) *Nursing action guides* (Program Guide: Nursing Service, Veterans Administration, No. G-10; M-2, Part V). Washington, D.C.: United States Government Printing Office, 1972.

Hall, B. Socializing hospitalized patients into the psychiatric sick role, *Perspectives in Psychiatric Care*, 1975, 13 (3), 123-129.

Hall, E. *The hidden dimension*. Garden City: Doubleday and Co., Inc., 1966.

Hein, E., and Leavitt, M. Providing emotional support to patients. *Nursing '77*, 1977, 7 (5), 38-41.

Kemp, R. Ambivalence. In C. Carlson (Ed.), *Behavioral concepts and nursing intervention*. Philadelphia: J. B. Lippincott, 1970.

Kiening, Sister M. M. Denial of illness. In C. Carlson (Ed.), *Behavioral concepts and nursing intervention*. Philadelphia: J. B. Lippincott Co., 1970a.

Kiening, Sister M. M. Hostility. In C. Carlson (Ed.), *Behavioral concepts and nursing interventions*. Philadelphia: J. B. Lippincott, 1970b.

Kolb, L. *Modern clinical psychiatry*. Philadelphia: W. B. Saunders, 1973.

Krieger, D. Therapeutic touch: the imprimatur of nursing, *American Journal of Nursing*, 1975, 75 (5), 784-787.

Long, E. How to survive hospitalization, *American Journal of Nursing*, 1974, 74 (3), 486-488.

Luckmann, J., and Sorensen, R. *Medical-surgical nursing: a psychophysiologic approach*. Philadelphia: W. B. Saunders, 1974.

Luparello, R. Chronic illness, conflict and the self: part II—for some, illness pays, *Medical Insight*, 1974, 6, 12-17.

Maher, B. *Principles of psychotherapy: an experimental approach*. New York: McGraw-Hill Book Company, 1966.

Maxon, K. Assuming the patient role, *Perspectives in Psychiatric Care*, 1975, 13 (3), 119-122.

Mead, M. (Ed.), *Cultural patterns and technical change*. New York: The New American Library, 1955.

Mischel, W. *Introduction to personality*. New York: Holt, Rinehart & Winston, Inc., 1971.

Parsons, T. *The social system*. New York: The Free Press, 1951.

Peplau, H. Experimental teaching, *American Journal of Nursing*, 1957, *57* (7), 884-886.

Robinson, L. *Psychological aspects of the care of hospitalized patients*. Philadelphia: F. A. Davis Co., 1968.

Sedgwick, R. Psychological responses to stress, *Journal of Psychiatric Nursing and Mental Health Services*, 1975, *13* (5), 20-23.

Ujhely, G. Two types of problem patients and how to deal with them, *Nursing '76*, 1976, *6* (5), 64-67.

Vincent, P. The sick role in patient care, *American Journal of Nursing*, 1975, *75* (7), 1172-1173.

2

BODY IMAGE

INTRODUCTION

The concept of body image has its roots in history. Its historical basis, however, cannot be traced, for in reviewing the literature, one finds the concept of body image applied in many diverse disciplines. Some of the disciplines influenced by the body image concept include neurology, psychiatry, hypnology, and psychosomatology (Fisher and Cleveland, 1968). Now nursing can be added to this list of disciplines, for the concept of body image has great relevance for comprehensive patient care.

If one attempted to find one definition of the concept of body image, one would find that an incomparable number of definitions exist. For example, Schilder (1950) describes the body image as the picture or schema of one's own body formed in one's mind as a tridimensional unity involving interpersonal, environmental, and temporal factors. Body image, as delineated by Jourard (1963), is the perceptions, beliefs, and knowledge an individual holds in regard to his or her body's structure, function, appearance, and limits. Fisher and Cleveland (1968) find the concept of body image too difficult to consolidate or methodize. Shontz (1974) tends to agree with the beliefs of Fisher and Cleveland (1968) by stating that the body image concept has lost its abstraction and has become a "thing" because such diverse definitions exist.

For the purpose of simplicity in dealing with such a complex and incommensurable concept, the authors of this book have chosen to describe the body image concept as the mental picture one uses to identify oneself as

21

being unique and different from everyone else. The view of being unique and different from others includes not only one's concept of one's physical structure, but it also includes one's concept of personal space.

Space, the area around us, is where our physical body boundaries end and some other object or person begins. Pluckhan (1968) refers to personal space as a nonentity that conveys meaning. This personal territory has meaning to the individual and conveys a message to those around the individual. We tend to stand close to friends and keep our distance from strangers. For example, note the reshuffling of people in an elevator when someone gets off the elevator and makes more room for the continuing passengers. The automatic reaction is to back away.

Hall (1966) has identified four distinct zones of space in which most people operate. He classifies these zones as (1) intimate distance, (2) personal distance, (3) social distance, and (4) public distance. As the terms imply, the zones are different areas in which we move, areas that either increase or decrease intimacy.

Intimate distance ranges from actual body contact up to 18 inches from the body. The close phase of intimate distance (body contact) is for making love, for very close friendships, and for children clinging to parents or to each other. A close intimate distance makes one overwhelmingly aware of the other individual. It is the most private zone of personal space. The far intimate phase ranges from 6 to 18 inches from the body. It is close enough for the clasping of hands, but the head, thighs, and pelvis are not easily placed in contact. The use of this distance in public is not considered appropriate by many adult, middle-class Americans (Hall, 1966).

Personal distance, the second zone of territory, ranges from a close distance of 1½ feet to 2½ feet to a far distance of 2½ feet to 4 feet. The close phase of personal distance allows one to hold or grasp the other individual's hand. This distance is frequently used between husband and wife. The far phase of personal distance lends a certain privacy to any encounter. The distance is close enough for personal discussion, yet one is unable to touch comfortably the other person. Hall (1966) refers to this distance as the limit of physical domination.

The third distinct zone, social distance, extends from a close distance of 4 feet to 7 feet to a far distance of 7 feet to 12 feet. Impersonal business is usually done at the close range. One usually assumes this distance at casual social gatherings. However, this distance also can be a manipulative distance, for it reminds the other individual of one's dominance (boss versus secretary). The far phase of social distance is more for formal social and business relationships. The husband and wife often assume this distance at home in the evenings while relaxing during conversation. This phase of social distance is almost a necessity in large families residing in the same household (Fast, 1971; Hall, 1966).

The fourth and final zone is public distance. Public distance is from 12 feet to 25 feet or more and is the farthest extension of our territorial bondage. The close phase of public distance ranges from 12 feet to 25 feet and is the most desirable range for informal gatherings, such as a teacher addressing a group of students. The far phase of public distance is any distance greater than 25 feet and is reserved for politicians and actors where space provides safety and security. This far distance makes it easier to hide the truth about motions of body language. It is a maneuver long used by stage actors.

In reviewing Hall's four distinct zones of space, one can see the relevance personal space can play in dealing with adult patients. For example, the nurse's invading the intimate zone of a patient while doing a dressing change may be interpreted by the patient as an extreme threat to privacy. The male patient may view the male nurse as invading his wife's personal zone if the nurse is standing too close to her while instructing her on her husband's home care. Needless to say, personal territory has multiple ramifications for patient care.

In order for the professional nurse to identify an appropriate role in dealing with patients who are experiencing alterations in physical structure and in personal space, the nurse must have a basic understanding of how an individual develops his or her body image. Erik Erikson's (1963) stages of personality development will be used as a framework for discussing an individual's body image development from birth through senescence.

DEVELOPMENT OF ONE'S BODY IMAGE

Trust Versus Mistrust
(Oral-Sensory Stage)

The first stage of development, the oral-sensory stage, occurs during the first year of life. It is during this developmental stage that the infant acquires a basic sense of trust. As the name of the stage implies, oral-sensory, the mouth is the predominant zone. The infant meets basic needs by way of the mouth. For these basic needs the infant is totally dependent upon the mother. The quality of care that the mother transmits to the infant in meeting the infant's basic needs will determine the infant's feeling of trust. The infant will either develop a sense of trust that the basic needs will be met or will feel that most of what is needed will be lost. The development of a sense of trust becomes the foundation for a healthy personality (Erikson, 1963).

At birth infants have no concept of physical body image except at the feeling level, for example, hunger, thirst, pain, comfort, and rage (Blaesing and Brockhaus, 1972). Infants have little knowledge about their bodies and relate to their body parts as though they were strange environmental objects. Throughout the first year of life the infant progressively acquires some degree of visual, tactile, and motor coordination that allows exploration of the body to a greater extent and allows the infant to bring objects to the mouth more easily (Kolb, 1973). For example, the infant gazes at his or her clenched fist as though it were a toy. The infant chews his or her fingers and toes and bangs the head in rage. However, the center of the child's body image remains the oral zone (Erikson, 1963).

As the infant reaches the end of the first year, the interest in observing the body has somewhat diminished. The infant becomes aware of the fact that his or her body is separate from mother's body and from those of others. This nuclear body image structure forms the basis of the individual's later personality and, to a great extent, the ability to cope with the stresses of illness, trauma, and physical change (Kolb, 1973).

Autonomy Versus Shame and Doubt (Muscular-Anal Stage)

The second developmental stage, the muscular-anal stage occurs in the second and third years of life. It is during this developmental stage that muscular maturation evolves. The child learns to walk, to eat, to communicate verbally, and to control anal sphincter muscles. With this increased muscular maturation comes the choice of two social modes: that of holding on or letting go. The child begins to attach tremendous value to autonomous will (Erikson, 1963).

It is during this second stage of development that parental figures become the most significant individuals to the child. The parents' approval or disapproval of the child's behavior and physical features impart an unforgettable impression on the child's self-concept. If the parents encourage the child to depend upon his or her own abilities and provide consistent and realistic support, the child will gain confidence in his or her own autonomy. Children who have been accepted by their parents usually do not underrate or overrate their body structures or functions (Blaesing and Brockhaus, 1972). However, if the parental figures are not accepting of the child's behavior or physical features, the child, according to Erikson (1963), will feel that his or her actions and body do not measure up to the expectations of others. For example, if the child is made to believe that his or her feces are bad and if the child is overrestrained, the child feels enraged at his or her incapabilities and there is danger of the development of shame and doubt. The child begins to expect defeat, in any venture, with those who are bigger and stronger.

The two- or three-year old child has a continuously changing body image because of rapidly changing motor activities. The child frequently has difficulties with definite body boundaries. The child may resist when the parental figure attempts to flush the feces away. The child may also be apprehensive when an adult attempts to cut the hair or nails. The child sees the feces, hair and nails as an extension of himself or herself. During this stage of motor and environmental mastery the child learns to relate to the world. If environmental mastery is not achieved, the child experiences feelings of helplessness, inadequacy, doubt, and shame (Erikson, 1963).

Initiative Versus Guilt
(Locomotor-Genital Stage)

The locomotor-genital stage, the third stage of development, begins at three years of age and ends at approximately the sixth year. The critical developments that take place during this period include: (1) start of sex typing and emergence of sexual curiosity, (2) identification with parental models, (3) rapid development of language and intellectual capacities, and (4) increased psychomotor skills (Blaesing and Brockhaus, 1972).

Sex typing and gender identification are the two primary tasks of this developmental stage. It is during this period of development that the parents impose their attitudes upon the child about the appropriate behavior for femaleness and maleness. It has been the general trend of our culture to deem muscular build, physical aggression, proficiency in athletics, and independence as desirable traits for males. Conversely, desirable female traits have been identified as neatness, politeness, social poise, inhibition of physical aggression, and dependency (Blaesing and Brockhaus, 1972). It must be recognized that social trends are changing and one can observe an intermingling of these male and female traits. For example, it is not uncommon to see girls playing on boy's baseball teams or to see girls setting up their own hockey and football teams. Traditionally, parental expectations and stigmas have been attached to the biological appearance of their offspring. In today's society with the ever growing recognition of the rights of sexually liberated persons, the identification of various activities and physical appearance with a particular sex has diminished. It is speculated that in the future there will be even less significance attached to maleness and femaleness during this developmental stage.

Because of the rapid growth of the child's language skills, intellectual capacities, and psychomotor abilities, the child becomes avidly curious about himself or herself. The "I" component of the personality becomes stronger. The child's curiosity and increase in hand coordination direct attention to the pleasurable sensation of touching and manipulating the genital area. According to Kaplan (1974), boys demonstrate an interest in manipulating their genitals as soon as hand coordination permits. During this developmental stage most children take part in some form of modified masturbation. Parental attitudes toward the child's masturbation is an important determinant of later sexual attitudes. If the parent attaches punishment to sexual curiosity and masturbation, the child may feel anxiety and guilt. The child's genitals become the focus of conflict which may result in a body image distortion of the genital region (Erikson, 1963).

Industry Versus Inferiority
(Stage of Latency)

From the ages of six to eleven years the child enters the fourth developmental stage, the stage of latency. It is during this developmental stage that the child develops the basic skills of technology. The child is in constant need to learn how to do things and how to make things for others. The child is developing skills in the use of adult materials while he or she waits, learns, and practices to be a provider. It is at this time that the child tries out new skills with his or her peer group.

The school becomes a way of life, whether the school be a formal classroom or a jungle. Since the school situation provides a less protective environment than home, for the first time the child may realize that he or she cannot perform as well as others. For example, the child may notice that his or her speech is not as clear as that of other children. The child may then feel inferior to peers. The presence of a physical alteration, such as defective vision or hearing, plays an important part in the schoolage child's body image concept (Blaesing and Brockhaus, 1972). Because of the presence of corrective lenses or hearing devices, the child may be led to feel inadequate or inferior to others. Inferiority and inadequacy are the greatest dangers during this stage of development and tend to occur more likely if the child does not receive recognition for his or her efforts (Erikson, 1963).

During approximately the tenth and eleventh years the child undergoes sudden body changes as the result of rapid growth, with females physically outgrowing males. During these natural increases in body changes the child becomes more self-conscious and focuses on his or her body and the bodies of others. The child may be particularly aware of his or her height and is very concerned about how he or she looks to others.

Identity Versus Role Confusion
(Stage of Puberty and Adolescence)

The fifth stage of development, adolescence, takes place during the eleventh to eighteenth years of life. It is during this period that childhood proper ends and youth begins. Erikson (1963) has referred to this developmental stage as a "moratorium, a psychosocial stage between childhood and adulthood, and between the morality learned by the child, and the ethics to be developed by the adult" (p. 263). The adolescent is faced with the task of opting for a career that receives parental consent or choosing one of his own. This indecision and perplexity in securing an occupational identity can lead to role confusion. In order for the adolescent to cope with such perplexities, he or she temporarily overidentifies with the leaders of cliques and crowds (Erikson, 1963). This overidentification can lead to a point of complete identity loss. The adolescent also tends to be "chummy," often to the point of ostracizing those who are different in manner of dress, cultural background, and/or financial status (Sullivan, 1953). However, the adolescent generally fears a negative identity and attempts to become what his or her parents and community members desire.

During this time rapid body growth and sexual maturity occur. Males become taller than females. The period of final growth occurs during late adolescence and this "last chance" for stature may carry special meaning for some adolescents (Dempsey, 1972). Body fat distribution, as well as height, plays a vital role in how adolescents view themselves. Females, especially when they are taller, tend to be heavier than males of the same age. The location of the body fat is probably the more important aspect because females and males are becoming more conscious of their body contours. The adolescent female body takes on a rounded feminine form while the adolescent male body assumes a muscular, masculine appearance. The adolescent sees the body as something that is useful and allows him or her to engage in activities. The success with which adolescents can utilize their bodies is important since it contributes to the value they place upon themselves.

Another important aspect of physical maturation during the stage of adolescence is the development of sex organs and the appearance of secondary sex characteristics. Since the scrotum and penis are external, adolescent males often compare sex organ size with their peers. Since females are unable to see their ovaries, they pay more attention to the menstrual cycle than to the existence of the ovaries themselves. This significance can be seen by the varied gynecological problems and complaints demonstrated during this developmental process. In addition, if social practices, such as calling the menstrual cycle "the curse are used, the female's concept of womanhood may suffer further destruction (Brown, 1972).

Secondary sex characteristics play a vital role in the adolescent's concept of his or her body image since they are more observable to others than the development of sexual organs. The quantity of development of secondary sex characteristics varies between adolescents. Some of the more valued characteristics in the female are development of breasts and pubic hair. The adolescent female often attempts to draw attention to her newly identifiable mark of femininity, her increased breast size. In the males the development of facial and body hair and voice changes are coveted signs of masculinity.

Intimacy Versus Isolation
(Stage of Young Adulthood)

Young adulthood, the sixth stage of development, begins at the eighteenth year and terminates approximately at forty-five years of age. This period of development continues to be a time of change, even though the biological aspects of adolescence are completed and a sense of identity should have been formulated. The young adult is ready and willing to merge his or her identity with that of others. It is during this period that the individual either shares himself or herself with others, both in friendship and a mutually satisfying sexual relationship, or because of the fear of losing individual identity, develops a sense of isolation (Erikson, 1963). If successful negotiation has occurred in previous stages of development, the young adult is able to accept his or her body without unnecessary preoccupation with its functions. The acceptance of one's body image plays a major role in one's ability to relate to others. In summary, an individual who successfully integrates his or her body image is more capable of developing meaningful and satisfying interpersonal relationships.

In Western society a greal deal of emphasis is placed upon the attractiveness of one's body (Woods, 1975). According to Cleveland and Morton (1962), the attitudes one has about oneself are influenced by one's physical appearance and ability. Research has demonstrated that members of society equate certain behavior with specific body builds. A person of "stocky" build is described as being lazy, less strong, good-natured, and trusting; an individual of muscular build is characterized as being strong, adventuresome, mature, and self-reliant; and an individual of slender build is rated as being tense, stubborn, pessimistic, and quiet (Well and Siegel, 1961). Even a difference in body image exists between the sexes. According to Fisher (1964), the female develops a more clearly defined and articulate concept of her body image than does the male. Therefore, the female's body awareness involves more defined boundary regions (high-barrier person) (Fisher, 1964). In addition, the female tends to devote more attention to her body than does the male and her feminine role tends to be more specifically identified with her body and its functions. The male's role is more likely to be defined in terms of achievement rather than bodily attributes. Since the female has more clearly defined body boundaries, she has a greater tendency to show reaction to boundary regions, such as the skin and muscle. The male, on the other hand, with a less defined body boundary (low-barrier person), when under stress, will experience an internal physiologic response, such as problems of the cardiac and gastrointestinal systems (Fisher, 1964).

In addition, Fisher and Cleveland (1968) found that individuals who have a firm body image and body boundary are more likely to be independent, goal-oriented, and influential group members. Conversely, individuals who have a poorly integrated body image and ill-defined body boundary are more likely to be passive, less influential in groups, and less achievement oriented. Such findings are of great importance to the professional nurse when dealing with ill adults.

In retrospect, we have seen that during the individual's life span large shifts in body image boundary occur. The infant has hazy boundaries and his or her more meaningful body experiences center around the mouth and stomach (Fisher and Cleveland, 1968). As the child develops, the boundaries approach the surface of the body wall; however, areas of intense contact with the world (mouth, anus) might reach the body wall earlier than the other body parts. Consequently, the child may perceive his or her contour to be highly irregular. Finally, the adult reaches the maximum regular contour consistent with the body wall (Fisher and Cleveland, 1968).

Generativity Versus Stagnation
(Stage of Adulthood)

The seventh developmental stage, adulthood, occurs approximately between the forty-fifth and sixty-fifth year. It is a stage that spans the middle years of life. It is during this period in one's life that a vital interest outside the home is founded. The major focus of one's interest is directed toward establishing and guiding future generations with an optimistic hope of bettering society. It must be kept in mind that being a biological parent does not make one inherently generative. It is an individual accomplishment and the unmarried or childless person is capable of being generative in his or her own right.

The middle-aged adult who feels that he or she has failed to accomplish his or her life-long goals may undergo a middle-aged crisis (Peplau, 1975) and feel incapable of being generative. As a result, the individual may become engulfed in satisfying personal needs and acquiring self-comforts because the individual feels that it is his or her last chance to succeed in life. The outcome is a sense of interpersonal impoverishment resulting from a state of self-absorption and stagnation (Erikson, 1963).

The fear of old age may be another concern of the middle-aged person. This fear can lead to inappropriate youthful behavior or dress (Murray, 1972). Ponytails, heavy eye makeup, and short shorts may be seen on some middle-aged females. Males, on the other hand, may wear necklaces and extremely "mod" clothing. The individual is unable to admit the existence of normal physical changes that are occurring, even though these changes are apparent to others (Murray, 1972). Conversely, the middle-aged adult may resign himself or herself to old age. The individual often identifies, in an exaggerated manner, every single physical change that occurs. Chronic defeatism and depression may result and the person may isolate himself or herself in self-pity. This middle-aged adult is likely to retire to the "rocking chair" prematurely.

Ego Integrity Versus Despair
(Stage of Maturity)

The eighth and final stage of development, the stage of maturity, occurs from sixty-five years of age and over. During this period the frequent thought of death and the concern about not being capable of caring for an ailing significant other become eminent. As a result, the mature adult may develop feelings of despair that are manifested by disgust. If the mature adult has developed a strong sense of self-worth and is able to place value on his or her past life experiences, feelings of despair will be overcome (Erikson, 1963). Strength is derived from satisfaction in one's life's experiences and accomplishments, the acceptance of triumphs and disappointments of the past.

Throughout life physiological changes are taking place, but when older individuals view themselves, they may find wrinkles and pigment changes in the skin, gray sparse hair, eyeglasses and hearing aids, dentures, enlarged knuckles, decreased taste sensations, body contour changes, and weight loss. With these internal and external changes mature adults may experience alterations in body-image boundaries and retreat their body boundaries to more internal sites (Fisher and Cleveland, 1968). An example of boundary retreat might be a constant fixation on bowel function, a manifestation often seen in the elderly. However, as with all the developmental stages, how mature adults view themselves is affected by how they feel others see them. The nurse's role in fostering a stable self-image in the elderly individual involves reassuring the individual that he or she continues to have something to offer others, whether it be a knowledge about making flies for trout fishing or the ability to read the paper or a book to another person.

SUMMARY

In reviewing the developmental stages of the body image, it can be seen that the individual's body image concept undergoes many changes. The infant starts with a hazy body boundary and the focus of his or her body image is the mouth. The child progresses to an image of distorted contours resulting from the difficulty in separating such items as feces and hair from the body proper, focuses on the genital regions, and finally develops gender identity. The adult develops a realistic contour consistent with his or her physical body wall and is able to accept the body without unnecessary preoccupation with its functions. The elderly invididual ends with a body image that retreats toward the interior of the body structure and may be preoccupied with certain body functions.

All these basic concepts are important when developing individualized patient care. The nurse must not only understand the normal developmental processes of the body image, but the nurse must also be aware of what developmental state the patient is exemplifying at any given time. To apply these basic concepts of body image, specific patient care problems dealing with alterations in body image will be presented in subsequent chapters.

REFERENCES

Blaesing, S., and Brockhaus, J. The development of body image in the child, *Nursing Clinics of North America*, 1972, 7 (4), 597-607.

Brown, F. Sexual problems of the adolescent girl, *Pediatric Clinics of North America*, 1972, *19*, 759-764.

Cleveland, S., and Morton, R. Group behavior and body image, *Human Relations*, 1962, *15*, 77-85.

Dempsey, N. O. The development of body image in the adolescent, *Nursing Clinic of North America*, 1972, 7 (4), 609-615.

Erikson, E. *Childhood and society*. New York: W. W. Norton and Co., 1963.

Fast, J. *Body language*. New York: Pocket Books, 1971.

Fisher, S. Sex differences in body perception, *Psychological Monographs*, 1964, *78*, 1-22.

Fisher, S., and Cleveland, S. *Body image and personality*. New York: Dover Publications, Inc., 1968.

Hall, E. T. *The hidden dimension*. Garden City: Doubleday and Co., Inc., 1966.

Jourard, S. M. *Personal adjustment: an approach through the study of healthy personality*. New York: Macmillan Publishing Company, 1963.

Kaplan, H. S. *The new sex therapy: active treatment of sexual dysfunction*. New York: Brunner-Mazel Publishers, 1974.

Kolb, L. *Modern clinical psychiatry*. Philadelphia: W. B. Saunders Co., 1973.

Murray, R. L. Body image development in adulthood, *Nursing Clinics of North America*, 1972, 7 (4), 617-630.

Peplau, H. Mid-life crisis, *American Journal of Nursing*, 1975, *75* (10), 1761-1765.

Pluckhan, M. L. Space: the silent language, *Nursing Forum*, 1968, 7 (4), 386-397.

Schilder, P. *The image and appearance of the human body*. New York: International Universities Press, Inc., 1950.

Shontz, F. C. Body image and its disorders, *International Journal of Psychiatry in Medicine*, 1974, 5 (4), 461-471.

Sullivan, H. S. *Interpersonal theory of psychiatry*. New York: W. W. Norton, 1953.

Well, W., and Siegel, B. Stereotyped somatotypes, *Psychological Reports*, 1961, *8*, 77-78.

Woods, N. F. *Human sexuality in health and illness*. St. Louis: The C. V. Mosby Co., 1975.

3

LOSS

INTRODUCTION

Loss is a fundamental human experience that spans the entire life continuum. No one can escape the experience of loss since it is ever present and ever occurring. An individual first encounters loss when he or she is expelled from the comforts of the mother's womb and continues to experience loss in many other forms throughout the life cycle. Loss of hearing, loss of mobility, loss of life-long friends and associates, and even loss of wellness are but a few examples of the losses experienced.

Members of the health care team face loss on a daily basis and must continually deal with the diverse reactions experienced by individuals to the various forms of loss. Nurses are confronted with the responsibility of contending with the loss itself, supporting the patient and the family's reaction to the loss and dealing with the responses to loss expressed by fellow health team members. Although each individual has created his or her own means of coping with loss, the concept of loss has been neglected in many health care curriculums because the major focus of concern deals with preservation and maintenance of life. Since the inability to maintain and preserve life may carry with it the act of personal failure, by and large, loss is ignored (Schoenberg, 1970).

FORMS OF LOSS

By definition, loss is a condition whereby an individual experiences deprivation of, or complete lack of, something that was previously present. Loss may be sudden or gradual, predictable or unexpected, traumatic or temperate. However, the manner in which each individual views the loss depends upon past experiences with loss, the value placed upon the lost object, and the cultural, psychosocial, economic, and family supports available for dealing with the loss. Loss of a significant other, loss of some part of one's physio-psychosocial well-being, and loss of one's personal possessions are three forms of loss seen in adult life.

Loss of a significant other

No doubt the most intense loss is the loss of a significant individual (Pretz, 1970a). Such a loss may occur by way of death, divorce, or separation. The loss may be permanent or temporary or complete or partial in character.

Loss by death is a permanent and complete loss that one experiences as the finale of the life of friends, associates, and loved ones. Never again can one make personal contact with the deceased. Whether death be sudden, as with some myocardial infarctions, or gradual, as with various forms of cancer, the impact of loss is traumatic to the individual who is experiencing the loss. Such a traumatic experience requires recognition on the part of the nurse. A crisis situation and nursing intervention should be initiated at this time in order to help the person cope with the loss.

Divorce implies a permanent loss, but it may be complete or partial in character. It is permanent in that both parties are no longer legally or emotionally committed to each other. Complete loss in divorce occurs when the husband and wife go their separate ways without ever seeing or requiring monetary or legal contact with each other. Partial loss occurs when the individuals are required to meet and/or either monetarily or legally contact each other because of visitation rights of children, alimony, child support payments, or property settlements and agreements.

Divorce may be the initial crisis that brings the patient to the health care clinic, as in the case of a situational adjustment reaction or may be the precipitating factor that leads to a physiological change, such as ulcer formation. Possibly the divorce is occurring simultaneously with other health care problems. Regardless of its relationship to existing health care problems, divorce is becoming an ever increasing form of loss and the psychodynamics of divorce must be taken into account by the nurse when caring for individuals experiencing such a loss (Lambert and Lambert, 1977).

Everyone contends with some form of separation, the third type of loss of a significant other, during his or her lifetime. Separation can be the result of numerous situational or functional states, such as war, work, travel, hospitalization, imprisonment, or estrangement. Loss created by separation is temporary and either complete or partial in character. It is temporary in that an individual has parted or withdrawn from another's company or presence for the time being; however, the possibility and potentiality for seeing or being with the other person does exist. Complete separation can occur in the case of war, imprisonment, or estrangement when no form of personal contact is made by means of letter, telephone calls, or any other forms of communication. Loss by separation becomes partial when personal contact can be made by some form of communication, such as letters to loved ones during vacations or visits and telephone calls made to the hospitalized patient. War, imprisonment, or estrangement may also create partial separations once personal contact is made with the individual(s) involved.

Loss of part of one's physio-psychosocial well-being

The second form of loss during adult life is loss of one's physio-psychosocial well-being. As the term implies, this form of loss includes three components: the individual's state of physiological function; the individual's ideas and feelings about himself or herself; and the individual's social roles. Alterations in any one of these three components of the individual's physio-psychosocial well-being do not occur independently. Alterations in any one of the components invariably affect the other two components. For example, if an individual encounters an alteration in physiological function, changes in feelings of self-worth may subsequently occur. On the other hand, as a result of the physiological alteration, the individual may be forced to change or alter his or her role(s) in society.

The components of one's physio-psychosocial well-being are intricate and intermeshed. Thus, the nurse's assessment of each individual constituent is necessary prior to determining the magnitude of loss. Loss of physiological functions may occur during partial or complete failure of body function and it may be permanent or temporary. Changes in vision and hearing that occur throughout the life cycle may be examples of partial failure of body function. The alteration is not complete because vision and hearing are not entirely lost, but the individual involved is unable to see and hear as well as when he or she was younger. The complete failure of a body function occurs in such instances as total renal failure, cardiac arrest, and paralytic ileus. If these conditions are not rectified, they could terminate in death.

The removal of a body part, such as a limb amputation, or the presence of a chronic illness, such as diabetes mellitus, may demonstrate a permanent loss of physiological function. It must be realized, however, that each individual's experience with a form of permanent loss of physiological function varies. Many individuals who have a permanent form of physiological dysfunction are capable of operating at an optimal level of wellness with the assistance of appropriate health care. By comparison, an alteration in breathing may be a temporary form of loss of physiological function, as in the case of an individual who has an obstructed airway. Once the obstruction is removed, most likely the patient will be able to breathe again in his usual manner. Regardless of whether the loss of physiological function is partial or complete, permanent or temporary, it demonstrates a loss that is real to the individual involved.

The second component of one's physio-psychosocial well-being is the loss of some part of the personal emotional well-being. In other words, it is an alteration in the individual's concept of his or her ideas and feelings about his or her worth, attractability, and desirability. Such a loss may be permanent or temporary.

A state of permanent loss may be seen in the individual who becomes unable to reestablish feelings of self-worth after removal of a body part. Such an individual may feel incomplete and, therefore, of little or no value to anyone. Subsequent acute and chronic emotional upheaval ensues and intense psychiatric care may be required. On the other hand, a temporary state of loss of self may occur, as in the case of a traumatic injury that creates a permanent disability or in the case of required hospitalization for minor surgery. These individuals may encounter difficulty with the changes they notice in their body functions or appearance and feel that these alterations make them "less than normal." Therefore, these individuals may doubt their capabilities and view themselves as undesirable. Once the individual begins receiving rehabilitation, as in the case of the individual who has a disability, or is discharged from the hospital after a successful surgery, as in the case of the individual requiring surgical intervention, the feelings of worthlessness and undesirability may suddenly or gradually dissipate. Hopefully, each individual now feels capable and complete and no longer questions his or her worth or desirability. The individual who has a permanent disability, however, may fluctuate between feelings of worthlessness and feelings of worth depending upon the present-day situation.

Loss of one's occupation or profession, status in the family setting, position in the community, and even one's sexuality comprise the third and final component of the loss of part of one's physio-psychosocial well-being. Each of these roles is temporary and either partial or complete in character.

Occupational or professional roles are temporary since an individual from the time of his or her first employment to his or her last working days assumes a variety of positions within the chosen occupation or profession. For example, college presidents, no doubt, began as college instructors and through time worked their way up the professional structural hierarchy to administrative positions. Similarly, the gas station attendant may have started out pumping gas, but eventually was required to assume the additional responsibilities of changing tires and doing mechanical work on cars. In addition, the positions and responsibilities maintained by both the college president and the gas station attendant may suffer partial or complete loss at any given time. To illustrate, if a stressor, such as illness, befalls either individual, his or her job responsibilities may require a partial or possibly a complete removal of accountability. Hence, partial or complete loss of the social role has occurred. Once the stressor, illness, is removed, total job responsibilities may again be resumed and the state of partial or complete loss of the social role is rectified.

One's position in a family structure is temporary in character since each individual assumes a variety of family roles throughout his or her lifetime. An individual can progress from child to adult-head-of-the-house, to parent, and on to grandparent. On the other hand, an individual may progress from child to adult and continue to live with his or her parents as their child. However, once the parents become elderly, the child may be required to assume the responsibility for their care, if possible, and hence becomes the adult-head-of-the-house.

Family roles may also oscillate between being complete or partial in character. A man in the household, for example, may be the source of total family income. If illness or a work slowdown occurs, other family members may have to assume additional responsibility for the family income. The man may demonstrate a partial social loss if his role as breadwinner is assumed in part by others. If the illness becomes acute and requires lengthy hospitalization and treatment or if the man is laid off from his job, complete loss of the family role of breadwinner may ensue because the man is no longer capable of maintaining total gainful employment.

Community roles, the third part of one's social role, are in a state of constant flux for each individual. Hence, they are by character temporary and either partial or complete. An individual can assume any number of roles at any given time during his or her life. For example, one can be the member of a church, the mayor of a town, and the participant in a voluntary fire department. Any one of these roles may last for a considerable length of time, but each role is subject to change and cancelation; consequently, these roles are temporary.

If a stressor such as illness or sudden additional family responsibilities occurs, the individual may be required to relinquish some components of his or her community role. Thus, partial loss develops. In the case of incompetent performance or total inability to carry out responsibilities as the result of lack of wellness, an individual may be totally removed from the role with the end result being a complete loss of the community role.

Loss of one's sexuality is the final part of one's physio-psychosocial well-being. Sexual roles have undergone great change during the past two decades. The realization of the importance of human sexuality has become of great concern to society and especially to the health care team. Sexuality consists of four major components and is temporary and either partial or complete in character. These four components are: (1) the presence of maleness and femaleness; (2) the existing feelings the individual holds concerning his or her sexual well-being; (3) the effects that maleness or femaleness has upon his or her daily living; and (4) the presence of reproductivity or nonreproductivity.

The presence of maleness or femaleness is the identification of one's biological sex by oneself and by others. In rare instances, individuals at birth may not be identified as one sex or the other because of genetic malfunctioning. In such cases, further medical studies and examinations may be required before the infant's sex is publicly determined (Money, 1975). In other instances, individuals have decided to change their sex by surgical intervention. These cases demonstrate that one's biological sex is temporary in form. However, almost all individuals elect to maintain their maleness or femaleness throughout their lifetimes.

An individual's feelings about his or her sexual well-being play an important part in the acceptance of his or her sexuality. Is the individual pleased about being a male or a female? Are sexual dysfunctions present? Does the individual have a satisfying sex life? Is the individual involved in sex therapy (Kaplan, 1974)? These are a few of the questions that play a part in determining one's feelings about his or her own human sexual response pattern. It is difficult for an individual to experience complete and satisfying sexuality if personal feelings about it are degrading. For example, if a stressor such as surgery occurs, the patient's sexual well-being may be threatened. If the surgery involves the individual's sex organs or structures close to the sex organs, the feelings of threat may be intensified. Such surgical interventions may include a vasectomy, hysterectomy, inguinal hernia repair, or a transurethral resection. Unless the feelings of threat toward sexual well-being are alleviated, the individual will continue to demonstrate a partial loss of sexuality.

Maleness or femaleness plays an important part in one's pattern of daily living and it affects the individual at home, at work, and in the social setting. Although sexual stereotypes are changing, one's biological sex continues to have an effect on the family, work, and social roles that are played. For example, since males have been considered physiologically stronger, it has not been unusual for them to be responsible for lifting heavy objects in the house. In the work setting, if an individual was the only male in an office of 30 females, attention was most likely focused on the male. Throughout history the presence of maleness in social settings has granted the individual the privilege to be assertive and offer to pick up the tab for an evening's entertainment. These practices, however, are currently undergoing change and the usage of one's biological sex in the home, at work, and in the social setting may be holding less meaning.

Partial loss of sexuality can also occur in the case of how one's femaleness or maleness affects patterns of daily living. For example, does the fact that an individual is a male in home economics affect the likelihood that he will not meet career aspirations? Is the individual suppressed because she is the only female in a class of 105 male medical students? Is the female patient neglected because the female nurses prefer to take care of the handsome young male patient? If the answers to these questions are yes, then a partial loss of sexuality has again developed.

Presence of reproductivity and nonreproductivity is the fourth and final component of one's sexuality. Today some heterosexual couples are selecting not to reproduce (Woods, 1975). By the same token, couples of similar sex, as in homosexual marriages and love affairs, are physiologically incapable of reproducing.

Since selected patterns of sexual activity vary among individuals, as can be seen in the presence of singleness, marriage, extramarital affairs, homosexual and heterosexual relationships, and self-sexual stimulation, what the individual finds as sexually satisfying is the important factor. If, however, the individual's sexual experiences fail to provide sexual satisfaction or offspring, when desired, then a partial loss of sexuality occurs. The complete loss of sexuality cannot develop unless all four components of the individual's sexual well-being are unmet. The chances of this happening are rare although the individual, at any time, may be unable to fulfill three of the components of his or her sexuality: satisfactory feelings toward sexual well-being; positive affects of biological sex upon daily living; and the presence or lack of reproductivity, depending upon desire. However, the presence of maleness or femaleness, the fourth component of sexuality, is ever present; consequently, one aspect of sexuality continually exists and complete loss of sexuality is not established.

Loss of one's personal possessions

The third and final form of loss during adult life is the loss of one's personal possessions. This form of loss may be permanent or temporary and it may be either partial or complete in character.

Personal possessions consist of such items as money, clothing, jewelry, habitation, and country. However, it must be realized that these possessions often represent an extension of one's being and loss of such items may demonstrate a true personal threat to the individual involved (Sloboda, 1977). Think of how you would feel if someone took or if you misplaced an item that you personally cherish.

Personal possessions may be lost in a variety of ways: robbery, misplacement, destruction, repossession, removal, or expulsion. Permanent loss occurs when the individual's possession is totally unretrievable. Such may be the case in destruction and expulsion. Never again will the individual be able to lay claim to the personal possession. A common example of permanent loss seen in the health care setting is when a member of the health team breaks a patient's dentures, eye glasses, or writing pen or puts the patient's rosary beads in the dirty-linen chute with the bed sheets. Loss of a personal possession becomes temporary if at some point the item is retrieved. Temporary loss of a personal possession may be in the form of robbery, misplacement, repossession, or removal. Temporary loss frequently occurs during hospitalization. One of the most ritualistic procedures carried out by nursing personnel that demonstrates temporary loss is removal of the patient's clothing, money, and medications at the time of admission and returning them upon discharge. Nurses should realize that such an act may well be interpreted by the patient as a personal assault on his or her being.

Partial loss of a personal possession occurs when some component or part of the possession is lost. An example is when an individual misplaces one piece in a set of jewelry or is asked to relinquish all medications except nitroglycerine at the time of hospital admission. Complete loss of one's possessions occurs when the entire item is lost, as in the case of expulsion from one's home or country.

Loss of one's personal possessions is undoubtedly the most frequent form of loss during adult life. Regardless of its frequency, one continues to view this form of loss as a threat both personally and monetarily.

Summary of forms of loss

An individual's adult life is confronted with three forms of loss: loss of a significant other, loss of some part of one's physio-psychosocial well-being, and loss of one's personal possessions. These losses vary in their ability to be permanent or temporary and complete or partial. During his or her lifetime an individual may be forced to deal with any number of losses. The manner in which the loss is viewed affects the individual's ability to cope with its presence and its recurrence.

REACTIONS TO LOSS

Regardless of what form of loss individuals encounter, be it death, separation, loss of a body part, or loss of home, individuals respond to loss with a sequential set of behaviors. The speed with which they progress through these reactions, the length of time spent dealing with each phase, and the intensity of each response to the loss depend upon many factors. These factors may include the value of the lost object, the rapidity of the occurrence of the loss, experience with similar losses, individual coping abilities, and cultural support systems. The following discussion will revolve around the three reactional phases experienced by the individual attempting to deal with loss. Related nursing interventions will be presented at the end of each developmental section.

Repudiation

An individual's initial reaction to loss is one of shock and disbelief (Engel, 1964). Comprehension and acknowledgment that the loss has occurred are repudiated. The individual refuses to recognize or accept that the loss has occurred. Common statements made by the individual experiencing the loss include: "No, it can't be true." "It's not possible." "I don't believe it."

In an attempt to protect themselves from the stress of the loss, some individuals may intellectualize the loss and proceed to carry out ordinary activities as though nothing had happened; others sit motionless in a dazed state (Engel, 1964). Either reaction prevents conscious access to the complete emotional impact of the loss. When the loss involves the diagnosis of a chronic illness, the individual may respond by refusing to believe the diagnosis and proceed to search for additional medical opinions (Kubler-Ross, 1969). Thus, the individual attempts to protect himself from having to face the overwhelming stress of the loss.

The act of repudiation may last a few minutes, several hours, days, or in some instances even months. However, the use of repudiation for extended periods, such as months, is an exception. Refusal to acknowledge the existence of loss is a temporary defense and eventually is replaced by, at least, partial acceptance of the loss (Kubler-Ross, 1969). Although repudiation is the initial reaction to loss, it must be recognized that the individual also may require its use in later phases of reaction to loss. The act of repudiation simply provides a buffer and allows individuals time to collect their thoughts and mobilize other less radical reactions to stress-producing circumstances.

Various physiological and emotional reactions accompany repudiation. These reactions may include fainting, pallor, excessive perspiration, increased heart rate, nausea, diarrhea, crying, confusion, and restlessness (Gray, 1974). However, the prevalence and intensity of these reactions will vary greatly among individuals experiencing loss. Some individuals may exhibit many of these reactions while others may exhibit few.

In summary, the major function of this initial reaction to loss, repudiation, is to protect oneself against the effects of overpowering stress created by the acknowledgment of the loss. Repudiation allows one time to collect oneself before attempting to face the loss and work toward accepting it.

Nursing Intervention During Repudiation.   Before initiating nursing intervention when dealing with individuals and families experiencing loss, the nurse must be cognizant of what phase of loss is being demonstrated.

This information must then be disseminated among all of the health team members dealing with the individual and with the individual's family. Information about the approaches to be used for each individual and his or her family must also be shared among the nurses and other members of the health care team in order to avoid conflicts in approach and to facilitate continuity of care.

The nurse's primary role during repudiation is to allow the individual the right to deny (Crate, 1965; Carlson, 1970). Listening intently to the individual's denial is important. Agreeing or arguing with the individual about the denial should be avoided, for denial is the only means of coping with the loss at the present time. If the individual were to say, "I don't need those medications!" the nurse must avoid responses such as, "I suppose you really don't!" or "You certainly do!" The first response supports the individual's denial and the second response is argumentative. Nothing is accomplished by such comments other than increasing the patient's already high anxiety level. It would be more advisable to respond in such a reflective manner as, "You don't believe that you need the medication?" or "You feel this medication will not be useful?" By responding this way the nurse requests additional information from the patient about the denial of loss. Additional communication avenues are opened and the patient is encouraged to talk about the denial.

In addition to encouraging the individual to express feelings about the loss, the nurse may have to manipulate the environment in order to assist the individual in maintaining the usual activities of daily living. Providing the patient with the opportunity to carry out personal hygiene or prescribed medical therapies and making sure that scheduled clinic appointments are kept are some possibilities. By so doing, additional threats of loss may be avoided.

On occasion the individual may be unable to carry out the usual life activities because of the energy expended in denying. During this period the nurse assumes the responsibility for the individual's care so that the individual is free to continue denial of the loss. Consequently, the nurse provides continuity in the patient's usual activities of daily living and assists in preventing possible additional losses from the environment.

While working with an individual experiencing loss, the nurse must recognize that the individual's family members also require support as they work through their individual feelings of shock and disbelief. Each family member may require separate intervention on the part of the nurse because all family members may not progress through the reactional phases of loss at the same pace. Some family members may repudiate the loss momentarily while others may carry on disbelief about the loss for extended periods of time. The expression of individual feelings by each family member should be encouraged since it is, as with the individual experiencing the loss, the one means of coping with loss at this time.

In addition, the nurse must determine which family member the remaining members rely upon for emotional support and guidance. This individual may require additional intervention from members of the health team while "working through" the repudiation of the loved one's loss.

Recognition

The second phase in the individual's reaction to loss involves recognition. Generally, within minutes or hours (possibly days or months for some individuals) recognition of the reality of the loss begins. The conscious has been penetrated and the increased awareness of the anguish of loss evolves. The loss now has been recognized.

Anger is likely to be elicited and projected upon other individuals or circumstances in the environment or directed toward oneself in the form of depression (Engel, 1964; Crate, 1965). Verbal attack, and aggressive or destructive acts, such as thrusting a fist through glass, are various demonstrations of the acting out of anger. In the hospital setting the patient may express anger by refusing medication or treatment. It is not uncommon to hear such verbal accusations as: "It is your fault that this medicine tastes so bitter." "I'm not going to physical therapy today. They don't know what they are doing. All they do is hurt me!" Regardless of what others do, individuals expressing anger due to loss may continually find fault.

Family and health team members often find it difficult to cope with the verbally abusive, angry individual experiencing loss, since they find it difficult not to take the expressed anger personally. Actually, the outwardly angry individual is not angry at them but at attributes which they represent, for example, wellness, purpose, freedom, vitality, cheerfulness, mobility, and the ability to control their own lives (Gray, 1974).

The individual who expresses anger about his or her loss in the form of depression also may be difficult for family and health team members to deal with. He or she expresses anger by being the "good patient" or by withdrawing into a room and being uncommunicative. Loss of appetite, sleep disturbances, decreased libido, and fatigability are additional manifestations of incipient depression arising due to loss (Beck, 1973). The following statements are often heard: "Don't waste your time nurse. The treatment won't help anyway." "Don't tell my family how I feel. They don't care about me either." The depressed patient may assume a bleak and fatalistic view about the loss and these feelings of helplessness and hopelessness only add to increasing biological vulnerability (Schmale, 1958; Parkes, 1964; Maddison and Viola, 1968).

After the individual has expressed anger, he or she then makes attempts to postpone the loss by negotiating and entering into the IF stage. The negotiation may be with a supreme being (Kübler-Ross, 1969), another individual, or with oneself. Common propitiatory attempts involving loss due to chronic illness or impending death may include such statements as: "If I can just go to my son's bar mitzvah." "If I could only see the seashore one more time." Negotiations involving loss of a personal possession may be made with oneself and include such statements as: "If only I had sent my wallet home with my family, the hospital staff couldn't have lost it." "If I only had put new locks on my doors, they never would have robbed me." It should be noted that negotiating statements inherently include or imply the word if. If the negotiation is fulfilled, the individual will most likely make another attempt to negotiate in order to extend further the trauma of dealing with the loss, since the act of negotiating is an attempt to deal with feelings of guilt. The individual may believe that his or her thoughts or actions had something to do with bringing about the loss (Marks, 1976). Not until the individual is ready to face the loss directly will the individual be capable of relinquishing the need for negotiating.

Once the individual has passed the IF stage, he or she then faces the painful absence of the lost object, whether it be another person, a body part, or an inanimate object. For a period of time there is a great deal of preoccupation with the lost object which is indicated by repetitive talks about the object (Engel, 1964). Idealization and any negative aspects about the lost object are repressed (Carlson, 1970) because the individual finds a need to identify with the positive qualities of the lost object. At this point the individual remains unable to replace the loss with a new object or relationship and may establish passive, dependent relationships with old well-established objects (Carlson, 1970). Given ample time and proper assistance, the individual can successfully work through the phase of recognition and be prepared to enter into the final reaction to loss, reconciliation.

Nursing Intervention During Recognition.   In dealing with the stage of recognition, the nurse's primary role is one of assisting the individual in coping with the loss and maintaining behavioral stability. Most likely, anger will be the first reaction to loss. In dealing with the individual's expressed anger, the nurse must not join the individual in the individual's anger. If the nurse joins in the anger, it is the same as retaliating against the individual's anger in an attempt to protect one's own ego. For example, suppose that the individual says, "Do you have to be so cheerful all the time? Your sweetness makes me sick." The nurse responds, "Well, excuse me for living!" The nurse's response would be retaliative and indicative of a personal threat. Remember that the individual experiencing loss becomes angry at others' attributes, such as cheerfulness, and not necessarily at the other individuals themselves.

An individual may have justifiable reason for anger. In such a case, the individual must not be reprimanded for expressing anger. Instead, the individual should be encouraged to vent his or her feelings verbally. By "talking out" the angry feelings about the loss, the individual is less likely to express anger in a socially unacceptable manner, such as throwing things or striking others. Take the case of the individual whose clothes have been lost by health care personnel during the hospital admission procedure. Does the individual not have justifiable reason for anger? By verbally attacking the individual or by making excuses for the loss, reinforcement of the individual's anger is intensified. A more therapeutic approach would be to say, "Your anger is certainly understandable. We will take appropriate steps in an attempt to retrieve your clothing. I will inform you step by step of the progress that we are making." Such a response by the nurse acknowledges the existence of the individual's anger, provides the individual concrete information on what attempts are going to be made to alleviate the anger, and provides follow up on health care actions. The nurse then *must* follow through and relay the actions to the individual; otherwise, mistrust may develop and further anger may be incited.

As mentioned previously, individuals may express anger about a loss in the form of depression. When dealing with depression, nurses must be aware that members of the health care team often unconsciously avoid individuals exemplifying this behavior. An atmosphere of personal isolation is created which may be interpreted by the depressed individual as rejection. Angry individuals demonstrating depression should not be avoided, for avoidance may intensify their depression. Instead, they need frequent personal contact and encouragement to express their feelings outwardly rather than expressing anger through internalization, such as, depression. Crying may be a means of such expression and value judgments regarding its use should not be made by the nurse (Engel, 1964). Privacy for the expression of such emotions should be made available for the individual's use (Schuster, 1973). Removing the individual from the chaos of the environmental surroundings and placing the individual in a quiet, private setting allows the expression of feelings with no reservation or embarrassment. When a private environment is provided for the expression of feelings, the nurse should avoid withdrawing from the situation. Withdrawing from the uncomfortable circumstance may be an easy way out for the nurse, but it is not necessarily a therapeutic maneuver for the individual's benefit. Sitting quietly with the individual as he or she begins to express anger, either in the form of verbal abuse or depression, demonstrates the nurse's acceptance of the individual and helps alleviate the individual's feeling of isolation and rejection. As the individual begins to verbalize feelings of depression about the loss, the nurse should provide appropriate feedback. The nurse can point out to the individual that it is obvious that he or she is depressed, but through time and with assistance the depression will subside. Asking the individual if he or she has ever been depressed and, if so, what actions he or she has taken to deal with the depression may provide avenues for a therapeutic intervention. Identifying what action the health care team can provide in assisting the individual to cope with the loss is another tangible way of dealing with the individual's depression. For example, necessary readjustments in job responsibilities because of an amputation may be disturbing the individual; hence, anger in the form of depression may ensue. With the assistance of social service and occupational therapy, alternatives in dealing with changes in work responsibilities may be developed and, in turn, the need for anger, in the form of depression, may be decreased. Regardless of what means are used in dealing with the individual's depression, it is important for the nurse to point out to the individual the individual's present positive attributes instead of feeding into the individual's negative feelings. Positive feedback may include making note of the individual's ability to walk farther today than yesterday or commenting on how much the individual's facial color has improved.

When dealing with negotiation, another behavioral manifestation during the stage of recognition, the nurse's primary responsibility is to guide the individual in looking at the reasons for using such a maneuver. The individual sometimes assumes that he or she must have done something wrong; therefore, the individual may think that he or she is guilty of some grievous act. It is necessary to assist the individual in identifying those acts and thoughts for which the individual believes he or she is guilty. Verbalization is one method that can be used to help the individual identify guilt feelings. It is important for the individual to talk out such feelings (Robinson, 1974). The nurse may want to respond to the individual with, "You keep saying *if* I only had done thus and such. Do you feel responsible for the loss?" A comment like this may guide the individual's thoughts and verbalization toward expressing repressed guilt. Above all, the nurse must avoid giving the individual "pat" answers, such as, "Oh, I'm sure everything will work out. It is not your fault!" This response is an abortive attempt to pacify the individual and direct the conversation away from a topic which, no doubt, is making the nurse uncomfortable.

As the individual passes the negotiation phase of recognition and begins to face the loss, intense preoccupation with the positive aspect of the loss evolves. During this phase of recognition the nurse must allow the individual to vent his or her feelings about all of the positive qualities of the loss and not expect the individual to establish relationships with new objects at this time. Not until the individual experiencing loss is allowed to be purged of the idealized beliefs about the loss will the individual be capable of viewing the aspects of the loss more objectively. Then the individual can begin to relinquish dependent relationships with old well-established objects and begin to organize new relationships with other objects.

The nurse must not only be available to assist the individual as he or she works through the loss, but the nurse must also be accessible to the family members as they work through the phase of recognition (Hampe,

1975). As with the stage of repudiation, each member of the family may be at a different level in the phase of recognition. Individual family members may require additional acceptance, support, and comfort from the nursing staff.

The basic concepts of nursing care for the individual experiencing loss during the phase of recognition also apply to the individual family members, but a few additional considerations must be identified. For one, the family may require frequent information about their loved one's reaction to loss. Such a maneuver provides the family with the feeling of some control over the situation and, in turn, facilitates in decreasing their anxiety levels about the loss. The family's anxiety level has a grave impact on the individual experiencing loss. If the family's anxiety is maintained at a low level, so might the individual's. Second, the family members may provide valuable information and suggestions on how to assist their loved one in dealing with loss; therefore, the family also must be consulted during the planning of nursing care. The nurse should remember that family members usually are most knowledgeable about how their loved one deals with life's stresses.

Once the individual and the individual's family have successfully completed all of the phases of recognition, they stand ready to deal with the final stage of loss, reconciliation.

Reconciliation

Reconciliation involves reorganization of one's feelings about the loss. The need for anger and depression no longer exists during this phase. Idealization of the lost object progresses to a detachment of the lost object from the self. The individual becomes less and less preoccupied with the lost object and begins to develop a more factual memory of the loss. For example, statements indicating reconciliation with loss of a significant other may include: "At times I'm sure I will miss my husband, but I'm so relieved that he isn't suffering anymore." "My baby is going to be in the hospital a long time, but the rest of my family needs me too; therefore, I'm going to spend more time at home. I'm confident that my baby is receiving good care while I'm gone." Reconciliation with loss of a body part may be indicated in a statement such as, "I have been so concerned about my appearance since my surgery, but with my new prosthetic device no one can tell that I've had a breast removed!" In the case of loss of a personal possession, a reconciliatory statement may be, "I really liked the coat I lost, but my new one is just as nice."

A gradual interest in new objects develops during reconciliation. In the case of loss of a significant other, new personal attachments begin and expand. When the loss involves a body part, as in the case of a colostomy or an amputation, interest is directed toward the new appliance or prosthetic device. When personal possessions have been lost, the individual may purchase a replacement and establish attachment to the newly acquired object. Final reconciliation is truly accomplished when the individual accepts the loss and with no hesitation is capable of openly ventilating and dealing with all feelings regarding the loss.

Nursing Intervention During Reconciliation. Even when the individual reaches the final phase of loss, reconciliation, the nurse's role is not finished, for during this phase the individual requires encouragement in expressing his or her views about himself or herself (Crate, 1965) and assistance in making plans for the future. The role of the nurse revolves around urging the individual to express his or her personal feelings now that the loss has been resolved. In what way does the individual see himself or herself now that he or she has experienced loss? How has the loss been incorporated into his or her body image? In what way has the individual assimilated the role of his or her present state of illness?

It is during this phase of loss that family members may require additional information about the individual's actions from members of the health care team. They may also need the opportunity to vent their personal feelings about the individual's present reaction to the loss. Not all family members are in the same stage of loss reaction and, therefore, they experience difficulty in understanding how the individual has come to accept the loss. The individual's reconciliation with loss does not inherently imply reconciliation by family members.

During the phase of reconciliation the nurse also may be required to assist the individual experiencing loss to plan and institute actions for his or her future. An individual experiencing loss of a significant other may express desire for companionship. The nurse may suggest various places, organizations, or ways of meeting new people. If the loss is caused by illness, the individual may require guidance in planning alternate ways of incorporating therapies into his or her busy work schedule. An individual experiencing loss of a personal possession may request nothing more than guidance in how to obtain a replacement for the lost object. Regardless of the kind of loss each individual experiences, his or her needs for future planning vary and these examples are but a few ways in which the nurse can intervene.

Summary of Reactions to Loss and
Related Nursing Interventions

An individual encountering loss progresses through three phases of development in an attempt to deal with the loss: repudiation, recognition, and reconciliation. All three phases must be worked through before the individual can be acknowledged as having successfully dealt with the loss.

The nurse must be aware that an individual experiencing loss may undergo the entire process of loss each time a new loss is encountered. Prior losses and how they have been resolved will affect an individual's ability to cope with the present loss (Kubler-Ross, 1969; Pretz, 1970b). The nurse plays a vital role in assisting the individual as he or she works through each stage in the reaction to loss. The intervention the nurse uses for each patient should be individualized and should include sound professional judgment.

REFERENCES

Beck, A. *The diagnosis and management of depression*. Philadelphia: University of Pennsylvania Press, 1973.

Carlson, C. Grief and mourning. In C. Carlson (Ed.), *Behavioral concepts and nursing interventions*. Philadelphia: J. B. Lippincott Co., 1970.

Crate, M. A. Nursing functions in adaptation to chronic illness, *American Journal of Nursing*, 1965, *65* (10), 72-76.

Engel, G. Grief and grieving, *American Journal of Nursing*, 1964, *64* (9), 93-98.

Gray, R. Grief, *Nursing '74*, 1974, *4* (1), 25-27.

Hampe, S. Needs of the grieving spouse in a hospital setting, *Nursing Research*, 1975, *24* (2), 113-119.

Kaplan, H. *The new sex therapy*. New York : Brunner/Mazel, Publishers, 1974.

Kubler-Ross, E. *On death and dying*. New York: The Macmillan Company, 1969.

Lambert C., and Lambert, V. Divorce: a psychodynamic development involving grief, *Journal of Psychiatric Nursing and Mental Health Services*, 1977, *15* (1), 37-42.

Maddison, D., and Viola, A. The health of widows in the year following bereavement, *Journal of Psychosomatic Research*, 1968, *12*, 297-306.

Marks, M. J. The grieving patient and family, *American Journal of Nursing*, 1976, *76* (9), 1488-1491.

Money, J. Sex assignment in anatomically intersexed infants. In R. Green (Ed.), *Human sexuality: a health practitioner's text*. Baltimore: The Williams & Wilkins Co., 1975.

Parkes, C. Effects of bereavement on physical and mental health: a study of the medical records of widows, *British Medical Journal*, 1964, *2*, 274-279.

Pretz, D. Development, object-relationships and loss. In B. Schoenberg, A. Carr, D. Peretz, and A. Kutscher (Eds.), *Loss and grief: psychological management in medical practice*. New York: Columbia University Press, 1970a.

Pretz, D. Reaction to loss. In B. Schoenberg, A. Carr, D. Peretz, and A. Kutscher (Eds.), *Loss and grief: psychological management in medical practice*. New York: Columbia University Press, 1970b.

Robinson, L. *Liaison nursing: psychological approach to patient care*. Philadelphia: F. A. Davis Company, 1974.

Schmale, A. Relationship of separation and depression to disease: a report on hospitalized medical population, *Psychosomatic Medicine*, 1958, *20*, 259.

Schoenberg, B. Management of the dying patient. In B. Schoenberg, A. Carr, D. Peretz, and A. Kutscher (Eds.), *Loss and grief: psychological management in medical practice*. New York: Columbia University Press, 1970.

Schuster, E. Privacy and hospitalization subject of nurse's investigation, *Nursing Research Report*, 1973, *8* (3), 1-8.

Sloboda, S. Understanding patient behavior, *Nursing '77*, 1977, *7* (9), 74-77.

Woods, N. *Human sexuality in health and illness*. St. Louis: The C. V. Mosby, Co., 1975.

PART
II

Alterations
in
Body Structure

4

The Patient with a
LIMB AMPUTATION

INTRODUCTION

Amputation surgery dates as far back as surgery itself. During the past quarter of a century, however, enormous progress has been made in the fields of medicine and surgery as they relate to amputations. With the advent of antibiotics, vascular surgery, and effective control of diabetes mellitus, the necessity for the amputation of limbs and appendages has decreased (Larson and Gould, 1974). Although great improvements in medicine and surgery have decreased the number of amputations, amputation remains a prevalent health care problem today.

During the initial impact of amputation the individual is faced with incorporating the sick role into his or her daily living.* Because of the individual's temporarily altered body function, the individual is exempt from social responsibility, unable to achieve wellness simply by will, obligated to seek wellness, and responsible for seeking and cooperating with technically responsible assistance (Parsons, 1951). Consequently, the impact of amputation affects the individual's emotional, somatic, sexual, occupational, and social well-being.

CAUSES FOR AMPUTATIONS

There are four major causes for amputations: trauma, disease, tumors, and congenital disorders (Larson and Gould, 1974). In the category of trauma,

*It is advisable for the reader to have read Chapter 1 before continuing with this chapter.

the amputation is required as a result of crushing or of extensive lacerations of the vascular and nervous structures in the extremity, thus rendering the extremity unsurvivable and in need of removal. Trauma generally involves individuals in the age group of twenty years to fifty-five years (Mital and Pierce, 1971) and is the most common cause for amputation of an upper extremity (Tooms, 1972).

The second cause for amputation, disease, comprises the largest percentage of amputations (Davies, Friz, and Clippinger, 1970). This category may include such maladies as extensive osteomyelitis, atherosclerosis, and arteriosclerosis, with diabetes mellitus often accompanying the two latter disease processes. At least three-fourths of all amputations are brought about by peripheral vascular changes. Thus, such changes are the most common disease processes causing the loss of a limb (McCollough, 1972; Warren, 1975). Lower extremities constitute the greatest number of limbs lost (Davies, Friz, and Clippinger, 1970). Rarely are upper extremity amputations performed to control peripheral vascular changes (Luckmann and Sorenson, 1974). Since peripheral vascular changes are enhanced by the aging process, people in the age category of fifty years and older constitute the largest percentage of individuals undergoing an amputation (Kerstein, Zimmer, Dugdale, and Lerner, 1975). Men experience nearly three-quarters of all amputations (Davies, Friz, and Clippinger, 1970). The amputee most frequently seen in the hospital setting is a male, fifty years of age or older, stricken with peripheral vascular changes, and who has lost a lower extremity.

Tumors, the third cause for amputation, comprise a small percentage of the total number of amputations. Tumor-related amputations generally are performed in order to prevent spread of the lesion (Davies, Friz, and Clippinger, 1970). Amputation due to tumor formation occurs with no apparent significant prevalence in any one age category (Mital and Pierce, 1971).

The fourth cause of amputation, congenital disorders, also makes up a small percentage of the total number of amputations (Davies, Friz, and Clippinger, 1970). Congenital disorders may consist of the absence of or severe malformation of a limb at birth resulting from faulty embryonic development. When a malformed limb does not respond to corrective therapy, its removal may be necessary. Removal of such a limb generally occurs prior to the age of thirty years (Mital and Pierce, 1971).

Thus, amputations can occur at any age and in the upper or lower extremities or appendages. The level of amputation may be proximal, distal, or total loss of structure. Regardless of whether the amputation is brought about by trauma, disease, tumors, or congenital malformation, the individual experiences the impact of loss and an alteration in body image.

IMPACT OF AMPUTATION

Emotional Impact*

The emotional impact of amputation on an individual is often underrated by members of the health team. In today's society the individual who is a highly mobile, physically attractive, independent achiever is admired. Communication media reinforce this concept in their advertisements for products that increase one's mobility, enhance one's beauty, and develop one's capabilities. For these reasons, the loss of a limb may signify more than just the relinquishing of a body part. Amputation may be viewed as the end of mobility, the loss of the capability for self-achievement, and the destruction of physical attractiveness.

When the individual first encounters the thought of an amputation, the initial reaction may include acute fear of impending death followed by a feeling of relief that he or she is alive. Such a reaction tends to be short-lived and occurs most frequently in individuals who have suffered a traumatic amputation, such as military personnel during wartime (Jeglijewski, 1973). However, this does not imply that individuals encountering an amputation brought on by disease, tumors, or congenital malformation may not experience the same reaction. Just the fear of surgical intervention to remove the limb or appendage can carry connotations of possible death for many people. The elderly individual may view the amputation as a prelude to his or her forthcoming death with the loss being the final blow to his or her usefulness (Caplan and Hackett, 1963). The individual's aged body is deteriorating, and the amputation is just one more aspect of failure in body function. The elderly individual subsequently may desire the cessation of life.

While the individual is experiencing the immediate fear of death the individual must be allowed to verbalize these feelings. How does the fear of death affect the individual? What are the individual's uppermost thoughts and concerns? During the individual's expression of feelings, a judgmental approach should be avoided as the individual's thoughts unfold. Value judgments conveyed by the nurse may cut off the individual's desire for expression. In addition, statements that change the subject should not be used, since the individual has a need to express these frightening thoughts. The use of statements that redirect the topic is often a defensive maneuver on the part of the nurse in an attempt to avoid an uncomfortable subject, such as death.

The individual's first reaction to the thought of an amputation may well be one of repudiation. However, with individuals encountering acute fear of impending death, repudiation may constitute the second emotional reaction to amputation. Repudiation is demonstrated by not believing that the limb

*It is advisable for the reader to have read Chapter 3 before continuing with this section.

or appendage will actually be removed and/or maintaining a state of disbelief even after the amputation has occurred. This happens despite the immediate intellectual observation that the body part is gone. Repudiation, like the acute fear of impending death, is generally short-lived. Some individuals, however, may use it for extended periods of time, possibly months. The amputee may demonstrate repudiation in such forms as refusing to look at the stump or attempting to ambulate, in the case of a lower limb amputation, before appropriate physical aides are provided.

Family members also may experience repudiation. Their disbelief may be manifested in such ways as refusing to sign a consent form for the amputation, as in the case of the parents of a child who has a malformed, untreatable extremity, or simply refusing to touch the loved one's stump. As the amputee must be assisted during the act of repudiation, so must the family members because their feelings may well affect the amputee's ability to cope with the loss.

The nurse must keep in mind that the act of repudiation is one way the individual and the family can cope with the experience of amputation at this point in their lives. Therefore, both the individual and the family must be allowed to express their denial of the loss. The nurse, however, must not join in the expression of this denial. For example, if the individual is experiencing peripheral vascular disease and requires an amputation because gangrene has set in, yet refuses the surgical removal of the limb because the individual feels that with time circulation will improve, the nurse must avoid supporting this decision. The individual requires assistance in exploring why he or she believes that circulation will improve and also what alternatives may result if the limb is not removed. By directing the individual's attention to the reality of the situation, but still allowing the expression of denial, the nurse is more likely to help the patient in making the best decision for this particular situation.

The amputee next enters the stage of recognition and it is during this emotional stage that anger, depression, and negotiation are demonstrated as the patient attempts to cope with the amputation.

The amputee's anger may be directed toward those in the environment, including the health team and family members. Statements like the following demonstrate anger: "You don't know what it is like to have a leg missing. So don't tell me I'll walk again." "You never wrap my ace bandage right. Don't you know anything?" The necessity for projecting blame elsewhere may exist regardless of what others do. It is the one way the amputee attempts to cope with the loss.

A growing awareness that the amputation has occurred will often elicit feelings of guilt. The amputee may feel that he or she contributed to the need for the amputation or that he or she did something for which the amputation is a punishment (Brown, 1964). The belief that an act of his or hers could have changed the situation may arouse acts of negotiation in an attempt to deal with these feelings of guilt. For example, the negotiating amputee might say: "If only I had not been driving in rainy weather, I wouldn't have had the accident and ended up like this (pointing to the stump)." "If I promise to move around in bed more, will you stop making me try to walk?"

Depression, generally a short-lived reaction, follows anger and guilt. Nurses may unintentionally inhibit the amputee's expression of anger and guilt and instead encourage the patient to be submissive and cooperative to the point of dependence (Zalewski, Geronemus, and Siegel, 1973). The individual who is basically a dependent person may relish the idea of having someone else care for his or her needs, since this relieves the individual of the responsibility (Severyn, 1969). Extreme mood swings tend to be the exception rather than the rule and most emotionally well-balanced individuals will not experience severe degrees of depression (Mital and Pierce, 1971). Nonetheless, some individuals may experience great difficulty in coping with the amputation and demonstrate deep-seated depression, thus requiring intense outpatient therapy or psychiatric hospitalization.

In dealing with amputees in the stage of recognition, the emotional impact of the loss can be minimized for most individuals by mobilizing the entire health care team for total care of the individual and the family. This care should begin before the amputation, if possible (probably not likely with a traumatic amputation), and continue until the amputee reenters society as a well-adjusted individual.

As the individual begins to express anger, he or she should be encouraged to do so without retaliative measures from others. The nurse must remember that the amputee sees others as mobile, self-sufficient, and physically attractive individuals. The amputee is likely to question whether or not he or she has these attributes. The expression of anger is directed toward these attributes held by others and not necessarily at others personally.

It is necessary to engage in frank discussion with the individual and the family before the amputation about the pathological processes that necessitate the amputation and the expected course of progression postoperatively. This discussion is the responsibility of *all* members of the health team, with particular emphasis on the physician and the nurse. During the discussion about the disease process the individual needs reassurance that the condition is something over which the individual has had no control. The individual should be informed that there is no reason to feel guilty about not coming for medical assistance sooner or for not carrying out measures that could have avoided the need for the amputation. In other words, the individual's guilt should be dealt with before the amputation instead of weeks later after the amputation so that the overall rehabilitative progress (Mital and Pierce, 1971) will not be delayed.

It is imperative that family members be included, as much as possible, in all explanations. Being aware of what their loved one faces allows concerned family members the opportunity to vent their own feelings to the health care personnel. It also provides the family with a better understanding of their loved one's personal needs while they are providing moral support (Cath, Glud, and Blane, 1957; Severyn, 1969). In addition, including family members also increases the number of people who may be able to assist the amputee in working through the reconciliation of the loss. Fear of the unknown is diminished by providing the individual and the family with information about the condition necessitating the amputation and about the expected course of progress during the postoperative period. The intensity of the individual's and family's depression about the loss may be held to a minimum.

As the amputee enters the stage of reconciliation, he or she begins to view the prosthetic device, if the amputee has one, more as a part of his or her body image than as an extemporaneous piece of equipment (Gerstmann, 1958). The amputee assumes greater responsibility and pride in caring for both the stump and the prosthetic device. No longer does the amputee shy away from social interaction and work responsibilities. The amputee who has reconciled the loss of a limb or appendage is now capable of resuming a life-style close to that which he or she had before the amputation (Martin, 1970). The amputee's life-style will never be exactly the same, but the reconciled amputee adapts to these necessary alterations and lives life to its fullest potential (Smith, 1970).

A general guide for the nurse to use in attempting to determine whether or not the individual is beginning to work toward the resolution of the amputation is to note his or her attempts to move about and to resume social interaction and work responsibilities (Mital and Pierce, 1971; Cath, Glud, and Blane, 1957). The nurse's primary responsibility to the amputee in the stage of reconciliation is one of supporting the individual's achievements and expressing positive feedback on the individual's accomplishments. The amputee also needs to verbalize his or her feelings now that he or she has learned to function with the loss. Only when the amputee can comfortably talk about the loss and view postamputation achievements and failures in a realistic manner will the amputee be in a total state of reconciliation.

Somatic Impact*

After an amputation most individuals experience the phenomenon of the phantom limb. The amputee describes the phantom limb phenomenon as a sensation of the lost limb's continuing presence. Although the extrem-

*It is advisable for the reader to have read Chapter 2 before continuing with this section.

ity is perceived as being whole, the amputee is most aware of the distal portions of the phantom limb, the toes and fingers. This is because fingers and toes have more nerves and cortical representation than any other body part (Frazier and Kolb, 1970). The phantom phenomenon usually is experienced immediately after surgery and may persist from 6 months to 20 years after the amputation (Frazier and Kolb, 1970). Since over the years an individual has built up a detailed mental picture of each body part, just as he or she has built up mental pictures of his or her surroundings, it is not amazing to find that image persisting even though the body has undergone drastic change (Parkes, 1976).

As can be expected, phantom phenomenon is not present in the individual who has a congenitally absent limb or in early childhood amputations, since the body image is minimally developed before the age of six years. Adults experiencing anesthesia to the limb for extended periods before the amputation do not encounter the phantom phenomenon (Frazier and Kolb, 1970). This can be attributed to the fact that the individual has had time to reestablish a body image void of the limb prior to its amputation.

The amputee may actually experience pain in the phantom limb. The pain can vary in severity from a mild tingling sensation to a cramplike or burning pain. This pain can be elicited by emotionally charged situations, such as anger or the discussion of the amputee's plight as it affects the amputee's family or occupational status. When the discussion is focused on pleasant, unrelated subjects, the pain tends to subside (Riding, 1976).

The nurse, in caring for the amputee, must not confuse phantom limb pain with stump pain. Stump pain does not occur immediately after surgery. It takes time to develop and occurs at the site of the surgical intervention. It can be brought on by touching the stump (Riding, 1976). Phantom limb pain, however, can be experienced at any time in the zone of the former limb.

The etiology of phantom pain is unknown and many methods of treatment have been attempted, but none has been universally successful (Larson and Gould, 1974). Some methods have included nerve blocks, reamputation, and hypnosis (Mital and Pierce, 1971).

A gradual fading of the phantom phenomenon takes place over time, with proximal portions fading first, then intervening parts, and finally distal parts. This fading is believed to be the result of the progressive increase of central suppression of afferent impulses as reorganization of the body image occurs (Frazier and Kolb, 1970). Some amputees have commented that the phantom phenomenon seems to disappear when they don their prostheses. No doubt it is at this time that the discrepancy between the visual presence of the lost limb and the sensation that the limb is present is reduced. Hence, the amputee thinks of the prosthesis as a limb (Parkes, 1976).

The likely existence of phantom limb phenomenon and phantom pain after amputation should be explained to the individual and the family *before* the surgical intervention. The sensations should be described to the individual and the family because they must be made aware that these sensations are normal (Parkes, 1975). Failure to carry out appropriate counseling on phantom phenomenon and phantom pain may lead to an emotionally frantic amputee who feels that he or she has "gone off the deep end." Anxiety is present and the amputee may not wish to describe these phantom sensations because the amputee believes that others will think he or she is emotionally disturbed. Hence, preoperative explanation of the phantom phenomenon is imperative.

In addition to the phantom phenomenon and phantom pain, one's altered body image constitutes part of the somatic impact of amputation. The trauma of amputation greatly changes the body image and no longer are the body boundaries the same. The amputee now is forced to reassess body boundaries. The kind of impact amputation imposes upon one's body image is greatly affected by the stage of development that one is experiencing at the time of the loss of limb or appendage. For example, the young adult amputee (eighteen years to forty-five years of age) is in the stage of intimacy versus isolation (Erikson, 1963). It is at this point in life that the individual is ready to merge his or her identity with others and to identify the body as a major factor in relating to others. Now that the young adult has experienced the loss of a limb or appendage, he or she may view his or her physical body as less than acceptable since Western society places a great deal of emphasis upon physical attractiveness (Woods, 1975). If the individual thinks that he or she is less than adequate because of his or her physical appearance, the individual may fail to establish a state of intimacy with others and may retreat into isolation.

The male, it will be recalled, is a low-barrier individual and defines his role in terms of achievement based upon his body function (Fisher, 1964). Thus, he may view his amputation as an assault that hinders his performance and ability to achieve. The female, on the other hand, is a high-barrier individual and identifies her role more specifically with her body and its functions (Fisher, 1964). Consequently, a female amputee may view her loss as an assault that affects her ability to carry out her "feminine role." Regardless of whether the amputee is male or female, the maximum regular contour consistent with the body wall has been reached as a young adult (Fisher and Cleveland, 1968). Amputation forces readjustment of body image.

The impact of an amputation is somewhat different in adulthood (forty-five years to sixty-five years of age). During this developmental stage the individual directs energy toward establishing and guiding future generations with the hope of improving society (Erikson, 1963). The presence of an amputation is likely to alter this goal and instead of being generative, the adult may enter a state of stagnation. Fear of old age often becomes uppermost in one's mind. The amputation may be viewed as an additional or unwanted bodily change related to old age.

The amputee in the final stage of life, maturity (sixty-five years of age and over), views the presence of loss differently. Since frequent thoughts of death occur during this stage (Caplan and Hackett, 1963), the existence of an amputation may be seen as the prelude to the termination of life. Hence, the mature adult may enter a stage of despair (Erikson, 1963) with a feeling of having little to offer others. Body boundaries have changed at the time of amputation and the individual's personal mental picture is altered, whatever his or her stage of development.

The nurse's role in dealing with altered body image revolves around assisting the individual in establishing a new image. In this regard, several points of patient care as pointed out by Friedmann and Friedmann (1975) are important. First, the amputee should be reassured that one can lead a functional and happy life whether or not a prosthesis is advisable. Second, if possible, the amputee should be introduced to another amputee of similar age, kind of amputation, and medical condition who has accomplished a readjustment in body image. Third, the amputee should be informed that it takes several weeks to become accustomed to the prosthetic device and that it will feel heavy and cumbersome at first. Fourth, the amputee should be told that a training period in the use of the prosthesis will be provided in order to prevent inappropriate use of the artificial limb. Fifth, the amputee should be made to understand that no cosmetic prosthesis is completely natural in appearance. Sixth, the lower limb amputee should be told that a change in gait is to be expected.

Nursing's focus in facilitating the readjustment of the amputee's body image is honesty, good preoperative teaching, reinforcement of teaching in the postoperative period, and listening to what the amputee has to say. Only then can the amputee come to accept a change in body structure.

Sexual Impact

The way an individual perceives his or her body may influence his or her sexual self-concept and sexual behavior (Woods, 1975) in both heterosexual and homosexual relationships. The limbs may be viewed as important to sexual attractiveness and sexual self-image (Parkes, 1976). The female amputee, for example, may view herself as less attractive to males who are sexually aroused by female legs. The amputee who feels unattractive or unlovable may feel inadequate in a sexual relationship. For example, the male amputee may equate the loss of a limb or appendage with castration, thereby, threatening his manhood (Cummings, 1975). In an attempt to maintain his masculinity, the male amputee may "act out" with such aggressive behavior as ramming doors with his wheelchair or balancing precariously on its rear wheels (Compton, 1973). Other means used to uphold an image of virility and "manliness" may be the displaying of pinup pictures, carrying out seductive, flirtatious acts toward nurses, or outright exhibitionism (Jeglijewski, 1973). The amputee may "act out" sexually in an attempt to test personal sexual image, to gain control of a situation that fosters dependence, and/or to attract attention from those in the environment (Woods, 1975).

Often the nurse's immediate reaction toward these flirtatious acts is to retreat and avoid. In dealing with sexual acting out from either a male or female amputee, the nurse must set firm limits, neither going along with the flirtatious acts nor rejecting them. For example, the nurse could say, "I would rather you not touch me. It makes me uncomfortable. However, I will still come and talk to you whenever you desire." This helps set limits, but it does not express rejection. In addition to setting limits, the nurse should assist the amputee in exploring such behavior and encouraging verbal expression of feelings (Kroah, 1973; Ujhely, 1976). The nurse may respond, "Your sexually aggressive behavior is not appropriate. I'd much rather talk to you about how you're feeling right now. It must be frustrating to be in the hospital not knowing how people will respond to you sexually." Such phrases attempt to guide the amputee's actions into words.

In addition to having a threatened sexual image, physical problems of carrying out the sex act may occur. The mechanics of positioning during sex play and intercourse may have to be altered. To illustrate, with the lower limb amputee, it may be desirable for the nonamputee to assume the superior position. Some male amputees may find this a further threat to their male ego and encounter additional difficulties with the sex act. In sidelying positions, an upper extremity amputee may want to switch sides so that the unaffected arm is free (Cummings, 1975). Regardless of the level or location of the amputation, the amputee and sex partner will have to experiment with various positions and techniques (Kaplan, 1975) so that they can find those which are satisfying for their particular sexual relationship.

Another physical problem that may be encountered is an increase in phantom pain after orgasm in the male amputee and during orgasm in the female amputee (Riding, 1976). Unless the amputee is made aware of this phenomenon, guilt feelings are likely to be aroused, since the amputee may believe that engaging in sex is "bad." In addition, the amputee's sexual enjoyment may be diminished. Unless both the amputee and sex partner are aware of the occurrence of phantom pain during sex, additional strains may be placed upon their sexual relationship.

The nurse, however, must be aware that the amputee's sexual dysfunction may not be directly related to the amputation. Alterations in sexual function may have been present before the amputation or may be related to various disease entities, such as diabetes mellitus (Babbott, Rubin, and Ginsburg, 1958; Kolodny, 1971). If the nurse detects a sexual dysfunction in the amputee, appropriate sex therapy should be suggested (Kaplan, 1974).

Occupational Impact

One's identity with an occupation is important since it provides the sense of doing or of having accomplished something constructive and worthwhile (Compton, 1973). This is demonstrated by the frequency with which one is asked, "What do you do for a living?" Now that the amputee has suffered the loss of a limb or appendage, he or she may ask "What has become of me? What am I going to do now?"

Depending upon the individual's prior occupation, some work adjustments may be necessary. These adjustments are either minor or major. For example, a minor adjustment could include placing left-handed banisters along the staircases at work for the individual who has a right arm amputation (McVittie, 1975). A major occupational adjustment may be completely changing jobs. If, for example, the individual's job requires the use of two functional hands, an upper extremity amputee will need occupational training for a new job. The nurse must remember that the amputee may require a change in employment. If so, the nurse should direct the amputee to seek assistance and guidance from the rehabilitation team. Having to change jobs can prove stressful to the amputee. Therefore, the nurse's role at this time will be one of listening to the amputee as he or she expresses fear about changing or modifying his or her occupation. One of the most important factors affecting an individual's ability to cope well with life as an amputee is the capacity to work (Parkes, 1975). The male amputee is likely to view his role as breadwinner endangered and he may imagine his family's affection dwindling as he sees himself being forced into idleness (Gruneberg, 1972). In addition, he might fear that his family's standard of living will drop because he might not be able to cope with the alteration in work status. The elderly amputee might even view the loss of a limb as the end of his or her occupational pursuits and the beginning of sedentary retirement sooner than desired.

Whether the amputee is young or old, the family must be used as a major source of encouragement. Providing support and acceptance as he or she attempts to reconquer simple physical tasks is a major role for family members. The family may be required to assume some of the responsibilities of breadwinner while the amputee is readjusting to a new occupational role. Frequent expressions of encouragement, stating that the amputee is a worthwhile and contributing member to the family, are necessary. The amputee's readjustment to a different occupation is not always rapid or easy, and patience is imperative. Since family members are the ones most directly affected (aside from the amputee) by the occupational readjustments, provisions should be made for them to verbalize their feelings about the impact of the amputation on occupational changes. These provisions can be through the rehabilitation team, the health care team in the hospital setting, or the spiritual advisor.

Social Impact

What one is to oneself and to others constitutes one's social identity. In other words, the inward assurance of expected recognition from oneself and from individuals of personal importance (Erikson, 1960), such as family, friends, and associates, makes up one's identity in society.

When the new amputee leaves the protective environment of the hospital and enters the world again, he or she must reestablish his or her social identity. This identity must incorporate the changed physical appearance and adaptations to daily living. Handrails next to the toilet and bathtub may be necessary for assistance in using these facilities. In addition, special devices may be required on the family automobile so that the amputee can drive. Such modifications in daily living become part of the amputee's identity and how he or she represents himself or herself in society.

Before the amputee is discharged from the hospital, he or she must be made aware that some individuals in society may stare, make comments about the missing limb, or ask numerous questions about the amputation. Amputees have commented that one of their most difficult social encounters is when an innocent child says, "Mommy, look, why does that man have only one leg?" The amputee must realize that some individuals are not probing to be personal but that they are actually uncomfortable and unable to handle the presence of an amputee. Their own anxiety and insecurity are demonstrated by their probing. It is vital to encourage the amputee before and after reentering society to verbalize how he or she may feel about such a situation and how he or she may handle the incident. Engaging amputees in sharing their individual social experiences and how they dealt with them often proves helpful. Society's reactions are reality and the amputee needs assistance in facing and dealing with these realities.

Reentering society demands a certain degree of independence. Since the hospital situation tends to foster dependence, amputees must be weaned from the dependent role early in therapy. Amputees need encouragement to do as much as possible for themselves, for example, their own personal hygiene and transfer techniques. As the lower limb amputee learns to ambulate with a prosthesis, the family, the nurse, and other members of the health team must avoid overprotection. If the patient falls while attempting ambulation, the nurse should ask if he or she needs assistance instead of running immediately to help. Immediate assistance in such an incident is not only degrading, but it fosters dependence on the part of the amputee. The amputee needs reassurance that many preamputation activities can be reestablished. Amputees have engaged in such sports as scuba diving, snow skiing, sky diving, and horseback riding (Smith, 1970). The amputee's personal drive to succeed and the family's support and understanding are vital in his or her reestablishment of preamputation activities.

If there were family problems before the amputation, the loss of a limb may be the final crisis that disrupts the family structure. In this case, psychiatric therapy may be needed for the amputee and the family since disruption of family structure may be interpreted by the amputee as further rejection. When the amputee feels rejection, he or she encounters difficulty in reestablishing a strong social identity.

Each amputee redevelops his or her social identity at a different pace. However, preparing the amputee for situations that might be encountered, allowing the amputee to verbalize feelings about how others react to him or her, fostering independence, and providing encouragement for all forms of progress can facilitate the reestablishment of a social identity.

SUMMARY

Amputation surgery is brought about by four major causes: trauma; disease; tumors; and congenital disorders. Nearly three-fourths of all amputations are brought about by peripheral vascular changes, thus making disease the most frequent cause of amputation. The greatest percentage of amputees are males fifty years old and older.

Amputation imposes a great impact upon both the individual involved and his family. The impact of amputation affects the amputee's emotional well-being, somatic identity, sexuality, occupational identity, and social role. The amputee contends with learning the sick role during the initial impact of amputation and goes on to experience loss, body image alterations, potential threats to sexuality, possible job alterations, and social reacceptance. Therefore, the psychosocial impact of amputation should never be underrated by members of the health care team. The major role of the health care team is to prepare the individual and the family for alterations in daily living which are likely to occur and to assist them in dealing with each of these changes.

Patient Situation

Mr. A. K., a fifty-five-year-old truck driver, has been a diabetic for the past 30 years. Because of chronic vascular changes that have accompanied his diabetes, a right lower limb amputation has been performed. Mr. A. K. is married and the father of two children. His elder child, a daughter, is married and his younger child, a son, is a sophomore in a local city college. Mr. A. K. is two days postamputation and demonstrates problems affecting his emotional well-being, somatic identity, sexuality, occupational identity, and social role. Following are Mr. A. K.'s nursing care plan and patient care cardex dealing with the above mentioned areas of concern.

NURSING CARE PLAN

Problems	Objectives	Nursing Interventions	Principles/Rationale	Evaluations
Emotional Impact Anger directed at health care team and family members.	To decrease Mr. A. K.'s anger.	Encourage the expression of feelings by using open-ended statements such as, "You seem upset today."	Expressing feelings may assist the amputee in identifying what is making him angry.	The nurse would observe for: Changes in Mr. A. K.'s expressions of anger.
	To demonstrate acceptance of Mr. A. K.	Avoid retaliative acts and statements when Mr. A. K. expresses his anger.	Retaliative acts and statements may further upset and anger the amputee. Retaliative acts may be interpreted by the health team as rejection by health team members and family members. Retaliative acts may be the family and health team members projection of their own anger.	Mr. A. K.'s ability to express himself freely without fear of retaliation from others.
	To support Mr. A. K.'s family during his expressions of anger.	Act as a sounding board for family members so that they might express their feelings of frustration when Mr. A. K. "strikes out" at them in anger.	A family frustrated by acts of anger directed at them by a loved one may be unable to provide necessary support to the loved one.	The family's ability to cope with Mr. A. K.'s anger.
		Provide explanations to Mr. A. K.'s family about reasons for his anger.	Expressions of anger are often directed at attributes, such as mobility, which others represent and not necessarily at others personally. Anger expressed in the form of blaming others is one way the amputee attempts	

66

Presence of phantom limb phenomenon and phantom pain.	To enhance Mr. A. K.'s and his family's understanding of phantom limb phenomenon.	Describe phantom limb phenomenon to Mr. A. K. and his family as the sensation at the amputated site that the limb is still present. Mention that the sensation is present in the majority of amputees and lasts anywhere from 6 months to 20 years.	Realizing that such a phenomenon exists and is experienced by the majority of amputees decreases the anxiety of both the amputee and his family.	The nurse would observe for: Anxiety and fear expressed by Mr. A. K. and his family related to the presence of phantom phenomenon and phantom pain.
	To enhance Mr. A. K.'s and his family's understanding of the difference between phantom limb pain and stump pain.	Describe the difference between phantom limb pain and stump pain to Mr. A. K. and his family. Describe stump pain as: 1. pain that does not occur immediately after surgery. 2. pain brought on by touching the stump. 3. pain that occurs at the site of surgical intervention.	By knowing the difference between phantom limb pain and stump pain, the amputee is better prepared to determine when pain medication is necessary for his stump pain.	Inappropriate use of pain medication (use of pain medication for phantom limb pain rather than stump pain).
		Describe phantom limb pain as: 1. pain in the phantom limb that often is elicited by an emotionally charged situation such as anger or talking about the amputation.	By realizing that phantom limb pain can be brought on by emotionally charged situations, the amputee and his family are better able to recognize and avoid such situations.	Identification and avoidance of situations by Mr. A. K. and his family which elicit phantom limb pain.
Body image change feared to be related to aging.	To assist Mr. A. K. in dealing with his fears of body change.	Encourage Mr. A. K. to verbalize his fears about how he views the amputation as an unwanted body change related to aging. The use of open-ended statements such as, "It must be frightening to lose a limb and not know what the future holds for you" may be helpful.	Verbalization about a fear tends to decrease the fear. Verbalization about a fear often assists the individual in identifying ways of dealing with the fear.	The nurse would observe for: Verbalization alluding to how Mr. A. K. views his body change.

NURSING CARE PLAN (cont.)

Problems	Objectives	Nursing Interventions	Principles/Rationale	Evaluations
Somatic Impact (cont.)		Provide privacy during Mr. A. K.'s discussions about his fears of body change related to aging.	Privacy enhances the likelihood that the amputee will express himself freely.	Mr. A. K.'s uninhibited verbalization of fears.
	To assist Mr. A. K. in analyzing the positive aspects of his life.	Assist Mr. A. K. in identifying and discussing those aspects of his life that he finds positive and supportive.	Recognizing the positive and supportive aspects of the amputee's life may provide him with a reason to be generative. Identifying and discussing positive aspects of life prevents a state of stagnation by the amputee.	Mr. A. K.'s verbalization of hopeful feelings and plans for the future.
Sexual Impact Inappropriate sexual statements and behavior toward female staff.	To alter Mr. A. K.'s inappropriate behavior.	Provide Mr. A. K. with limits for his behavior while never going along with nor rejecting his inappropriate behavior (i.e., inform him that you find his behavior unpleasant, but reassure him that you accept *him.*)	Providing a sexually aggressive individual with well-defined limits for his inappropriate behavior, yet expressing acceptance of him as a person, aids in decreasing inappropriate sexual behavior.	The nurse would observe for: A decrease in Mr. A. K.'s inappropriate sexual statements and behavior.
		Encourage Mr. A. K. to examine his behavior.	Looking at one's own behavior aids in identifying ways of dealing with the behavior.	
	To enhance Mr. A. K.'s feelings of self-worth.	Encourage Mr. A. K. to express his feelings.	Verbalization aids in decreasing anxiety and helps in identifying	Mr. A. K.'s positive expression about his self-worth.

Expressed concern about an alteration in the family's standard of living.	To assist Mr. A. K. in examining his concerns about the family's financial status.	Encourage Mr. A. K. to discuss his concerns about his family's financial security with his wife and children. Notify social service about Mr. A. K.'s expressed concern.	Financial concerns affect the entire family; therefore their knowledge and input in developing a solution is imperative. Social service is a component of the health team prepared to assist the amputee and his family with financial concerns.	The nurse would observe for: Expressed satisfaction by Mr. A. K. of possible solutions of his financial concerns. Increased communication between Mr. A. K. and his family concerning their financial situation.
		Encourage Mr. A. K. to continue to verbalize his concern about his family's financial status.	Internalizing a concern can lead to undue anxiety.	Decreased anxiety in Mr. A. K. about family financial concerns.
Social Impact Expressed concern about how society will accept his altered physical structure.	To assist Mr. A. K. in dealing with his concern about society's acceptance of his altered physical structure.	Encourage Mr. A. K. to verbalize how he may react and deal with people staring at him, commenting about his lost limb, or asking probing questions about the amputation.	Verbalizing feelings about social acceptance and possible ways of dealing with these feelings assists the amputee in preparing for a potentially traumatic social reality.	The nurse would observe for: Open expression by Mr. A. K. about his feelings and his possible reactions to society's response to his altered physical structure.
		Encourage Mr. A. K. to express his concerns about society's acceptance of him with his family.	Family members who are cognizant of a loved one's concerns are better prepared to provide support during a traumatic situation.	Supportive statements from the family related to society's acceptance of Mr. A. K.'s altered physical structure.

PATIENT CARE CARDEX

PATIENT'S NAME: ___Mr. A. K.___ DIAGNOSIS: ___Right lower limb amputation___

AGE: ___55 years___ SEX: ___Male___

MARITAL STATUS: ___Married___ OCCUPATION: ___Truck driver___

SIGNIFICANT OTHERS: ___Wife and two children (one married and one attending local college)___

Problems	Nursing Approaches
Emotional: Anger directed at health care team and family members.	1. Encourage the expression of feelings by use of open-ended statements (i.e., "You seem upset today"). 2. Avoid use of retaliative acts and statements when patient expresses anger. 3. Act as sounding board for family so that they might express their feelings of frustration when patient "strikes out" at them in anger. 4. Provide explanations to family about reasons for patient's anger.
Somatic: Presence of phantom limb phenomenon and phantom pain.	1. Describe phantom limb phenomenon to patient and family. 2. Mention that phantom limb phenomenon is present in the majority of amputees and lasts anywhere from 6 months to 20 years. 3. Describe difference between phantom limb pain and stump pain to patient and family. Describe stump pain as: (a) pain that does not occur immediately after surgery. (b) pain brought on by touching the stump. (c) pain that occurs at the site of surgical intervention. Describe phantom limb pain as: (a) pain in the phantom limb which often is elicited by an emotionally charged situation such as anger or talking about the amputation.

aging.

Sexual: Inappropriate sexual statements and behavior toward female staff.

Occupational: Expressed concern about an alteration in the family's standard of living.

Social: Expressed concern about how society will accept his altered physical structure.

related to aging.
2. Provide privacy during discussions about fears of body change related to aging.
3. Assist in identifying and discussing those aspects of life which are positive and supportive.

1. Provide with limits for behavior while never going along with nor rejecting inappropriate behavior (i.e., inform that you find behavior unpleasant, but reassure that you accept *him*.)
2. Encourage to examine behavior.
3. Encourage to express feelings.

1. Encourage to discuss concerns about family's financial security with family.
2. Notify social service about expressed concern.
3. Encourage to continue to verbalize concern about family's financial situation.

1. Encourage to verbalize how he may react and deal with people staring at him, commenting about lost limb, or asking probing questions about the amputation.
2. Encourage to express with family concerns about society's acceptance of him.

REFERENCES

Babbott, D., Rubin, A., and Ginsburg, S. J. Reproductive characteristics of diabetic men, *Diabetes*, 1958, 7, 33-35.

Brown, F. Knowledge of body image and nursing care of the patient with limb amputation, *Journal of Psychiatric Nursing*, 1964, 2, 397-409.

Caplan, L., and Hackett, T. Emotional effects of lower limb amputation in the aged, *The New England Journal of Medicine*, 1963, 269 (22), 1166-1171.

Cath, S., Glud, E., and Blane, H. The role of the body image in psychotherapy with the physically handicapped, *Psychoanalytic Review*, 1957, 44, 34-40.

Compton, C. War injury: identity crisis for young men, *Nursing Clinics of North America*, 1973, 8 (1), 52-66.

Cummings, V. Amputees and sexual dysfunction, *Archives of Physical Medicine and Rehabilitation*, 1975, 56 (1), 53-66.

Davies, E., Friz, B., and Clippinger, F. Amputees and their prothesis, *Artificial Limbs*, 1970, 14, 19-48.

Erikson, E. *Childhood and society*. New York: W. W. Norton and Co., 1963.

Erikson, E. The problems of ego identity. In M. Stein, A. Vidich, and D. White (Eds.), *Identity and anxiety*. Glencoe, Ill.: The Free Press, 1960.

Fisher, S. Sex differences in body perception, *Psychological Monographs*, 1964, 78, 1-22.

Fisher, S., and Cleveland, S. *Body image and personality*. New York: Dover Publications, Inc., 1968.

Frazier, S., and Kolb, L. Psychiatric aspects of pain and the phantom limb, *Orthopedic Clinics of North America*, 1970, 1 (2), 481-490.

Friedmann, L., and Friedmann, L. The quality of hope for the amputee, *Archives of Surgery*, 1975, 110, 760.

Gerstmann, J. Psychological and phenomenological aspects of disorders of the body image, *Journal of Nervous and Mental Disease*, 1958, 126 (6), 499-512.

Gruneberg, R. Psychological assessment in trauma, *The Journal of Trauma*, 1972, 12 (4), 364-365.

Jeglijewski, J. Target: outside world, *American Journal of Nursing*, 1973, 73 (6), 1024-1027.

Kaplan, H. S. *The illustrated manual of sex therapy*. New York: Quadrangle/The New York Times Book Co., 1975.

Kaplan, H. S. *The new sex therapy*. New York: Brunner/Mazel, 1974.

Kerstein, M., Zimmer, H., Dugdale, F., and Lerner, E. What influence does age have on rehabilitation of amputees? *Geriatrics*, 1975, 30 (12), 67-71.

Kolodny, R. C. Sexual dysfunction in diabetic females, *Diabetes*, 1971, 20, 557-559.

Kroah, J. How to deal with patients who act out sexually, *Nursing '73*, 1973, 2 (12), 38-39.

Larson, C., and Gould, M. *Orthopedic Nursing.* St. Louis: The C. V. Mosby Co., 1974.

Luckmann, J., and Sorensen, K. *Medical-surgical nursing: a psychophysiologic approach.* Philadelphia: W. B. Saunders, 1974.

Martin, N. Rehabilitation of the upper extremity amputee, *Nursing Outlook,* 1970, *18* (2), 50-51.

McCollough, N. C. The dysvascular amputee, *Orthopedic Clinics of North America,* 1972, *3* (2), 303-321.

McVittie, C. K. Traumatic amputation of the right arm, *Nursing Mirror,* 1975, *141* (9), 147-148.

Mital, M., and Pierce, D. *Amputees and their prosthesis.* Boston: Little, Brown and Co., 1971.

Parkes, C. M. The psychological reaction to loss of a limb: the first year after amputation. In J. G. Howells (Ed.), *Modern perspectives in the psychiatric aspects of surgery.* New York: Brunner/Mazel, 1976.

Parkes, C. Reaction to loss of limb, *Nursing Mirror,* 1975, *140* (1), 36-40.

Parsons, T. *The social system.* New York: The Free Press, 1951.

Riding, J. Phantom limb: some theories, *Anaesthesia,* 1976, *31,* 102-106.

Severyn, B. R. Nursing implications with a loss of body function, *ANA Regional Clinical Conference,* 1969, 233-241.

Smith, J. P. In what sports can patients with amputations and other handicaps successfully and actively participate? *Physical Therapy,* 1970, *50* (1), 121-126.

Tooms, R. E. Amputation surgery in the upper extremity, *Orthopedic Clinic of North America,* 1972, *3* (2), 383-395.

Ujhely, G. Two types of problem patients ... and how to deal with them, *Nursing '76,* 1976, *6* (5), 64-67.

Warren, R. Amputation in the lower limb, *Surgery Annual,* 1975, *7,* 331-346.

Woods, N. F. *Human sexuality in health and illness.* St. Louis: The C. V. Mosby Co., 1975.

Zalewski, N., Geronemus, D., and Siegel, H. Hemipelvectomy: the triumph of Ms. A., *American Journal of Nursing,* 1973, *73* (12), 2073-2077.

5

The Patient with a

MASTECTOMY

INTRODUCTION

Approximately 88,000 women are diagnosed each year as having cancer of the breast (Cancer Statistics, 1976). In other words, 1 out of every 15 women in the United States will be affected by breast cancer at some time during her life (Cancer News, 1976). The majority of cases of breast cancer have been found in women over the age of forty-five years, with the incidence increasing with age (Haagensen, 1971). Studies reveal that cancer occurs most frequently in the outer quadrant of the left breast and in women who have not borne or breast fed infants (Luckmann and Sorensen, 1974). However, cancer of the breast diagnosed in a localized stage has been treated with considerable success with five-year survival rates for white females (84 percent) and black females (77 percent) (Cancer Statistics, 1976).

Although cancer of the breast remains the leading cause of cancer deaths in women, it must not be forgotten that males are also susceptible to tumors of the breast. Tumors of the male breast, however, are not as common as those that occur in the female organ. In addition, males affected by tumors of the breast have been slightly older than females so affected (Wakeley, 1973).

When an individual first detects the presence of a lump in the breast, nursing intervention is required. The nurse's role is to recognize the impact that detection of a lump has upon one's life and the results that a mastectomy does and will have upon the individual.* This chapter will deal with the impact of mastectomy on both the female and male's emotional well-being, somatic identity, sexuality, occupational identity, and social role.

*It is advisable for the reader to have read Chapter 1 before continuing with this chapter.

SIGNIFICANCE OF DISCOVERY AND DIAGNOSIS

The presence of a lump in the breast, in the majority of cases, is found during bathing, dressing, examination by the individual, or during manipulation of the breast by the sex partner (Maguire, 1975a). Discovery of a lump in the breast often elicits an immediate reaction of concern for life (Katz, Weiner, Gallagher, and Hallman, 1976; and Kent, 1975). A palpable lump denotes the possible presence of cancer and the fear of impending death is usually uppermost in the individual's mind (Akehurst, 1974), since many individuals equate the word cancer with death. The individual's response may be one of repudiation and may be demonstrated by such a statement as, "No, this can't be happening to me." Repudiating the existence of the lump or the fear of a possible mastectomy may lead to the individual's delay in seeking medical treatment (Leis and Pelnik, 1974; The controversy over breast cancer, 1974). The fear of mutilation is often as intense as the fear of cancer (Leis, 1974).

Once the presence of the lump has been noted, the individual involved is concerned about how others will respond to the presence of the lump or is concerned about the possibility of a mastectomy. The mastectomy candidate may wonder how his or her sex partner will respond to the mutilating effects of surgery. A mother may be concerned about the welfare of her children should something happen to her as a result of the breast lump. The model, no doubt, will fear the effects that a mastectomy may have upon his or her professional career.

The individual's response to a mastectomy is affected by both the cultural and the personal importance of the breast. In today's dress, clothing often accentuates the bustline, such as a low-cut evening dress or a tight fitting T-shirt. By the same token, the choice of going braless can be a female's way of expressing her liberation (Woods, 1975b) while the male can express his liberation with an open shirt. Because of the similarities in manner of dress and hair style between males and females, the presence of the protruding breast is often the only publicly visible mark of femininity (Renneker and Cutter, 1952).

The female breast is a symbol of motherhood both from a nutritious and nurtural point of view. The infant can be fed by the female breast or the child can be cuddled close to the breast in a protective manner. The importance of the breast to the female becomes apparent during adolescence when the young girl focuses a great deal of attention on the development of her bustline and goes to great effort to draw attention to her new identifiable marks of femininity. The attention may be brought about by the clothing that she wears or by the posture she maintains. The breast also plays a role in sexual stimulation (Anstice, 1970a), and it may assume an important role in adult sex play for both sexes (Woods, 1975a; Woods, 1975b). Thus, it can be seen that the breast has a variety of functions in both personal and cultural life.

In today's society the impact of mastectomy on the sex partner often has been overlooked. Frequently, he or she is the first to be told whether the breast mass was cancerous. The sex partner is usually the first person called upon to provide emotional support to the mastectomee (Downie, 1974). However, little support and understanding are provided by the health care team to this individual. Yet the sex partner is often required to suppress his or her feelings and keep a "stiff upper lip" in an attempt to be that supportive "significant other."

The sex partner has equal need for support and understanding. The fear of whether the loss of a partner will occur, what needs the mastectomee may have which require assistance, and how the sex partner will react to the surgical experience are but a few of the concerns expressed by the mastectomee's sex partner. A sex partner who is uncertain and full of conflicting emotions may project an attitude of rejection (Klein, 1971), the very attitude most feared by the mastectomee. The health care team must provide the sex partner with honest answers to questions and encourage him or her to ventilate openly his or her feelings to them. If adequate preparation and support are not provided for the individual who is the mastectomee's major source of emotional support, the sex partner, may not be prepared to cope with the demands placed upon him or her.

Generally, the second individual to discover that the lump was cancerous and that the breast has been removed is the patient. The first act carried out by the patient immediately postoperative is touching and palpating the appropriate chest area in an attempt to determine whether or not the breast has been removed. This maneuver is usually done in the recovery room while the patient is recuperating from anesthesia, a time when few emotional support systems are available. Once the individual discovers that the breast is gone, the process of loss begins.

IMPACT OF MASTECTOMY

Emotional Impact*

When the individual first discovers that the breast has been removed, the act of repudiation occurs. Repudiating the loss of the breast generally lasts from a few minutes to several days. In some cases, however, the use of repudiation may extend for months. As with any loss, repudiation is the "buffer" that allows the individual time to activate thoughts and mobilize other means of coping with the loss.

*It is advisable for the reader to have read Chapter 3 before continuing with this section.

After the stage of repudiation, the mastectomee enters the stage of recognition and it is during this emotional stage that anger, depression, or negotiation may be elicited. The most common emotional reaction of the mastectomee during this stage of loss is depression (Maguire, 1976; 1970b). Most female mastectomees experience depression within a week or so after the operation. This depression frequently lasts several months, but it may last as long as two years (Anstice, 1970b). The woman feels that her life is ended and that no one understands how she feels. Every time she bathes, undresses, or looks in a mirror, she is faced with the fact that a potentially fatal disease may be present (Maguire, 1975b). Some women may demonstrate their depression by failing to carry out necessary household or work responsibilities. Instead, they may retreat to bed and assume the role of an invalid. These women often view themselves as worthless and noncontributing members of society. The following statements are examples of expressed worthlessness: "What good am I to myself and my family now that I'm not a whole person." "I can't carry out my usual duties since I have had a surgery like this one." Feelings of depression may be apparent in other forms, such as insomnia or inability to concentrate. The use of group sessions consisting of individuals in similar stages of loss has proven effective (Schmid, Kiss, and Hibert, 1974). Mastectomees, thus, are able to empathize and provide support to one another during this period.

The male mastectomee, no doubt, goes through a stage of depression after the loss of his breast. It must not be forgotten that male mastectomees are also reminded that they may have a potentially fatal disease each time they touch or view their chest area.

Crying plays an important role for the female mastectomee in dealing with her depression (Anstice, 1970b; Harrell, 1972). It can be her means of expressing her feelings out in the open. At no time should the individual be reprimanded for crying or should the presence of crying be interpreted as a sign of weakness. Privacy should be provided during crying and the individual should be reassured that there is nothing wrong with expressing one's feelings in the form of tears. Family members, if present during the mastectomee's crying, may feel embarrassed and encourage the woman not to cry. It is the nurse's responsibility at this point to explain to the family that the individual has a need to cry. The following kind of statement may prove beneficial: "Crying is one way of relieving pent-up frustrations and your wife needs to cry at this time in order to express her feelings about her mastectomy."

To assist family members with their feelings of discomfort during the mastectomee's crying, the nurse should encourage them to provide support in the form of listening, holding her hand, or simply touching the woman's arm in an expressive, gentle manner. In addition, the nurse may find it helpful to discuss with the family members their feelings about crying after the incident is over. Possibly expressing that they are uncomfortable during the mastectomee's crying will help them identify why they feel uncomfortable and how they might best deal with their own feelings.

Men are less likely to express their depression in the form of crying because of the societal "taboos" for such behavior in males. The nurse is more likely to observe the male mastectomee retreat into his room, remain uncommunicative, or play the role of the "good patient." It is imperative for the nurse to encourage him to verbalize how he feels about himself. A leading statement such as, "You seem 'low' today," may initiate verbalization. Suppressing feelings of self-worth only add to prolonging the expression of depression.

Feelings of guilt may also be expressed by the mastectomee during the stage of recognition. Possibly misconceptions about cancer or fear of surgery delayed the seeking of medical attention. Common misconceptions include the belief that cancer is inherited, contagious, or caused by a blow or injury to the breast (Women's attitudes regarding breast cancer, 1974). The mastectomee may feel that delay in seeking medical attention added to the severity of the disease process. Thus, the extensiveness of the surgical intervention, the individual may believe, is punishment for such actions. Again, it is imperative that this individual verbally express any feelings of guilt. Reassurance that the surgical intervention is not punishment for some wrongdoing on the part of the mastectomee should be provided. Misconceptions about cancer require clarification and the nurse must take an active role in providing accurate information.

During the stage of recognition the mastectomee needs assistance from the nurse in dealing with attitudes that will be present in the environment outside the hospital. Friends may suddenly stay away once they have heard about the surgical intervention or totally avoid the discussion of cancer because of their own discomfort in dealing with the topic. Conversations between the nurse and the mastectomee regarding how these situations will affect the individual and how the mastectomee intends to deal with them are imperative. It is a grave injustice not to prepare the mastectomee for such confrontations (Harrell, 1972).

When the mastectomee enters the final stage of loss, reconciliation, he or she is ready to reenter society with a note of confidence. No longer does the mastectomee feel a need for isolation from social interaction or work responsibilities. If a prosthesis is used, it becomes a part of the body image and not just a piece of necessary equipment. Clothing issues are resolved and the mastectomee again presents an appearance that is both attractive and well-groomed. A feeling of self-worth is reestablished and the need to resume the role of a contributing member of society again becomes apparent. It must not be overlooked, however, that the mastectomee continues to live with the fear of possible metastasis and possible loss of the second breast (Leis, 1971; Schmid, Kiss, and Hibert, 1974). Therefore, fluctuations in emotional well-being do occur and the mastectomee may move back and forth between the stages of repudiation, recognition, and resolution.

Somatic Impact*

The breast is an important part of one's body image. This image is not necessarily an objective or accurate picture of oneself, but rather an accumulation of thoughts that one has about oneself. Loss of any body part, such as a breast, disrupts one's body image and, with it, the sense of naturalness and wholeness. The female mastectomee views her breasts as a symbol of her femininity (Woods, 1975b). Now that a breast is gone, is her femininity gone? This may be a question mulled over and over by the female mastectomee. The male mastectomee, by the same token, may equate the removal of a breast with castration since his masculine physique has been altered. He may now view his manly appearance as being inferior.

The somatic impact of a mastectomy is affected by the individual's stage of development at the time of the loss. The majority of female mastectomees are in the stage of adulthood (forty-five to sixty-five years of age) when the major focus of interest is directed toward establishing and guiding future generations (Erikson, 1963). Now that the woman has lost a breast she may feel that her ability to "mother" and guide future generations is no longer present. Instead of becoming generative, she may withdraw from others, become self-absorbed, and enter a stage of stagnation.

In addition to the task of generativity during the stage of adulthood, the female is concerned about maintaining an attractive physical appearance. She often identifies, in an exaggerated manner, each single physical change related to aging. The loss of a breast may be viewed by the female mastectomee in the stage of adulthood as an additional unwanted bodily change related to the aging process. Consequently, she may feel resigned to old age. Since she feels unattractive physically and incapable of achieving the task of generativity, chronic defeatism and depression may result and the woman isolates herself in self-pity.

Male mastectomees tend to be older than female mastectomees (Wakeley, 1973) and are more likely to fall in the stage of maturity (sixty-five years of age and older) when frequent thoughts of death occur (Erikson, 1963). If feelings of despair are present, the occurrence of a mastectomy may add additional despondent thoughts of impending death. In addition, the male mastectomee may be unable to derive satisfaction from his life's experiences and accomplishments, especially if he has not developed a strong sense of self-worth. The presence of the mastectomy may add to his decreased feel-

*It is advisable for the reader to have read Chapter 2 before continuing with this section.

ings of self-worth. Consequently, he manifests his feelings of despair in expressions of disgust. Regardless of the developmental stage demonstrated by the individual at the time of the mastectomy, body boundaries have been altered and the individual is forced to readjust his personal mental picture of his body structure.

How the mastectomee believes significant others view him or her is of vital importance. The mastectomee is concerned about how the sex partner will react to the missing breast and to the large scar that exists. "Will my sex partner be repulsed by the appearance of my chest wall?" "Will my sex partner replace me with some one else because of the change in my body structure?" These are but a few of the concerns with which the mastectomee must deal.

Following a mastectomy, lymphedema of the extremity on the affected side may occur, rendering that extremity larger than the extremity on the nonaffected side (Healey, 1971; Golemastic, Delikaris, Balarustsos, and Karamonakos, 1975). Hence, special precautions of arm and hand care are necessary. These precautions include such things as wearing rubber gloves when gardening or using harsh detergents, wearing thimbles when sewing, using electric razors when shaving under the arm, and avoiding injections, infusions, and finger pricks in the affected arm (Schmid, Kiss, and Hibert, 1974). In addition, since the extremity on the affected side may be larger than on the nonaffected side, the individual should be encouraged not to wear constrictive sleeves, restrictive jewelry, or a tight bra strap on that side. The emotional impact of these restrictions only adds to the mastectomee's already altered body image. The mastectomee may be concerned about how the enlarged arm appears to others. The mastectomee might say, "This enlarged arm makes me look like a freak." The nurse may want to respond in a reflective expression of personal feelings about the altered body image.

Numbness and tingling along the inner aspect of the arm on the affected side are likely to occur in most patients (Schmid, Kiss, and Hibert, 1974; Harrell, 1972). The fact that peripheral nerves are cut during the surgery helps explain the occurrence of this sensation. As the peripheral nerves regenerate, sensation gradually resumes. In some instances, mastectomees will have permanent residual loss of sensation in the arm on the affected side (Schmid, Kiss, and Hibert, 1974). The individual must be advised of these changes before surgery in order to avoid undue anxiety after surgery that something went wrong. With the presence of numbness and tingling the mastectomee must now reestablish body boundaries. Not only is a breast missing, but sensation in the arm on the affected side is also altered.

Phantom phenomenon, often an issue overlooked by nursing, is not uncommon in the mastectomee. The phantom breast may be experienced in its entirety or only specific regions of the breast may be felt. Some mastectomees have reported a phantom pain in the missing breast. Although the phantom phenomenon or phantom pain may not be so vivid as that felt in a limb amputation, nonetheless, these sensations do exist in some individuals (Weinstein, Vetter, and Sersen, 1970). Phantom phenomenon of the breast, just like phantom phenomenon of the limb, yields a more vivid phantom in the proximal area. Thus, the nipple is the single most common area felt in breast phenomena. In addition, research has indicated that the tendency for phantoms of the left breast appeared significantly sooner after surgery than phantoms of the right breast (Weinstein, Vetter, and Sersen, 1970). The mastectomee must be made aware of the fact that such sensations can exist after surgery and that these sensations are normal. If the mastectomee is not forewarned of the possibility of these sensations, the individual may believe that the phantom pain is an abnormal occurrence. Such beliefs will only increase the mastectomee's anxiety and cause concern about possible complications.

The breast prosthesis plays a major role in the female mastectomee's reestablishment of body image. It is advisable for a lightweight soft prosthesis to be provided soon after the surgical dressings are removed. Although the initial prosthesis is temporary, it helps raise the woman's self-image while she is vulnerable to feelings of depression (Kent, 1975). It is possible to wear a lightweight prosthesis as early as the second or third postoperative day as a result of contemporary suction techniques and lightweight dressings. A permanent prosthesis should not be fitted until the wound has healed completely. A variety of prostheses are available and they vary in cost. They may be silicone-gel, oil-filled, granule-filled, or air-filled (Breast prosthesis, 1975; Winkler, 1977). The one the women selects should be based upon cost, comfort, and what she finds most suitable to restore her figure. The sex partner may wish to take an active role in helping in the selection of the prosthesis. Some prosthetic devices assume a very human-like texture and may be found desirable by the sex partner. If the woman wants information about breast prostheses, the nurse should direct her to surgical appliance firms, women's wear departments, and drugstores. A list of establishments that carry permanent breast prostheses can be obtained through the American Cancer Society.

If the mastectomy is not radical, the woman may want a silicone implant instead of a breast prosthesis (Leis and Pelnick, 1974). The use of a silicone implant is a tentative decision made preoperatively by the woman and her physician. If during the course of the operation the physician finds that it is possible to carry out the silicone implant, he may do so. However, some authorities question the value of such a surgical maneuver since it has been found that the detection of new lumps by palpation is very difficult (Weiss, 1975). In addition, if the woman's hopes for such a breast reconstruction is shattered, she is robbed of the opportunity to begin her loss process preoperatively. In addition to doing silicone implants during the surgical intervention, some surgeons have grafted the nipple back or fashioned a nipple from the labia and grafted it in place (Leis, 1974; Leis and Pilnik, 1974; Thomas and Yates, 1977). Such a surgical maneuver can provide a positive effect upon the individual's reestablishment of body image, since the chest area now may have a closer resemblance to its premastectomy state.

When the mastectomee returns for the first postoperative checkup, the individual should be instructed and advised on the technique for breast self-examination. Pictorial pamphlets are helpful and can be obtained from the American Cancer Society (Byrd, 1974). Introducing this procedure may elicit some feelings of anxiety, since it reminds the mastectomee that recurrence of the cancer is possible. The individual should be encouraged to verbalize these feelings since suppression and internalization of them may lead to depression. If the mastectomee finds it difficult to carry out breast self-examination, the sex partner may prove helpful (Anstice, 1970a).

Sexual Impact

A mastectomy is one of the most prevalent sexually threatening experiences. In the case of the female mastectomee, a normally visible organ has been removed and in its place remains a flattened or concave chest. The sexual significance of the breast to the individual plays a major role in the process of adaptation to the loss of a breast. For many women the breast is a significant indication of femininity. To some men the presence of a muscular breast can represent masculinity. The value assigned to the lost breast by the individual is of personal importance. If the individual is greatly concerned with bodily appearance, the loss of a breast, no doubt, is more threatening to the self-image than the individual who is not so concerned with bodily appearance. A patient of either sex who perceives himself or herself as mutilated because of the mastectomy is likely to feel that he or she is unacceptable both to society and to significant others, especially the sex partner. Many a woman has actually moved out of her bedroom into a guest bedroom in an attempt to prevent her sex partner from viewing her altered body structure.

Females whose breasts were either very large or very small are likely to be especially sensitive about the altered appearance of their breasts (Woods, 1975b). To add to the trauma of the mastectomy, these women can encounter difficulty in obtaining an adequate prosthesis without the assistance of a skilled prosthetist. Very large breasted women may have difficulty in obtaining a prosthesis of adequate weight to resemble the remaining breast. Women with very small breasts often experience problems both in obtaining a prosthesis of representative size and in keeping the prosthesis in place, since it is relatively lightweight (Woods, 1975b).

The presence of the breast plays an important part in sex play in many relationships. If the individual finds breast stimulation both desirable and essential in foreplay, the absence of a breast could affect sexual satisfaction. The presence of the breast can also serve as a source of sexual excitement for the sex partner. Seeing and touching the breast may have provided sexual pleasure for the sex partner. Now that the breast is gone the sex partner may interpret its absence as interference with his or her own sexual satisfaction (Shope, 1975).

An individual may feel that personal sexual identity is dependent upon the sexual image projected by one's sex partner. Thus, the presence of a mastectomy may be perceived by the individual as a threat to one's personal sexual image. If an individual is revulsed by the appearance of the mastectomy, personal sexual satisfaction may be threatened (Woods, 1975a). Unless the individual is assisted in expressing these feelings, extreme guilt may be aroused as a result of the uncontrollable thoughts. If the individual attempts to hide such feelings, the sexual enthusiasm displayed by the sex partner will probably decrease. This decrease in sexual enthusiasm, in turn, can be interpreted by the mastectomee as rejection (Bard and Sutherland, 1955).

Witkin (1974) suggests that the mastectomee and sex partner share their fears and emotions with each other and avoid the pretense of being unaffected by the operation. The sex partner should make it clear to the mastectomee that any hesitant response does not imply rejection, but rather an expression of empathy. The sex partner must be encouraged to express to the mastectomee that he or she does not desire separate sleeping accommodations. Allowing the mastectomee to retreat to another bedroom is not being helpful and can lead to marital and sexual problems (Maguire, 1975a). To aid in the expression of acceptance of the mastectomee by the sex partner, resumption of intercourse as soon as possible is suggested. When intercourse takes place early in the postoperative period, the chances for the development of a sense of impairment and valuelessness by the mastectomee are much less. Early intercourse provides proof of continued affection by the sex partner (Witkin, 1974). In addition, it assists the mastectomee in accepting himself or herself as an undiminished sexual being.

The issue of whether or not marital stability will be affected by the loss of a breast is often present in the mind of the mastectomee. A Gallup Poll conducted among women indicated that an already happy marriage would not be endangered by a mastectomy, but many of the women felt that a mastectomy would interfere with the establishment of a new sexual relationship (Women's attitudes regarding breast cancer, 1974). Bard and Sutherland (1955) found that couples whose preoperative relationships were burdened with problems encountered the most difficulty after a mastectomy. By the same token, Schoenberg and Carr (1970) feel that if the marital relationship is supportive and good sexual adjustment exists prior to the mastectomy, postoperative adjustment is less difficult.

In some cases, the surgery may be used as an excuse for avoiding intercourse in sexually unsatisfying or unpleasant relationships (Woods, 1975b). In this instance, the surgical intervention is used as a means of avoiding an unpleasant situation, the sexual relationship. It would be advisable to assess the sexual relationship preoperatively. If difficulties are identified, counseling may be needed in an attempt to minimize the strain that will be placed upon the relationship caused by the mastectomy.

Occupational Impact

The occupational impact that a mastectomy will have upon an individual varies. For some, a mastectomy may end a career. For others, no alterations in occupational pursuits will occur. No doubt, the individual affected the most by the existence of a mastectomy is one who must rely heavily upon natural body appearance for occupational reasons. Models, for example, may encounter changes in work assignments or complete loss of job should a mastectomy be performed. The appearance of the body in clothing with varying degrees of exposure is an occupational necessity for most models. For example, the female model who frequently wears evening gowns with plunging necklines or wears blouses designed to enhance the "natural" look may find the presence of a mastectomy a hindrance. In such a situation, if possible, the surgeon is encouraged to use a transverse incision or a modified radical procedure for a mastectomy because it avoids scars in the neck, shoulder, and apex of the axilla (Burdick, 1975; Leis, 1974). Silicone implants and the use of a modified radical procedure have permitted some women to resume their modeling careers after a mastectomy (Leis, 1974; *Cancer News*, 1976).

Many individuals may be concerned about their ability to resume activities involving the arm on the affected side. The patient should be reassured that motion of the arm on the affected side will be regained with the consistent use of arm exercises that are taught for use in the postoperative period (Mamaril, 1974). However, the mastectomee must be instructed not to lift heavy objects, carry heavy packages, or move furniture. Assistance with these activities is important. In addition to the routine exercises that may be prescribed for the mastectomee, various household tasks are beneficial in exercising the arm on the affected side. Making beds, sweeping, vacuuming, washing and ironing clothes, cleaning windows and mirrors, hanging curtains, or cleaning the bathtub are just a few of the household activities the mastectomee can do to enhance arm motion (Lasser, 1969). These household activities also may not seem so monotonous to the individual as routine arm exercises.

Activities and hobbies that involve the use of one's hands are beneficial. Such activities as playing the piano, painting (both household and artistic), typing, cutting with scissors, sewing, gardening (with gloves), and driving the car are but a few activities that develop strength in the arm on the affected side. In addition, these activities supplement the necessary arm exercises (Lasser, 1969).

The mastectomee must be encouraged by health team members and family members to resume premastectomy activities as soon as possible, whether it be at home or with a career. Resuming activities done prior to the mastectomy or finding new ones not only provides physical benefits but emotional benefits as well.

Social Impact

The effect that the mastectomy has upon social contact is of utmost importance to both the mastectomee and the family involved. If feelings of shame or embarrassment are prevalent, the mastectomee may withdraw from others and avoid contact with family members, friends, or acquaintances. After a mastectomy, social contacts with individuals outside a marital relationship are most vulnerable to decay (Maguire, 1975b). Recognition that the mastectomee requires some privacy in adjusting to the altered body image is necessary. However, firm yet gentle, encouragement to be with others is necessary for reestablishment of social status.

Since body boundaries have been altered, the actual personal space one needs is disrupted. The individual is aware of the space normally occupied by the breast and makes an unconscious allowance for its existence by keeping a set distance from others. Now that a breast has been removed, it no longer occupies the usual space. Maguire (1975a) noted that personal space may become suddenly excessive as the mastectomee begins to integrate new body boundaries. Family members must be alerted to the existence of such behavior, for they may interpret the increase in personal distance as a sign of rejection on the part of the mastectomee.

Unless family members are prepared preoperatively for the possibility of the mastectomee's withdrawal and avoidance of others, feelings of anger and frustration may result. It is vitally important that family members realize that the time immediately after the mastectomy is a difficult period of adjustment for both the mastectomee and the family. The mastectomee must not be pitied. Encouragement to return to premastectomy activities as soon as possible should be provided. It is helpful to consider the individual's likes and dislikes. Encourage the likes and try to eliminate the dislikes (Lasser, 1972). If the mastectomee enjoyed golf, bowling, swimming, or tennis, he or she should be encouraged to take an active part with family and friends. The mastectomee's initial limitations should be recognized, but positive reinforcement for improvements in performance is necessary.

A mastectomee who is unattached emotionally to another's affections prior to the surgical procedure may express concern about setting up a new relationship now that a breast has been lost. The fear of possible rejection is a major concern (Bower, 1975; Kent, 1975). Discussing this concern with members of the health team and other mastectomees may prove helpful. The mastectomee may want to express to the nurse how he or she will deal with the situation should it arise. Generally, the mastectomee is advised not to discuss the fact that a breast has been removed until the relationship is comfortable and the mastectomee does not feel threatened about discussing the issue. In addition, the seriousness of the relationship plays a major role in the mastectomee's decision of whether or not the new acquaintance should be told about the missing breast.

Clothing concerns are of vital importance to the mastectomee's social reestablishment. When the female mastectomee is tired and depressed, she may express little desire to alter clothes that no longer fit. Regardless of when the clothing alterations are made, some women will find this task an unpleasant reminder of a changed body image (Anstice, 1970a). It may prove helpful to have a friend or dressmaker provide suggestions and work with the woman on required alterations. Halter neck dresses require minimal adjustments other than building up under both arms to produce a balanced look. Bathing suits can be worn with ease as long as they are built up under the arms. Some designers have created swimwear that is exclusively styled for the mastectomee (Aves, 1973). Strapless gowns can be converted into halters or provided with shrug attachments by using contrasting material. Some strapless dresses may not require alterations if they are well boned and have high support under the arms (Lasser, 1969). The female mastectomee will find, no doubt, that most of her clothing can be worn without alterations and, if necessary, a little filling can be sewn into a garment to give it that "just-right look." Above all, the female mastectomee must be encouraged to stand erect with head and shoulders back since one's personal appearance is enhanced by excellent posture.

The male mastectomee will encounter fewer required alterations in clothing. One of the major clothing concerns expressed by the male mastectomee is appearance in swimwear. Now that a breast has been removed, he may find the appearance of his trunk displeasing for public viewing. In this case, he can be encouraged to wear a tank-top with his swim trunks so that his scar is covered in a fairly unobvious manner.

Without necessary support and understanding with clothing needs, the mastectomee can easily drift into carelessness in personal appearance and into wearing sloppy clothing in an attempt to conceal the missing breast. This only further undermines one's morale and, in turn, prolongs adequate reestablishment of social identity.

SUMMARY

In the United States approximately 1 out of every 15 women will be affected by breast cancer at some time during her life. Women most frequently affected are over forty-five years of age and have not borne or breast-fed children. Cancer of the breast remains the leading cause of cancer deaths in women. However, if diagnosed when in a localized stage, breast cancer is treated with considerable success.

It must not be forgotten that males are also susceptible to breast cancer. However, tumors of the male breast are not so common as those occurring in the female breast. In addition, the male involved tends to be slightly older than the female affected by cancer of the breast.

The presence of a breast lump is usually found by the individual involved or by the sex partner. At the time of discovery the most frequent thought of the individual involved is the fear of impending death. Many individuals equate the word cancer with death. Repudiating the existence of the lump and the fear of a possible mastectomy are two major reasons for delaying the individual's move to seek medical attention.

The presence of a mastectomy imposes a great impact upon both the individual affected and his or her family. The impact of mastectomy affects the mastectomee's emotional well-being, somatic identity, sexuality, occupational identity, and social role. The mastectomee is faced with learning the sick role during the initial impact of the mastectomy and goes on to experience loss, body image alterations, and social readjustment. Therefore, the psychosocial impact of mastectomy must never be underrated by members of the health care team. The major role of the health care team is to prepare the individual and his or her family for alterations in daily living which may occur because of the impact of the mastectomy. The health care team should also assist the individual in dealing with each of these changes.

Patient Situation

Ms. R. M. is a forty-nine-year-old married woman with three children, ages 20, 18, and 13. Mr. R. M. is an executive for a large business firm and is required to do a great deal of entertaining. Consequently, Ms. R. M. is kept busy planning social events for her husband. In addition to her social entertaining, she enjoys playing tennis at the country club.

Ms. R. M. detected a lump in her breast one day while bathing. A frozen section determined that the lump was cancerous; subsequently, a mastectomy was performed. During her hospital stay the nursing staff felt that it was advisable for a community health nurse to visit Ms. R. M. after discharge. Ms. R. M. is now three weeks postmastectomy and the community health nurse has identified problems affecting Ms. R. M.'s emotional well-being, somatic identity, sexuality, occupational role, and social identity.

Following are Ms. R. M.'s nursing care plan and patient care cardex dealing with the above mentioned areas of concern.

NURSING CARE PLAN

Problems	Objectives	Nursing Interventions	Principles/Rationale	Evaluations
Emotional Impact Frequent crying spells related to depression.	To decrease Ms. R. M.'s depression.	Encourage Ms. R. M. to express her feelings to her husband and children.	Expressing feelings may assist the mastectomee in identifying what is making her depressed.	The nurse would observe for: Ms. R. M.'s increased verbalization about feelings to her husband and children.
	To demonstrate acceptance of Ms. R. M.	Encourage Ms. R. M. to become involved in mastectomee group sessions.	Groups of mastectomees are able to empathize and provide support to one another since they are experiencing or have experienced similar problems.	Ms. R. M.'s involvement in mastectomee groups.
		Encourage Ms. R. M. to become involved in her premastectomy activities.	Becoming involved in premastectomy activities demonstrates to the mastectomee that she is still a contributing member of society.	Ms. R. M.'s involvement and increased enjoyment in premastectomy activities. Ms. R. M.'s ability to express herself without fear of rejection from others.
	To assist Ms. R. M.'s family in ways of dealing with her depression.	Encourage Mr. R. M. and the children to take an active part in getting Ms. R. M. involved in her premastectomy activities.	Mastectomees are more likely to become involved in activities when family members are encouraging and supportive.	Active involvement of Ms. R. M.'s family in dealing with her depression.
		Encourage Mr. R. M. and the children to compliment Ms. R. M. on any accomplishments made in her involvement in premastectomy activities.	Positive feedback for accomplishments facilitate feelings of self-worth.	
		Encourage Mr. R. M. and the children not to reprimand her for crying.	Demonstrations of disgust toward a crying mastectomee can be interpreted by the mastectomee as rejection.	

NURSING CARE PLAN (cont.)

Problems	Objectives	Nursing Interventions	Principles/Rationale	Evaluations
		Explain to Mr. R. M. and the children the need for Ms. R. M. to cry.	Crying is a means of expressing feelings in the open and family members who understand this are more capable of providing necessary emotional support.	
		Encourage Mr. R. M. and the children to sit with Ms. R. M. as she cries and to make body contact by holding her hand or touching her arm.	Body contact and human presence are means of demonstrating acceptance.	
Somatic Impact Expressed fear that her bustline will not have a normal appearance.	To decrease Ms. R. M.'s fear about an abnormal appearance of her bustline.	Encourage Mr. R. M. and the children to allow Ms. R. M. to verbalize her concerns about her appearance.	Verbalization of a fear may assist the mastectomee in identifying ways of dealing with that fear.	The nurse would observe for: Free verbalization by Ms. R. M. about her fear of an abnormal appearance of her bustline.
	To restore Ms. R. M.'s feminine image.	Direct Ms. R. M. to a surgical appliance firm, an appropriate women's wear department, or an appropriate drugstore.	Mastectomees aware of the appropriate place to obtain a prosthesis will have less anxiety about the availability of the item.	Ms. R. M.'s selection of a prosthesis with which she feels comfortable.
		Provide Ms. R. M. with information about the various types of available prostheses.	A mastectomee aware of the various types of prostheses is better able to select the type most appropriate for her.	
		Encourage Ms. R. M. to involve Mr. R. M. in taking an active part in choosing the prosthesis.	Involving the sex partner of the mastectomee in the selection of the prosthesis prevents placing the entire responsibility upon	

Problem	Goal	Nursing Intervention	Rationale	Evaluation
		until her wound is healed before being fit with a permanent prosthesis.	permanent prosthesis before the wound is entirely healed may lead to improper fitting since some edema of the wound may still be present.	
		Encourage Mr. R. M. and the children to compliment Ms. R. M. on her personal appearance when she begins to wear her permanent prosthesis.	How a mastectomee appears to others is important to her.	Ms. R. M.'s demonstration of a sense of pride in her personal appearance.
Sexual Impact Avoidance of sexual relationship with husband.	To assist Mr. and Ms. R. M. in returning to their premastectomy sexual activities.	Encourage Mr. R. M. to express to his wife his feelings about viewing the mastectomy scar.	Feelings of guilt about one's reaction to the mastectomy scar are difficult to hide and may affect the sex partner's sexual enthusiasm.	The nurse would observe for: Open expression of feelings between Mr. and Ms. R. M. about their sexual activity and whether or not they have returned to their premastectomy level of sexual activity.
	To assist Mr. and Ms. R. M. in dealing with feelings of guilt.	Encourage Mr. R. M. to tell his wife that any hesitant response toward her is not rejection, but rather an expression of empathy.	A mastectomee who is aware of her sex partner's true feelings is less likely to misinterpret his actions.	
		Encourage Ms. R. M. to express to Mr. R. M. her feelings about engaging in sexual relations with him.	Expressing feelings about sexual relations assists the mastectomee and her sex partner in identifying possible reasons for feelings of anxiety and guilt related to the sex act.	
		Encourage Mr. and Mrs. R. M. to resume sexual activity as soon as possible.	Early resumption of sexual activity provides recognition of continued affection on the part of the sex partner.	

NURSING CARE PLAN (cont.)

Problems	Objectives	Nursing Interventions	Principles/Rationale	Evaluations
Occupational Impact Expressed concern about not being able to carry out usual household activities.	To increase Ms. R. M.'s feelings of self-worth.	Encourage Ms. R. M. to resume usual household responsibilities with the exception of lifting heavy objects. Encourage Ms. R. M. to resume entertaining in her home.	Taking part in premastectomy activities helps reestablish the mastectomee's feelings of self-worth.	The nurse would observe for: Increased resumption of premastectomy household activities.
	To decrease Ms. R. M.'s concern about resuming her household responsibilities.	Reassure Ms. R. M. that activities such as bedmaking, sweeping, vacuuming, washing, and ironing are a few of the household duties that will enhance arm action on her affected side.	Resuming activities done prior to the mastectomy provides physical benefits for arm movement on the affected side.	
Social Impact Refusing to visit friends and associates because of feelings of embarrassment or shame.	To decrease Ms. R. M.'s feelings of embarrassment or shame.	Encourage Ms. R. M. to express her feelings of embarrassment or shame about her altered body structure.	Verbalizing the feelings of embarrassment or shame about altered body structure may assist the mastectomy in identifying ways of dealing with such feelings.	The nurse would observe for: Ms. R. M.'s open verbalization about feelings of embarrassment or shame.
	To increase Ms. R. M.'s contact with friends and associates.	Encourage Mr. R. M. and the children to be firm, yet gentle, in encouraging Ms. R. M. to be with friends and associates. Suggest to Ms. R. M. that she resume playing tennis.	Reestablishment of social contacts with individuals outside the marital relationship are most vulnerable to decay. Taking part in premastectomy activities that involve,individuals outside the marital relationship helps to reestablish these social	Increased contact with friends and associates by Ms. R. M.

Goal	Nursing Actions	Rationale	Expected Outcome
To increase Ms. R. M.'s satisfaction with her personal appearance.	children, and family friends to compliment Ms. R. M. on improvements in tennis.	plishments facilitate feelings of self-worth.	Ms. R. M.'s increased pride and satisfaction with personal appearance.
	Discuss with Ms. R. M. clothing alterations that she feels may be necessary.	Clothing concerns are of vital importance to the mastectomee's social reestablishment.	
	Encourage Ms. R. M. to utilize the assistance of a dress-maker or a friend in making clothing alterations if she feels it would be helpful.	Assistance in making the necessary alterations in clothing makes the task less burdensome.	
	Encourage Ms. R. M. to stand erect with good posture at all times.	A mastectomee's personal appearance is enhanced by excellent posture.	
	Suggest to Mr. R. M. and the children that they compliment Ms. R. M. on her personal appearance.	Without necessary support and feedback on personal appearance, the mastectomee can easily drift into carelessness.	

PATIENT CARE CARDEX

PATIENT'S NAME: Ms. R. M.   DIAGNOSIS: Mastectomy

AGE: 49 years   SEX: Female

MARITAL STATUS: Married   OCCUPATION: Housewife

SIGNIFICANT OTHERS: Husband and three children (20, 18, and 13 years)

Problems	Nursing Approaches
Emotional: Frequent crying spells related to depression.	1. Encourage to express feelings to husband and children.
	2. Encourage to become involved in mastectomee group sessions.
	3. Encourage to become involved in premastectomy activities.
	4. Encourage family to take an active part in getting her involved in premastectomy activities.
	5. Encourage family to compliment her on accomplishments made in her involvement in premastectomy activities.
	6. Encourage family not to reprimand her for behavior during spells of depression.
	7. Explain to family the purpose of her crying.
	8. Encourage family to sit with her as she cries and to make body contact by holding her hand or touching her arm.
Somatic: Expressed fear that her bustline will not have a normal appearance.	1. Encourage family to allow her to verbalize concerns about herself.
	2. Direct to surgical appliance firm, an appropriate women's wear department, or an appropriate drugstore.
	3. Provide with information about the various types of available prostheses.
	4. Encourage to involve husband in taking an active part in the decision regarding the choice of prosthesis.
	5. Encourage to wait until wound is healed before being fit with a permanent prosthesis.
	6. Encourage family to compliment her on personal appearance when she begins to wear permanent

with husband.

2. Encourage husband to tell her that any hesitant response toward her is not rejection, but rather an expression of empathy.
3. Encourage to express to husband her feelings about engaging in sexual relations with him.
4. Encourage husband and wife to resume sexual activity as soon as possible.

Occupational: Expressed concern about not being able to carry out usual household activities.

1. Encourage to resume usual household responsibilities with the exception of lifting heavy objects.
2. Encourage to resume entertaining in her home.
3. Reassure that activities such as bedmaking, sweeping, vacuuming, washing, and ironing are a few household duties that will enhance arm action on the affected side.

Social: Refusing to visit friends and associates because of feelings of embarrassment or shame.

1. Encourage to express feelings of embarrassment or shame about altered body structure.
2. Encourage family to be firm, yet gentle, in encouraging her to be with friends and associates.
3. Suggest resumption of tennis.
4. Encourage family and friends to compliment her on improvements in tennis.
5. Discuss any clothing alterations that may be necessary.
6. Encourage to utilize the assistance of a dressmaker or friend in making clothing alterations.
7. Encourage to stand erect with good posture at all times.
8. Suggest to family that they compliment her on her personal appearance.

REFERENCES

Akehurst, A. C. Post-mastectomy morale, *Nursing Mirror*, 1974, *139* (21), 66.

Anstice, E. Coping after a mastectomy, *Nursing Times*, 1970a, *66* (28), 822-883.

Anstice, E. The emotional operation.I, *Nursing Times*, 1970b, *66* (27), 837-838.

Aves, B. D. Swimwear for the post-mastectomy patient, *Radiography*, 1973, *39*, 159.

Bard, M., and Sutherland, A. Psychological impact of cancer and its treatment— Part IV—Adaptation to radical mastectomy, *Cancer*, 1955, *8* (4), 656-672.

Bower, P. Nursing care in breast surgery, *Nursing Mirror*, 1975, *140* (14) 51-52

Breast prosthesis, *Nursing Mirror*, 1975, *140* (14), 60-61.

Burdick, D. Rehabilitation of the breast cancer patient, *Cancer*, 1975, *36* (2), 645-648.

Byrd, B. *Standard breast examination*. New York: American Cancer Society Professional Education Publication, 1974.

Cancer News, Spring 1976, *60* (2), 1-22.

Cancer Statistics, 1976. New York: American Cancer Society, Inc., 1976.

The controversy over breast cancer, *AORN Journal*, 1974, *19* (4), 864-869.

Downie, P. Breast surgery, *Nursing Times*, 1974, *70*, 1311-1312.

Erikson, E. *Childhood and society*. New York: W. W. Norton & Co., 1963.

Golemastic, B., Delikaris, P., Balarutsos, C., and Karamanakos, P. Lymphedema of the upper limb after surgery for breast cancer, *The American Journal of Surgery*, 1975, *129* (3), 286-288.

Haagensen, C. D. *Diseases of the breast*. Philadelphia: W. B. Saunders, 1971.

Harrell, H. To lose a breast, *American Journal of Nursing*, 1972, *72* (4), 676-682.

Healy, J. Role of rehabilitation medicine in the care of the patient with breast cancer, *Cancer*, 1971, *28* (6), 1666-1671.

Katz, J., Weiner, H., Gallagher, T., and Hallman, L. Stress, distress, and ego defenses, *Archives of General Psychiatry*, 1976, *23*, 131-142.

Kent, S. Coping with sexual identity crises after mastectomy, *Geriatrics*, 1975, *30* (10), 145-146.

Klein, R. The crisis to grow on, *Cancer*, 1971, *28* (6), 1660-1665.

Lasser, T. *A message to husbands from Terese Lasser*. New York: American Cancer Society, Inc., 1972.

Lasser, T. *Reach to recovery: a manual for women who have had breast surgery*. New York: American Cancer Society, 1969.

Leis, H. Selective, elective, prophylactic contralateral mastectomy, *Cancer*, 1971, *28* (4), 956-961.

Leis, H. Surgical procedures for breast cancer, *RN*, 1974, *37* (1), OR1-OR6.

Leis, H., and Pilnik, S. Breast Cancer, a therapeutic dilemma, *AORN Journal*, 1974, *19* (4) 813-820.

Luckmann, J., and Sorensen, K. *Medical-surgical nursing: a psychophysiologic approach.* Philadelphia: W. B. Saunders, Co., 1974.

Maguire, P. Emotional responses after mastectomy, *Contemporary Obstetrics and Gynecology,* 1975a, *8,* 34-48.

Maguire, P. The psychological and social consequences of breast cancer, *Nursing Mirror,* 1975b, *140* (14), 54-57.

Maguire, P. The psychological and social sequelae of mastectomy. In J. Howells (Ed.), *Modern perspectives in the psychiatric aspects of surgery.* New York: Brunner/Mazel, Publishers, 1976.

Mamaril, A. Preventing complications after radical mastectomy, *American Journal of Nursing,* 1974, *74* (11), 2000-2003.

Rennker, R., and Cutter, M. Psychological problems of adjustment to cancer of the breast, *Journal of the American Medical Association,* 1952, *148* (10), 833-838.

Schmid, W., Kiss, M., and Hibert, L. The team approach to rehabilitation after mastectomy, *AORN Journal,* 1974, *19* (4), 821-836.

Schoenberg, B., and Carr, A. Loss of external organs: limb amputation, mastectomy and disfiguration. In B. Schoenberg, A. Carr, D. Peretz, and A. Kutscher (Eds.), *Loss and grief: psychological management in medical practice.* New York: Columbia University Press, 1970.

Shope, D. *Interpersonal sexuality.* Philadelphia: W. B. Saunders Co., 1975.

Thomas, S., and Yates, M. Breast reconstruction after mastectomy, *American Journal of Nursing,* 1977, *77* (9), 1438-1442.

Wakeley, C. Tumors occurring in the male breast, *Nursing Mirror,* 1973, *137* (7), 26-27.

Weinstein, S., Vetter, R., and Sersen, E. Phantoms following breast amputation, *Neuropsychologia,* 1970, *8,* 185-197.

Weiss, M. A word of caution, *American Journal of Psychiatry,* 1975, *132* (11),1220.

Winkler, W. Choosing the prosthesis and clothing, *American Journal of Nursing,* 1977, *77* (9), 1433-1436.

Witkin, M. Sex therapy and mastectomy, *Journal of Sex and Marital Therapy,* 1974, *1* (4), 290-304.

Women's attitudes regarding breast cancer, *Occupational Health Nursing,* 1974, *20,* 20-23.

Woods, N. F. *Human sexuality in health and illness.* St. Louis: The C. V. Mosby Co., 1975a.

Woods, N. F. Influences on sexual adaptation to mastectomy, *JOGN Nursing,* 1975b, *4* (3), 33-37.

6

The Patient with an
ALTERATION
IN
SEXUAL FUNCTION

INTRODUCTION

There is increasing interest in the psychological effects that surgical alterations in sexual function have upon the individual and his or her family. For
some time medical science has been aware of some of the psychosocial
effects that various surgical alterations in sexual function have upon the
female. However, the psychosocial effects of surgical alterations in the
male's sexual function have become an issue of increasing interest in the
health care field. With the concern over limiting one's family size, the request for and performance of vasectomies have been on the increase (Craft,
1975; Doty, 1974). No doubt the economic pressures of living and the increased liberation of the female have added to this increase in demand.
Regardless of whether an individual is undergoing a vasectomy or a hysterectomy, surgical alterations in sexual function create an impact upon one's
emotional well-being, somatic identity, sexuality, occupational identity, and
social role. This chapter will deal with the impact that the hysterectomy and
the vasectomy have upon each of these areas.

SEXUAL ALTERATION PROFILES

The individual undergoing a vasectomy is most often white, middle-class,
well educated, in the fourth decade of life, the father of two or three children, of the Protestant religion, and in his first marriage (Swenson, 1975;
Moss, 1975; Ager, Werley, Allen, Shea, and Lewis, 1974). The major

reason he gives for obtaining a vasectomy is that it is a safe, effective means of contraception that does not interfere with sexual activity (Swenson, 1975). Physical illness of either partner or the presence of hereditary diseases are reasons given less frequently (Hackett and Waterhouse, 1973).

Certain men are considered poor risks for vasectomies and are generally discouraged from obtaining them. According to Swenson (1975), these poor risk individuals include men under twenty-five years of age, with preexisting marital or sexual problems, with psychopathology or whose wives demonstrate psychopathology, and whose wives oppose a vasectomy. If an individual falls into any one of these categories, extensive counseling or even psychotherapy may be required before a vasectomy is performed. The young male (twenty-five and younger) may not be completely cognizant of the impact that a vasectomy could have upon his future. A man, or his sex partner, with preexisting sexual difficulties, marital problems, or psychopathology may be using the vasectomy as an easy solution to more complex problems. Finally, the wife's consent is necessary since the possibilities of legal suits at a later date could occur should she decide that she was not appropriately informed about the procedure (Wallace, 1974; Foreman, 1973).

Once the man has decided to have a vasectomy, and if he does not fall into any of the above categories, he should be provided with adequate information about the procedure, its desired effects, and the finality of the structural alteration (Wolfers, 1970; Bennett, 1976). In addition, he should be encouraged to express his feelings or doubts about the vasectomy. The individual's questions must be answered and any misconceptions must be clarified. Only after such interventions should the man undergo a vasectomy.

The individual undergoing a hysterectomy presents a different profile. She is generally married and in her fifth decade of life. It is a time when her financial contributions to the family as a working woman are no longer pressing. Her children are grown and are ready to leave home. Her husband has reached the peak of his career (Holm, 1971). Thus, her role as a major contributing factor to the family structure may be undergoing change.

Removal of the uterus can result from various factors. Such factors include the presence of nonmalignant tumors, cancer of the uterus, menorrhagia, endometriosis, pelvic inflammatory disease, or a ruptured uterus (Carbary, 1975). Whatever the reason, unlike the vasectomy, the hysterectomy generally is not performed as a form of birth control. Rather, tubal ligation is utilized for this purpose.

Regardless of the reason for the hysterectomy, the impact of the loss can affect various facets of the female's life. Just like the male undergoing a vasectomy, the female undergoing a hysterectomy needs to be provided with adequate information about the procedure and the finality of the structural alteration. She must have her questions answered and any misconceptions clarified. Ideally, this should be done before the hysterectomy.

Whether the individual is male or female, loss is experienced. Regardless of the reasons for the changes in sexual structure, the individual's ability to reproduce has been permanently altered. As a result, an impact occurs.

IMPACT OF SEXUAL ALTERATIONS

Emotional Impact*

Unlike many other surgical interventions, a vasectomy generally is an operation of choice. In other words, a male undergoing a vasectomy has selected to have this surgical alteration. Thus, for a short period of time the individual has selected to assume the sick role. More than 500,000 men a year in the United States have vasectomies for the purpose of sterilization (Montie and Stewart, 1974).

Men have expressed that one of the most difficult aspects of the vasectomy is deciding to have it done; no doubt this is because of the finality of the alteration. No longer will he be able to father children. Although attempts are being made to develop reversible forms of vasectomy, these surgical procedures are still very new and are not completely effective at this time (Montie and Stewart, 1974).

If the man is married, it is imperative that the decision to have a vasectomy be a cooperative decision between the man and his wife. Many men feel that it would be more of a health risk for their sex partner to undergo a surgical procedure, such as a tubal ligation, for sterilization than for them to have a vasectomy (Wallace, 1974). Also more emphasis is being directed toward the male's assumption of equal responsibility in fertility control.

Birth control is no longer viewed primarily as the female's task. However, should the man feel pressure from his wife to obtain a vasectomy, the emotional impact of the sterilization procedure may produce untoward effects. He may view himself as emasculated and, as a result, become extremely sensitive about how others view him (Davis and Lubell, 1975; Doty, 1974).

If the man does not feel pressured to have a vasectomy and if he has chosen to undergo the sterilization process on his own, he is unlikely to exhibit emotional problems as a result of the vasectomy. He will feel comfortable with the decision and, most likely, will not be oversensitive about continuing to carry out household tasks that he did prior to the vasectomy or about the connotations others may attach to them (Rodgers, Ziegler, and Levy, 1976). Some authorities disagree with this concept and feel that a vasectomy is a means for emotionally sick women to castrate their hus-

---

*It is advisable for the reader to have read Chapters 1 and 3 before continuing with this section.

bands (Erickson, 1954). However, this concept tends to be in the minority and is not widely accepted. By contrast, other authorities question whether vasectomy candidates deny the anxiety produced by the operation or defensively distort their feelings about the effects of the surgical intervention (Hornstein and Houston, 1975; Hamersma, Anderegg, Miller, and Rudolph, 1975; Bloom and Houston, 1976).

The woman undergoing a hysterectomy is generally doing so because of some underlying medical problem. The removal of the uterus thus becomes the surgical procedure of choice to correct or alleviate the pathological alteration. Historically, many individuals in medicine felt that the removal of the uterus would automatically induce emotional problems. Thus, the term hysterectomy was coined to describe the "hysterical" or uncontrollable emotional state that occurred because of the loss of the uterus (Williams, 1973). This theory has since been proven ill-founded and no direct link can be made between emotional disorders and hysterectomy. This is not to say, however, that there is no emotional impact. The removal of the uterus creates a loss, and the woman is faced with the responsibility of dealing with the loss.

It has been found that women who have encountered difficulty in handling losses in the past develop more problems in dealing with the loss of a body part, such as the uterus, than women who have been able to deal with past losses successfully (Drake and Price, 1975). The fantasy of pregnancy can no longer be maintained, and some women find this hard to handle (Mathis, 1973).

The anxiety created by the loss of the uterus tends to be greater in separated and divorced women than in married women (Polivy, 1974). No doubt this is because separated and divorced females are faced with loss beyond that of a significant other. In addition, some women may find the loss of the uterus a great threat to their femininity, since they may not have the "sense of security" that the presence of a significant male companion can offer.

Research has demonstrated that pelvic surgery, such as a hysterectomy, tends to create greater anxiety in the female than does upper abdominal surgery (Janis, 1958), such as a cholecystectomy. It is not uncommon for a woman to experience depression following her sexual surgical alteration. It is very normal for the woman to feel "low" or "weepy" for a few days during the postoperative period. In fact, depression tends to be more common after a hysterectomy than after many other operations (Mathis, 1973).

To deal with this depression, the woman and her family need to be informed before the hysterectomy that depression after surgery is not uncommon. They must be reassured that these feelings are normal. As the woman begins to deal with her loss, her feelings of depression will start to subside. However, the nurse must be aware that some women may experience depression for extended periods of time and thus require profes-sional counseling. During the woman's feelings of depression she needs encouragement to express her feelings, whether it be in the form of crying or verbalization. In addition, members of her family need to be reminded of the importance of allowing her to express her feelings to them. Family members also may require support from health team members in the form of listening to their feelings about dealing with their loved one's depression after a hysterectomy.

For some women, a hysterectomy may be viewed as a welcome relief. They see the removal of the uterus as a new found freedom. No longer will they have to fear the possibility of pregnancy or contend with menstruation. If the hysterectomy resolved underlying pathology, the woman now may be exempt from contending with the concern for an annoying gynecological problem.

Regardless of whether the woman views her hysterectomy as a wel-come relief or as an emotional trauma, the nurse must be cognizant of the individual's concept of her newly acquired loss. Only then can appropriate emotional support be provided. However, if a female nurse is unstable in her own femininity, she may encounter difficulty in providing the necessary support.

Somatic Impact*

The ability to reproduce is an important aspect of one's body image. The capability of creating another human being contributes to the indi-vidual's feelings of manliness and womanliness. Thus, when a man selects to have a vasectomy, he must explore how he will feel about his manly image once he has lost the ability to reproduce, especially since the surgical procedure is usually irreversible. Some men may postpone, or completely refuse, a vasectomy because they feel that loss of reproductivity would make them less manly. In addition, a fear that the vasectomy will affect one's masculine appearance, a concern about whether or not voice changes will take place, apprehension about an increase in promiscuity, and anxiety about whether or not physical weakness will result are potential concerns. The male and his sex partner require reassurance and information that all of these beliefs are ill-founded and do not occur as a result of the sterilization procedure. Only with time and a better understanding about the effects of vasectomy will some individuals select it as a means of birth control.

The majority of vasectomies occur during young adulthood. This is a time when the individual is ready and willing to merge his identity with that of others. It is during young adulthood that the individual either shares himself with others, both in friendship and in a mutually satisfying sexual

---

*It is advisable for the reader to have read Chapter 2 before continuing with this section.

relationship, or develops a sense of isolation (Erikson, 1963). Therefore, the male must examine how he believes a vasectomy will affect his ability to merge his identity with others. If he sees himself as "less than a man," he may retreat into isolation and fail to set up both friendships and a mutually satisfying sexual relationship. Since setting up a mutually satisfying sexual relationship is likely to occur before the age of twenty-five, authorities have discouraged a vasectomy prior to that age. A man past twenty-five is more likely to have established a sexual relationship and thus may not feel that his ability to procreate is essential in maintaining this relationship.

In the case of the male who is married and over twenty-five years of age, a concern may exist as to how he is perceived by his wife. If he fears that she views him as "less than a man," counseling of both the husband and wife should be done before a vasectomy is performed. If the man's masculine concept is destroyed, he may retreat from his wife and fail to establish or maintain a mutually satisfying sexual relationship.

The somatic impact of a hysterectomy on the female is somewhat similar to that of the somatic impact of a vasectomy on the male. Just as the male may view a vasectomy as an assault on his masculine image, so may the female view a hysterectomy as an assault on her feminine image. The female may view her hysterectomy as a surgical procedure in which everything was "taken away." She no longer visualizes herself as being physically attractive to others. In fact, some women view a hysterectomy as a psychologically mutilating experience. The somatic impact of the hysterectomy is particularly acute in women who feel that it is punishment for past errors, especially those who have been sexually oriented (Woods, 1975). Feelings of guilt are aroused that may further add to feelings of depression.

Since the majority of hysterectomies occur during the developmental stage of adulthood, alterations may occur in the woman's interest in establishing and guiding the future generations, the major focus in life at this time (Erikson, 1963). If the woman feels that she is "less than a woman," she may perceive herself as unfit to guide future generations. Instead of becoming generative, she may become increasingly concerned over premature aging. She may believe that her hysterectomy contributes to the acceleration of her aging process. Preoccupation with every single physical change becomes the focus of her life. She becomes engulfed in satisfying personal needs, acquiring self-comforts, and enters a life of self-absorption and stagnation. To aid the woman in dealing with her concerns of physical attractability, the nurse and family should encourage her to maintain her physical appearance. The nurse and family should urge her to use makeup appropriately and style her hair attractively. In addition, the family should be encouraged to compliment her on her attractive personal appearance. Not until the woman feels that she is attractive to herself and others will she change her preoccupation with aging.

Sexual Impact

The sexual impact of surgical alterations in sexual function is one of the greatest concerns of the individual affected. The man undergoing a vasectomy usually does so as a means of birth control (Bennett, 1976). He frequently fears the effects of other methods of contraception on his wife's health, namely, the pill (Ager, Werley, Allen, Shea, Lewis, 1974). Therefore, the man feels that the effects of a vasectomy are minimal compared to the effects encountered by his wife when using other means of birth control. Even with these thoughts in mind, prior to a vasectomy the man may be concerned about a possible decrease in sexual desire as a result of the surgical intervention (Doty, 1974). Such a concern may be the primary reason for postponing the vasectomy for an extended period of time. However, since the fear of pregnancy is removed from the sexual relationship, many men have noted an increase of enjoyment in their sexual relationship (Wallace, 1974).

A major fear of men preparing to undergo a vasectomy is the fear of castration, the removal of the gonads (Ferber, Tietze, and Lewit, 1967; Bumpass, 1974). These fears are compounded when the male has limited knowledge about the surgical procedure. Since the surgical incision is located on the scrotum, many men have their fears of castration intensified. Unless thorough preoperative explanation about the procedure is provided, fear of castration may be great at the time of the procedure. However, even with thorough preoperative explanations, some men are not completely convinced that no alterations to their testicles occur.

In addition to the fear of castration is the fear of pain resulting from the surgical intervention. The male is well aware of the sensitivity of his genital region and thoughts of having a surgical procedure in this region may cultivate intense concern about the pain. To decrease the fear of pain, thorough preoperative explanation about the surgical procedure and the postoperative course is necessary. During the explanation the male must be reassured that the discomfort is minimal. He requires information about the use of ice packs to the area and the use of mild analgesics to control the discomfort that can exist in the immediate postoperative period.

How soon one can resume sexual activity is a question frequently asked by the man undergoing a vasectomy. Since the concerns about sexual desire and castration frequently exist, the need to prove himself sexually to both his sex partner and himself may be important. Therefore, during the preoperative explanation the man should be instructed that he may resume sexual intercourse as soon as he desires (Craft, 1975). However, he and his sex partner must be encouraged to continue previous means of birth control until semen analysis demonstrates the absence of sperm. This time period may extend from 6 to 15 ejaculations which may take as long as 3 months (Foreman, 1973; Craft, 1975; Freund and Davis, 1969).

The effect that the vasectomy will have upon the marital relationship is important. As pointed out earlier, when the man's wife is adamantly against the procedure, it is not performed. By the same token, if the man's wife pressures him into having a vasectomy, the impact of the sterilization has a greater chance of creating emotional problems for him (Erickson, 1954). Thus, how the wife reacts to her husband's vasectomy can have an effect upon the marital relationship.

When the marital relationship is not laden with problems, the performance of a vasectomy that has been selected willingly is unlikely to cause difficulties in the marriage (Swenson, 1975). However, a marital relationship undergoing difficulties may find the vasectomy just one more problem with which to contend. Therefore, during preoperative counseling the husband and wife must be instructed that a vasectomy is not an easy solution to existing marital problems and must not be viewed as such. In some cases, it may be necessary for the husband and wife to deal with existing marital problems before consenting to the performance of a vasectomy.

Just as the male undergoing a vasectomy, the female undergoing a hysterectomy can encounter difficulties in dealing with the sexual impact of surgical alterations of sexual function. The hysterectomy is most frequently performed on women during the fifth decade of life, a time when sexual drive tends to be reduced (Amias, 1975). However, the effects of the surgical procedure on a sexual relationship can be great. The woman involved may question her sexual desirability to her husband (Woods, 1975). Such fears are intensified when the woman and her husband are of a cultural background in which the presence of the woman's uterus is a way of satisfying *macho* desires (Williams, 1973). In such instances, the woman may be viewed as being less than perfect now that she is unable to bear children, which is a primary role of her femininity in such a culture (Williams, 1973; Williams, 1976). Women affected by such cultural influences may postpone a much needed hysterectomy. This postponement may be caused by fears about her spouse's possible attitude toward her once the operation has been performed. Fear of being rejected sexually by her husband may become a primary concern. Now that she is unable to bear children she wonders whether her husband will leave her or find another sex partner.

Since some women are hesitant to express their concerns about the marital ramifications of a hysterectomy, health team members may have to approach the topic for the woman. Even though a woman does not openly express her feelings about the sexual impact of a hysterectomy, it does not mean that concerns do not exist. A leading statement that may encourage the verbalization of feelings about the forthcoming hysterectomy might be, "Many women have expressed anxiety about the effects that a hysterectomy will have upon their femininity. How do you feel your surgery will affect you?"

It is important that the husband be made aware of his wife's potential or actual fears of rejection. He should be encouraged to carry out methods he has used in the past for expressing his affection for her. These methods may include giving her "feminine type" gifts or physically caressing her. Regardless of what means the husband uses to express his affection, he must be alerted to the fact that his wife may need frequent reminders of his continued affection for her.

To deal adequately with the woman's fear about her sexuality, it is vitally important that both the husband and wife be counseled before the hysterectomy. They must be given explanations about the surgical procedure and what structures are to be removed (Vernon, 1973; Piver, Rutledge, and Smith, 1974; Carbary, 1975). If the ovaries are to be removed along with the uterus, and if the woman's age makes reasonable the use of hormonal replacement therapy, such facts must be provided (Higgins, 1971). If the ovaries are not to be removed along with the uterus, the woman and her husband require information that she will not require adjunctive hormone therapy. Above all, the husband and wife must be reassured that the woman will not lose her ability to be "female" even though she will be unable to bear children. In no way should her sexual activity be hindered.

A common concern of the woman in the immediate postoperative period is when she can resume coitus. Women are generally advised not to resume intercourse for approximately six weeks after surgery (Williams, 1976). The woman should be advised that she may experience some discomfort initially because of the tightening of the vaginal walls and a decrease in natural vaginal lubrication if the ovaries were removed along with the uterus. However, this discomfort will subside, for intercourse actually helps the tissues become supple again (Steele and Goodwin, 1975). In addition, the use of vaginal creams or lubricants may prove helpful if the discomfort is brought on by the decrease in natural vaginal lubrication. The woman, however, must be told not to use lubricants containing estrogens if she has a history or diagnosis of malignancy (Keaveny, Hader, Massoni, and Wade), 1973). For some women, total enjoyment of sexual intercourse may not occur for three to four months after the surgical intervention since tenderness of the abdomen may be present this long. This is especially true if the hysterectomy was done abdominally. To alleviate this discomfort, the woman may want to try positions for coitus that do not place weight upon the abdomen. Some examples of such positions include a side-to-side position, female superior position, a male superior "dog-fashion" position (Kaplan, 1975). The woman and her sex partner will have to determine which position is most enjoyable for them.

Fear may be a significant factor in the resumption of sexual activity. Anxiety that intercourse was the cause of the disease that led to the hysterectomy, that intercourse might reactivate the prehysterectomy pathology, or that intercourse will harm the woman can produce a loss of sex drive for both the woman and her sex partner (Amias, 1975). These misconceptions must be clarified so that unnecessary anxiety is alleviated and so that the woman and her sex partner can resume prehysterectomy sexual activity.

The frequency of sexual activity after a hysterectomy remains individual. Some women have noted an increase in their sexual activity after a hysterectomy (Craig and Jackson, 1975). This is particularly true if the fear of a possible pregnancy existed prior to the surgical intervention. Since the potential threat of pregnancy has been removed, the woman may find the enjoyment of the sex act to be greater.

Occupational Impact

The occupational impact of the vasectomy is generally minimal. Since the procedure is not considered a major surgical intervention by medical standards, it is not uncommon for the vasectomy to be performed in a clinic or office setting (Squires, Barb, and Pinch, 1976). Some physicians, however, may prefer a hospital environment.

It is common for the procedure to be performed toward the end of the working week (Craft, 1975) so that the individual has an opportunity to rest for several days over the weekend before resuming work again. If the individual is not able to have a weekend free from job responsibilities, he is encouraged to rest completely for 12 hours following surgery and to take time off the following day if his occupation requires heavy labor (Foreman, 1973).

Generally, the male will not be required to lose working days after the operation. However, if he has to miss work, the number of days missed is rarely over three (Sobrero and Kohli, 1975). Thus, it can be seen that the performance of a vasectomy places a minimal economic impact on the individual and society.

The occupational impact of a hysterectomy proves to be greater than that of the vasectomy. One of the greatest occupational concerns expressed by the housewife is her fear of being unable to carry out her domestic duties. Generally, the woman is advised to do only light housework for the first two weeks upon her return home and to avoid such activities as vacuuming, lifting, and sports for four to seven weeks after surgery (Williams, 1976). It is advisable to suggest to the woman that spacing her household responsibilities with rest periods will decrease her chances of excessive fatigue. This practice is especially important the first few days at home when fatigue and weakness are common.

If the female is employed outside the home, she may be required to avoid total resumption of her job responsibilities for a month or two. This, of course, depends upon her job. Such a practice can produce a financial burden upon the individual. In addition, a hysterectomy, unlike a vasectomy, is performed in a hospital environment. The expense of the surgical procedure and hospitalization, plus the lost working days, produces an economic impact for both the individual and society.

Social Impact

The general popularity of a vasectomy stems from the increasing awareness of an improved standard of living resulting from a small-sized family unit (Craft, 1975). Many individuals request the sterilization procedure because a colleague or friend has undergone the procedure and expressed satisfaction with the outcome. Since today's society discusses sex more freely, the topic of vasectomy is dealt with more openly. It no longer is only a bedroom topic.

Males undergoing a vasectomy are younger and have smaller family units. In addition, these individuals tend to be from a higher income bracket and tend to be a better educated group than the general population. It has been noted that minority groups consistently have been underrepresented in the performance of vasectomies (Westoff, 1972; Bumpass, 1974; Phillips, 1971). Reasons cited for this social phenomenon include fear of genocide, concern over an altered masculine gender role, fear of surgery, and feelings of threat to one's masculinity as a result of the inability to father children (Davis and Lubell, 1975).

In addition to these reasons for the minority social phenomenon, some individuals exhibit concerns over societal views about the continuation of tasks that the vasectomized male performs around the house, such as washing dishes. A fear may exist that others will label him as a "sissy" if he is caught doing household chores felt to be "woman's work." Because of these concerns, the male undergoing a vasectomy may hesitate to discuss with others the fact that he has undergone a sterilization process or he may hesitate doing household chores that he carried out in the past. Thus, the individual requires information to the effect that more people are receiving vasectomies as a means of birth control, vasectomies are more openly discussed by society than in the past, and a vasectomy is an acceptable means of birth control. However, not until the male feels secure with his public masculine image will he be able to discuss openly or deal with the fact that he has undergone a vasectomy.

The social effects of a hysterectomy are different from those of a vasectomy. The female often views her hysterectomy as a social disruption of her previous way of life. Menstruation is a concrete cyclic symbol of femininity (Mathis, 1973) and now it is absent since the uterus has been removed. No longer can the woman either consciously or unconsciously plan social events around the occurrence of menstruation. For example, in the past she may have made arrangements for vacations, active sports, or cocktail parties at a time when menstruation did not occur. Now that menstruation is suddenly absent, her cyclic manner of social planning will be altered and she will be forced to adapt.

In addition to the disruption of a cyclic routine of life, women may express concern over their bodily appearance now that their uterus has been removed. Questions frequently asked include whether a swimsuit or other revealing clothing can be worn and whether or not weight will be a problem. The woman should be informed that the position of the abdominal scar does vary frequently with it often being below bikini level (Steele and Goodwin, 1975). Thus, if she desires to wear swimwear or other revealing clothing, she can do so with relative ease. Weight is a problem only if less exercise is carried out and more food is consumed than before the operation. Adequate nutritional intake generally controls this problem. The woman, however, may find that her abdomen bulges initially after surgery, but as the abdominal muscles regain strength the bulging will subside.

Approval from significant others is important to the woman who has undergone a hysterectomy. She may question her feelings of self-worth now that one of her marks of femininity has been lost. This is especially true in women of the lower socioeconomic level, since they frequently view their major feminine role as child bearer (Polivy, 1974). To enhance feelings of self-worth, family members should encourage the woman to become involved in activities outside the home, especially if her children are grown and have moved away. The woman's interests will affect her choice of activities, and these interests need to be considered as a family assists her in selecting social activities. However, possible activities to consider are volunteer work, adult education classes, or learning a new hobby. Positive reinforcement from significant others is important as the woman's interests and involvement in social functions increase. Since approval from her significant others is so important, she may require compliments for accomplishments made so that her feelings of self-worth can be reestablished. Only when feelings of self-worth have been reestablished can the woman resolve the loss of her uterus.

SUMMARY

Alterations in sexual function are becoming increasingly prevalent in today's society. More men are selecting the vasectomy as a means of controlling family size, and women continue to have hysterectomies as a necessary treatment for various forms of gynecological pathology.

The male undergoing a vasectomy is generally young, at the beginning of his career, and has young children at home. By contrast, the female undergoing a hysterectomy tends to be in the menopausal stage of life and has a grown family. Her husband is at the peak of his career and, since the children have often left home, her financial contributions to the family may no longer be pressing.

Unlike most hysterectomies, the vasectomy usually is a surgical procedure of choice. Nonetheless, in both cases, an impact in the life of the individual involved occurs. The presence of surgical sexual alterations can affect one's emotional well-being, somatic identity, sexuality, occupational identity, and social role. The feelings expressed by the spouse or sex partner of the man or woman undergoing a surgical sexual alteration play an important part in how the individual adapts to such loss. Therefore, members of the health care team must prepare both the individual and his or her family for alterations in daily living which may occur as a result of the impact of the vasectomy or hysterectomy and assist them in dealing with each of these changes.

Patient Situation

Mr. V. is a twenty-five-year-old, white, middle-class Methodist with three children. He is a chemical engineer by profession. Mr. V. and his wife do not desire more children and hence have been using birth control. However, Mrs. V. has encountered difficulties and displeasure with the various forms of birth control that she has used. Consequently, she has requested Mr. V. to undergo a vasectomy. Mr. V. has consented to the surgical procedure, but he is experiencing doubts about whether or not he really wants to be sterilized because he has many unanswered questions about the procedure and its effects. Mr. and Mrs. V. are currently being counseled by a nurse in a vasectomy clinic. During the initial assessment the nurse identified patient-centered problems related to emotional stability, somatic identity, sexuality, occupational identity, and social role.

Following are Mr. V.'s nursing care plan and patient care cardex related to the above mentioned areas of concern.

NURSING CARE PLAN

Problems	Objectives	Nursing Interventions	Principles/Rationale	Evaluations
Emotional Impact Expressed ambivalent feelings about having a vasectomy.	To enhance Mr. V.'s verbalization of his feelings.	Encourage Mr. V. to express to his wife how he feels about having a vasectomy.	Verbalizing feelings can assist the individual in identifying possible solutions to a problem. A sex partner who is aware of the individual's feelings about a surgical sexual alteration is more likely to be able to provide necessary emotional support.	The nurse would observe for: Mr. V.'s expressed feelings about the surgery to his wife.
	To support Mr. V.'s male ego.	Reassure Mr. V. that having a vasectomy does not make him any less a man.	A man who has a threatened male ego due to a vasectomy will encounter difficulty in coping emotionally with his surgical sexual alteration.	
	To increase Mr. and Mrs. V.'s awareness of the importance of mutual consent about the performance of a vasectomy.	Encourage Mrs. V. to allow Mr. V. to reexamine his feelings about having a vasectomy.	A man who is pressured into making the decision to have a vasectomy is more likely to undergo emotional problems as a result of the surgical intervention.	Mutual reexamination by Mr. and Mrs. V. for the desire for a vasectomy. Definitive plans, by Mr. and Mrs. V., for or against the performance of a vasectomy.
Somatic Impact Expressed anxiety about being emasculated.	To enhance Mr. V.'s examination of his self-image.	Encourage Mr. V. to verbalize how he feels the vasectomy will affect him.	Some men feel that the loss of reproductivity makes them less manly.	The nurse would observe for: Mr. V.'s open verbalization about his masculinity.
		Encourage Mrs. V. to verbalize how she feels the vasectomy will affect Mr. V.	A man who is aware of how his sex partner will view him after a vasectomy is better prepared to make a decision on whether or not he desires it.	

NURSING CARE PLAN (cont.)

Problems	Objectives	Nursing Interventions	Principles/Rationale	Evaluations
Somatic Impact (cont.)		Inform Mr. and Mrs. V. that a vasectomy does not alter: 1. masculine appearance. 2. voice tone. 3. sexual activity. 4. physical strength.	With a better understanding about the effects of the vasectomy, individuals are more capable of making the decision of whether or not it is their desired means of birth control.	
	To increase Mr. V.'s recognition of the possibility of retreating into isolation.	Encourage Mr. V. to discuss how he feels a vasectomy will affect his ability to relate to others.	A man who views himself as "less of a man" because of the vasectomy may retreat into isolation and fail to set up friendships or a mutually satisfying sexual relationship.	Mr. V.'s discussion of how the vasectomy will affect his social and sexual relationships.
Sexual Impact Verbalized fear of possible castration.	To decrease Mr. V.'s fear of castration.	Reassure Mr. and Mrs. V. that castration (removal of the gonads) does not take place during the surgical procedure.	Fear of castration is compounded when an individual has limited knowledge about the surgical procedure.	The nurse would observe for: A decrease in Mr. V.'s expressed fear of castration.
	To enhance Mr. and Mrs. V.'s knowledge about the vasectomy procedure.	Inform Mr. and Mrs. V. that either a short midline incision is made in the scrotum or a half-inch incision is made on both sides. Both vas deferens (excretory ducts of the testes) are lifted out and a small section is removed. The duct is closed off and		

...about the possibility of missing work.	...apprehension about the effect which the vasectomy will have upon occupational responsibilities.	...the procedure is performed at the end of the work week (generally on Friday) so that Mr. V. has an opportunity to rest over the weekend before returning to work. If Mr. V. is unable to have a weekend free from his job, he should be informed that he needs to rest completely for 12 hours after the surgery with time off the following day if his work requires heavy labor. Reassure Mr. V. that generally a man undergoing a vasectomy will not be required to lose work days. However, if he has to miss work, the number of days missed is rarely over three.	...knowledge about the specifics of a surgical procedure can decrease unnecessary apprehension.	...A decrease in Mr. V.'s expressed concern about missing work days as a result of the vasectomy.
Social Impact Expressed anxiety about what friends will think and say about him once he has had a vasectomy.	To decrease Mr. V.'s anxiety about what others think and say about him.	Encourage Mr. V. to verbalize how he feels the vasectomy will affect him.	The male who feels insecure with the masculine image he portrays will be less likely to admit openly and deal with the fact that he has undergone a vasectomy.	The nurse would observe for: Mr. V.'s decreased anxiety about what others think and say about him.
		Inform Mr. and Mrs. V. that: 1. More people are receiving vasectomies as a means of birth control. 2. Vasectomies are more openly discussed by society than in the past. 3. A vasectomy is an acceptable means of birth control.	Increased knowledge and understanding about an issue tend to decrease one's apprehension.	

PATIENT CARE CARDEX

PATIENT'S NAME:	Mr. V.	DIAGNOSIS: Desiring vasectomy for purpose of birth control
AGE: 35 years		SEX: Male
MARITAL STATUS: Married		OCCUPATION: Chemical Engineer
SIGNIFICANT OTHERS: Wife and three children		

Problems	Nursing Approaches
Emotional: Expressed ambivalent feelings about having a vasectomy.	1. Encourage to express to wife how he feels about having a vasectomy. 2. Reassure that having a vasectomy does not make him any less of a man. 3. Encourage wife to allow him to reexamine his feelings about having a vasectomy.

Somatic: Expressed anxiety about being emasculated.	1. Encourage to verbalize how he feels a vasectomy will affect him.
	 2. Encourage wife to verbalize how she feels the vasectomy will affect husband.
	 3. Inform patient and wife that a vasectomy does not alter:
	   (a) masculine appearance.
	   (b) voice tone.
	   (c) sexual activity.
	   (d) physical strength.
	 4. Encourage to discuss how he feels a vasectomy will affect his ability to relate to others.

Sexual: Verbalized fear of possible castration.	1. Reassure patient and wife that castration does not take place during the surgical procedure. 2. Inform patient and wife that either a short midline incision is made in the scrotum or a half-inch incision is made on both sides. 3. Inform patient and wife that both vas deferens are lifted out and a small section is removed. The

possibility of missing work.

there is an opportunity for rest over the weekend before returning to work. If patient is unable to have a weekend free from work, he should be informed that he needs to rest completely for 12 hours after the surgery with time off the following day if work requires heavy labor.

2. Reassure that generally a man undergoing a vasectomy will not be required to lose work days, but if days are missed, they rarely number more than three.

Social: Expressed anxiety about what friends will think and say about him once he has had a vasectomy.

1. Encourage to verbalize how he believes the vasectomy will affect him.
2. Inform patient and wife that:
   (a) more people are receiving vasectomies as a means of birth control.
   (b) vasectomies are more openly discussed by society than in the past.
   (c) a vasectomy is an acceptable means of birth control.

REFERENCES

Ager, J., Werley, H., Allen, D., Shea, F., and Lewis, H. Vasectomy who gets one and why? *American Journal of Public Health,* 1974, *64* (7), 680-686.

Amias, A. Sexual life after gynaecological operations—I, *British Medical Journal,* 1975, *2,* 608-609.

Bennett, A. Vasectomy without complication. *Urology,* 1976, 7 (2), 184-185.

Bloom, L. and Houston, K. The psychological effects of vasectomy for American men, *Journal of Genetic Psychology,* 1976, *128,* (2), 173-182.

Bumpass, L. The increasing acceptance of sterilization in U. S. In M. Schima, I. Ludbell, J. Davis, and E. Connell (Eds.), *Advances in voluntary sterilization.* (Proceedings of the Second International Conference, Geneva, 1973), *Excerpta Medica,* 1974, 104-111.

Carbary, L. The hysterectomy patient, *Nursing Care,* 1975, *8* (2), 8-12.

Craft, I. Problems of vasectomy, *The Practitioner,* 1975, *214,* 70-74.

Craig, G. and Jackson, P. Sexual life after vaginal hysterectomy, *British Medical Journal,* 1975, *3* (5975), 97.

Davis, J., and Lubell, I. Advances in understanding the effects of vasectomy, *The Mount Sinai Journal of Medicine in New York,* 1975, *42* (5), 391-397.

Doty, F. Emotional aspects of vasectomy: a review, *Journal of Reproductive Medicine,* 1974, *10* (4), 156-161.

Drake, R., and Price, J. Depression: adaptation to disruption and loss, *Perspectives in Psychiatric Care,* 1975, *13* (4), 163-169.

Erickson, M. H. The psychological significance of vasectomy. H. Rosen (Ed.), In *Therapeutic Abortion.* New York: Julian Press, 1954.

Erikson, E. *Childhood and society.* New York: W. W. Norton & Co., 1963.

Ferber, A., Tietze, C., and Lewit, S. Men with vasectomies: a study of medical, sexual, and psychosocial changes, *Psychosomatic Medicine,* 1967, *29,* 354-366.

Foreman, J. Vasectomy clinic, *American Journal of Nursing,* 1973, *73* (5), 819-821.

Freund, M., and Davis, J. Disappearance rate of spermatozoa from the ejaculate following vasectomy, *Fertility and Sterility,* 1969, *20,* 163-169.

Hackett, R., and Waterhouse, K. Vasectomy reviewed, *American Journal of Obstetrics and Gynecology,* 1973, *116* (3), 438-455.

Hamersma, R., Anderegg, R., Miller, C., and Rudolph, B. Psychological dynamics and self-perceptions of vasectomy candidates, *Perceptual and Motor Skills,* 1975, *40,* 1004-1006.

Higgins, J. More hysterectomies—fact, fantasy, or fad? *Canadian Nurse,* 1971, *67,* 33-35.

Holm, L. Nursing care of patients having a hysterectomy, *Canadian Nurse,* 1971, *67,* 36-37.

Hornstein, D., and Houston, B. The effects of vasectomy on postoperative psychological adjustment and self-concept, *The Journal of Psychology,* 1975, *89,* 167-173.

Janis, I. *Psychological stress.* New York: John Wiley Sons, Inc., 1958.

Kaplan, H. S. *The illustrated manual of sex therapy.* New York: Quadrangle/The New York Times Book Co., 1975.

Keaveny, M., Hader, L., Massoni, M., and Wade, G. Hysterectomy: helping patients adjust, *Nursing '73*, 1973, *3* (2), 8-12.

Mathis, J. Psychologic aspects of surgery on female reproductive organs, *JOGN Nursing*, 1973, *2*, 50-53.

Montie, J., and Stewart, B. Vasovasostomy: past, present, and future, *The Journal of Urology*, 1974, *112* (11), 111-113.

Moss, W. Attitudes of patients one year after vasectomy, *Urology*, 1975, *6* (3), 319-322.

Phillips, N. The prevalence of surgical sterilization in a suburban population, *Demography*, 1971, *8*, 261-270.

Piver, M., Rutledge, F., and Smith, J. Five classes of extended hysterectomy for women with cervical cancer, *Obstetrics and Gynecology*, 1974, *44* (2), 265-272.

Polivy, J. Psychological reactions to hysterectomy: critical review, *American Journal of Obstetrics and Gynecology*, 1974, *118* (3), 319-322.

Rodgers, D., Ziegler, F., and Levy, N. Prevailing cultural attitudes about vasectomy: a possible explanation of postoperative psychological response, *Psychosomatic Medicine*, 1976, *24* (5), 367-375.

Sobrero, A., and Kohli, K. Two years' experience of an outpatient vasectomy service, *American Journal of Public Health*, 1975, *65* (10), 1091, 1094.

Squires, J., Barb, M., and Pinch, L. The morbidity of vasectomy, *Surgery, Gynecology and Obstetrics*, 1976, *143* (2), 237-240.

Steele, S., and Goodwin, M. A pamphlet to answer the patient's questions before hysterectomy, *Lancet*, 1975, *2* (7933), 492-493.

Swenson, I. Psychologic considerations in vasectomy: a review of literature, *JOGN Nursing*, 1975, *4* (6), 29-32.

Vernon, A. Explaining hysterectomy, *Nursing '73*, 1973, *3* (9), 36-38.

Wallace, D. Vasectomy, *Nursing Mirror*, 1974, *138*, 58-59.

Westoff, C. The modernization of U. S. contraceptive practice, *Family Planning Perspectives*, 1972, *4*, 9-12.

Williams, M. Cultural patterning of the feminine role: a factor in the response to hysterectomy, *Nursing Forum*, 1973, *12* (4), 379-387.

Williams, M. Easier convalescence from hysterectomy, *American Journal of Nursing*, 1976, *76* (3), 438-440.

Wolfers, H. Psychological aspects of vasectomy, *British Medical Journal*, 1970, *4*, 297-300.

Woods, N. *Human sexuality in health and illness.* St. Louis: C. V. Mosby, 1975.

7

The Patient with a
WEIGHT PROBLEM

INTRODUCTION

Excessive weight is an ever-increasing concern for the health care professions. Approximately one-third of the people in the United States are above their ideal weight (Gold, 1976) and approximately one-quarter of a million of them are on some form of diet most of the time to control their weight (Lindner, 1974). Undoubtedly, the affluence of Western society contributes greatly to the occurrence of weight related health problems. Food is abundant and accessible for most people. In addition, the standard of living is high so that a fair amount of time is available for recreational activities. Unfortunately, a large percentage of the population only takes part in sedentary recreational activities. Television and spectator sports are forms of such recreation. Thus, physical inactivity has become one of the greatest contributing factors to the weight problem (Seltzer and Stare, 1973; Kalisch, 1972).

The literature has attempted to describe the varying degrees of weight. Some authorities have described overweight as being an excess of weight in comparison to a set standard without consideration for fat deposit, bone structure, or muscle mass (Seltzer and Stare, 1973). Obesity is frequently referred to as a condition in which there is an excess of adipose tissue (Seltzer and Stare, 1973). The easiest and most direct means of determining the presence of obesity is by measuring the thickness of the individual's skinfold because large quantities of adipose tissue are located under the skin. Detailed studies of skinfolds on many sites of the body show that the amount of fat at the upper arm site, over the triceps and at the subscapular site, correlates highly with total body fat (Damon and Goldman, 1964; Hansman, 1970). An upper arm skinfold measurement of 3.0 centimeters and above for a woman and a measurement of 2.3 centimeters and above for a man are considered standard measurements of obesity by many authorities (Seltzer and Stare, 1973).

However, regardless of whether the individual is excessively overweight or is actually obese, similar problems are encountered by both. For clarity of the topic related to an individual experiencing a weight problem, this chapter will refer to these individuals as obese.

OBESITY PROFILE

Obesity is generally recognized by health care professionals as a major health hazard both physically and emotionally (Musante, 1974). Research has demonstrated that individuals who are obese are more prone to additional health care problems, such as diabetes mellitus, cardiovascular disorders, and renal disease (Kalisch, 1972). Unfortunately, few individuals in the general population view obesity as ill health. For many it has become a way of life, since through history obesity has frequently been viewed as a weakness, a sin, or as inadequate self-control rather than as a medical condition (Salzman, 1972).

Obesity, undoubtedly, is the most common chronic illness in American women (Winick, 1975). Obese men outnumber obese women in the early adult years, but women increasingly outnumber men after age thirty-five (U.S. Public Health Service, 1965). Nearly two and one-half times more obese women than nonobese women were overweight as children (Rimm and Rimm, 1976). Obese children and adolescents are a major reservoir for obesity in adults (Seltzer and Stare, 1973) since over 80 percent of them go on to become obese adults (Brook, 1972).

In addition, a familial tendency exists in obesity. It has been found that if one parent is obese, then 40 percent of the children are obese; if both parents are obese, 80 percent of the children are obese. Generally, only 7 percent of the children with nonobese parents become obese (Mayer, 1972).

Socioeconomic factors play an important part in the prevalence of obesity. Studies have demonstrated that obesity is six times more common in women of lower socioeconomic class than in women of higher socioeconomic class (Goldblatt, Moore, and Stunkard, 1965; Stunkard, 1959). For men, social class also has a significant relationship to obesity, but the relationship is less pronounced than in women (Bray, 1976).

Cultural background also contributes to the development of obesity. Bray (1976) and Stunkard (1976) note that individuals originating in Eastern Europe and living in the United States have a higher incidence of obesity than individuals from Western Europe. The incidence of obesity increases steadily as one moves eastward across Europe, starting with Great Britain and continuing with Ireland, Germany, Italy, Czechoslovakia, Hungary, and a Polish-Russian group. Stunkard (1976), however, notes that one ethnic group, the Czechoslovakians, does not fit this pattern. The Czechoslavakians demonstrate the highest rate of obesity among any of the groups, with 34 percent of them being obese. Research also demonstrates that the time spent in the United States has an effect upon the frequency of obesity. The lowest incidence of obesity is among individuals whose families have been in the United States for a long period of time (Stunkard, 1976). Consequently, recent immigrants to the United States have a higher incidence of obesity than fourth-generation Americans of the same cultural heritage.

Religion has a decided relationship to the frequency of obesity. Stunkard (1976) found obesity to be most common among Jews, followed by Catholics, and then Protestants. When the Protestant religion is further broken down into some of its denominations, the occurrence of obesity mirrors the social class stereotyping conventionally ascribed to each of these divisions. Baptists have the highest incidence of obesity, followed by Methodists, Presbyterians, and finally Episcopalians (Stunkard, 1976).

Although various interpretations can be placed upon these findings, major contributing factors to the prevalence of obesity are, most likely, increased standard of living, abundance of food, decreased physical activity, and basic food habits. Food of high carbohydrate and caloric content may frequently comprise the diet of individuals of lower socioeconomic status. One-dish meals designed to stretch meat allowances for a family often contain high carbohydrate foods, such as noodles or macaroni. Thus, caloric consumption increases. In addition, increased use of "junk foods" has affected the additional caloric intake of many individuals, regardless of social class. Cultural food patterns in which potatoes, pastas, and sweet pastries are important constituents can also contribute to increased weight. If the main meal of the day is high in calories and if physical activity becomes increasingly less, obesity is likely to ensue.

Regardless of the factors that contribute to obesity, its presence can create problems that affect emotional well-being, somatic identity, sexuality, occupational identity, and social role. The remainder of the chapter will discuss how obesity can affect each of these areas.

IMPACT OF OBESITY

Emotional Impact*

The presence of obesity has many emotional ramifications. A question frequently asked by members of the health care team is, "Which came first, the emotional difficulties or the obesity?" Advocates for both sides exist.

*It is advisable for the reader to have read Chapters 1 and 3 before continuing with this section.

However, regardless of which occurred first, emotional difficulties or obesity, both facets greatly contribute to the survival of the other.

Obese individuals are frequently seen by others as stubborn, defiant, and wary, characteristics that form the basis for a passive-aggressive personality organization (Castelnuovo-Tedesco and Schiebel, 1975). They may intentionally miss clinic appointments or they may take their daily prescribed vitamins and minerals haphazardly, even though the importance of adhering to both regimes is explained.

When asked to describe themselves, the obese individuals are ambivalent. Obese individuals are unaware of the esthetic drawbacks of obesity, yet they are very embarrassed about viewing themselves in a mirror or in photographs (Castlenuovo-Tedesco and Schiebel, 1975). Some obese individuals refuse to shop for clothing because they dislike having to view themselves in a mirror when trying on garments. In addition, the environment (ill-fitting clothing, small dressing rooms, and narrow seats) frequently reminds them of their size.

Obese individuals usually view food as a self-administered gratification to decrease emotional upheavals. Although such individuals are aware that the food they eat is not good for them (Plutnick, 1976), they have an intense desire to eat it. Thus, a strong sense of denial is manifested. External stimuli such as the smell of food, the sight of food, and the discussion of food play a vital role in encouraging obese individuals to eat. Unlike the case for nonobese individuals, internal stimuli, such as gastric contractions and changes in blood sugar levels, play a minor role in initiating the obese individuals drive to consume food (Schachter, 1971). Rodin (1975) found that obese individuals perceive time as passing more slowly than nonobese individuals and thus eat sooner. Consequently, obese individuals are greatly affected by the stimuli from the environment and, because of these stimuli, increase their food consumption. Such findings lend themselves to the belief that eating disorders are learned behaviors that have become reflexive in the obese individual's pattern of daily living (Musante, 1974).

Obesity, like alcoholism, drug abuse, and gambling, is a complex problem. Individuals exhibiting any one of these disorders frequently demonstrate an obsessive-compulsive syndrome. According to Salzman (1972), such individuals are rigid and controlled, especially in those areas of their emotional life which are not completely under voluntary control. Since they are unable to be in absolute control, they often attempt to control by totally avoiding any kind of control. They are either totally organized or totally unorganized, meticulously clean or very sloppy. The obsessive-compulsive individual tends to be concerned about being in control either through extreme active attempts at control or complete abandonment of all efforts to control (Salzman, 1972). This behavior is manifested by the obese individual's obsession to eat and the compulsion to eat. "What difference does it make how much I eat? Everything turns to fat anyway!" These are common statements made by the obese person demonstrating an obsessive-compulsive syndrome.

On the other end of the continuum of weight problems, the individual manifesting anorexia nervosa may reject food because he or she is afraid that everything that is eaten contributes to the deposition of body fat (Bruch, 1973; Bruch, 1977). The fear of obesity for the anorectic is so intense that the rejection of food overrides powerful hunger pangs, and ultimately even the grasp on life itself (Stunkard, 1976).

As mentioned earlier, children and adolescents are a major reservoir for obesity in the adult years. Research has demonstrated that adults who were obese as children encounter more difficulties in the treatment of their weight problem (Gold, 1976). The prognosis and psychological aspects of obesity are different in individuals who have become obese in their middle adult years from those who have been obese since early life. According to Seltzer and Stare (1973), individuals who were obese as children are more likely to be obsessively concerned about their self-image than persons who have middle-age, adult-onset obesity. The child-onset obese individual tends to view his or her obesity as a badge of shame rather than a medical problem. In addition, the individual usually demonstrates a long history of repeated failures to control weight.

By contrast, middle-age, adult-onset obesity is less inundated with diffuse psychological factors. The adult-onset obese individual generally views his or her condition as reversible, provided he or she obtains appropriate medical guidance. In addition, the individual tends to realize the health hazards of obesity, thus creating a more cooperative and conducive climate with the health care team and their approach to the obesity problem. This is not necessarily true of the person with child-onset obesity who does not view the excessive weight as harmful to physical health and thus demonstrates less cooperation in the institution of therapy. Consequently, one can see the importance of knowing the age of the individual's obesity onset in developing and implementing an appropriate plan of care.

In summary, the obese individual often portrays to others a picture of stubbornness, defiance, wariness, cynicism, passive-aggressive behavior, and obsessive-compulsive manifestations. The obese individual is ambivalent about the obesity and has a strong desire for food as gratification for his or her emotional disequilibrium. The obese individual becomes reliant upon the need for food to deal with emotional upheavals, but this only accentuates the problems.

Since treatment of obesity is complex, a multidimensional approach is necessary for successful treatment. Simply placing the individual on a weight reduction diet and encouraging more physical activity are often not enough in accomplishing the goal of taking off pounds.

To deal with the individual's emotional aspects of the weight problem, one of the first goals in therapy is to establish sound rapport with the individual. A nurse, or any other member of the health care team, who holds unwarranted prejudices about obesity must identify these prejudices before attempting therapy with the individual manifesting a weight problem. If the health team member views obesity as incurable or only slightly amenable to therapy, these feelings may be transmitted to the obese individual. Such prejudices of health care members may have contributed to the low success rate experienced by the individual in past attempts at weight reduction.

Acceptance of the individual must occur before weight reduction therapy is instituted (Kalisch, 1972). Since the obese individual harbors feelings of shame and guilt about his or her condition, the individual may find it difficult to express these feelings if he or she feels that the therapist is not accepting of him or her; consequently, treatment efforts are doomed before they start.

Throughout the obese individual's life he or she has, most likely, frequently been reminded of the negative effects of eating to excess. The use of negative reinforcement of the problem may often intensify the existence of that problem (Pierre and Warren, 1975). Instead of using negative feedback, positive reinforcement on the part of those in the environment of the obese individual may prove more beneficial. For example, health team members and family members should comment in a positive way about the individual's decrease in food consumption instead of commenting that he or she still is eating too much even though the individual has cut down some. Statements like these may prove beneficial: "I've noticed that you are eating less at each meal. It must be difficult and I'm proud of your attempts."

During weight reduction the obese individual may need frequent positive feedback, for it is not uncommon for depression to occur during therapy. Most periods of depression occur during the first 12 months of weight reduction, with the first 6 months being the most difficult (Kalucy and Crisp, 1974). Once weight reduction is stabilized at the lower desired weight, emotional upheavals tend to disappear (Glucksman and Hirsch, 1968). The obese individual and the family need to be reassured that feelings of depression during this initial period of weight loss are not uncommon. Since feelings of discouragement are evident, frequent, strong, positive encouragement to continue with the therapy may be necessary. Encouraging the dieting individual to verbalize his or her feelings to significant others and the therapist is vital. By the same token, the significant others must provide positive reinforcement for the accomplishment in weight loss that has been made.

As previously mentioned, environmental factors play a major role in contributing to the obese individual's compulsion to eat. Therefore, one of the first acts that the nurse or another member of the health team must carry out is an assessment of the individual's eating behaviors. The obese person requires instructions on how to keep a record of eating patterns for approximately one week. This record must include the following: when eating takes place, what is eaten, where eating takes place, what is being done while eating, and how the individual feels prior to eating. Depending upon the data obtained from this assessment, the appropriate interventions then can be instituted.

To assist the obese person in controlling the effects that external stimulation have upon eating patterns, attempts must be made to decrease such environmental stimuli. Mustante (1974), Jordan, Kimbrell, and Levitz (1976) suggest the following maneuvers to accomplish this goal:

1. Eat meals slowly so that they last at least 20 minutes.
2. Chew each mouthful of food ten times.
3. Place the utensils on the plate between mouthfuls.
4. Decrease the size of food portions.
5. Serve the meals restaurant style.
6. Discard leftover food immediately after the meal is completed.
7. Avoid keeping prepared snack food in the house.
8. Leave small portions of food on the plate at each meal.
9. Alter the composition of foods (if possible) high in caloric content. For example, over a period of days or weeks decrease the amount of bread used to make a sandwich until no bread is used at all.
10. Use low-calorie substitutes with meals, such as low-calorie sodas.
11. Shop for groceries after eating a full meal.
12. Shop from a prepared grocery list.
13. Turn off the bulb in the refrigerator.
14. Keep all foods in covered containers.
15. Eat only in one room and in one chair.
16. Avoid carrying out household and personal activities, such as telephone calls or letter writing, in the kitchen.
17. Reward appropriate dietary behavior (preferably not with food).

As the obese individual attempts the above suggested measures to decrease the external stimulation to eat, he or she may identify other maneuvers that are helpful, for example, using a small dinner plate to eat from or placing a picture of a slender person on the door of the refrigerator as a reminder to decrease food consumption. Some individuals resort to chewing gum each time they feel the urge to eat. Regardless of which measures an individual uses, those that are helpful in decreasing environmental stimuli are the ones of importance.

Family members and friends can play a vital role in assisting the obese individual in carrying out diet therapy. They can help in the decrease of environmental stimuli and by providing positive reinforcement for accomplishments made. Thus, the obese individual does not feel alone in the effort for weight reduction.

In addition to the support provided by family and friends, some obese individuals find the use of group interaction helpful. Group interaction can take several forms. Group therapy sessions with a physician or the use of organized societal groups such as Weight Watchers or TOPS (Take Off Pounds Sensibly) are examples. The use of group interactions provides a means for obese individuals to share similar problems and possible solutions to their problems. Since the obese person has a great need to be liked, peers in group interaction provide a possible means for such acceptance. In addition, group interactions provide another available source of positive reinforcement for continuation with weight-reduction therapy and for accomplishments achieved.

Somatic Impact*

The presence of obesity can play a vital role in the development of one's body image. Three components have been identified as major contributing factors to the development of a disturbed body image in an obese individual: age of obesity onset, presence of emotional problems, and negative appraisal of obesity by other individuals during the formative years (Stunkard and Mendelson, 1967).

Disturbances in body image occur primarily among individuals who became obese during childhood and adolescence. Generally, an individual who is obese in childhood also tends to be obese in adolescence (Stunkard and Burt, 1967). Adolescence is the developmental stage when a disturbed body image usually occurs (Stunkard and Mendelson, 1967). It is during this developmental stage that the individual becomes concerned about his or her body contour. The female adolescent takes on a rounded feminine form and the male assumes a muscular masculine appearance. However, both the male and the female adolescent see their bodies as something useful to them that allows engagement in activities valued by their peers. The success with which the adolescent utilizes his or her body is important because the body contributes to the value that he or she places upon himself or herself. If the adolescent views his or her body as "less than desirable" because of the obesity, he or she will encounter difficulties in establishing a healthy view of his or her capabilities and, in turn, the body image will be distorted.

According to Stunkard (1976), the basic feature of the obese individual's disturbed body image is a constant preoccupation with obesity. This preoccupation may actually lead to the exclusion of other personal character-

---

*It is advisable for the reader to have read Chapter 2 before continuing with this section.

istics. Even if the obese individual is intelligent, wealthy, or talented, his or her weight becomes the major concern. The obese person often views the entire world in terms of body weight and divides society into classifications of differing weight and responds to them accordingly. The thinner individual is viewed with envy, while someone fatter is looked upon with contempt. The obese person appraises his or her body as grotesque and feels that others view his or her body with horror. These feelings are exemplified in such statements as, "Who would want to marry an elephant?"

Long-term results for weight reduction in the juvenile-onset obese individual are poor. Studies have demonstrated that when undergoing weight reduction a variety of behavioral changes such as distortions of time, inaccuracies on body size estimations, and depressive symptoms occur in juvenile-onset individuals. Adult-onset individuals do not experience any of these alterations (Grinker and Hirsch, 1972; Grinker, 1973). Thus, it is apparent that the age at which obesity occurs has profound effects on both the individual's body image and the success encountered in dealing with weight loss.

The second contributing factor in the alteration of the obese individual's body image is the presence of emotional disturbances. The juvenile-onset obese individual frequently manifests emotional disorders (Stunkard and Mendelson, 1967). By contrast, the adult-onset obese individual tends to demonstrate a variety of emotional disorders with few, if any, related to their obesity (Stunkard and Mendelson, 1967). Emotional disturbances can contribute to a disruption in body image, but they are not necessarily a primary constituent to its development.

Negative evaluation of obesity by significant others comprises the third predisposing factor to a disturbed body image in the obese individual. Today's society has an almost universal devaluation of obesity. The obese individual frequently is ostracized by others during social functions and becomes the target of jokes. He or she is often viewed with hostility and contempt. How others view the obese person is important not only to the obese adult, but to the obese child as well. Fat children are known to encounter more difficulties with interpersonal relationships and are discriminated against by peers (Alessi and Anthony, 1969; Matthews and Westie, 1966). Richardson and Goodman (1961) investigated children's reaction to the physical attributes of other children. Their findings indicate that almost unanimously the nonobese child was the most preferred and the obese child was the least desired. In addition, physicians have been found to harbor negative feelings toward the obese female whom they describe as ugly, awkward, and weak-willed (Maddox and Liederman, 1968).

The occasional existence of juveniles who do not face censorship because of their size reinforces the importance that this factor can play in the formation of a disturbed body image. Stunkard and Mendelson (1967) found that men coming from families in which large body size was valued and overweight was viewed as a sign of strength and health escaped body image disturbances. This favorable evaluation of body size was also shared by peers. Such individuals frequently are in demand as football players.

One reason given for society's negative attitudes toward obesity is that to a large degree success depends upon physical attractiveness. Another justification offered is that excess weight is detrimental to health, and health is an important measure of status and security (Kalisch, 1972). Regardless of the justifications offered by society, the views society holds and the feelings society expresses play a vital role in the individual's development of his or her body image in childhood and in adolescence. Without a doubt, the most devastating result of the stigmatizing attitude displayed by society is that the afflicted individuals come to accept the negative evaluation placed upon them (Goffman, 1963).

The negative feelings the obese individual harbors because of his obesity can have an effect upon the stage of development that he or she is currently experiencing. If the obese individual is in the stage of young adulthood (eighteen to forty-five), the individual is in the period in which merging his or her identity with others is vital to maturation. Since the obese individual feels grotesque and believes that others view him or her with contempt, the individual will undoubtedly experience difficulty in sharing himself or herself with others, both in friendships and in a mutually satisfying sexual relationship. In fact, studies have indicated that obese women encounter more difficulty in establishing a satisfying sexual relationship with members of the opposite sex than nonobese women (Stunkard and Mendelson, 1967). Because of the fear of negative evaluation by significant others, the obese young adult may retreat into isolation instead of establishing a sense of intimacy with other individuals. The existing state of isolation leads to boredom and boredom can lead to a need to eat in an attempt to cope with the feelings of loneliness. Thus, a vicious cycle develops and obesity ends up generating obesity.

The developmental stage of adulthood (forty-five to sixty-five years) may create problems of stagnation for the obese individual. The middle years are a time when vital interests outside the home are founded and a concern for guiding future generations evolves. If obese individuals view themselves with contempt and become preoccupied with their obesity, they devalue their other personal attributes. Regardless of the positive characteristics that they may have, they see only the negativeness of their obesity and consequently become self-absorbed and stagnate. They feel that they have nothing of value to offer the forthcoming generations. Chronic defeatism results and they isolate themselves in self-pity.

The stage of maturity (sixty-five and over) is a period when the individual derives satisfaction from life's past experiences and accomplishments. Obese individuals may not be satisfied with their past accomplishments and have developed a weak sense of self-worth. In addition to the impact of obesity upon their body structure, they now must contend with the frequent body changes brought about by aging. Their ego integrity is weak and it is not uncommon for a state of despair to exist for obese individuals experiencing the final developmental stage of life. Thus, it can be seen that obesity can have an adverse affect upon their successful accomplishment of each developmental stage of adulthood. Obesity does alter one's mental picture of oneself.

The nurse's role in dealing with an obese individual's altered body image revolves around assisting him or her in reestablishing a new body image. It has been found that a formerly obese person who has not reestablished his or her self-image will most likely be unable to retain weight loss (Kalisch, 1972). This is often the result of harbored feelings of self-hate and inadequacy. The individual must be assisted in examining his or her feelings. Encouraging the obese person to verbalize feelings may assist him or her in recognizing possible ways of dealing with his or her feelings. It also provides a means of releasing pent-up emotions so that these internalized emotions do not further intensify feelings of self-hate and inadequacy.

The obese individual needs encouragement to express how he or she feels that he or she is viewed by members of society. The individual requires assistance in awareness of and resistance to stigmatizing attitudes that the community may express. Instead of retreating into isolation and further compounding these feelings of inadequacy, the obese individual must be assisted in understanding why people react the way they do. The obese individual needs help to realize that ostracizing and stigmatizing someone who is different is often the way people deal with their own insecurities. If the obese person can understand and accept this, he or she may encounter fewer difficulties in relating to members of society who shun him or her.

In addition to verbalizing personal feelings and attempting to understand other individuals' reactions, the obese individual requires positive feedback for attempts and accomplishments made in weight reduction. The feedback may be encouragement about the use of willpower at a party serving many high-caloric foods or compliments about weight lost. Since the obese person has frequent moments of discouragement and depression, positive feedback is necessary both from significant others and members of the health care team. Not until the obese individual reevaluates and restructures his or her body image will the individual consistently be able to lose the necessary amount of weight and maintain the desired level of weight (Jordan, Levitz, and Kimbrell, 1977).

Sexual Impact

Sexual behavior is affected by the way an individual perceives his or her body (Woods, 1975), and the obese individual certainly is no exception. Obese individuals find their bodies ugly and loathsome and continually avoid mirrors and scales. They tend to think of themselves as fat, and awareness of their size is rarely far from their conscious thoughts. Displeasure at looking at their nude bodies is not uncommon. Obese people dislike having others see them in the nude and they even avoid being seen in bathing suits. Therefore, it is not uncommon for obese individuals to carry out sexual intercourse in the dark or while partially clothed (Castelnuovo-Tedesco and Schiebel, 1975). In addition, sexual activity is significantly diminished (Crisp, 1967). This, surely, is related to the fact that obese individuals encounter serious difficulties in relationships with members of the opposite sex. Such difficulties seem to stem from self-consciousness about how others view their obesity (Stunkard and Mendelson, 1967). Such self-consciousness may range from avoidance to hateful devaluation of the opposite sex. Obese females actually hesitate to become emotionally involved with a member of the opposite sex. As a result, they may cynically view the male's intentions (Castelnuovo-Tedesco and Schiebel, 1975). However, obese individuals who do not demonstrate disturbances in body image have fewer difficulties in their relationships with the opposite sex (Stunkard and Mendelson, 1967).

Some obese individuals have used their obesity as a protective means of lessening heterosexual opportunities. Such a maneuver is related to fears about their own sexual potential. When obesity is removed from such persons, they are suddenly confronted with feelings they cannot handle (Kalucy and Crisp, 1974). Frigidity or increased anger with individuals who "come too close" are two possible examples.

Obese individuals do, however, tend to be attracted to other obese persons. Research has shown that obese men tend to be married to obese women. By the same token, obese women tend to marry obese men at every decade level from the third through the seventh (Garn, 1976). Thus, it appears that the obese person seeks out another obese person in marriage, a phenomenon referred to as homogamy or assortative mating (Garn, 1976).

In addition to the psychological effects that obesity may have upon one's sexual activity, physical difficulties in carrying out intercourse also may be encountered. Because of the excessive body fat, the ability to assume various coital positions may be difficult. Also, vaginal penetration may become complicated because there is an excess of adipose tissue in the pelvic region. Such distribution of excessive body fat does not lend itself to close body positioning. The obese individual may find it necessary to experiment with various coital positions before deciding which one(s) provides the greatest comfort and enjoyment. For example, the male superior position may create breathing difficulties for the female because of either her own obese state or the weight of her sex partner. The "doggy-fashion" position may be impossible because of the excessive fat on the female buttocks. The inability to carry out the sex act satisfactorily can create problems in the sexual relationship and/or intensify existing difficulties.

Proper feminine hygiene after intercourse may pose problems for the obese female. Because of the excessive body fat the woman may encounter difficulties in adequately cleansing the perineal area. She may be unable to see or to reach her perineum so that she can clean herself properly. As a result, the woman may hesitate to engage in intercourse. Again, the results may be the creation of difficulties or intensification of existing problems within the sexual relationship.

The nurse's role in assisting the obese individual encountering sexual difficulties caused by obesity includes encouraging the expression of feelings by both sex partners about their sexual relationship. Both partners need to discuss openly how they feel about the existing physical and emotional difficulties they encounter. It is very possible that neither member has openly expressed his or her emotions about the sex act to the other member. Unless feelings are expressed, the identification of problems is difficult and the internalization of ill feelings can only add to the creation of tension in the sexual relationship.

Once feelings have been openly expressed, the nurse can more easily identify existing and potential problems in the sexual relationship. If such problems exist, the nurse's next responsibility is to direct the individuals to appropriate members of the health team who are prepared in the counseling of individuals with sexual difficulties. If the nurse is a prepared sex therapist, then necessary interventions can be carried out.

If the obese female has difficulty in cleansing the perineal area, the nurse should instruct her how to use a small hand mirror to assist in the visualization of the perineum. Assuming a sitting position on the toilet may facilitate the ability to reach the area. Also the use of a bidet or a squeeze bottle with a spray tip for external cleansing may prove helpful.

Unless the obese individual's sexual difficulties are identified and dealt with appropriately, the sexual impact of obesity will continue to present problems. These problems subsequently can aid in the intensification of other difficulties resulting from the impact of obesity.

Occupational Impact

Obese individuals often find their condition a barrier to obtaining privileges, opportunities, and status granted to others. They may encounter difficulties in acquiring the necessary preparation for certain jobs or in securing employment. For example, admission to college may be a problem for the obese individual. Obese applicants to college are less likely to be admitted than nonobese applicants, even when there is no measurable difference in academic achievement, social class, and motivation (Canning and Mayer, 1966). In addition, many companies have regulations for acceptable body weight that hinder the obese individual from securing a job. Such occupational and educational problems only add to the obese person's already existing low self-concept.

Even if the individual is not discriminated against because of weight, the job requirements may make it difficult, if not impossible, for the individual to function. To illustrate, body fat may actually get in the way if the obese individual is required to operate certain machinery or if he or she is expected to maneuver down small passageways or sit on small stools. In addition to increased size, the obese individual demonstrates a decrease in physical capabilities (Curtis and Bradfield, 1971). The obese individual tires more easily and is not able to tolerate the same amount of physical strain as a nonobese individual.

Aside from the fact that certain occupations are unsafe and/or impossible for the obese person, certain jobs actually foster the potential occurrence of obesity. Consider the businessman or woman who frequently is expected to "wine and dine" clients as part of his or her job responsibilities. The owner of a delicatessen or a bakery easily may become a "nibbler" since pieces of food often are left over. The factory worker who is required by union law to take coffee breaks may munch on "goodies" from the ever-present vending machine during these breaks. Finally, the housewife may put on excessive weight because food is always available. She also may find herself eating the leftovers from the family meals or eating what the children have left on their plates because she cannot tolerate seeing food wasted. As a result, it is evident that the obese individual not only encounters problems in obtaining employment but also in losing and maintaining weight because he or she is constantly bombarded by external stimuli related to job responsibilities.

The role of the nurse in assisting the obese individual to deal with the occupational impact of obesity consists of two major goals. First, the nurse and other members of the health team need to guide the obese individual in recognizing ways in which obesity is affecting his or her occupation. The obese person needs to verbalize how excessive weight is affecting work performance and occupational advancements. Unless the individual is aware that this obese state has an impact upon employment, the obese individual may not be ready to deal with its control.

Second, if the work situation tends to foster obesity, means of dealing with the situation should be identified. For example, the individual who frequently is required to "wine and dine" clients as part of the job needs assistance in learning how to select low-calorie foods from a menu. Also, the individual requires encouragement to set limits prior to the meal on how much he or she intends to eat and drink. The individual then must function within these self-imposed limits. The obese individual who usually eats high-calorie goodies from the vending machine during coffee breaks may find it helpful to take breaks where the vending machines are not accessible.

If this is not possible or if the obese individual has a great need to eat during the coffee break, encouragement to drink low-calorie beverages and to bring low-calorie foods from home, such as celery and carrot sticks, may prove beneficial. In the case of the housewife or the delicatessen owner, suggestions on ways to discard leftover foods are important. Possible ways of decreasing the availability of such food is to dispose of it immediately in the garbage or to package and put it in the freezer for future use. The major purpose in the second goal for dealing with the occupational impact of obesity is to decrease or eliminate external stimuli that foster food consumption.

Only when the obese individual recognizes the effect obesity has upon his or her occupation and learns ways to control the environmental stimuli that affect food consumption will the individual be ready to deal with the occupational impact of obesity.

Social Impact

The meaning of food in the social structure has greatly contributed to the occurrence of obesity. For centuries food has been the symbol of many religious and secular rituals (Salzman, 1972). For example, weddings, baptisms, confirmations, and bar mitzvahs are religious rituals in which food is usually served in abundance. Fund raising banquets, cocktail parties, and graduation galas are but a few secular examples of where food is ever present. In fact, people cannot escape the existence of food when relaxing in front of the television set. Commercials for hamburgers, sodas, candy, and ice cream continually are being aired. Consequently, even when the obese individual identifies that obesity is a personal problem, he or she soon realizes that it is his or her individual concern. Even though society believes that fatness is unacceptable, it does little to assist the individual in achieving the goal of weight reduction.

Obesity presents a greater social disadvantage for women than it does for men. Physical attractiveness becomes a major factor in a woman's social success. The obese female finds it difficult to progress up the social ladder, relate to others, and find a suitable marriage partner (Kalisch, 1972). Since physical desirability is not one of her outstanding features, she finds herself often taking second best. For men, educational achievement, occupation, and financial status are the valued social traits. Hence, physical attractiveness plays less of a role in their social achievements.

Clothing plays a part in the social impact of obesity. Men's clothes often are designed to conceal body form and thus hide bulges. Women's clothes, however, frequently are fashioned to reveal body configurations and hence expose fat bulges. Because of this, some women hesitate to be seen at social functions. In addition, when extra weight is acquired new clothing may not be purchased. Consequently, the tight-fitting clothes intensify the fat bulges to a greater extent. However, should the obese female purchase new clothing because of her weight gain she may look at her new wardrobe with feelings of despair. After all, she may feel that "one can't be choosy when Omar the tentmaker is your dressmaker!"

One of the most frequent complaints related to the social impact of obesity is the feeling of humiliation at parties (Stunkard and Mendelson, 1967). The obese person often is found sitting along the sidelines at a dance or standing alone at a cocktail party. "Who wants to dance with a blimp!" is a statement frequently made by the obese person in reference to social functions.

Obese individuals are extremely concerned about being liked by others, but they frequently worry about being too agreeable lest they be "used" or "put down" (Castelnuovo-Tedesco and Schiebel, 1975). They often appear awkward, tense, withdrawn, and seclusive during social contacts. Thus, the comment that an obese individual is inherently jolly and the life of the party is a fallacy. Diminished social contact may further intensify the tendency to overeat, one of the obese individual's few remaining gratifications (Gold, 1976). Obese individuals bemoan the fact that they are fat and frequently use it as an alibi for other handicaps (Bruch, 1973). Yet they feel helpless, trapped, and incapable of altering their sad state of affairs.

One of the nurse's roles in assisting the obese individual to cope with the social impact of obesity is to assist the individual in developing adaptive responses to unavoidable social situations, such as banquets and weddings (Jordan, Kimbrell, and Levitz, 1976). The obese individual must be taught strategies for dealing with the presence of attractive and abundant foods. However, realistic expectations of his or her behavior at such functions must be considered when planning these strategies. Setting extremely high goals that are unachievable and unrealistic can only lead to discouragement and failure.

Preplanning eating behavior, standing away from the serving table at a cocktail party, leaving small amounts of each kind of food on the dinner plate at a banquet, and constantly "thinking thin" are a few possible strategies the obese person can use. The primary goal is to enjoy the food at the social function while eating less of it.

The obese person must be encouraged by the health team members and significant others to maintain a high standard of personal appearance. The woman should be urged to apply makeup routinely, to style her hair frequently, and to wear clothing that does not accentuate her body size. For example, clothing made of dark colors and designed with vertical lines tends to deemphasize body size. Obese men and women must maintain good personal hygiene, for body odor is often a problem in the obese individual. In addition, tight-fitting clothing should be avoided because it tends to emphasize fat bulges. The primary purpose for carrying out each of these maneuvers is to appear as attractive as possible.

The obese individual should not avoid social functions because isolation and loneliness often encourage the tendency to overeat. Some obese persons have found group interaction with other obese persons (e.g., Weight Watchers and Overeaters Anonymous) helpful in identifying and sharing ways of coping with social difficulties. Such groups may not be helpful for everyone; therefore, the nurse and other members of the health team must identify which obese individuals would benefit from such interactions.

Above all, the obese person needs encouragement from the nurse and significant others not to use obesity as an excuse to avoid social interactions. In addition, the result of social isolation should be made known to the individual. Since the obese person has frequent feelings of helplessness and hopelessness, constant positive feedback is a must. Unless the obese person's attitude toward social interaction is altered, he or she will continue to be socially isolated and to indulge in self-pity.

SUMMARY

Obesity is a prevalent and ever-increasing health care problem. It affects individuals of all ages and it is a hazard both physically and emotionally. Research has demonstrated that obesity tends to be more common in women of lower socioeconomic class, individuals originating from Eastern Europe, persons of recent immigration to the United States, and individuals of the Jewish faith. However, regardless of the factors that contribute to a person's obesity, its presence can create difficulties in the individual's emotional well-being, somatic identity, sexuality, occupational identity, and social role.

The obese person often is forced to deal with his or her health care problem alone. Society frowns on obesity, but it does little to assist the obese person in losing weight or maintaining weight already lost. Therefore, the role of the health care team is to assist the obese person in identifying how obesity affects his or her everyday life and guide the person in dealing with each of these alterations.

Patient Situation

Mrs. O. is a twenty-eight-year-old married woman with children ages two and four. Mrs. O's parents were immigrants from Hungary, but Mrs. O. was born in the United States. Her husband is currently employed as a gas station attendant. Mrs. O. has had a weight problem since the birth of her second child. She has come into the free clinic requesting assistance in dealing with her obesity. During the initial assessment the nurse identifies patient-centered problems related to emotional stability, somatic identify, sexuality, occupational identity, and social role.

Following are Mrs. O's nursing care plan and patient care cardex related to the above mentioned areas of concern.

NURSING CARE PLAN

Problems	Objectives	Nursing Interventions	Principles/Rationale	Evaluations
Emotional Impact Inability to control eating habits.	To assist Mrs. O. in identifying uncontrollable eating behavior.	Instruct Mrs. O. how to keep a record of her eating habits. The record must include: 1. when she eats. 2. what she eats. 3. where she eats. 4. what she is doing while she eats. 5. how she feels prior to eating.	Identifying eating patterns assists the individual in recognizing her eating behavior.	The nurse would observe for: Recognition by Mrs. O. that her eating habits are uncontrollable.
	To identify means of controlling Mrs. O.'s eating behavior.	Involve Mrs. O. in group interactions in weight control programs.	Interacting with individuals with similar problems can provide emotional support and may facilitate in the solution of individual problems.	A change in Mrs. O.'s eating habits.
		Instruct Mrs. O. on ways to decrease environmental stimuli that may be affecting her eating patterns. Include the following maneuvers: 1. Eat meals slowly so that they last at least 20 minutes. 2. Chew each mouthful of food 10 times. 3. Place the utensils on the plate between mouthfuls. 4. Decrease the size of food portions. 5. Serve the meals restaurant style on small plates. 6. Discard leftover food immediately after the meal is	Increasing understanding about factors that contribute to obesity can enhance the desire to control eating habits. Prolonging the meal can aid in the prevention of rapidly consuming excessive amounts of food. Decreasing the amount of readily available food for consumption can decrease food intake.	

Problem	Goal	Nursing Intervention	Rationale	Evaluation
		...snack food in the house.		
		8. Leave a small portion of food on the plate at each meal.	Decreasing the amount of calories consumed can lead to a loss in weight.	
		9. Alter the composition of foods high in caloric content (if possible).		
		10. Use low-calorie substitutes with meals.		
		11. Shop for groceries after eating a full meal.	Shopping from a prepared list while not hungry can prevent the purchase of unnecessary food items.	
		12. Shop from a prepared grocery list.		
		13. Turn off the bulb in the refrigerator.	Decreasing the visibility of food can decrease the urge to eat.	
		14. Keep all foods covered in containers.		
		15. Eat only in one room and in one chair.	Increasing the difficulty to eat can decrease the desire to eat.	
		16. Avoid carrying out household and personal activities in the kitchen.		
		17. Reward appropriate dietary behavior.	Positive feedback for accomplishments facilitates the feelings of self-worth.	
Somatic Impact Devaluation of self.	To assist Mrs. O. in establishing a new body image.	Encourage Mrs. O. to verbalize the feelings she has about herself.	Verbalization of feelings can assist the individual in recognizing possible ways of dealing with feelings.	The nurse would observe for: A decrease in Mrs. O.'s verbalization that she is of little importance. An increase in Mrs. O.'s pride about herself.
		Encourage Mrs. O. to express how she feels members of society view her.	Verbalizing feelings provides a release of pent-up emotions.	
		Assist Mrs. O. in understanding that individuals who may ostracize and stigmatize her often do so because of their own insecurities.	Understanding the reasons for others' actions can aid the obese person in relating to other members of society.	

NURSING CARE PLAN (cont.)

Problems	Objectives	Nursing Interventions	Principles/Rationale	Evaluations
Somatic Impact (cont.)		Encourage Mr. O. to provide positive feedback to Mrs. O. for attempts and accomplishments made in weight reduction.	Positive feedback for accomplishments facilitates feelings of self-worth.	
Sexual Impact Expressed concern about increased avoidance of sexual relationship with husband.	To facilitate a healthy and satisfying sexual relationship between Mr. and Mrs. O.	Encourage Mrs. O. to express her feelings about her sexuality.	Expression of feelings about one's sexuality may assist the individual in identifying a specific problem.	The nurse would observe for: Open expression of feelings between Mr. and Mrs. O. about an increased satisfaction with their sexual relationship.
		Encourage Mr. and Mrs. O. to discuss openly with each other their feelings about their sexual relationship.	Expression of feelings between sex partners assists in their identifying specific sexual problems and aids in the prevention of internalized feelings that can create tension in the sexual relationship.	
		Reassure Mrs. O. that her expressed concern about avoiding sexual contact with her husband is not abnormal.	Providing reassurance can decrease anxiety that can interfere with sexual activity. Diminished sexual activity is not uncommon for obese persons. In addition, they often encounter difficulties in relationships with members of the opposite sex because they are self-conscious about how others view them.	
Occupational Impact Increased tendency	To assist Mrs. O. in	Encourage Mrs. O. to verbalize	Being aware of the impact that	The nurse would observe for:

when at home.	her household duties.	individual's readiness to deal with its control.	performance as a housewife.
To decrease external stimuli in the occupational situation that foster food consumption.	Encourage Mrs. O. to discard leftover foods immediately after the meal by disposing of them in the garbage or freezing them for future use. Encourage Mrs. O. not to eat the food her children leave on their plates and to dispose of it instead. Encourage Mrs. O. not to purchase snack foods high in calories, such as potato chips and cookies.	Decreasing the amount of available food for consumption can decrease food intake.	

Social Impact
Avoidance of social contacts.

To enhance Mrs. O.'s social interaction.	Encourage Mrs. O. to take part in social functions because avoidance of social contact can be detrimental to the obese person.	Isolation and loneliness often encourage the tendency to overeat.	The nurse would observe for: Mrs. O.'s increased involvement in social functions.
To facilitate Mrs. O.'s feelings of comfort when at social functions.	Instruct Mrs. O. on various strategies to use in social situations for dealing with the presence of attractive and abundant food (e.g., pre-planning of eating behavior, standing away from the serving table at a cocktail party, and constantly thinking thin). Encourage Mrs. O. to maintain an attractive appearance by wearing makeup and clothing that deemphasize her size (i.e., dark colors and slenderizing lines).	Developing adaptive responses to eating for social situations that are unavoidable and unchangeable can facilitate the obese person's comfort in taking part in social contacts. Feeling attractive to oneself and others facilitates feelings of self-worth.	Mrs. O.s verbalization about increased comfort and enjoyment at social functions.

PATIENT CARE CARDEX

PATIENT'S NAME: _____ Mrs. O. _____ DIAGNOSIS: _____ Obesity

AGE: _____ 28 years _____ SEX: _____ Female

MARITAL STATUS: _____ Married _____ OCCUPATION: _____ Housewife

SIGNIFICANT OTHERS: _____ Husband and two children (2 and 4 years)

Problems	Nursing Approaches
Emotional: Inability to control eating habits.	1. Instruct how to keep a record of eating habits. The record must include: (a) when she eats. (b) what she eats. (c) where she eats. (d) what she is doing while she eats. (e) how she feels prior to eating. 2. Involve in group interactions in weight control programs. 3. Instruct on ways to decrease environmental stimuli that may be affecting eating patterns. Include the following: (a) Eat meals slowly so that they last at least 20 minutes. (b) Chew each mouthful of food 10 times. (c) Place the utensils on the plate between mouthfuls. (d) Decrease the size of food portions. (e) Serve the meals restaurant style on small plates. (f) Discard leftover food immediately after the meal is completed. (g) Avoid keeping prepared snack food in the house. (h) Leave a small portion of food on the plate at each meal. (i) Alter the composition of foods high in caloric content (if possible). (j) Use low-calorie substitutes with meals. (k) Shop for groceries after eating a full meal. (l) Shop from a prepared grocery list. (m) Turn off the bulb in the refrigerator. (n) Keep all foods in covered containers.

(q) Reward appropriate dietary behavior.

Somatic: Devaluation of self.	1. Encourage to verbalize the feelings she has about herself. 2. Encourage to express how she feels members of society view her. 3. Assist in understanding that individuals who may ostracize and stigmatize her often do so because of their own insecurities. 4. Encourage husband to provide positive feedback to patient for attempts and accomplishments made in weight reduction.
Sexual: Expressed concern about increased avoidance of sexual relationship with husband.	1. Encourage to express feelings about sexuality. 2. Encourage husband and patient to discuss openly with each other their feelings about their sexual relationship. 3. Reassure that her expressed concern about avoiding sexual contact with husband is not abnormal.
Occupational: Increased tendency to eat excessive amounts of food when at home.	1. Encourage to verbalize how excessive weight is affecting ability to perform household duties. 2. Encourage to discard leftover foods immediately after the meal by disposing of them in the garbage or freezing them for future use. 3. Encourage not to eat food her children leave on the plates and to dispose of it instead. 4. Encourage not to purchase snack foods high in calories, such as potato chips and cookies.
Social: Avoidance of social contacts.	1. Encourage to take part in social functions because avoidance of social contact can be detrimental to the obese person. 2. Instruct on various strategies to use in social situations for dealing with the presence of attractive and abundant food (e.g., preplan eating habits). 3. Encourage to maintain an attractive appearance by wearing makeup and clothing that deemphasizes her size (e.g., dark colors).

REFERENCES

Alessi, D., and Anthony, W. The uniformity of children's attitudes toward physical disabilities, *Exceptional children*, 1969, *35* (7), 543-545.

Bray, G. The overweight patient, *Advances in Internal Medicine*, 1976, *21*, 267-308.

Brook, C. Consequences of childhood obesity, *World Medical Journal*, 1972, *19*, 45-46.

Bruch, H. Anorexia nervosa. In E. Wittkower and H. Warnes (Eds.), *Psychosomatic medicine: its clinical applications*. New York: Harper & Row Publishers, 1977.

Bruch, H. *Eating disorders*. New York: Basic Books, Inc., 1973.

Canning, H., and Mayer, J. Obesity—its possible effect on college acceptance, *New England Journal of Medicine*, 1966, *275* (21), 1172-1174.

Castelnuovo-Tedesco, P., and Schiebel, D. Studies of superobesity: I—psychological characteristics of superobese patients, *International Journal of Psychiatry in Medicine*, 1975, *6* (4), 465-480.

Crisp, A. The possible significance of some behavioural correlates of weight and carbo-hydrate intake, *Journal of Psychosomatic Research*, 1967, *11* (6), 117-131.

Curtis, D., and Bradfield, R. Long-term energy expenditure of obese housewives, *American Journal of Clinical Nutrition*, 1971, *24* (12), 1410-1417.

Damon, A., and Goldman, R. Predicting fat from body measurements: densitometric validation of ten anthropometric equations, *Human Biology*, 1964, *36*, 32-44.

Garn, S. The origins of obesity, *American Journal of Diseases of Child*, 1976, *130* (5), 465-467.

Glucksman, M., and Hirsch, J. The response of obese patients to weight reduction: a clinical evaluation of behavior, *Psychosomatic Medicine*, 1968, *30* (1), 1-11.

Goffman, E. *Stigma: notes on the management of spoiled identity*. Englewood Cliffs, N.J.: Prentice-Hall, Inc., 1963.

Gold, D. Psychologic factors associated with obesity, *American Family Physician*, 1976, *13* (6), 87-91.

Goldblatt, A., Moore, M., and Stunkard, A. Social factors in obesity, *Journal of the American Medical Association*, 1965, *192* (12), 1039-1044.

Grinker, J. Behavioral and metabolic consequences of weight reduction, *Journal of the American Dietetic Association*, 1973, *62* (1), 30-34.

Grinker, J., and Hirsch, J. Metabolic and behavioural correlates of obesity, *Ciba Foundation Symposium*, 1972, *8*, 349-374.

Hansman, C. Anthropometry and related data; anthropometry skinfold thickness measurement. In R. McCammon (Ed.), *Human growth and development*. Springfield, Illinois: C. C. Thomas, 1970.

Jordan, H., Kimbrell, G., and Levitz, L. Managing obesity—why diet is not enough, *Postgraduate Medicine*, 1976, *59* (4), 183-186.

Jordan, H., Levitz, L., and Kimbrell, G. Psychological factors in obesity. In E. Wittkower and H. Warnes (Eds.), *Psychosomatic medicine: its clinical applica-tions*. New York: Harper & Row Publishers, 1977.

Kalisch, B. The stigma of obesity, *American Journal of Nursing*, 1972, *72* (6), 1124-1127.

Kalucy, R., and Crisp, A. Some psychological and social implications of obesity, *Journal of Psychosomatic Research*, 1974, *18* (6), 465-473.

Linder, D. The nurse's role in a bariatric clinic. *R.N.*, 1974, *37* (2), 28-33.

Maddox, G., and Liederman, V. Overweight as social deviance and disability, *Journal of Health and Social Behavior*, 1968, *9*, 287-298.

Matthews, V., and Westie, C. A preferred method for obtaining rankings: reactions to physical handicaps, *American Sociological Review*, 1966, *31*, 859.

Mayer, J. Obesity, *Postgraduate Medicine*, 1972, *51* (6), 99-105.

Musante, G. Obesity: a behavioral treatment program, *American Family Physician*, 1974, *10* (6), 95-102.

Pierre, R., and Warren, C. Smoking and obesity: the behavioral ramifications, *Journal of School Health*, 1975, *45* (7), 406-408.

Plutnick, P. Emotions and attitudes related to being overweight, *Journal of Clinical Psychology*, 1976, *32* (1), 21-24.

Richardson, S., and Goodman, N. Cultural uniformity and reaction to physical disability, *American Sociological Review*, 1961, *26*, 241-247.

Rimm, I., and Rimm, A. Association between juvenile onset obesity and severe adult obesity in 73,532 women, *American Journal of Public Health*, 1976, *66* (5), 479-481.

Rodin, J. Causes and consequences of time perception differences in overweight and normal weight people, *Journal of Personality and Social Psychology*, 1975, *31* (5), 898-904.

Salzman, L. Obsessive-compulsive aspects of obesity, *Psychiatry in Medicine*, 1972, *3*, 29-36.

Schachter, S. *Emotion, obesity and crime.* New York: Academic Press, 1971.

Seltzer, C., and Stare, F. Obesity, *Medical Insight*, 1973, *5* (4), 10-22.

Stunkard A. Eating patterns and obesity, *Psychiatric Quarterly*, 1959, *33*, 284-295.

Stunkard, A. *The pain of obesity.* Palo Alto, Calif.: Bull Publishing Co., 1976.

Stunkard, A., and Burt, V. Obesity and the body image: II—age at onset of disturbances in the body image, *American Journal of Psychiatry*, 1967, *123* (11), 1443-1447.

Stunkard, A., and Mendelson, M. Obesity and the body image: I—characteristics of disturbances in the body image of some obese persons, *American Journal of Psychiatry*, 1967, *123* (10), 1296-1300.

U.S. Public Health Service. *Weight, height and selected body dimensions of adults: United States, 1960-1962.* Washington: U.S. Government Printing Office, 1965.

Winick, M. Nutritional disorders of American women, *Nutrition Today*, 1975, *10* (5, 6), 26-30.

Woods, N. F. *Human Sexuality in health and illness.* St. Louis: The C. V. Mosby Co., 1975.

8

The Patient with a
BURN

INTRODUCTION

To be burned is one of the most devastating, dehumanizing experiences known. Not only is the injury frightening, but the individual involved may be faced with pain, helplessness, dependency, prolonged sick role assumption, possible disfigurement, and death.

Between 2½ million and 3 million people are burned yearly (*American Burning*, 1973). Approximately 3 percent of these individuals require hospitalization, with less than four-tenths of a percent dying (Luckmann and Sorensen, 1974; Jacoby, 1970; Hartford, 1973).

Burns are usually acquired in an uncontrolled fire or explosion or through contact of some body part with a hot liquid or object, an acid, or a flame. Involvement in an uncontrolled fire or explosion and contact with a hot object constitute the most common causes of burns that lead to death, while nonfatal injuries caused by burns are more likely a result of hot liquids, acids, or flames (Luckmann and Sorensen, 1974; Artz and Moncrief, 1969).

The individual sustaining a burn is most often a nonwhite female living in a low-income area (Luckmann and Sorensen, 1974; MacArthur and Moore, 1975). The individual's home is usually the site of the burn incident with hair or clothing, a mattress, bedclothes, or an overstuffed chair being the items of initial ignition. In addition, certain predisposing factors tend to contribute to the likelihood of a burn. Alcoholism is the most frequent factor, with senility, psychiatric disorder, and neurological disease following in order (MacArthur and Moore, 1975). A burned patient is somewhat likely to be a female with a history of alcoholism, igniting her own clothing or hair, or being burned while sitting in a burning overstuffed chair.

TYPES OF BURNS

The depth of a burn depends upon the intensity and duration of the heat. Below 45° centigrade injury from heat does not occur. Above 65° centigrade cell death takes place. Between 45° and 65° centigrade the amount of injury that occurs depends upon the duration of exposure (Hartford, 1973). For example, in a hot water burn, the body temperature cools the heat from the hot water. The result is generally a superficial second-degree burn. The heat from a flame burn, however, cannot be rapidly cooled by the body and the result is usually a deep second-degree or third-degree burn.

According to Artz and Moncrief (1969), burns may be classified in the following manner:

First-degree burn: a burn caused by brief contact with hot liquids or prolonged exposure to sunlight. The burn area appears red, dry, and generally is free from blisters. The area is painful.

Second-degree burn: a burn caused by short periods of exposure to intense flash heat or contact with hot liquids. The burn area is moist, and is mottled red or pink in color. Blister formation is a characteristic feature. The area is very painful.

Third-degree burn: a burn caused by flames or contact with hot objects. Electrical burns are generally third-degree. The burn area is dry and pearly white or charred in appearance. The area is not very painful since terminal nerve endings are destroyed by the deep injury.

As mentioned previously, the majority of burns do not require hospitalization. These are generally nonextensive first-degree burns, superficial second-degree burns of less than 15 percent of the body, deep second-degree burns of less than 6 percent of the body, and third-degree burns that cover small areas of the body (Luckmann and Sorensen, 1974). Most other burns, however, do require hospitalization.

Once the individual is admitted to the hospital, maintenance of the burned individual's life becomes the primary goal and concern of the health care team. The outcome of the burn therapy depends upon the extent and degree of the burn. The very young and the elderly have the lowest survival rate (Luckmann and Sorensen, 1974). In addition, supporting nutrition, antibiotic resistance, and the individual's will to live become major factors contributing to a successful recovery.

Once the acute phase has passed and death no longer is the major concern, the health care team turns its focus toward cosmetic reconstruction and rehabilitation. At this time many burned individuals also change their focus of concern from the strangeness of the hospital and the fear of impending death to the total impact of their experience. Thoughts of what effects the burn will have upon their future are common.

A burn experience creates an impact upon one's emotional well-being, somatic identity, sexuality, occupational identity, and social role. The remainder of this chapter will discuss how a burn experience can affect each of these areas.

IMPACT OF BURNS

Emotional Impact*

The individual undergoing a burn experience not only is faced with physiologic shock resulting from hypovolemia, but also emotional shock resulting from the burn experience. According to Andreasen, Noyes, Hartford, Brodland, and Proctor (1972), the initial emotional shock of burns can take one of two forms. The burned individual may enter a calm dreamlike state with little awareness of his or her surroundings. During this time the individual may talk lucidly. Later in recovery, however, the individual will have little or no recollection of these conversations.

The other, and more common, initial emotional reaction to a burn experience is an acute traumatic reaction. Such a reaction is characterized by insomnia, an exaggerated startle response, anorexia, emotional liability, and nightmares about the burn incident (Andreasen, Noyes, Hartford, Brodland, and Proctor, 1972; Davidson, 1973).

During the initial emotional shock of a burn experience the individual is rarely troubled about deformity (Andreasen, Noyes, Hartford, Brodland, and Proctor, 1972). Some individuals manifest confusion about the burn experience and express fears of impending death. However, their major concerns deal with the strangeness of the hospital, the cost of hospital care, and who is caring for their affairs and family.

In dealing with the initial shock reaction to a burn experience, one of the major nursing interventions is to provide the individual with reassurance that he or she will not be abandoned (Davidson, 1973). A trusting relationship between the individual and the staff is crucial. It should be established at the time of admission and continued through discharge. Explaining procedures, responding promptly to individual needs, being available to listen and talk to the individual and the family, and providing explanations about the body's reaction to burn are interventions that enhance a trust relationship.

*It is advisable for the reader to have read Chapters 1 and 3 before continuing with this section.

If nightmares are present, informing the individual that this reaction is normal, but temporary, may assist in decreasing anxiety elicited by such dreams (Davidson, 1973). Encouraging the individual to describe the dream can provide an additional outlet for anxiety, but the individual should be told that he or she can stop at any time he or she wishes.

If the nurse notices that the burned individual is extremely restless during sleep, it is likely that a nightmare is occurring. Gently awakening and encouraging the individual to verbalize these feelings and fears not only decrease anxiety caused by the nightmares, but they also provide positive reinforcement that someone is always close by. In addition, they may assist in alleviating fears of what sleep may bring and hence prevent insomnia.

After going through the initial period of shock, burned individuals frequently become acutely aware of their environment. Every minute noise or movement in their surroundings is noticed. This initial lucidity, however, usually is short-lived and periods of delirium soon follow (Davidson, 1973).

Delirium is characterized by impaired orientation, restlessness, agitation, altered cognitive abilities, fluctuating levels of awareness and consciousness, visual hallucinations, and insomnia (Andreasen, Noyes, Hartford, Brodland, and Proctor, 1972; Noyes, Andreasen, Hartford, 1971; Hinsie and Campbell, 1974). The manifestations of delirium tend to worsen at night when the individual is deprived of familiar, orienting environmental cues (Andreasen, Noyes, Hartford, Brodland, and Proctor, 1972), such as the face of a staff or family member. The degree and duration of delirium are variable. However, the frequency tends to increase with the individual's age and the severity of the burn (Andreasen, Noyes, Hartford, Brodland, and Proctor, 1972).

A burned individual who is delirious requires reassurance and reorientation. Ongoing orientation to time, place, and person is necessary. Such statements as the following provide such orientation: "Good morning, Mr. B. Today is Monday, January 13th. You are in your room at University Medical Center. It is 8:00 a.m. and I have your breakfast." Repetitive orientation may be necessary because the burned individual frequently may fade in and out of periods of disorientation.

A clock, a calendar, or a radio often prove helpful in assisting the individual in orientation. In addition, when possible, the attendance of a familiar individual, such as a family member or friend, is often beneficial. To prevent unnecessary disorientation at night, a light should be kept on in the individual's room to prevent misinterpretation of the surroundings. Placement of the light should be such that there will be no unnecessary shadows because shadows can increase illusions.

Physical restraint of the delirious individual should be avoided, if possible, since it frequently arouses additional fears and anxieties. The restrained individual may feel that he or she is unable to protect himself or herself against illusions such as snakes and bugs which are believed to be harmful (Davidson, 1973). Restraint also may be interpreted by the individual as a threat to his or her sexuality, since during the illusions the burned individual may interpret restraint as castration or rape. Medication to control the individual's restlessness and agitation can prove beneficial, but barbiturates should be avoided because they further decrease cerebral function and enhance confusion (Andreasen, Noyes, Hartford, Brodland, and Proctor, 1972).

Above all, the burned individual and the family require reassurance that the manifestations of delirium are frequent in individuals sustaining severe burns. They must be informed that such manifestations do not imply the existence of a severe emotional disorder and that as the individual's physical condition improves, generally, so will the level of orientation (Andreasen, Noyes, Hartford, Brodland, and Proctor, 1972).

Because of the overwhelming stress of the situation, burned individuals often utilize the mechanism of regression which appears to be the psyche's attempt to conserve energy (Noyes, Andreasen, and Hartford, 1971). Regression is the act of returning to an earlier level of adaptation (Hinsie and Campbell, 1974). In other words, the individual reverts to childlike ways of adapting and dealing with others. Regressive behavior is manifested by a low tolerance for frustration, hypochondriasis, dependency, temper tantrums, poor cooperation, and demanding, infantile behavior (Andreasen, Noyes, Hartford, Brodland, and Proctor, 1972). This behavior is demonstrated by such acts as complaining about mistreatment, threatening to sign out, ordering staff and family members to leave the room, threatening to strike someone, and using foul and abusive language that contains sexual overtones. The degree of regression is variable. Mild regression is common and benign (Andreasen, Noyes, Hartford, Brodland, and Proctor, 1972), but marked regression, unfortunately, becomes difficult for health team members to handle.

Since the health care team members are closest to the burned individual, they frequently become the object of abuse. This is especially true of the nurse because of the frequent interactions with the individual. Unless each member of the health care team recognizes and understands the basis for the burned individual's behavior, a vicious cycle of attack and counterattack is likely to occur.

To deal with regressive behavior, the nurse and other members of the health team must realize that the individual requires acceptance at his or her own regressed level. The individual must be dealt with in a firm, kind, and nonrejecting manner. The burned individual needs assurance that when he or she is unable to control his or her behavior, limits and controls will be provided. The health team basically assumes a parental role. For example, if the burned individual refuses to eat, he or she should be informed of the importance of nutrition in a nonpunitive manner and be offered a choice between nasogastric feedings and eating self-selected food (Andreasen, Noyes, Hartford, Brodland, and Proctor, 1972).

Limits must be specifically described, agreed upon, and consistently carried out by the health care team. Thus, team conferences are imperative in developing each burned individual's care. If individual members of the health team are inconsistent in the planned approach, double messages may be given to the burned individual. As a result, further confusion and anxiety will be produced and the burned individual may demonstrate greater degrees of regression.

Conversation with the burned individual during periods of regression should be simple and concrete. Short frequent visits throughout each shift by a variety of health team members who utilize a consistent, supportive approach are beneficial (Davidson, 1973). Prolonged visits by a few select members of the health team can result in a vicious cycle of hostility when they no longer can tolerate the burned individual's regressive acts.

As the burned individual becomes less regressed, positive feedback on his or her behavior is important. For example, providing the individual with additional choices about his or her care can be helpful. Such an act assists in the preservation of the individual's autonomy and can enhance cooperation (Davidson, 1973).

As with delirium, concerned and embarrassed family members require reassurance that the regressive acts of their loved one are not unusual. As the individual's physical condition improves, so does the behavior. Allowing the family the opportunity to ventilate their feelings about the burned individual's actions is important because they too may become intolerant of these regressive acts. In addition, the family should be informed about the approach to be used when the burned individual demonstrates regressive behavior; otherwise inconsistency in care can develop. If the family does not understand the rationale for a prescribed approach to care, feelings of hostility may arise between the family and the health team. The results can be undue anxiety in the burned individual's environment.

If the burned individual is hospitalized more than a month, depression is likely to occur (Andreasen, Noyes, Hartford, Brodland, and Proctor, 1972). Although the onset is frequently during the middle of hospitalization, the time of occurrence does vary. Depression in its mildest form is manifested by loss of interest in one's self and surroundings, anorexia, frequent crying spells, insomnia, and helplessness about the future. In its severest form, depression is demonstrated by refusal to eat, lethargy, severe insomnia, loss of the desire to cooperate with health team members, inability to cry, and a desire to be left alone to die in peace. Thus, severe forms of depression can hinder the efforts of the health team to carry out necessary treatments such as nutritional intake and physical therapy.

In dealing with the burned individual's depression, it is helpful to identify the cause. Often the existence of depression has been precipitated by a specific problem that possibly can be relieved. For example, some burned individuals experience depression as a result of their silent frightening fantasies, such as fears of impotence when a burn has occurred in the genital region. If the depression is precipitated by such a problem, clarification of the situation may relieve the burned individual's anxiety and hence lessen his or her depression. If the problem is a realistic one, such as depression precipitated by viewing one's scarred face in the mirror for the first time, the individual requires assistance in ventilating his or her feelings and identifying ways of dealing with the problem. The nurse and other members of the health team must be cognizant of what has occurred each day in the life of the burned individual. Then assessment and identification of possible precipitating factors leading to the depression can be made. Above all, the burned individual and the family require reassurance that feelings of depression are typical and that such feelings will subside with time.

In summary, the individual sustaining a burn is likely to experience a variety of emotional reactions. Initially, he may undergo an acute traumatic reaction followed by a keen awareness of the environment. This initial lucidity may be followed by a state of delirium that varies in degrees and duration. Next, in order to cope with the overwhelming stress of the burn, the individual also may manifest behaviors of regression ranging from mild to severe. Finally, a state of depression can develop, especially when the burned individual is hospitalized more than a month. The nurse's primary role in dealing with the emotional impact of burns is to be cognizant of the manifestations of each behavioral reaction and to initiate the appropriate intervention.

Somatic Impact*

An alteration in body image is undoubtedly one of the most devastating impacts of a burn. The burn injury and the necessary treatments that follow often disrupt the body boundary concept. Such disruptions are the result of alterations in bodily appearance, in sensation, and in perception of the body surface (Liviskie, 1973). Dressing changes, whirlpool baths, and pain alter the limits of one's body boundary. Dressing changes and whirlpool baths may produce a loss of body boundaries. On the other hand, dressing application may represent the reestablishment of an intact body surface. Pain can distort the body boundaries to the point of producing a sense of swelling (Schilder, 1950). Thus, the burned individual undergoes contractions of and expansions of the body boundaries at various times during the sick role.

*It is advisable for the reader to have read Chapter 2 before continuing with this section.

Pain varies in character and severity among burned individuals. However, pain suffering tends to be most intense at the time of dressing changes and during débridement (Davidson, 1973). As the individual's hospitalization progresses, the pain threshold and the ability to withstand pain decrease. No doubt, the anxiety caused by the expectation of pain related to anticipated dressing changes or forthcoming surgery contributes to this reduction in pain tolerance. Pain also reminds the individual of the initial injury, thus creating anxiety and, possibly, a decreased pain tolerance (Andreasen, Noyes, Hartford, Brodland, and Proctor, 1972).

When in a state of regression, the burned individual may be unable to control his or her emotions during pain. The individual may find it necessary to lash out at others, for example, the health care team and family members. Less regressed and more controlled individuals may fear the consequences of exhibiting anger toward health care members who directly care for them. Instead, they may vent their feelings of anger and frustration on individuals indirectly responsible for their care (Davidson, 1973), such as housekeeping personnel or dietary staff.

When pain becomes inevitable, and irreducible, often health team members tend to direct their interests to other concerns (Fagerhaugh, 1974). For example, concern over the complexities of dressing changes may become their primary focus. Thus, pain management and its psychosocial implications may receive minimal attention. To avoid this situation, the nurse must directly approach the individual's reactions to pain. Allowing free ventilation of feelings about the anticipation and sensations of pain is necessary.

The burned individual often views the availability of pain medications as a sign of the health care team's interest in his or her welfare (Andreasen, Noyes, Hartford, Brodland, and Proctor, 1972). The patient's requests for analgesics, however, may become a means of expressing fears and seeking much needed reassurance. Andreasen and associates (1972) suggest that some form of pain medication be available to the burned individual at all times, even if it is a mild analgesic or if the burned individual does not believe that it is helpful. The lack of available pain medication can be interpreted by the burned individual as evidence of little or no concern for his or her welfare by health team members. The administration of pain medication prior to painful dressing changes and débridement does seem to assist in alleviating a fair amount of pain for the burned individual and to decrease some of the anxiety. In addition, allowing for free expression about the pain experience is imperative.

Some burned individuals have found pain more tolerable after talking to a burned individual who is in a more advanced stage of therapy (Fagerhaugh, 1974). "Just knowing that someone else has made it through a similar experience is comforting" may be a typical statement expressed by a newly burned individual after conversing with another burned individual.

The sharing among burned individuals of various ways to distract one's attention from the pain also has proven helpful. Some means of distraction include watching T.V., walking around, or doing craft work, if possible.

Some degree of moaning and yelling is acceptable during treatment, but if such a practice is continued for a long period of time, it can have a demoralizing effect upon other burned individuals in the immediate area. Therefore, in addition to distracting their attention during a painful experience, burned individuals find that they must also develop various ways of controlling pain expression during uncomfortable therapies. Such maneuvers can include placing something in the mouth to bite on; using self-hyponosis by loudly saying, "It doesn't hurt. It doesn't hurt"; or distracting oneself by turning up the volume on radio earphones (Fagerhaugh, 1974). Simply knowing that a great deal of pain will subside once grafting has occurred gives many burn victims a feeling of hope. Reinforcement of this fact by a grafted burn victim to a newly burned individual may prove beneficial.

Pain not only exists during dressing changes and débridement, but many burned individuals have described its presence in donor sites once grafting has occurred. Some individuals believe that the pain experienced in the donor site is more intense than the pain experienced in the burn site. This will vary among individuals and depends upon such factors as the severity and depth of the burn, the individual's anxiety level, and the individual's pain tolerance at the time of grafting. Nonetheless, pain in the donor site can exist and the previously mentioned interventions for dealing with pain should be instituted.

The presence of pain creates a powerful urge to touch the part that has elicited the pain (Schilder, 1950; Szasz, 1957). Touch provides stimulation of a body part where perception has been altered by pain. When an individual sustains a burn, body boundaries are altered. To aid in redefining one's body boundaries after a burn, touching of the dressing and affected parts is necessary (Liviskie, 1973; Cleveland, 1960). Tactile stimulation of the body surface not only assists in reidentifying one's body surface, but it also enhances one's awareness of one's true body boundaries. Allowing the burned individual to touch the dressings and body parts can facilitate the necessary relinquishment of dressings (a temporary body boundary) with little or no anxiety. Thus, the new body surface will more readily be accepted as the new body boundary. If the burned individual is not allowed to carry out necessary tactile stimulation, difficulties in establishing a new body image may ensue.

Fears of deformity and mutilation start to develop once the acute phase of injury passes (Andreasen, Noyes, Hartford, Brodland, and Proctor, 1972). By this time the burn victim is familiar with the hospital surroundings and routine and now focuses attention upon the future. The individual mulls over such questions as, "Will I ever look normal again?" and "How can anyone love someone that looks like me?" Thus, the two most commonly voiced fears deal with the loss of function, especially the hands, and cosmetic deformities (Andreasen, Noyes, Hartford, Brodland, and Proctor, 1972).

Men are usually more concerned about loss of function, whereas women have a greater fear of cosmetic deformity (Noyes, Andreasen, and Hartford, 1971). Most likely, this results from a man's concern about being able to function in order to continue with his job. A woman, however, may feel greater pressure than a man to appear physically attractive in order to achieve in the occupational and social world. Therefore, cosmetic deformity can be of more importance to a woman than the ability to function.

During the early phases of the sick role burned individuals usually require assistance in dealing with their concern about possible deformities. At this time the burn victim still is suffering from the shock of the injury and its stresses. Therefore, it is advisable that there be no mirrors in the individual's room. Most burned individuals will wait until they are ready to view their faces in the mirror (Andreasen, Noyes, Hartford, Brodland, and Proctor, 1972). When they are ready, a supportive individual must be present. This person should be either a member of the health team or a stable family member. The initial reaction to viewing one's facial disfigurement may be repudiation of the existence of the deformity or a severe state of depression. Regardless of the individual's reaction, a hopeful, yet honest, attitude must be maintained. Statements commenting on the improvement of the wounds are important because such statements supply both honesty and optimism.

The fear of rejection may arise when the burned individual realizes the full impact of his or her deformity. This rejection may be demonstrated by a strong tendency to increase personal space. The burned individual may avoid intimate and personal distances, function in a zone of social distance but prefer a public distance of 12 feet or more (Bernstein, 1976; Hall, 1966). Unless health team members and family members are aware of these maneuvers carried out by the burned individual, they unconsciously may allow this increase in personal space to occur.

Standing close and touching in an accepting manner can aid in preventing the burned individual's loneliness and withdrawal. Pointing out what the individual is doing and encouraging him or her to identify ways in which to avoid increasing personal space may prove beneficial. Frequent reminders of the individual's importance to others are also helpful in preventing withdrawal and loneliness. Family pictures and get well cards placed around the room act as reminders of the individual's value to others. Most importantly, there must be reassurance from both health team members and family members that the individual is important to them and that he or she is accepted as he or she is.

The impact the trauma of a burn imposes upon body image is greatly affected by the stage of development that the individual is experiencing at the time. For example, the young adult (eighteen to forty-five years) is in the stage of intimacy versus isolation (Erikson, 1963). It is during this developmental stage that the individual is ready to merge his or her identity with others, both in friendship and in a mutually satisfying sexual relationship. The body becomes a major factor in relating to others. If the individual experiences disfigurement when a burn is sustained, he or she may view his or her physical appearance as unacceptable, since Western society places a great deal of emphasis upon physical attractiveness (Woods, 1975). If the burned individual feels less than acceptable because of his or her physical appearance, the individual may retreat into isolation instead of establishing a state of intimacy with other individuals.

The impact of a burn is somewhat different in the developmental stage of adulthood (forty-five to sixty-five years). The middle years are a time when the individual directs energies toward establishing and guiding future generations with the hope of improving society (Erikson, 1963). The presence of a burn may alter this goal and instead of being generative, the adult may become self-absorbed and stagnate. The middle-aged burned individual may feel that he or she has nothing of value to offer other generations. Chronic defeatism may result and the individual may become isolated in self-pity.

The burned individual in the final stages of life, maturity (sixty-five years and over), views the presence of a burn differently. Since thoughts of death occur during this stage, the presence of a burn may be seen as a prelude to the end of life. Hence, the mature adult may enter a stage of despair (Erikson, 1963) and have the feeling of having little to offer others. Whatever the individual's stage of development, the individual's body boundaries have changed at the time of the burn and his or her personal mental picture is altered.

The nurse's role in dealing with an altered body image revolves around assisting the burned individual in establishing a new body image. The burned individual requires assistance in examining his or her feelings. If the individual believes that he or she is "a freak" or "a monster," or if he or she encounters problems in dealing with questions that society poses about the burn incident, the individual will experience difficulties relating and interacting with others.

Group sessions with burn victims may be helpful, for they allow for the opportunity of sharing ideas on ways to cope with society. Instead of retreating into isolation and further compounding the sense of rejection, burned individuals require assistance in understanding why society may react the way it does. Burned individuals need to realize that other people may view them with a sense of curiosity, sympathy, and fear. They are curious about how the incident occurred, they sympathize with them about how they live with the disability, and they fear that a burn incident could easily happen to them.

Sexual Impact

The sexual impact of burns is frequently overlooked by members of the health care team. Often it is a topic not openly approached by the burned individual, but this does not mean that the burned individual is unconcerned about his or her sexuality.

The fear of personal rejection becomes a grave fear for many burned individuals. They believe that their disability threatens their capacity to be loved by others (Hamburg, 1974); this is especially so if the burn occurs on the face or genital region (Schneider and Stone, 1971). Such beliefs make them hypersensitive to the reactions of others. The slightest indication of possible rejection may be blown out of proportion. Consequently, they are in need of constant reassurance of being accepted and loved.

Military and industrial populations are particularly susceptible to burns of the genitalia and perineum (Hamburg, 1974). A minor burn of the genitalia may evoke more emotional distress than more serious burns elsewhere on the body. Females are likely to be concerned about their fertility, especially if the menses are interrupted as a result of the physical or emotional stress of the burn experience (Hamburg, 1974). By the same token, castration anxiety can occur in the male when perineal burns are present (Bernstein, 1976). The male may become convinced that he is sterile as a result of the trauma to his perineum. He may feel embarrassed and ashamed about his imagined inadequacy (Andreasen, Norris, and Hartford, 1971; Sanders, 1974).

Since the sexual impact of burn trauma usually is not approached by the individual involved, the nurse and other members of the health team may have to initiate discussion on the topic. Leading statements such as, "Individuals sustaining burns similar to yours have indicated a concern about being rejected by others. How do you feel about this?" may initiate a much needed discussion about the sexual impact of burns. The burned individual's significant others must be informed that the fear of rejection is common. Therefore, they may need encouragement to show outward signs of acceptance and love for the burned individual. Whatever means were used to demonstrate affection before the burn incident should be used at this time. Such means may include physical caressing, giving gifts, or including the burned individual in family decision making.

The sex partner must be aware that the burned individual may encounter difficulties in the sexual relationship because of his or her fear of infertility or impotence. Open discussion about these fears must be encouraged between the burned individual and sex partner. As with any physical disability, if the sex partner is revulsed by the appearance of the burn, personal sexual satisfaction may be threatened. Unless the sex partner is assisted in expressing these feelings, extreme guilt may be aroused as a result of thoughts which are uncontrollable. In an attempt to hide these feelings, the sexual enthusiasm displayed by the sex partner will probably decrease. In turn, this decrease in sexual enthusiasm can be interpreted by the burned individual as rejection. Thus, it is advisable that the burned individual and sex partner share their fears and emotions with each other and avoid the pretense of being unaffected by the presence of the burn. The sex partner needs to make it clear to the burned individual that any hesitant response does not imply rejection, but rather an expression of empathy.

If the sexual impact of the burn becomes too difficult for the burned individual and sex partner to resolve, counseling may be in order. The burned individual and sex partner should be directed to a member of the health team experienced in sex counseling.

Occupational Impact

Recovery of the burned individual is never totally dependent upon one person; it is dependent upon every member of the health care team. But since the professional nurse spends more time in direct contact with the burned individual than anyone else, potentially, the nurse has the greatest influence on the success of the rehabilitation program.

Total rehabilitation is accomplished when the burned individual returns to society as a contributing member and is living to his or her fullest capacity. In order for the individual to achieve a successful rehabilitation, the process must begin at the time of admission to the burn-care facility. Everything that is done for the burned individual from the time of admission contributes in some way to a successful return to society.

During the acute phase of treatment the burned individual is dependent upon the health care team for his or her total care. As therapy progresses, however, the individual should become more responsible for his or her own care. Personal hygiene is vital and is an activity that the burned individual should be carrying out as much as possible. This activity includes bathing, ambulation, shaving, combing hair, and brushing the teeth. The nurse is responsible for supervising these activities and providing assistance when needed. In addition to providing the individual with a sense of self-pride and independence, these activities require muscle movements needed to prevent contracture formation.

As the burned individual assumes more responsibility for self-care, fears of neglect and abandonment by the health care team may be elicited. The burned individual may feel that he or she is physically and emotionally unprepared to deal with this increased independence (Feller, Jones, Koepke, Withey, and Whitehouse, 1973). Thus, constant reinforcement is necessary for small improvements and accomplishments. The individual requires reassurance that his or her fears are not unnatural and that many other individuals sustaining burns have encountered the same fears.

Physical therapy continues throughout the rehabilitation period. It includes hydrotherapy (to assist in exercise and with the removal of wound crusts), active and passive range of motion, and ambulation (Feller, Jones, Koepke, Withey, and Whitehouse, 1973). In addition, splints or functional devices may be necessary to control contracture formation. The burned individual needs constant encouragement and assurance that all physical therapy activities are as important to a successful recovery as are medications and grafting procedures.

Since the burned individual may require a lengthy rehabilitation program, family members must be incorporated into the program early in its development. During periods of physical therapy, family members must be taught how to carry out needed exercise programs, dressing applications, and splint applications. Before sending the burned individual home, the health care team must be sure that written instructions for care are ready and that the family is capable of carrying out necessary therapies. Having a family member demonstrate to a health team member the necessary therapies proves very beneficial. If home follow-up is necessary, a community health nurse should be notified so that appropriate exchange of information can take place before the burned individual is discharged. If possible, the community health nurse should visit the burned individual and the family in the burn-care facility to help allay unnecessary fears and concerns of being left alone to deal with their problems.

Before he or she is discharged the burned individual requires a realistic appraisal of what to expect at home. For example, once the initial excitement of returning home subsides, the individual is likely to experience feelings of depression (Feller, Jones, Koepke, Withey, and Whitehouse, 1973). A sense of being overwhelmed is not unusual, for therapies that seemed so simple in the hospital setting may now seem burdensome. If the burned individual and family feel unable to cope with the home situation, they should be instructed to contact the community health nurse or the burn-care facility. However, if the burned individual and the family are adequately prepared prior to discharge, they are not likely to encounter extreme difficulties in their new situation.

Occupational retraining may be necessary for some burned individuals. The effect that the burn has upon one's future plans is a common concern (Hamburg, 1974). For example, if the burned individual's former occupation depended upon the use of his or her hands, and if the hands were badly burned, retraining may be in order. By the same token, nonvocational activities are also affected by the presence of a burn. If an individual derives great satisfaction from physical activities such as basketball or cycling, leg burns may prove extremely threatening. Consequently, the burned individual may require introduction to and training in some other form of recreation.

Andreasen, Norris and Hartford (1971) found that the burned individual's capacity and desire to work are not significantly affected. Adults who encounter exaggerated feelings of inadequacy and are disturbed by their dependency upon others because of their physical helplessness are, most likely, individuals who had difficulty coping with adult responsibility prior to their burn incident (Hamburg, 1974). Often disabled individuals, such as severely burned people, thrust ahead vocationally. They become obsessed with achieving and reaching a goal (Kleck, 1968). Thus, many burned individuals emerge with a new identity because they have been able to triumph over external limitations.

The financial impact of the burn may be voluminous. The burned individual, especially if the burns are extensive and severe, will require lengthy health care treatment, reconstructive surgery, and rehabilitation. If the burned individual is employed, he or she will not be able to work during the duration of the hospitalization. If the hospital period extends for any length of time, accumulated sick leave will undoubtedly be used up. Thus, in some instances, the burned individual may be dismissed. This puts an additional financial burden on family members and they may be required to go to work. Consequently, the standard of living may change. If the family is unable to meet the high cost of burn therapy, the financial impact becomes an economic burden upon society. Thus, it can be seen that a burn incident not only affects the individual involved, but it may also affect other members of society.

Social Impact

How well the burned individual will be received by society is a common concern of the burn victim. If scarring and contractures are readily visible, the burned individual may go into isolation and hesitate to be seen socially. The individual fears what others may think of his or her appearance. Thus, reconstructive surgery, whether cosmetic or functional, becomes important. Cosmetic surgery may improve the burned individual's appearance only slightly, but it may provide needed emotional support (Boswick, Dimick, Larson, Longmire, Rivas, Schrang, and Smith, 1971).

In addition to concerns about how others view him or her, the burn victim finds it necessary to seek a socially acceptable reason for the burn incident. The individual may seek to justify the reason for the burn from a religious perspective. His or her religious perspective, however, may not reflect a specific religious institution. The burned individual may have thoughts about judgment or punishment related to the incident, especially if he or she is held accountable for the accident by law or by significant others. In addition, the burn may be interpreted by the burned individual as a test of faith.

During this justification period it is the nurse's responsibility to convey acceptance of the burned individual's religious frame of reference. This is done by providing him or her with nonjudgmental reassurance that someone will always be present to meet his or her needs. When the health team conveys acceptance instead of judgment of the burned individual, the concepts of forgiveness and reconciliation can be reinforced in the individual's own religious frame of reference (Davidson, 1973). In addition, a hospital chaplain may prove helpful for interpreting and meeting the burned individual's specific religious needs.

As the burned individual extends social contacts, he or she generally finds most people supportive. Those who appear tactless, curious, and hostile tend to be strangers or casual acquaintances (Andreasen, Norris, and Hartford, 1971). The burned individual may require assistance in how to contend with these people. Encouraging the burned individual to verbalize how he or she may deal with such a situation is beneficial because it prepares the individual for the situation before it occurs. Burned individuals in group sessions often share ideas on how they personally have contended with awkward situations involving tactless and curious people. Some suggestions have included directly approaching the curious or tactless person and introducing oneself or walking away from the situation and ignoring the individual.

Many burned individuals resolve their crisis concerning other's response toward them by reformulating their sense of identity (Hamburg, 1974). Instead of developing an identity based upon physical appearance, they construct an identity emphasizing inner self-worth and religiousity. By means of reassurance of continued affection, the burned individual shifts his or her orientation toward the internal "good-self" which has not been damaged by the burn. Often the burned individual feels that the burn experience has made him or her a better person. The burned individual now feels that he or she is more resourceful and compassionate. Concern for others, solidarity of family relationships, and a renewed religious faith may become important components of his or her life.

SUMMARY

Almost 3 million people are burned each year. Such an experience can be devastating and dehumanizing. The individual sustaining a burn is most often a nonwhite female living in a low-income area. The home is the usual site of the burn incident with the hair, clothing, a mattress, or an overstuffed chair being the items of initial ignition. Predisposing factors such as alcoholism, senility, psychiatric disorders, or neurological disease may contribute to the likelihood of the burn.

If the burn is severe and/or extensive, hospitalization may be required, but most burns are not treated in a hospital setting. If hospital care is required, the treatment, most likely, will be lengthy and expensive. Thus, the burned individual often is forced to assume the sick role for an extended period of time and is faced with pain, helplessness, dependency, possible disfigurement, or death.

Regardless of the extent or the degree of the burn, each burned individual undergoes an impact to his or her emotional well-being, somatic identity, sexuality, occupational identity, and social role. Members of the health care team must assist the burned individual in identifying how the presence of the burn affects his or her everyday life and must assist the burned individual in dealing with each of these alterations.

Patient Situation

Miss B. is a twenty-two-year-old single, engaged, black salesgirl who sustained burns over 20 percent of her body. She fell asleep one evening in an overstuffed chair while smoking a cigarette. The lit cigarette caused the chair and her clothing to ignite. As a result, she suffered burns of the perineum, thighs, and abdomen. The fire was extinguished by the fire squad and Miss B. was admitted to the burn-care facility at the University Medical Center.

Miss B. is currently ten days postburn. The nurse caring for her has identified patient-centered problems related to Miss B.'s emotional well-being, somatic identity, sexuality, occupational identity, and social role.

Following are Miss B.'s nursing care plan and patient care cardex dealing with each of these areas of concern.

NURSING CARE PLAN

Problems	Objectives	Nursing Interventions	Principles/Rationale	Evaluations
Emotional Impact Refusal to eat.	To avoid fostering Miss B.'s regressive behavior.	Approach Miss B. in a firm, kind, and nonrejecting manner (e.g., "I'll position your breakfast tray to facilitate your eating").	Demonstrating acceptance can decrease the need for using regressive behavior as a means of relieving anxiety.	The nurse would observe for: A decrease in Miss B.'s regressive behavior.
		Inform Miss B. that when she is unable to control her behavior, limits and controls will be provided.	Providing limits creates a consistent and stable environment. Providing limits shows the individual that when she is un-controlled she will not be allowed to harm herself or others.	
	To increase Miss B.'s food consumption.	Inform Miss B. of the importance of nutrition in a nonpunitive manner (e.g., give her a choice between nasogastric feedings and eating self-selected foods).	Allowing the patient the right to control her environment implies respect for her as an adult. Decision making fosters autonomy and can enhance cooperation.	An increase in Miss B.'s food consumption.
		Keep conversation simple and concrete during periods of regressive behavior.	Preventing sensory overload can decrease the need for regressive behavior as a means to deal with anxiety.	
		Utilize a variety of health team members who maintain a consistent supportive approach with Miss B.'s behavior.	Prolonged visits by a few select members of the health team can result in a vicious cycle of hostility and counterhostility when the team members no longer can tolerate the burned individual's regressive behavior. Conflicting approaches toward an individual can foster regressive behavior.	

NURSING CARE PLAN (cont.)

Problems	Objectives	Nursing Interventions	Principles/Rationale	Evaluations
Somatic Impact Excessive and prolonged screaming during and after painful dressing changes.	To decrease Miss B.'s pain during dressing changes.	Encourage Miss B. to verbalize her feelings about the anticipation of and sensation of pain.	Ventilating feelings about pain can assist in decreasing anxiety related to the pain experience.	The nurse would observe for: A change in Miss B.'s expression of pain.
	To assist Miss B. in venting her expression of pain in a more acceptable manner.	Administer analgesics *prior to* the dressing change.	Administering analgesics *prior to* a dressing change assists in alleviating pain and decreasing anxiety associated with the dressing change.	Miss B.'s increased use of less demoralizing means of pain expression.
	To prevent demoralizing effects that Miss B.'s screaming may have upon other burned individuals in the immediate area.	Encourage the discussion of pain and ways of dealing with it between Miss B. and an individual in a more advanced stage of burn therapy.	Knowing that someone else has made it through a similar experience can be comforting.	
		Suggest various maneuvers to be used to control the expression of pain during painful dressing changes, for example: Placing something in the mouth to bite on. Using self-hypnosis by loudly saying, "It doesn't hurt."	Sharing and developing ways of distracting one's attention during a painful dressing change can decrease the patient's need to express pain inappropriately for extended periods of time.	
		Reassure Miss B. that a great deal of the pain will subside once grafting takes place.	Knowing that pain will decrease with grafting leaves a feeling of hope for many burned individuals.	
Sexual Impact Expressed fear of being rejected by fiancé because of perineal	To decrease Miss B.'s fear of rejection.	Encourage Miss B. to express her fear of possible rejection by her fiancé.	Expressing feelings of rejection may assist the patient in developing ways of dealing with such	The nurse would observe for: A decrease in Miss B.'s expressed fear of rejection by

	To assist Miss B. in dealing with her fears of rejection.	Encourage Miss B.'s fiancé to discuss with each other her fears of rejection.	Knowing how an individual reacts to a crisis situation can assist significant others in understanding and dealing with the individual's behavior.	An increase in discussion between Miss B. and her fiancé about her fears of rejection.
		Encourage Miss B.'s fiancé to express to her his feelings about her perineal burn.	Feelings of guilt about one's reaction to a perineal burn are difficult to hide and may affect the fiancé's sexual enthusiasm.	
		Encourage Miss B.'s fiancé to tell her that any hesitant response toward her is not rejection, but rather an expression of empathy.	An individual with perineal burns who is aware of her sex partner's true feelings is less likely to misinterpret his actions.	
	To increase Miss B.'s feminine self-concept.	Encourage Miss B.'s fiancé to demonstrate affection toward her by carrying out maneuvers used prior to the burn to express such feelings. Such acts may include physical caressing or the giving of gifts.	Expression of acceptance by significant others can aid the individual with perineal burns in decreasing fears of rejection.	An increase in Miss B.'s expressed feelings of feminine self-worth.
Occupational Impact Expressed fear of being unable to resume the duties of a salesgirl.	To decrease Miss B.'s fear of physical incapacity.	Encourage Miss B. to take an active part in daily personal hygiene. Encourage Miss B. to carry out her required physical therapy each day.	Taking an active part in one's own therapy program assists in the achievement of physical function and fosters independence.	The nurse would observe for: Miss B.'s increased participation in her burn therapy program.
		Explain to Miss B. the importance of carrying out all components of her burn therapy.	Understanding that all components of burn therapy are vital for a successful recovery facilitates the individual's likelihood of adhering to prescribed therapies.	Miss B.'s decreased verbalization about her fear of not being able to resume occupational activities.

NURSING CARE PLAN (cont.)

Problems	Objectives	Nursing Interventions	Principles/Rationale	Evaluations
Occupational Impact (cont.)	To increase Miss B.'s feelings of self-worth.	Compliment Miss B. on each improvement and accomplishment made during her rehabilitation program.	Positive feedback for accomplishment fosters a feeling of self-worth and a feeling of achievement.	Miss B.'s expression of the fact that she is still a worthwhile human being.
Social Impact Expressed belief that the burn incident was a punishment from God.	To assist Miss B. in dealing with her thoughts about justification for the burn incident.	Convey acceptance of Miss B.'s religious frame of reference by providing nonjudgmental reassurance that someone will always be present to meet her needs.	Demonstration of acceptance of the burn individual reinforces concepts of forgiveness and reconciliation within the individual's religious frame of reference.	The nurse would observe for: Miss B.'s decreased expression about the belief that her burn incident was a punishment from God.
		Notify the hospital chaplain of Miss B.'s feelings.	A member of the health team prepared in religious thought may prove helpful for interpreting and meeting the burn individual's religious need.	Miss B.'s verbalization of the fact that the burn was an accident.

PATIENT CARE CARDEX

PATIENT'S NAME:	Miss B.	DIAGNOSIS:	Burns
AGE:	22 years	SEX:	Female
MARITAL STATUS:	Single	OCCUPATION:	Salesgirl
SIGNIFICANT OTHERS:	Fiancé		

Problems	Nursing Approaches
Emotional: Refusal to eat.	1. Approach in a firm, kind, and nonrejecting manner (e.g., "I'll position your breakfast tray to facilitate your eating"). 2. Inform that when she is unable to control her behavior, limits and controls will be provided. 3. In a nonpunitive manner inform of the importance of nutrition (e.g., give her a choice between nasogastric feedings and eating self-selected foods). 4. Keep conversation simple and concrete during periods of regressive behavior. 5. Utilize a variety of health team members who maintain a consistent supportive approach with the patient's behavior.

Somatic: Excessive and prolonged screaming during painful dressing changes.	1. Encourage to verbalize feelings about the anticipation and sensation of pain.
	2. Administer analgesics prior to the dressing change.
	3. Encourage the discussion of pain and ways of dealing with it between the patient and an individual in a more advanced stage of burn therapy.
	4. Suggest various maneuvers to be used to control the expression of pain during painful dressing changes, such as:
	  (a) placing something in the mouth to bite on.
	  (b) using self-hypnosis by loudly saying "It doesn't hurt."
	5. Reassure that a great deal of pain will subside once grafting takes place.

Sexual: Expressed fear of being rejected by fiancé because of perineal burns.	1. Encourage to express fear of possible rejection by fiancé. 2. Encourage patient and fiancé to discuss with each other patient's fears of rejection. 3. Encourage fiancé to express to patient his feelings about her perineal burns. 4. Encourage fiancé to tell patient that any hesitant response toward her is not rejection, but rather an expression of empathy.

165

PATIENT CARE CARDEX (cont.)

Problems	Nursing Approaches
Sexual (cont.)	5. Encourage fiancé to demonstrate affection toward her by carrying out maneuvers used prior to the burn.
Occupational: Expressed fear of being unable to resume the duties of a salesgirl.	1. Encourage to take an active part in daily personal hygiene. 2. Encourage to carry out required physical therapy each day. 3. Explain importance of carrying out all components of burn therapy. 4. Compliment on each improvement and accomplishment made during rehabilitation program.
Social: Expressed belief that the burn incident was a punishment from God	1. Convey acceptance of religious frame of reference by providing nonjudgmental reassurance that someone will always be present to meet her needs. 2. Notify hospital chaplain of patient's feelings.

REFERENCES

American Burning. Final report of the National Commission on Fire Prevention and Control. U.S. Government Printing Office, Washington, D.C., May, 1973.

Andreasen, N., Norris, A., and Hartford, C. Incidence of long-term psychiatric complications in severely burned adults, *Annals of Surgery,* 1971, *174* (5), 785-793.

Andreasen, N., Noyes, R., Hartford, C., Brodland, G., and Proctor, S. Management of emotional reactions in seriously burned adults, *The New England Journal of Medicine,* 1972, *286* (2), 65-69.

Artz, C., and Moncrief, J. *The treatment of burns.* Philadelphia: W. B. Saunders Co., 1969.

Bernstein, N. *Emotional care of the facially burned and disfigured.* Boston: Little, Brown and Co., 1976.

Boswick, J., Dimick, A., Larson, D., Longmire, W., Rivas, J., Schrang, E., and Smith, E. The critically burned patient: helping the patient heal without undue physical and emotional scars, *Patient Care,* 1971, *5,* 118-136.

Cleveland, S. Body image changes associated with personality reorganization, *Journal of Consulting Psychology,* 1960, *24* (6), 256-261.

Davidson, S. Nursing management of emotional reactions of severely burned patients during the acute phase, *Heart and Lung,* 1973, *2* (3), 370-375.

Erikson, E. *Childhood and society.* New York: W. W. Norton and Co., Inc., 1963.

Fagerhaugh, S. Pain expression and control on a burn care unit, *Nursing Outlook,* 1974, *22* (10), 645-650.

Feller, I., Jones, C., Koepke, G., Withey, L., Whitehouse, R. The team approach to total rehabilitation of the severely burned patient, *Heart and Lung,* 1973, *2* (5), 701-706.

Hall, E. *The hidden dimension.* Garden City: Doubleday and Co., Inc., 1966.

Hamburg, D. Coping behavior in life-threatening circumstances, *Psychotherapy and Psychosomatics,* 1974, *23,* 13-25.

Hartford, C. The early treatment of burns, *Nursing Clinics of North America,* 1973, *8* (3), 447-455.

Hinsie, L., and Campbell, R. *Psychiatric dictionary.* New York: Oxford University Press, 1974.

Jacoby, F. Current nursing care of the burned patient, *Nursing Clinics of North America,* 1970, *5* (4), 563-575.

Kleck, R. Self-disclosure patterns of the nonobviously disabled, *Psychological Reports,* 1968, *23,* 1239-1248.

Liviskie, S. Definition of body boundaries after burn injury, *Maternal-Child Nursing Journal,* 1973, *2* (2), 101-109.

Luckmann, J., and Sorensen, K. *Medical-surgical nursing: a psychophysiologic approach.* Philadelphia: W. B. Saunders Co., 1974.

MacArthur, J., and Moore, F. Epidemiology of burns, *Journal of the American Medical Association*, 1975, *231* (3), 259-263.

Noyes, R., Andreasen, N., and Hartford, C. The psychological reaction to severe burns, *Psychosomatics*, 1971, *12* (6), 416-422.

Sanders, R. The burnt patient: a general view, *British Medical Journal*, 1974, *3*, 460-463.

Schilder, P. *The image and appearance of the human body.* New York: John Wiley & Sons, Inc., 1950.

Schneider, J., and Stone, N. Burn patient care: The psychiatrist's role, *AORN Journal*, 1971, *14* (4), 58-61.

Szasz, R. *Pain and pleasure.* New York: Basic Books, Inc., 1957.

Woods, N. F. *Human sexuality in health and illness.* St. Louis: The C. V. Mosby Co., 1975.

PART
III

Alterations in Life-Sustaining Functions

9

The Patient with an

ALTERATION IN CARDIOVASCULAR FUNCTION

INTRODUCTION

Western society's standard of living has created the existence of many luxuries and comforts. People no longer have to fight for survival from the elements but are able to partake of many of the "finer" things in life. Sedentary activities are prevalent and one's life span has grown longer. However, with these luxuries and comforts come disadvantages. One such disadvantage is the increased prevalence of coronary heart disease. Sedentary living, increased longevity, and the increased anxiety and emotional stress under which many individuals function contribute greatly to this rising incidence of coronary heart disease. At the present, coronary disease constitutes the leading cause of incapacitation and death in both Europe and the United States (Luckmann and Sorensen, 1974; Kleiger, Martin, Miller, and Oliver, 1975). Coronary disease has become the ailment of the leisure person.

Historically, the heart has been identified as the maintainer of life, since it pumps life-giving blood throughout the body. The heart's continual beating provides people with an ever-present reminder of its value. Early medical observers held romantic notions about the pathology of the heart. For example, they described fibrinous pericarditis as "hair" and associated its presence with a heroic death (Spodick, 1970). As a result, the heart has been credited with the expression of such emotions as fear, courage, sadness, desire, and love (Rodbard, 1975). Religiously, the heart has been designated as a substitute for the body and the spirit. This belief was demonstrated by the heart burials of the rulers of the Holy Roman Empire. Thus, the importance of the heart was identified and acknowledged long ago.

PATIENT PROFILE

Research has demonstrated that the presence of various factors increases the incidence of coronary heart disease. Such predisposing factors can be physiologic and/or psychosocial in nature. Obesity, cigarette smoking, consumption of a high-caloric, high-fat diet, a sedentary life-style, seasons of the year, hypertension, stress, and the presence of specific personality traits are such possible factors (Protos, Caracta, and Gross, 1971; Jenkins, 1975; Luckmann and Sorensen, 1974).

The presence of physiological factors such as cigarette smoking, hypertension, consumption of a high-caloric, high-fat diet, and obesity creates such changes as vasoconstriction, myocardial damage, lipid abnormalities, and an increased cardiac workload. Psychosocial factors such as sedentary life-style, stressful situations, and the existence of certain personality traits often lead to overeating, smoking, and elevation in blood pressure, all of which produce deleterious effects upon cardiac function. The exact effect, however, that emotional factors have upon the occurrence of coronary heart disease is not known and all theories at the present are speculative.

Some authorities advocate that individuals who manifest a certain behavior pattern are more likely to be prone to coronary heart disease (Friedman, 1969; Rosenman, 1967). Friedman (1969) has defined the coronary-prone behavior pattern as a "type A personality." Such an individual is very goal-oriented, gestures with abrupt assertive movements, speaks rapidly with bursts of loudness for emphasis, demonstrates intensity of involvement, and lacks an openness to extraneous stimuli not directly related to his or her identified goal.

According to Jenkins (1975), if one were to examine a diverse picture of characteristics of the type A personality, one could identify the following traits:

Values

1. Sets high standards for self.
2. Critical of self and others when self-established standards are not met.
3. Is intense and inflexible.
4. Prefers respect for achievements made rather than for who he or she is.
5. Feels a need to maintain productivity in order to maintain a feeling of self-worth.
6. Craves recognition and power.
7. Is competitive with self and others.
8. Is gratified primarily by occupation and aggressive avocational pursuits (e.g., political and community affairs).

Style of thought

1. Simultaneously pursues several lines of thought and action (e.g., eats while working).
2. Anticipates the future and begins to react prematurely.
3. Appears alert and ready to move.
4. Is compulsive about completing tasks.
5. Demonstrates poor observation skills.

Interpersonal relationships

1. Is self-centered.
2. Feelings of anger easily aroused.
3. Is easily frustrated in a work situation.
4. Is aggressive sexually, but enjoys the chase more than the consummation.
5. Emits a certainty about his or her own correctness.
6. Becomes a victim of his or her own behavior pattern (e.g., pushes beyond his or her limits).

Style of response

1. Reacts rapidly.
2. Speaks with certainty and emphasis.
3. Does not waste words.
4. Gives nods and "ahems" while listening to another speaker.
5. Becomes emotionally and physically involved when describing a situation that characteristically frustrates him or her.
6. Finds it uncomfortable to slow down the speed of his or her speech or writing when requested to do so.

Gestures and movements

1. Uses tense, energetic movements.
2. Clenches fists when tense.
3. Shakes hands with a firm grip and uses active motion.
4. Finds it difficult to remain still when sitting or standing.

Facial expression

1. Uses momentary tense smiles with a tight horizontal lip line.
2. Uses brief smiles to emphasize comments or reveal impatience.
3. Tenses jaw muscles or grits teeth when emphasizing comments.

Breathing

1. Has frequent breaks in breathing rhythm.
2. Inhales more air than necessary when speaking.

It must be emphasized that no type A individual demonstrates all of the characteristics listed. Whether or not an individual is characterized as being a type A personality depends upon the number of characteristics possessed and their intensity. Also, when examining the relationship between the type A personality and coronary heart disease, one must realize that most research has been limited to male members of industrialized societies. Two studies, however, do suggest that type A females may also be subject to an increased incidence of coronary heart disease (Rosenman and Friedman, 1961; Kenigsberg, Zysanski, Jenkins, Wardwell, and Licciardello, 1974). In addition, the incidence of type A personality tends to be highest among young males and decreases with age (Jenkins, 1975). To date no research speaks to whether or not the type A personality is a risk factor after the age of sixty-five.

The importance of the identification of type A behavior patterns among individuals with cardiovascular disease is multidimensional. Understanding its foundation in personality structure, realizing how it is reinforced by our society, knowing what effect it has upon cardiac medical therapy, and identifying possible approaches to modifying it are all part of a long-term rehabilitation program for the individual sustaining coronary heart disease. Just as the individual is instructed in ways to alter the predisposing physiologic factors to coronary heart disease, so must he or she learn about altering predisposing psychosocial factors.

Not until the industrialized individual is willing to and capable of adjusting his or her life-style will the incidence of coronary heart disease be altered. As long as coronary heart disease remains a major health care problem, nursing must be cognizant of the effects that it has upon the individual's total way of life. Therefore, the remainder of this chapter will deal with the impact that coronary heart disease, namely, myocardial infarction, has upon an individual's emotional well-being, somatic identity, sexuality, occupational identity, and social role.

IMPACT OF MYOCARDIAL INFARCTION

Emotional Impact*

The use of denial to protect oneself from facing the full impact of impending death, impaired function, and disability is a phenomenon that has been noted clinically in every type of disease and disability (Levine and Zigler, 1975). The individual sustaining a myocardial infarction is no exception and the use of denial can be identified as early as the preadmission period. A typical response of actual or potential coronary patients just prior

*It is advisable for the reader to have read Chapters 1 and 3 before continuing with this section.

to hospital admission is to delay in seeking medical advice or treatment (Gentry, 1975). This delay can range from less than one hour up to several days (Moss and Goldstein, 1970). However, the average time for hospital arrival is between two and one-half to four hours after the onset of symptoms (Moss and Goldstein, 1970; Simon, Feinleib, and Thompson, 1972). This time period is often referred to as the individual's *decision time,* the period of time starting from the onset of symptoms until the individual obtains medical assistance. The prolongation of the decision time concerns medical authorities since approximately 50 to 70 percent of the individuals experiencing a myocardial infarction die within one hour after the onset of acute symptoms and prior to obtaining medical treatment (Gentry, 1975).

Gentry (1975) has identified three factors that determine an individual's preadmission behavior. These factors include demographic characteristics, perception of the illness, and the social context at the onset of symptoms.

Demographic characteristics include the individual's age, sex, educational background, occupation, socioeconomic class, ethnic background, and history of coronary disease. Research indicates that older individuals tend to take longer to seek medical attention than younger individuals (Moss and Goldstein, 1970; Moss, Wynar, and Goldstein, 1969). Men demonstrate a shorter decision time than women. Education, occupation, and socioeconomic class appear to have no relation to preadmission behavior (Gentry, 1975). Ethnic background, however, appears to have a decided effect upon preadmission behavior, with individuals of Jewish and Italian origins demonstrating a higher proportion of denial than individuals from the Irish and British old American groups (Croog, Shapiro, and Levine, 1971). Individuals with a past history of myocardial infarction generally are better able to diagnose their initial symptoms as a cardiac problem than are individuals without such a history (Moss and Goldstein, 1970). However, a history of coronary disease either has no effect or actually increases the individual's decision time (Alonzo, 1973; Goldstein, Moss, and Green, 1972), hence prolonging the seeking of medical attention.

How the individual perceives the illness is the second factor determining preadmission behavior. According to Moss, Wynar, and Goldstein (1969), three cognitive functions are required in an individual's ability to seek medical attention following the occurrence of symptoms. These three functions include perception of the symptoms, recognition of their meaning, and realization that medical attention is necessary. If the individual follows this cognitive sequence (perception-recognition-realization), he or she will seek medical attention in a reasonably short period of time. However, if the individual does not follow the sequence, he or she will delay in obtaining medical care. Research has demonstrated that although individuals often perceive the symptoms, they either attribute them to other causes or assess the symptoms as being less severe than they actually are (Olin and Hackett,

1964; Hackett and Cassem, 1969). Thus, the individual utilizes denial in recognizing the seriousness of the symptoms. Although the denial may serve as a temporary means of reducing anxiety about the immediate situation, it also serves to decrease the long-term chances of adequate care and survival.

The third factor determining preadmission behavior is the social context in which the symptoms occurred. Investigators have found that preadmission behavior is affected by the time of day of the week. Decision time tends to increase when the symptoms occur during the day and on weekends (Moss, Wynar, and Goldstein, 1969; Tjoe and Luria, 1972). Decision time is shorter when the symptoms occur during working hours as opposed to nonworking hours, when others (especially the spouse) are present, and when the individual involved makes the decision to seek medical assistance (Alonzo, 1973; Goldstein, Moss, and Green, 1972; Moss, Wynar, and Goldstein, 1969).

No single factor determines whether or not and when an individual seeks medical attention. Rather, several factors are involved. Gentry (1975), however, believes that the most important factor is the social context at the time of symptom onset. If others are around, if the individual is not involved in an activity that is difficult to terminate, and if the symptoms occur at a time when they appear more serious (the middle of the night), the individual is likely to respond with greater speed in seeking medical attention. Without a doubt, educating the public concerning the symptoms of a myocardial infarction and the necessity of seeking appropriate medical attention is one important intervention for decreasing the incidence of death caused by a prolonged decision time.

Once the individual is diagnosed as having sustained a myocardial infarction, he or she is faced with a loss, the loss of wellness. Since the individual sustaining a myocardial infarction generally losses wellness suddenly, he or she is thrust into sick role assumption with little time for role change preparation. Thus, the individual responds to the loss of wellness with a sequential set of behaviors.

The first reaction to a myocardial infarction is one of repudiation. This response occurs immediately after the myocardial infarction and generally lasts from 24 to 48 hours (Scalzi, 1973). It is during repudiation that the individual refuses to believe what has occurred and demonstrates a stunned numbness about the experience. The use of repudiation appears to be more prolonged in the younger individual, someone thirty to forty years of age (Rosen and Bibring, 1966). Manifestations of repudiation may include avoidance of discussing the myocardial infarction and its significance, minimizing the seriousness of the condition and its consequences, engaging in social, humorous interactions with health members, and asking different staff members the same questions in an attempt to find the desired answer.

During the stage of repudiation the myocardial infarction victim must be allowed to deny the loss of wellness. Encouraging free verbalization about his or her feelings is important, but at no time should the nurse or other members of the health team join the individual in denial. For example, if the individual verbalizes that increasing activity has no effect upon the heart, the nurse should not agree. Such a comment is the individual's way of telling health team members that he or she is not ready to accept the myocardial infarction or its restrictions.

The nurse's response to such a statement should be open-ended so that it allows for additional verbalization. For example, the nurse could say, "You don't believe that increasing your activities affects your heart." "Why don't you feel that you need restricted activity?" Also, forcing the individual to accept the fact that he or she has sustained a myocardial infarction should be avoided. The individual is not ready to cope with such a realization. Removing his or her denial at this point could prove detrimental if no support system is available to put in its place.

In addition to allowing the individual the right to deny the loss of wellness, the nurse must assess whether or not the denial is interfering with medical and nursing therapies. Accurately assessing the consequences of the individual's not following the prescribed therapy is necessary. For example, monitoring vital signs and observing for fatigue and shortness of breath when restricted activities are carried out by the individual are such means of assessment. Based upon these assessments, alterations in activity orders may be needed. The individual may find such alterations less threatening and hence he or she may be more willing to follow them.

Conveying concern and allowing the individual more control over the environment may prove beneficial in modifying behavior. Providing the cardiac patient the opportunity to be involved in deciding the sequence and manner in which morning care is carried out is a possible approach. Thus, by compromising and allowing involvement in care, the nurse assists the individual in altering or modifying his or her behavior to an acceptable therapeutic level.

The second behavioral reaction to a myocardial infarction is one of recognition. It generally begins 48 hours from the time of diagnosis (Scalzi, 1973) and extends into the discharge period. During the stage of recognition the individual's physiologic condition becomes more stable and the fear of impending death decreases. The cardiac patient begins to think about the myocardial infarction and how it may alter or change his or her life-style. The patient may wonder how the illness will affect his or her job, whether or not he or she will become dependent upon others, and if this illness is a prelude to a premature old age (Scalzi, 1973). During this stage of loss the use of denial becomes more difficult to maintain and the reality of the situation begins. Depression, overt anger, and negotiation are likely to be demonstrated.

Depression results when the individual is unable to express his or her feelings outwardly and instead internalizes them. Cardiac victims fifty to sixty years of age appear to be more likely to demonstrate signs of depression than are younger individuals (Rosen and Bibring, 1966). This is not to say, however, that younger individuals may not manifest depression.

When dealing with the depressed cardiac patient, the nurse may note a sense of listlessness, expressions of hopelessness, loss of appetite, crying, and slowness in movement and speech. If these manifestations, are not dealt with successfully, they could hinder the individual's recovery by preventing the institution of various medical and nursing therapies. Essential nursing interventions for dealing with depression caused by myocardial infarction include reflection of observations made, informing the individual that these feelings are typical and that many people feel depressed about their hospital situation, and soliciting and listening to the individual's feelings about himself or herself and about the illness.

Instead of internalizing feelings in the form of depression, the heart-attack victim may overtly express feelings in the form of anger. He or she may verbally strike out at members of the health team and the family or at circumstances in the environment. Overt anger may be expressed by refusing to remain in bed, failing to take prescribed medications, or accusing others of not caring about his or her well-being. If the individual expresses anger toward health team members, they should try not to take it personally or become defensive about these statements. It must not be forgotten that the angry individual experiencing loss is not necessarily angry at them but at their attributes, such as wellness, freedom, vitality, mobility, and the ability to control their own lives.

To deal with the individual's anger, the nurse and other members of the health care team need to remain matter-of-fact about the anger. They must listen to the individual's expression of anger and show neither approval nor disapproval of this behavior. By their being matter-of-fact, the patient is less likely to feel guilty about expressing his or her feelings. Allowing the individual to express anger also aids in preventing the individual from internalizing his or her feelings into depression.

Negotiation also may be used by the individual with a myocardial infarction. Common negotiating statements may include: "If I hadn't been in such a hurry to catch that train, I wouldn't be in the hospital now" or "If *only* I had lost weight as the doctor told me." The act of negotiation in the heart attack victim is an attempt to deal with feelings of guilt. The individual may believe that his or her actions had an effect upon the present dilemma. The individual has a need to be purged of such beliefs and, therefore, finds it necessary to make negotiating statements. Not until the individual with a myocardial infarction is ready to face the loss of wellness directly will the individual be capable of relinquishing the need for negotiation.

During the phase of negotiation the nurse's primary role is to guide the cardiac patient in looking at the reasons for using such a maneuver. Encouraging the patient to verbalize these feelings of guilt is vital because he or she needs to be purged of these feelings. Above all, the nurse must avoid such statements as, "Oh, I'm sure everything will work out and you will be out of C.C.U. in no time." This response is a clumsy attempt to pacify the individual and direct the conversation to a topic that the nurse may find more comfortable.

The third emotional response to a myocardial infarction is reconciliation. This emotional response tends to take place after the individual is discharged from the acute care setting. It is at this time that the cardiac patient reorganizes his or her feelings about the loss of wellness and the need for anger, depression, and negotiation no longer exists.

During reconciliation the individual becomes less preoccupied with the illness and starts to develop a more factual approach to the myocardial infarction. The patient begins to deal with the consequences of the myocardial infarction by giving up some of his or her dependency upon others and assuming responsibilities in identifying realistic goals to health care and ways of achieving these goals. For example, the individual more readily accepts the effects that smoking has upon the heart condition (Fuhs, 1976). He or she noticeably may decrease the number of cigarettes smoked or even stop smoking altogether. The need for weight reduction might be taken more seriously and attempts may be made to follow a reducing diet. Open discussion of how stressful situations, such as an occupation, affect him or her may take place between the individual and the family. In other words, the cardiac patient in reconciliation is demonstrating gradual assumption of interests in new ways of dealing with health care needs.

The nurse's role is to encourage the cardiac patient who is in the stage of reconciliation to verbalize how he or she feels now that he or she has resolved the occurrence of the myocardial infarction. Does the individual see himself or herself as being different from before the heart attack? In what way has the individual assimilated the current state of health into his or her life-style? How does he or she view the effects of his or her state of health upon his or her occupation, social life, or sexuality? These may be but a few of the cardiac patient's concerns and feelings that should be expressed verbally.

Final reconciliation of the myocardial infarction is accomplished when the individual accepts his or her state of health and, with no hesitation, is able to ventilate openly and to deal with these feelings about his or her condition. The nurse must be cognizant of the fact, however, that an individual experiencing a loss, such as a myocardial infarction, may undergo the entire process of loss (repudiation, recognition, and reconciliation) each time a new loss of wellness is encountered. Such a loss of wellness may be another myocardial infarction or an entirely different health care situation.

In addition to the cardiac patient's emotional response to the myocardial infarction itself, there is also an emotional reaction to the coronary care unit. The coronary care unit may be viewed as a threat by the individual who has sustained a myocardial infarction. Hence, the most frequent response to this strange complex of people and machines is anxiety.

Anxiety is an uncomfortable feeling or dread associated with an unrecognizable source of anticipated danger (Freedman, Kaplan, and Sadock, 1975). The anxious individual will manifest such behaviors as increased verbalization, inability to concentrate, restlessness, insomnia, tachycardia, and palmar sweating. For the individual who has sustained a myocardial infarction, three periods of time can be identified as producing unusually high levels of anxiety: admission to the coronary care unit, transfer from the coronary care unit to the step-down unit, and discharge from the hospital (Scalzi, 1973). The nurse must be alert to these time periods so that appropriate nursing assessment and intervention can take place.

Upon admission and during the individual's stay in the coronary care unit, orientation to the unit's routines, procedures, and equipment is beneficial. Repeated orientation may be necessary since during periods of high anxiety an individual's ability to retain information is decreased. Emphasizing the positive features of the coronary care unit is helpful (Cassem, 1975). For example, explaining that monitoring equipment is a safeguard for the patient's welfare is one suggestion. This can be done as the equipment is being connected and started. Explaining that routine vital signs and intravenous medications are a standard procedure in a coronary care unit can aid in decreasing some of the individual's anxiety as he or she observes these procedures.

Encouraging the expression of feelings, concerns, and questions is imperative because it enables the nurse to identify situations which the individual with a myocardial infarction finds anxiety producing. For example, not understanding why bed rest is necessary may provoke unnecessary anxiety in some people. Concerns about one's sexuality may prove extremely upsetting for another individual. Each person's perception of a situation is different and what one individual finds anxiety producing another individual may not. Therefore, clarifying areas of concern and misunderstanding is necessary to aid in decreasing a cardiac patient's anxiety.

Consistent and continuous nurse-patient contact must be maintained during periods of severe anxiety. If possible, the cardiac patient should be assigned to the same nurse each shift so that a trust relationship can be formed. The need for the same nurse during each shift cannot be emphasized enough. Above all, the nurse must convey a feeling of competence in both performance and abilities because such an atmosphere encourages a feeling of security in the cardiac patient. Feeling insecure about the manner in which he or she is cared for can provoke additional and unnecessary anxiety.

Since transfer from the coronary care unit and discharge from the hospital are times of increased anxiety, the individual with a myocardial infarction must be prepared for these environmental changes. This preparation should begin shortly after admission. The individual must be told that the stay in the coronary care unit is temporary and that the transfer out of the unit and eventually home is a positive step toward recovery (Scalzi, 1973).

If possible, it is helpful for the nurses from the cardiac step-down unit to visit the individual in the coronary care unit prior to the individual's transfer. During their visit, the nurses from the cardiac step-down unit can explain how the environment and routines in their unit differ from that of the coronary care unit. This interaction not only provides the cardiac patient with information about the environment, but it also aids in preparing the patient emotionally for the transfer. When the individual is transferred, it is helpful to have a relative present to provide additional support and comfort. In addition, if possible, it is advisable to avoid transferring the cardiac patient at night, for such a maneuver tends to increase anxiety and disorientation.

If the cardiac patient does not require cardiac monitoring once he or she leaves the coronary care unit, it is advisable to remove the monitor one to two hours before the transfer (Scalzi, 1973). Some patients develop a great attachment to the monitor and feel that their heart's function is dependent upon the machine, even after explanations to the contrary. Removal of the monitor several hours before the transfer provides the individual time to adjust to the fact that he or she can survive without it.

Last, but not least, many cardiac patients transferred out of the coronary care unit find it comforting to be visited occasionally by the nursing staff from the unit since an emotional attachment for those working in the coronary care unit often develops. The individual may find it easier to relate to the staff on the cardiac step-down unit when he or she does not feel abandoned by the staff of the coronary care unit. Knowing that communications exist between the nurses in both units creates a sense of security in the cardiac patient. He or she feels that there is continuity in care as he or she moves toward a state of recovery.

In summary, the cardiac patient undergoes a variety of behavioral manifestations as he or she deals with the emotional impact of the myocardial infarction. Prior to the actual diagnosis of the myocardial infarction the cardiac patient sustaining signs and symptoms of coronary disease often tends to deny the existence of illness. Once the condition is diagnosed, the cardiac patient goes through the stages of loss: repudiation, recognition, and reconciliation. During repudiation the patient suffers from emotional shock and denies the circumstances. As he or she enters the stage of recognition, the cardiac patient may manifest anger, depression, and negotiation. In addition to these behavioral manifestations, the cardiac patient also demonstrates anxiety as he or she learns the expected role that must be played during illness and as he or she is confronted with the strangeness of the environment, the coronary care unit. Additional anxiety-provoking situations occur when the cardiac patient is transferred from the coronary care unit to the cardiac step-down unit and then eventually to the home environment. The patient finally reaches the stage of reconciliation to the loss of wellness when he or she is at home. It can be seen that a myocardial infarction creates many emotional responses for an individual. Therefore, the professional nurse must be cognizant of these responses, how these responses are manifested, and how best to assist the individual in coping with each response.

Somatic Impact*

A major source of stress for the cardiac patient is the alteration of his or her life-style caused by the illness. Such alterations may include losing weight, changing dietary habits, abstaining from smoking, and changing occupations. The cardiac patient is confronted with these alterations while in the hospital, but their total impact has no affect until after he or she is discharged.

How well an individual accepts his or her altered life-style affects the ability to formulate a new body image. The individual who was well-adjusted and stable before the myocardial infarction will probably accept his or her new body image without extreme difficulty (Bragg, 1975), but the individual who is less able to deal with crisis situations may encounter problems in accepting his or her changed body image caused by the illness.

An individual who encounters problems in accepting himself or herself after the heart attack may manifest regressive behavior and become as passive and dependent as a child. The individual allows and expects others to take charge and tell him or her what he or she should and should not do. In the early course of illness such behavior is acceptable, but as the recovery period progresses this dependency should begin to subside. When passive-dependent behavior continues, most likely, difficulties in accepting one's new body image have occurred.

The individual who does not want to step out of the sick role and who continues to be dependent often enjoys the secondary gains offered by the existence of the myocardial infarction. The cardiac status becomes a central part of his or her way of life and the individual uses this physical condition as a means of exploiting interpersonal relationships. The individual not only expects to be cared for, but he or she also demands it. Such an individual may view himself or herself as being weak, as less than a man or woman

*It is advisable for the reader to have read Chapter 2 before continuing with this section.

and requiring constant care and attention. Thus, the individual truly becomes a "cardiac invalid."

In such a situation, the cardiac patient must be provided with limits in which to function. The cardiac patient must not be allowed to exploit interpersonal relationships by refusing to step out of the sick role. What is expected of him or her should be well defined and this information then should be relayed to the patient. For example, if the patient manifests passive-dependent behavior by expecting to be fed when he or she is capable of such a task, the food should be prepared, it should be placed in front of him or her, and he or she should be given 30 minutes to finish the meal. At the end of the 30 minutes the food should be removed. During the meal the cardiac patient may require encouragement to the effect that he or she is physically capable of feeding himself or herself and that each additional acitivty assumed is a step closer to recovery.

The cardiac patient may continue or resume the role of a "cardiac invalid" in the home setting. Therefore, family members need encouragement not to support such behavior. By having well-defined written home-going instructions for the cardiac patient and the family, uncertainties related to the cardiac patient's activity at home are alleviated. In addition, the family members will feel more secure in enforcing the cardiac patient's independence.

How the cardiac patient feels about himself or herself as a result of the heart attack is also affected by the stage of development that the individual is currently experiencing. If the individual is in the stage of young adulthood (eighteen to forty-five years), he or she may encounter problems in sharing himself of herself with others both in friendship and in a mutually satisfying sexual relationship (Erikson, 1963). Because of the heart attack, the individual may feel that his or her body is less than perfect for interactions with others and hence the individual may retreat into isolation. Because he or she is unable to integrate successfully a new image that incorporates the required alterations in life-style, the individual may find it difficult to develop or to maintain interpersonal relationships. For example, the cardiac patient in young adulthood may feel that he or she is less than a man or woman and not worthy of socializing with his or her friends as they carry out their social interactions. Also, the individual may feel less than sexually desirable as a result of the myocardial infarction and be unable to maintain a mutually satisfying sexual relationship with the sex partner.

The individual in the stage of adulthood (forty-five to sixty-five years) confronts different problems after a myocardial infarction as he or she attempts to incorporate the new body image. The major focus of one's interest during this period of life is directed toward establishing and guiding future generations (Erikson, 1963). If the cardiac patient believes that the illness has made him or her an unfit person to guide others, the patient may become engulfed in meeting his or her own needs and acquiring self-comforts, and hence enters a state of stagnation. In addition to stagnation, the adult may view the myocardial infarction as a prelude to premature old age. Since the illness may require alterations in life-style, the cardiac patient may see the future less optimistically (Gentry and Haney, 1975). He or she may view the myocardial infarction as a deterrent to future aspirations and successes and may retreat into isolation and self-pity or retire to the "rocking chair" before his or her time.

The stage of maturity (sixty-five years and over) is a time when many individuals have frequent thoughts of death. As a result, the cardiac patient in the stage of maturity may consider the heart attack a prelude to death. Physiological changes have occurred throughout life, but the myocardial infarction may be seen as the "final blow" of old age. Hence, the mature adult sustaining a myocardial infarction may feel despair (Erikson, 1963) and question his or her life's accomplishments. Thus, it can be seen that a myocardial infarction can have adverse effects upon the individual's successful accomplishment of each developmental stage of adulthood.

The nurse's role in dealing with the cardiac patient's altered body image revolves around assisting him or her in integrating the changed image into his or her life-style. It is important to encourage the individual, regardless of developmental stage, to verbalize how he or she feels about himself or herself. Does the individual feel incapacitated and less than acceptable to others? How does the individual feel the illness affects his or her relationship with others? As the cardiac patient verbalizes these feelings, the nurse can assess the individual's reactions to the illness. Once it is determined how the individual feels, members of the health team can then assist the individual in identifying ways of dealing with these feelings.

If the individual describes himself or herself as weak, worthless, or less than a man or woman because of the cardiac condition, the nurse should point out the positive aspects of his or her life. For example, if the individual is in business, bookwork and business calls may be carried out at home. The individual who enjoys walks can still engage in walking, but instead of taking long walks, the individual should take short but frequent strolls because they are less tiring and less physically demanding. If the individual finds luncheon engagements a necessary part of life, a dietician can instruct him or her on ways to select low-sodium, low-caloric, and low-cholesterol foods. The major goal, when emphasizing to the cardiac patient the positive aspects of life, is to demonstrate that with alterations many of his or her premyocardial infarction activities can be carried out. It is important to stress this fact because research has shown that when an individual develops the ability to focus attention from somatic concerns to other objectives he or she more readily demonstrates the ability to return to work (Lebovitz, Shekelle, Ostfeld, and Oglesby, 1967).

Sexual Impact*

The effect that a myocardial infarction has upon one's sexuality is an area that is all too often avoided by members of the health care team. The sexual ramifications of a myocardial infarction generally begin early in the hospitalization period. Once the threat of death is no longer the major concern, the cardiac patient's behavior may shift from concern for life to concern for the quality of remaining life (Woods, 1975). As a result, the cardiac patient's behavior may manifest sexual overtones.

Anxiety resulting from threats to one's self-image as an adult and from fear of sexual inadequacy (Scalzi, 1973) are possible reasons for the cardiac patient's sexually oriented behavior. Postmyocardial infarction patients question their sexual identity and thus find a need to test their feelings of sexuality. As a result, the cardiac patient may respond to some members of the health care team with sexually aggressive behavior such as grabbing and touching body parts of health care providers. This behavior demonstrates a maladaptive effort on the part of the individual to test his virility, autonomy, and external achievement (Scalzi, 1973).

Often the nurse's initial response to such behavior is embarrassment, fright, discomfort, and finally withdrawal from the individual. Such reactions feed into flirtatious behavior by demonstrating to the sexually oriented individual that the nurse is being manipulated and/or demoted as an authority figure. If the sexually aggressive patient does not elicit such a response, he possibly would alter his behavior.

Instead of supporting such behavior by reacting to it or withdrawing from it, the nurse must provide limits for the sexually aggressive individual. This can be done by informing the cardiac patient that his sexual behavior makes the nurse uncomfortable. It is necessary to ask the individual if the nurse's actions in anyway led to his sexually aggressive behavior. This is a reasonable question because the nurse may have been seductive without realizing it.

In addition, the nurse should explore with the cardiac patient what his behavior means to him. Does he perceive his myocardial infarction as a threat to his sexuality? Is he attempting to counteract his fears of sexual inadequacy or impotence by being sexually aggressive? In addition to exploring the patient's feelings, the nurse should direct his focus to his positive attributes, such as accomplishments made in his recovery. He must be reassured that the members of the health care team accept him as he is but that his sexually aggressive behavior is not acceptable or necessary for obtaining attention. As the individual feels more competent as a person he

*Since limited research exists on the sexual impact of a myocardial infarction on the female patient, this section will deal exclusively with the male patient who has sustained a myocardial infarction.

hopefully will find less of a need to prove his sexuality by being sexually aggressive. The individual's sexually aggressive behavior provides the nurse with an overt clue to the patient's concerns and fears about his sexual well-being. However, not all patients manifest overt sexual aggression in the hospital setting. Nonetheless, all patients have concerns about resuming sexual activity. Many of the fears experienced by the cardiac patient and the sex partner about sexual activity after a myocardial infarction are created by misconceptions and the lack of knowledge about sexual capabilities.

The most common misconceptions include the beliefs that even mild exertion will kill the cardiac patient, sexual intercourse should never again be attempted, and repeated infarctions tend to occur at orgasm (Hackett and Cassem, 1973). Such misconceptions often lead to a decrease in sexual activity. Often the sex partner of a cardiac patient becomes passive in response to sexual activity out of fear that it may be too strenuous for the postmyocardial infarction patient. Research has demonstrated that the average middle-aged man engages in sexual intercourse twice a week (Kent, 1975; Green, 1975). Six months after a myocardial infarction, sexual activity often is decreased to one and six-tenths times per week (Kent, 1975). This decrease in sexual activity tends to be more marked in older cardiac patients, but it is present in all age groups (Block, Maeder, and Haissly, 1975). Unless the cardiac patient and the sex partner are counseled on postmyocardial infarction sexual activity, unnecessary strains caused by suppressed sexual needs can be created.

The use of masturbation in the hospital setting may prove helpful in providing visible proof that sexuality still remains. Masturbation is a natural form of sexual self-expression used by many individuals from infancy through senescence. During the convalescent period of hospitalization masturbation can be considered an acceptable activity when the cardiac patient is capable of walking two lengths of a hospital corridor (Watts, 1976) or is capable of tolerating an accelerated heart rate of 130 beats per minute without undue side effects (Wagner, 1975). The health care team, however, should create a climate of acceptance of masturbation or else the cardiac patient may experience feelings of guilt and anxiety. According to Watts (1976), most cardiac patients masturbate at some time prior to discharge from the hospital.

The cardiac patient will resume sexual activity within 4 to 16 weeks from the time of the myocardial infarction (Hellerstein and Friedman, 1970; Zohman, 1973; Puksta, 1977). Most often physicians will use the tolerance of exercise as a guideline for determining tolerance of sexual intercourse. According to Hellerstein and Friedman (1970), marital coitus for the postmyocardial infarction patient requires caloric expenditure of approximately 4½ calories, with peak effort at about 6 calories, for less than

30 seconds. The heart rate generally increases up to 117 beats per minute. This physical stress very closely equals the rapid ascent of two flights of stairs or a brisk walk down the street. As a result, the postmyocardial infarction patient's tolerance of such activity can be used as a guideline for determining tolerance of sexual activity. It can be seen that the usual cardiac demands of sexual activity fall well within the range of capabilities of 70 to 80 percent of the middle-aged men recovering from an uncomplicated myocardial infarction (Hellerstein, 1972).

Before the patient is discharged from the hospital both the cardiac patient and the sex partner should receive verbal and written instructions on the important issues of sexual activity. The primary goals are to assist the individual and sex partner in reestablishing their pre-illness state of sexuality, to educate the couple about sexual adaptations imposed by the myocardial infarction, and to facilitate communications between the couple for optimal sexual satisfaction (Watts, 1976).

Some of the important points to include in the patient's sexual counseling and written going-home instructions are as follows:

1. Utilize positions and maneuvers that impose less strain upon the cardiac patient.
   (a) A back-lying position for the cardiac patient with the sex partner kneeling (so that full body weight is not upon the patient) is less demanding for the individual who has sustained a myocardial infarction (Scalzi, 1973). Some men, however, may find this position demeaning and unacceptable, especially if they identify their role as dominant and controlling. To enforce an abrupt change in sexual style or role could further disrupt the equilibrium of the sexual relationship. Therefore, other alternatives may be suggested during the recovery period, with encouragement to resume pre-illness sexual patterns as the patient's state of wellness progresses.
   (b) A side-lying position (rear and front entry) produces less strain on the cardiac patient (Scalzi, 1973; Moore, Folk-Lighty, and Nolen, 1977).
   (c) Having the cardiac patient sit in an armless chair with the sex partner sitting on his lap and facing him tends to decrease strain on the cardiac patient. It is advisable, however, for the couple to use a chair that is low enough so that they can place their feet on the floor (Scalzi, 1973).
   (d) Encouraging the patient to concentrate on breathing regularly during coitus because breathholding prior to orgasm may trigger a Valsalva maneuver. This maneuver causes a transient decrease in venous return and precipitates hypotension and

reflex tachycardia. These factors lead to inadequate coronary perfusion and hence may cause palpitations and anginal pain in the final stage of the sexual response (Watts, 1976; Lefkowitz, 1975).

(e) Encourage the avoidance of acts, such as penial and digital insertion into the anus, that create vagal excitement and subsequent bradycardia.

2. Avoid intercourse in certain situations.

(a) Coitus should be avoided when extremely fatigued, when emotionally upset, and for at least three hours after consuming a heavy meal or after drinking alcohol (Watts, 1976; Puksta, 1977) because each of these situations places an additional workload upon the cardiac system.

(b) An environment in which there is excessive heat or excessive cold should not be used for sexual activity since the heart has to increase its activity to maintain the body's normal temperature. Excessive temperature alterations imply the patient's awareness of physical discomfort in the environment (Scalzi, 1973).

(c) Illicit sexual encounters are generally not advised during the recovery period from a myocardial infarction because they tend to increase the risk of reinfarction and death (Lawson, 1974; Massie, Rose, Rupp, and Whelton, 1969; Ueno, 1963). "Death in the saddle syndrome" tends to occur more frequently when the cardiac patient engages in sex with a much younger partner in an unfamiliar milieu. The danger to the cardiac patient is related to deviating from one's usual partner or usual sexual pattern.

3. Be aware of warning signals that may indicate a decreased tolerance of sexual activity.

(a) Prolonged (more than 15 minutes) rapid heart rate and rapid breathing after sexual intercourse (at rest) should be noted and reported (Scalzi, 1973; Moore, Folk-Lighty, and Nolen, 1977).

(b) An extreme feeling of fatigue on the day after intercourse should be noted and reported (Scalzi, 1973; Moore, Folk-Lighty, and Nolen, 1977).

(c) Chest pain during or after intercourse should be noted and reported. In some instances, individuals who experience anginal pain during and after intercourse are advised to take prophylactic nitroglycerine prior to the sex act (Watts, 1976; Moore, Folk-Lighty, and Nolen, 1977).

In summary, the initial impacts of a myocardial infarction on an individual's sexuality are anxiety concerning self-image and fear of sexual inadequacy. In response to these feelings, an individual may react by becoming sexually aggressive toward others, namely, members of the health care team. The postmyocardial infarction patient may continue to question his sexuality as he progresses toward wellness. Thus, use of masturbation in the hospital setting may prove helpful in providing tangible proof that one's sexuality still remains. Once the patient can tolerate an accelerated heart rate of 130 beats per minute without undue effect, the patient most likely can tolerate masturbation. If masturbation is utilized, members of the health care team should not create an atmosphere of disgust, for such a climate may create unnecessary guilt and anxiety for the cardiac patient.

In the early stage of convalescence at home the cardiac patient and sex partner may require counseling on various alterations and guidelines to use in coitus. However, both the patient and the sex partner require reassurance that sexual activity is not harmful for the patient and that as the patient progresses toward wellness the primary goal is to reestablish the state of sexuality before the myocardial infarction. Unless the cardiac patient and the sex partner are adequately advised on postmyocardial infarction sexual activity, unnecessary strain may result in the relationship because of misunderstandings and lack of knowledge.

Occupational Impact

Since the majority of individuals sustaining a myocardial infarction are males and breadwinners, the source of family income may be discontinued for a period of time. As a result, the occurrence of a myocardial infarction often creates a financial strain upon the family structure. In some instances, men even are requested to retire on disability pensions or are reassigned to less strenuous tasks at a reduced income (Tyzenhouse, 1973). In addition, the expense of the hospitalization creates an added unexpected financial burden. Mortgage payments, house improvement costs, and school expenses for children may become difficult to meet. Savings may dwindle and spouses may feel the need to secure employment. Often the employment the wife obtains does not defray expenses since her income is often well below that of her husband, especially if she had not worked before. The wife may feel additional pressures going back to work and she may experience tension if she also continues to assume all of her domestic responsibilities.

Fortunately, 80 to 85 percent of all cardiac patients are able to return to the same job after a myocardial infarction with little modification in responsibilities (Bowar-Ferres, 1975). Any individual suffering from a myocardial infarction, however, will be out of work for at least three months following the onset of illness (Scanlon, 1972).

A social worker, an occupational therapist, or a rehabilitation counselor can increase the individual's chances of returning to work by directly talking to the employer (Wells, 1974). Thus, the employer is kept up to date on the medical status of the employee, the employee's physical capabilities, and projected date of return to work. The counselor can discuss with the employer the cardiac patient's concerns about resuming occupational pursuits. In addition, the patient, the employer, and the cardiac counselor together can identify stressful situations within the work environment that may require alterations. Unfortunately, many work situations in our society tend to support type A personality behavior (Jenkins, 1975), which is a predisposing factor to myocardial infarction.

The greatest single physical factor related to a safe return to work is the ability to resume gradually those activities which were usual for the post-myocardial infarction patient prior to the illness (Rubin, Grass, and Arbeit, 1972). For example, the cardiac patient may want to start out by working several hours a day, then advance to half-days and then three-quarter days, and finally resume full-day employment. Most men can progressively return to the job responsibilities they had prior to illness without angina, dyspnea, palpitations, or excessive fatigue. If any of these symptoms appears, it should be reported to the physician so that appropriate interventions can be instituted.

The remaining 20 percent of postmyocardial infarction patients who encounter difficulties in returning to the same job do so because of either physical limitations or anxiety related to resumption of work responsibilities (Bowar-Ferres, 1975). These anxieties can be the individual's concerns or they can be concerns expressed by the spouse. It is not uncommon for the spouse to believe that the work situation was the greatest contributing factor to the occurrence of the myocardial infarction. A common statement expressed by the spouse is, "He just worked himself into a heart attack."

It has been found that the longer an individual is out of work after physical recovery is complete, the more difficult the rehabilitation becomes (Crawshaw, 1974). In addition, the spouse's anxiety generally diminishes markedly once the postmyocardial infarction patient successfully resumes work responsibilities (Skelton and Dominian, 1973).

The 20 percent who encounter difficulties resuming work responsibilities generally require selective placement, psychiatric assistance, vocational counseling and testing, or job retraining (Bowar-Ferres, 1975). Such activities may be initiated by either a social worker, an occupational therapist, or a rehabilitation counselor. Idleness leads to boredom and unhappiness and they are not healthy. In fact, Kjøller (1976) found that the incidence of recurrences of myocardial infarction was higher among individuals who had abandoned work after a myocardial infarction than among those who resumed work shortly after recovery. Thus, resumption of meaningful and productive activity is important in the rehabilitative process for both the postmyocardial infarction patient and the family.

Social Impact

The nurse must not overlook the response of the cardiac patient's significant others toward a myocardial infarction. The spouse, children, and even friends tend to react to a myocardial infarction with anxiety, fear, hostility, depression, and overprotective behavior (Granger, 1974). Generally, the spouse is relieved when the cardiac patient is discharged from the hospital; nevertheless, many wives find the convalescent period the most stressful. Especially difficult is the period after discharge until the cardiac patient returns to work. The two major reasons for this stress have been identified as a fear of recurrence of the myocardial infarction and difficulties created by the cardiac patient's reaction after returning home (Skelton and Dominian, 1973).

It is not uncommon for the wife of a man who has sustained a myocardial infarction to feel guilty about the occurrence of the illness. The wife may blame herself for her husband's illness (Skelton and Dominian, 1973). The following statements express feelings of guilt and blame: "I never should have let him work that hard." "Maybe I nagged him too much?" Because of her feelings of guilt, the spouse often searches for a cause of the illness and frequently identifies it as overwork (Skelton and Dominian, 1973). In response to this identification, the spouse feels a need to protect her husband so that there will not be a recurrence. The following comments express a sense of overprotection: "I will never let him work that hard again." "I'll make sure that he relaxes more." Even such maneuvers as listening for her husband's heartbeat and breathing while he sleeps are common. Some wives even have gone to the extreme of awakening their husbands to make sure that they are still alive and well.

The cardiac patient's wife does not want her husband to overexert and she does not want anything in the environment to upset him. As a result, she may assume the role of both decision maker and breadwinner. This overprotective manner may further intensify the cardiac patient's feelings of dependency and helplessness. He may respond to this overprotective behavior with either anger or a demonstration of excessive helplessness and dependency.

In response to her overprotective behavior toward her husband, the wife often tends to inhibit her own expression of hostility (Adsett and Bruhn, 1968). She fears that any expression of anger or upset may initiate another myocardial infarction. Consequently, to deal with her own suppressed feelings she may become solicitous. Her solicitousness carries a punitive quality as she attempts to release her own internalized anger (Granger, 1974).

Often the overprotective behavior of the spouse and the excessively dependent or angry behavior of the cardiac patient are the result of a lack of understanding about the illness and the prescribed therapies (Wishnie, Hackett, and Cassem, 1971). In addition, the cardiac patient is often afraid to share his fears with his family and he becomes resentful and angry with them when they attempt to shield him from unpleasant information. Therefore, detailed home care instructions are necessary for both the patient and his family. The instructions should include the amount of activity to engage in at a prescribed stage of recovery and include a means of assessing the tolerance of the increased activity (e.g., changes in pulse rate and respiratory rate.)

Since family members are expected to make drastic role and interactional changes because of the myocardial infarction, they require assistance from members of the health care team. Family members must be encouraged to verbalize their fears, concerns, and feelings of anger. The wife especially must be encouraged not to internalize any hostility she may harbor. Instead, she must be encouraged to vent her feelings to a member of the health care team. It should be pointed out to the spouse that solicitousness that is punitive in nature may be the result of her internalized anger and that such behavior only intensifies the fears and uncertainty already harbored by the cardiac patient.

When a myocardial infarction occurs, the spouse also experiences loss: loss of the mate's wellness and loss of the sense of strength that the partner once represented (Skelton and Dominian, 1973). Reactions to these losses are frequently exemplified by sleep disturbances and alterations in appetite. Such reactions tend to be more common among wives under forty-five years of age than in wives who are older (Skelton and Dominian, 1973).

To assist the spouse in coping with her loss, she should be encouraged to verbalize her feelings to a member of the health care team or be encouraged to take part in a cardiac club, if one is available. These clubs are often available through the hospital, a rehabilitation center, or a local chapter of the American Heart Association. Cardiac clubs generally meet once or twice a week and give patients and family members an opportunity to express and share feelings and experiences with each other. Such a maneuver can aid in alleviating the patient's and the family's distress and better prepare them to cope with their newly inflicted loss, the lack of wellness. A member of the health care team (cardiac rehabilitation nurse, liaison nurse, psychiatrist, hospital chaplain) generally serves as the group leader (Harding and Morefield, 1976).

In addition, the wife should be encouraged to discuss her feelings with her husband. She must be reassured that he also is hesitant to verbalize his fears and feelings. Since they both are reluctant to express themselves openly, both partners internalize feelings that further add to manifestations of anger, hostility, and guilt. The wife needs assurance that open discussion between her and her husband is much better for both of them than silence that leads to internalization of feelings. Both partners are better able to cope with the cardiac patient's loss of wellness when each of them is aware of the other's feelings.

SUMMARY

Western society's increased standard of living has led to more comforts and luxuries. No longer do people have to fight the elements for survival, but Western society's luxurious living has brought misfortune, an increased incidence of coronary heart disease. Today coronary disease constitutes the leading cause of incapacitation and death in Europe and the United States. Coronary disease has become the illness of the leisure person.

When coronary heart disease, such as a myocardial infarction, results, the impact of the illness is multidimensional. The individual afflicted is faced with alterations in his or her emotional well-being, somatic identity, sexuality, occupational identity, and social role. The role of the health care team is to help the cardiac patient and the family identify the alterations in lifestyle that will be necessary as a result of the illness and to assist them in incorporating these alterations into their activities of daily living.

Patient Situation

Mr. C. P. is a fifty-three-year-old, married, certified public accountant who has one daughter who is currently enrolled in medical school. He is employed by a large accounting firm and has been very busy the past couple months completing clients' income tax forms. Five days ago while rushing home for a quick dinner before returning to the office to complete some urgent work he suffered severe chest pains. When he arrived home, he told his wife who encouraged him to notify the family physician about the complaint. The family physician instructed him to go directly to the community hospital emergency room. Upon examination, Mr. C. P. was diagnosed as having sustained a myocardial infarction and subsequently was admitted to the coronary care unit.

Now that his condition is stable, Mr. C. P. is being transferred from the coronary care unit to the cardiac step-down unit. One of the staff nurses from the cardiac step-down unit has just interviewed Mr. C. P. and his wife. During the interview the nurse identified problems related to Mr. C. P.'s emotional well-being, somatic identity, sexuality, occupational identity, and social role.

Following are Mr. C. P.'s nursing care plan and patient care cardex which deal with the above mentioned areas of concern.

NURSING CARE PLAN

Problems	Objectives	Nursing Interventions	Principles/Rationale	Evaluations
Emotional Impact Expressed anxiety about impending transfer from the coronary care unit to the cardiac step-down unit.	To increase Mr. C. P.'s knowledge of the reason for transfer from the coronary care unit to the cardiac step-down unit.	Explain to Mr. and Mrs. C. P. that transfer from the coronary care unit to the cardiac step-down unit is a positive progression toward recovery.	Understanding that transfer from the coronary care unit is standard procedure and a sign of progression toward recovery can aid in decreasing an individual's anxiety about his transfer.	The nurse would observe for: Mr. C. P.'s expression that his anxiety about being transferred from the coronary care unit has decreased.
	To decrease Mr. C. P.'s anxiety about the transfer from the coronary care unit to the cardiac step-down unit.	Provide Mr. and Mrs. C. P. with information about the cardiac step-down unit. For example, explain the environment and routines and how they differ from the coronary care unit.	An individual provided with information about an impending, unfamiliar situation is less likely to become anxious due to fear of the unknown.	Mr. C. P.'s increased ease with the nursing staff of the cardiac step-down unit. Mr. C. P.'s increased ease in the environment of the cardiac step-down unit.
		Encourage Mrs. C. P. to be present, if possible, during Mr. C. P.'s transfer from the coronary care unit to the cardiac step-down unit.	Having a family member present during transfer from the coronary care unit provides additional support and comfort for the patient.	
		Transfer Mr. C. P. during the daylight hours.	Moving a patient during the night from familiar surroundings to unfamiliar surroundings tends to increase anxiety and disorientation.	

NURSING CARE PLAN (cont.)

Problems	Objectives	Nursing Interventions	Principles/Rationale	Evaluations
Emotional Impact (cont.)				
		Remove Mr. C. P.'s cardiac monitor several hours prior to transfer from the coronary care unit.	Some patients develop a great attachment to the cardiac monitor and feel that their heart's function is dependent upon the machine, even after it is explained to them that it is not. Removing the monitor several hours before transfer allows the patient time to deal with the fact that he can survive without the monitor.	
		Encourage the nursing staff of the coronary care unit to visit Mr. C. P. after his transfer to the cardiac step-down unit.	Patients often become emotionally attached to the nursing staff in the coronary care unit. Therefore, a patient may find it easier to relate to the nursing staff of the cardiac step-down unit if he does not feel abandoned by the staff of the coronary care unit.	
Somatic Impact Manifestations of the image of a "cardiac invalid" (passive-dependent behavior).	To assist Mr. C. P. in integrating his changed body image into his life-style.	Provide Mr. C. P. with limits in which to function. For example, instruct him on what physical activities are expected of him and encourage him to carry them out.	Setting limits for an individual provides him with a structured environment and communicates what is expected of him.	The nurse would observe for: A decrease in Mr. C. P.'s passive dependent behavior.
		Provide positive feedback for achievements in physical activity.	Receiving positive feedback enhances an individual's feelings	An increase in Mr. C. P.'s independence.

Problem	Objective	Nursing Intervention	Rationale	Evaluation
		Encourage Mr. C. P. to verbalize how he feels about himself. For example, does he view himself as incapacitated and less than acceptable to himself and others or does he feel his illness has affected his relationship with others?	...feels about himself as a result of his illness assists the health care team in identifying ways of helping the individual deal with his feelings.	
	To direct Mr. C. P.'s focus from somatic concerns to other objectives.	Point out to Mr. C. P. the positive aspects of his life, for example, possible ways in which he can carry out some of his public accountant responsibilities at home.	Emphasizing to the cardiac patient the positive aspects of his life demonstrates to him that, with alterations, many of his pre-M.I. activities can be carried out. In addition, when an individual develops the ability to focus his attention from somatic concerns to other objectives he more readily demonstrates the ability to return to work.	An increase in Mr. C. P.'s interest in concerns other than those of somatic nature.
Sexual Impact Verbalized fear about not being able to resume sexual activity.	To clarify possible misconceptions that Mr. and Mrs. C. P. may have about post-M.I. sexual activity.	Inform Mr. and Mrs. C. P. that resumption of sexual activity will be determined by the physician, but it is usually dependent upon the patient's ability to tolerate the rapid ascent of two flights of stairs.	Providing the cardiac patient and his sex partner with information about the patient's sexual capabilities in the post-M.I. recovery period assists in preventing the couple from avoiding sexual encounters and aids in assisting the couple in achieving their pre-illness state of sexuality.	The nurse would observe for: Mr. and Mrs. C. P.'s verbalization about their decreased fear related to engaging in sexual activity.

NURSING CARE PLAN (cont.)

Problems	Objectives	Nursing Interventions	Principles/Rationale	Evaluations
Sexual Impact (cont.)	To provide Mr. and Mrs. C. P. with information about sexual activity in the post-M.I. recovery period.	Provide Mr. and Mrs. C. P. with the following information both in written and verbal form: **1.** Utilize positions and maneuvers that impose less strain upon the cardiac patient. (a) A back-lying position for the cardiac patient with the sex partner kneeling (so that full body weight is not upon the patient) is less demanding. (b) A side-lying position (rear and front entry) is less strenuous than many other positions. (c) Having the cardiac patient sit in an armless chair with the sex partner on his lap and facing him tends to decrease strain on the cardiac patient. The couple, however, must be encouraged to use a chair that is low enough so that they can place their feet on the floor. (d) Encourage the patient to concentrate on breathing	Knowing that certain alterations in sexual activity can reduce the strain upon the heart may increase the cardiac patient's likelihood of engaging in sexual activity.	

place an additional workload upon the heart increases the cardiac patient's likelihood of avoiding such situations prior to coitus.

Knowing the warning signals that may indicate a decreased tolerance to sexual activity may aid in decreasing the incidence of subsequent cardiac complications.

situations.
  (a) Coitus should be avoided when extremely fatigued, when upset, and after consuming a heavy meal or after drinking alcohol.
  (b) Environments in which there is excessive heat or excessive cold should not be used for sexual activity.
  (c) Illicit sexual encounters are generally ill-advised during the recovery period.

3. Be aware of warning signals that may indicate a decreased tolerance of sexual activity.
  (a) Prolonged (more than 15 minutes) rapid heart rate and rapid breathing after sexual intercourse should be noted and reported to the physician.
  (b) An extreme feeling of fatigue on the day after intercourse should be noted and reported to the physician.
  (c) Chest pain during and after intercourse should be noted and reported to the physician.

NURSING CARE PLAN (cont.)

Problems	Objectives	Nursing Interventions	Principles/Rationale	Evaluations
Occupational Impact Expressed concern about not being able to return to work.	To decrease Mr. C. P.'s concern about being incapacitated because of his myocardial infarction.	Inform Mr. C. P. that 85 percent of all cardiac patients are able to return to the same jobs with little modification in responsibilities.	By knowing that the odds of an individual's returning to work after an M.I. are very good, the cardiac patient is less likely to become extremely anxious about his work situation.	The nurse would observe for: Mr. C. P.'s verbalization of possible ways to alter his work situation so that he can gradually return to work.
		Encourage Mr. C. P. to think of ways he can alter his work pattern so that he can make a gradual return to his work responsibilities (e.g., doing bookwork and making business phone calls at home).	The greatest single physical factor related to a safe return to work is the ability to resume gradually activities that were usual for the post-M.I. patient prior to his illness.	Mr. C. P.'s verbalization that with alterations he feels that he will eventually be able to resume many of his pre-M.I. work responsibilities.
		Contact social service, occupational therapy, or a cardiac rehabilitation counselor about setting up communications with Mr. C. P.'s employer about Mr. C. P.'s return to work.	By utilizing members of the health care team prepared in occupational rehabilitation, the individual's chances of returning to work are increased because there are direct dealings with the employer. The employer is kept up to date on the employee's medical status, physical capabilities, and projected date of work	

Mrs. C. P.'s expressed feelings of guilt about the occurrence of Mr. C. P.'s myocardial infarction.	To assist Mrs. C. P. in dealing with her feelings of guilt.	Encourage Mr. and Mrs. C. P. to discuss their feelings with each other.	The wife who does not discuss personal feelings with her husband about her reaction to his myocardial infarction is likely to suppress her feelings. To deal with her own suppressed feelings she, in turn, may become punitively solicitous toward her husband. In addition, both marital partners are better able to cope with the loss of wellness when each of them is aware of the other's feelings.	The nurse would observe for: Open discussion of feelings between Mr. and Mrs. C. P. Mrs. C. P.'s verbalization that her feelings of guilt are beginning to subside.
		Encourage Mrs. C. P. to discuss her feelings with other members of the cardiac club.	Sharing feelings with individuals who have sustained the same loss often helps in identifying ways of coping with one's own loss.	
	To assist Mrs. C. P. from becoming overprotective of Mr. C. P. because of her feelings of guilt.	Encourage Mrs. C. P. to avoid demonstrating overprotective behavior (e.g., assuming role of decision making) toward Mr. C. P.	Overprotective behavior on the part of the spouse can cause the cardiac patient to respond with impatience and extreme irritability because he may find such behavior demeaning.	Mrs. C. P.'s encouraging Mr. C. P. to increase his independence as he progresses toward recovery.
		Provide Mr. and Mrs. C. P. with well-defined home-going instructions related to Mr. C. P.'s prescribed therapies. They should include the amount of activity to engage in at each prescribed stage of recovery and how to assess exercise tolerance.	Overprotective behavior on the part of the spouse is caused by lack of understanding about the cardiac patient's prescribed therapies.	

PATIENT CARE CARDEX

PATIENT'S NAME: _____ Mr. C. P. _____ DIAGNOSIS: _____ Myocardial Infarction _____

AGE: _____ 53 years _____ SEX: _____ Male _____

MARITAL STATUS: _____ Married _____ OCCUPATION: _____ Certified public accountant _____

SIGNIFICANT OTHERS: _____ Wife and daughter _____

Problems	Nursing Approaches
Emotional: Expressed anxiety about impending transfer from coronary care unit to cardiac step-down unit.	1. Explain that transfer from the coronary care unit to the step-down unit is a positive progression toward recovery. 2. Provide information about the routines and environment of the step-down unit. 3. Encourage Mrs. C. P. to be present during transfer to the step-down unit. 4. Transfer during the daylight hours. 5. Remove the cardiac monitor several hours before the transfer from the coronary care unit. 6. Visit after transfer from the coronary care unit.
Somatic: Manifests image of cardiac invalid.	1. Define expected physical activities. 2. Provide positive feedback for achievements in physical activities. 3. Encourage verbalization of feelings about self. 4. Point out positive aspects of life (e.g., ways to do job-related activities in the home).

Sexual: Verbalized fear about not being able to resume sexual activity.	1. Inform that resumption of sexual activity will be determined by physician and may depend upon physical tolerance of rapid ascension of two flights of stairs.
	2. Inform of sexual maneuvers that prevent extensive cardiac strain:
	  (a) Utilize a side-lying coital position (rear or front entry).
	  (b) Utilize a back-lying coital position with the sex partner kneeling.
	  (c) Utilize a sitting position in an armless chair with the sex partner on the lap of the patient. (Be sure that a low chair is used so that it allows for both individuals to place their feet on the floor).
	  (d) Encourage to concentrate on breathing regularly during coitus.

(a) When extremely fatigued, when upset, and for at least three hours after consuming a heavy meal or after drinking alcohol.

(b) In excessively warm or cold environments.

(c) Illicit sexual encounters.

4. Inform of warning signals that may indicate intolerance of sexual activity:

(a) Prolonged (more than 15 minutes) rapid heart rate and rapid breathing after sexual intercourse.

(b) Extreme fatigue on day after intercourse.

(c) Chest pain during and after intercourse.

Occupational: Expressed concern about not being able to return to work.

1. Inform that majority of cardiac victims are able to return to same job with little modification of responsibilities.

2. Encourage to think of ways to alter work pattern to allow for a gradual return to work responsibilities.

3. Contact social service, occupational therapy, or cardiac rehabilitation counselor about setting up communications with employer about patient's resumption of work responsibilities.

Social: Wife's expressed feelings of guilt about the occurrence of the M. I.

1. Encourage discussion of feelings between patient and wife.

2. Encourage wife to discuss her feelings with other members of a cardiac club.

3. Encourage wife to avoid overprotective behavior.

4. Provide with detailed home-going instructions on prescribed therapies.

REFERENCES

Adsett, C., and Bruhn, J. Short-term group psychotherapy for post-M.I. patients and their wives, *Canadian Medical Association Journal,* 1968, *99* (28), 577-584.

Alonzo, A. *Illness behavior during acute episodes of coronary heart disease.* Unpublished Ph.D. thesis, University of California, Berkley, 1973.

Block, A., Maeder, J., and Haissly, J. Sexual problems after myocardial infarction, *American Heart Journal,* 1975, *90* (4), 536-537.

Bowar-Ferres, S. Returning to work—another stage of recovery and growth for the M.I. patient, *Occupational Health Nursing,* 1975, *23* (11), 18-25.

Bragg, T. Psychological response to myocardial infarction, *Nursing Forum,* 1975, *14* (4), 383-395.

Cassem, N. The nurse in the coronary care unit. In W. Gentry and K. Williams, Jr. (Eds.), *Psychological aspects of myocardial infarction and coronary care.* St. Louis: The C. V. Mosby Co., 1975.

Crawshaw, J. Community rehabilitation after acute myocardial infarction, *Heart and Lung,* 1974, *3* (3), 258-262.

Croog, S., Shapiro, D., and Levine, S. Denial among male heart patients, *Psychosomatic Medicine,* 1971, *33* (5), 385-397.

Erikson, E. *Childhood and society.* New York: W. W. Norton & Co., 1963.

Freedman, A., Kaplan, H., and Sadock, B. *Comprehensive textbook of psychiatry — II.* Baltimore: The Williams & Wilkins Co., 1975.

Friedman, M. *Pathogenesis of coronary artery disease.* New York: McGraw-Hill Book Company, 1969.

Fuhs, M. Smoking and the heart patient, *Nursing Clinics of North America,* 1976, *11* (2), 361-369.

Gentry, W. Preadmission behavior. In W. Gentry and R. Williams, Jr. (Eds.), *Psychological aspects of myocardial infarction and coronary care.* St. Louis: The C. V. Mosby Co., 1975.

Gentry, W., and Haney, T. Emotional and behavioral reactions to acute myocardial infarction, *Heart and Lung,* 1975, *4* (5), 738-745.

Goldstein, S., Moss, A., and Green, W. Sudden death in acute myocardial infarction, *Archives of Internal Medicine,* 1972, *129* (5), 720-724.

Granger, J. Full recovery from myocardial infarction: psychosocial factors, *Heart and Lung,* 1974, *3* (4), 600-610.

Green, A. Sexual activity and the postmyocardial infarction patient, *American Heart Journal,* 1975, *89* (2), 246-252.

Hackett, R., and Cassem, N. Factors contributing to delay in responding to the signs and symptoms of acute myocardial infarction, *American Journal of Cardiology,* 1969, *24* (11), 651-658.

Hackett, R., and Cassem, N. Psychological adaptation in myocardial infarction patients. In J. Naughton and H. Hellerstein (Eds.), *Exercise testing and exercise training in coronary heart disease.* New York: Academic Press, 1973.

Harding, A., and Morefield, M. Group intervention for wives of myocardial infarction patients, *Nursing Clinics of North America*, 1976, *11* (2), 339-347.

Hellerstein, H. Rehabilitation of the post-infarction patient, *Hospital Practice*, 1972, *7* (7), 45-53.

Hellerstein, H., and Friedman, E. Sexual activity and the post-coronary patient, *Archives of Internal Medicine*, 1970, *125* (6), 987-999.

Jenkins, C. The coronary-prone personality. In W. Gentry and R. Williams, Jr., (Eds.), *Psychological aspects of myocardial infarction and coronary care*. St. Louis: The C. V. Mosby Co., 1975.

Kenigsberg, D., Zyzanski, S., Jenkins, C., Wardwell, W., and Licciardello, A. The coronary-prone behavior pattern in hospitalized patients with and without coronary heart disease, *Psychosomatic Medicine*, 1974, *36* (4), 344-351.

Kent, S. When to resume sexual activity after myocardial infarction, *Geriatrics*, 1975, *30* (8), 151-153.

Kleiger, R., Martin, T., Miller, J., and Oliver, G. Mortality of myocardial infarction treated in the coronary-care unit. *Heart and Lung*, 1975, *4* (2), 215-226.

Kjøller, E. Resumption of work after acute myocardial infarction, *Acta Medica Scandinavica*, 1976, *199*, 379-385.

Lawson, B. Easing the sexual fears of the cardiac patient, *R.N.*, 1974, *37* (4), ICU-1-5.

Lebovitz, B., Shekelle, R., Ostfeld, A., and Oglesby, P. Prospective and retrospective psychological studies of coronary heart disease, *Psychosomatic Medicine*, 1967, *29* (3), 265-272.

Lefkowitz, S. Breathholding and orgasm, *Medical Aspects of Human Sexuality*, 1975, *9* (10), 106.

Levine, J., and Zigler, E. Denial and self-image in stroke, lung cancer, and heart disease patients, *Journal of Consulting and Clinical Psychology*, 1975, *43* (6), 751-757.

Luckmann, J., and Sorensen, K. *Medical-surgical nursing: a psychophysiologic approach*. Philadelphia: W. B. Saunders, 1974.

Massie, E., Rose, E., Rupp, J., and Whelton, R. Sudden death during coitus: fact or fiction? *Medical Aspects of Human Sexuality*, 1969, *3* (6), 22-26.

Moore, K., Folk-Lighty, M., and Nolen, M. The joy of sex after a heart attack, *Nursing '77*, 1977, *7* (6), 52-55.

Moss, A., and Goldstein, S. The pre-hospital phase of acute myocardial infarction, *Circulation*, 1970, *41* (5), 737-742.

Moss, A., Wynar, B., and Goldstein, S. Delay in hospitalization during the acute coronary period, *American Journal of Cardiology*, 1969, *24* (11), 659-665.

Olin, H., and Hackett, T. The denial of chest pain in 32 patients with acute myocardial infarction, *Journal of the American Medical Association*, 1964, *190* (11), 977-981.

Protos, A., Caracta, A., and Gross, L. The seasonal susceptibility to myocardial infarction, *Journal of the American Geriatrics Society*, 1971, *19* (6), 526-535.

Puksta, N. All about sex after a coronary, *American Journal of Nursing*, 1977, *77* (4), 602-605.

Rodbard, S. The heart as hostile witness, *Perspectives in Biology and Medicine*, 1975, *18* (3), 375-378.

Rosen, I., and Bibring, G. Psychological reactions of hospitalized male patients to a heart attack, *Psychosomatic Medicine*, 1966, *28* (6), 808-821.

Rosenman, R. Emotional patterns in the development of cardiovascular disease, *Journal of the American College Health Association*, 1967, *15* (2), 211-214.

Rosenman, R., and Friedman, M. Association of specific behavior patterns in women with blood and cardiovascular findings, *Circulation*, 1961, *24* (11), 1173-1184.

Rubin, I., Grass, H., and Arbeit, S. *Treatment of heart disease in the adult.* Philadelphia: Lea & Febiger, 1972.

Scalzi, C. Nursing management of behavioral responses following an acute myocardial infarction, *Heart and Lung*, 1973, *2* (1), 62-69.

Scanlon, M. An industrial visiting nurse: occupational health outside the plant, *Nursing Clinics of North America*, 1972, *7* (1), 143-152.

Simon, A., Feinleib, M., and Thompson, H. Components of delay in the prehospital phase of acute myocardial infarction. *American Journal of Cardiology*, 1972, *30* (10), 476-482.

Skelton, M., and Dominian, J. Psychological stress in wives of patients with myocardial infarction, *British Medical Journal*, 1973, *2*, 101-103.

Spodick, D. Medical history of the pericardium: the hairy hearts of hoary heros, *The American Journal of Cardiology*, 1970, *26* (11), 447-454.

Tjoe, S., and Luria, M. Delays in reaching the cardiac care unit: an analysis, *Chest*, 1972, *61* (7), 617-621.

Tyzenhouse, P. Myocardial infarction, *American Journal of Nursing*, 1973, *73* (6), 1012-1013.

Ueno, M. The so-called coition death, *Japanese Journal of Legal Medicine*, 1963, *17*, 330-340.

Wagner, N. Sexual activity and the cardiac patient. In R. Green (Ed.), *Human sexuality — a health practitioner's text.* Baltimore: Williams & Wilkins Co., 1975.

Watts, R. Sexuality and the middle-aged cardiac patient, *Nursing Clinics of North America*, 1976, *11* (2), 349-359.

Wells, C. Rehabilitation counseling of the heart patient in an outpatient rehabilitation center, *Heart and Lung*, 1974, *3* (4), 594-599.

Wishnie, H., Hackett, T., and Cassem N. Psychological hazards of convalescence following myocardial infarction, *Journal of the American Medical Association*, 1971, *215* (8), 1292-1296.

Woods, N. *Human sexuality in health and illness.* St. Louis: The C. V. Mosby Co., 1975.

Zohman, B. Emotional factors in coronary disease, *Geriatrics*, 1973, *28* (2), 110-119.

10

The Patient with an
ALTERATION
IN
RESPIRATORY FUNCTION

INTRODUCTION

Respiration is essential to life. The ability to breathe is generally taken for granted by most individuals. Since respiration is the only essential bodily activity under both voluntary and involuntary control, people tend not to be aware of respiratory function until they consciously change their breathing patterns to meet their needs, as in taking a deep breath before diving into a pool of water. The individual suffering from chronic obstructive pulmonary disease (COPD), however, has frequent thoughts about the ability to breathe. Since the respiratory function is impaired, many, if not all, of his or her daily activities are affected by the inability to breathe effectively and efficiently.

Chronic obstructive pulomonary disease is a term applied to respiratory alterations that involve persistent obstruction of bronchial airflow. Various diseases are associated with chronic obstructive pulmonary disease, but the conditions that most frequently give rise to COPD are bronchial asthma, chronic bronchitis, and pulmonary emphysema (American Lung Association, 1973a). Each of these disorders can occur independently or in combination, with bronchitis and emphysema coexisting most frequently (American Lung Association, 1973a).

Nearly 14 million people are afflicted with some form of COPD (American Lung Association, 1973b) with approximately 41,000 dying annually (American Lung Association, 1976a). Following heart disease, pulmonary emphysema is the second leading cause of disability among American workers receiving Social Security disability payments (American Lung Association, 1976b). Thus, respiratory conditions create an economic impact on both the individual and society with the total annual cost of pulmonary emphysema and other chronic respiratory diseases being more than $400 million a year (American Lung Association, 1976b).

ETIOLOGIC FACTORS

The exact causes of COPD have not been identified. However, various etiologic factors are considered of importance in the development of chronic obstructive pulmonary disease. These factors include smoking, air pollution, recurrent or chronic respiratory infections, occupational exposure to irritating fumes and dusts, genetic factors, aging, and allergic factors (American Lung Association, 1973a). However, research has identified *smoking* to be of greatest importance in the development of chronic obstructive pulmonary disease (Department of Health, Education, and Welfare, Public Health Service, 1973; Spain, Siegel, and Bradess, 1973; Mueller, Keble, Plummer, and Walker, 1971).

An unfortunate factor in COPD is that early detection is difficult and afflicted individuals often are unable to recognize the development and progression of this respiratory disorder. Often by the time an individual is seen in the doctor's office the structural damage to the lung is irreversible and the individual no longer has adequate cardiopulmonary reserve to meet his or her physiological needs. Only when adequate and consistent preventive measures for facilitating respiratory function are enforced will the incidence of chronic obstructive pulmonary disease be reduced. Therefore, the public must be educated about factors that contribute to formation of COPD with particular emphasis upon the hazards of pulmonary irritants and the necessity of prompt treatment of respiratory disorders.

Individuals afflicted with COPD are required to make many alterations in their life-styles as their disease process progresses. The impact of this chronic condition is extensive and affects the individual's emotional stability, somatic identity, sexuality, occupational identity, and social role. The remainder of this chapter will deal upon each of these areas of concern and how members of the health care team can assist the individual in dealing with the illness.

IMPACT OF CHRONIC OBSTRUCTIVE PULMONARY DISEASE

Emotional Impact[*]

Some individuals are able to deal with the limitations that chronic obstructive pulmonary disease impose upon their life-styles. More commonly, however, the individual with a chronic respiratory alteration experiences a

[*]It is advisable for the reader to have read Chapters 1 and 3 before continuing with this section.

variety of emotional responses. The presence of increased weakness, dyspnea, cough, and sputum production seems overwhelming and the individual with COPD generally feels anger, fear, anxiety, apathy, and/or depression (Dudley, Wermuth, and Hague, 1973): anger because of the inability to carry out daily activities as others do; fear of smothering to death because of impaired respiration; anxiety about what the future will hold as a result of the chronic illness; apathy toward therapies which may seem, at times, to do little good; and depression as the individual moves between exacerbations and remissions of the disease process. Unfortunately, these emotional reactions only create additional stress for the individual's already inefficient respiratory process.

Anxiety, anger, and fear are psychological variables that tend to be associated with increased skeletal muscle activity and increased energy expenditure that can lead to an elevated ventilatory rate and an increase in oxygen consumption. Since the individual with COPD has an inefficient respiratory system, he or she is unable to supply the air exchange necessary to meet the metabolic demands of the increase in energy expenditure brought about by such emotions.

Psychological variables such as apathy and depression, however, are associated with decreased skeletal muscle activity and decreased energy expenditure. The outcome can be a ventilation below that which is necessary to provide sufficient oxygen and to remove accumulated carbon dioxide. A decrease in ventilation associated with depression is insufficient to maintain homeostasis and the individual with chronic obstructive pulmonary disease may experience additional insult to the already compromised respiratory system.

In summary, emotional states, whether they increase or decrease energy expenditure, can rapidly upset the precarious cardiopulmonary system of the individual with chronic obstructive pulmonary disease. The end results are respiratory imbalance and decompensation.

In an attempt to prevent the emotional stimulation that can lead to symptom production and physiological decompensation, the individual may develop obsessional traits and compulsive rituals or retreat into isolation (Fuhs and Stein, 1976). In addition, the individual may internalize emotional feelings in order not to evoke a physiological response within his or her body. As a result, the individual with COPD literally lives in an emotional straitjacket. The individual's rigid avoidance of emotionally charged situations and the use of obsessional patterns, however, tend to perpetuate those frustrations which the individual finds he or she cannot manage adequately. In turn, the inability to handle feelings of frustration creates an increased metabolic demand that requires additional oxygen consumption. Symptoms of respiratory distress are provoked and a vicious cycle ensues. Unless the individual with chronic obstructive pulmonary disease learns techniques of handling changes in his or her emotional state, he or she will be unable to maintain the necessary therapeutic program and will decrease the chances for long-term survival.

It is the responsibility of the nurse to work with the individual with COPD and the family on ways of coping with emotionally charged situations. It is vital that the individual with respiratory problems ventilate feelings to members of the health care team and to the family. By so doing, situations that provoke emotional responses can be identified more easily. For example, anger may occur if other members of the family use the family bathroom during the time the patient usually attends to morning hygiene. Members of the family should be encouraged to discuss ways of dealing with such situations. A possible solution is to set up a time schedule for each individual's use of the bathroom. In addition to bathroom occupancy, watching certain programs on television may elicit an emotional response in the individual with COPD. If so, the family may find it necessary to avoid watching these programs in the presence of the respiratory patient.

Once emotionally charged situations are identified, if possible, the individual with COPD needs to be encouraged to avoid them. These situations can prove to be life-threatening, especially when the individual is experiencing acute respiratory decompensation.

In addition to identifying and dealing with situations that provoke emotional responses, the individual with COPD needs encouragement to verbalize his or her feelings about the illness. It must not be forgotten that the individual with COPD has a chronic illness and, as a result, must repeatedly deal with the impact of loss of wellness. Since COPD frequently fluctuates between periods of remission and exacerbation, the individual affected may reexperience the stages of loss (repudiation, recognition, and reconciliation) each time an exacerbation of symptoms occurs. This needs to be explained to family members so that they are better prepared to understand why their loved one may have variations in emotional responses. When symptoms of dyspnea, weakness, cough, and sputum production become acute, the respiratory patient may exhibit more intense responses of anger, fear, anxiety, apathy, or depression. Knowing that emotional responses become more acute during periods of exacerbation, family members and the respiratory patient may desire to be more active in identifying and in avoiding situations that provoke undue emotional stimulation for the afflicted individual.

Somatic Impact*

Coping with changes in bodily appearance is important to the individual with chronic obstructive pulmonary disease. Common bodily changes may include the presence of a barrel-shaped chest, excessive sputum production,

*It is advisable for the reader to have read Chapter 2 before continuing with this section.

pallor or an ashen tint to the skin, noisy respirations, and the assumption of a leaning-forward, arms supported, sitting position. The individual with COPD is well aware of the changes that have occurred in his or her appearance and may be self-conscious about these changes.

The presence of a barrel chest may embarrass the individual affected. He or she may find his or her appearance grotesque and verbalize anger with such comments as, "I feel like a walking beer keg!" or "I look like an upside down coke bottle!" In addition, the individual with a barrel chest occasionally may encounter difficulties in obtaining clothing that does not confine the upper torso.

Excessive sputum production may hinder the individual with COPD from engaging in social contacts because the individual may feel that frequent coughing and expectorating are not conducive to social conversation. He or she may feel that members of society find the frequent expectoration distasteful and hence avoid him or her. Skin color change, another body alteration, is a difficult manifestation to hide. Each time the individual looks in the mirror, he or she may note pallor or a bluish tint to the skin. As a result, the individual may not wish to look in the mirror or to be seen by others.

Noisy respirations and a sitting position of leaning forward with the arms supported may create difficulties for the individual with COPD. Again, the individual may avoid social contacts because he or she feels that these bodily changes are not conducive to contact with others. The individual fears that the noisy respirations might be distracting to others. The individual also believes that the unusual sitting position could portray an appearance of disinterest in social conversation since the individual looks ready to leap from the chair.

How well the adult experiencing any of these bodily changes can cope with them is affected by how effectively he or she handled the earlier developmental stages of life (Paley and Luparello, 1973). If the individual progressed through childhood and adolescence with a favorable view of himself, he or she will be better able to cope with the difficulties imposed by the chronic illness. Therapies will be adhered to more readily and periods of exacerbations will be approached with a feeling of optimism.

If, however, the individual encountered difficulties during developmental stages of childhood and adolescence, feelings of helplessness, weakness, and depression are more likely to develop. Such an individual may take on the demanding qualities of the child who feels miserable, bad, and guilty about the illness. As a result, the individual may express feelings of anger toward others. Expressions of being mistreated by those upon whom he or she depends (health team members and family) are not uncommon. As a result, tensions are created and relationships become strained. These stressful situations may then trigger emotional responses which, in turn, often lead to respiratory difficulties.

The stage of development being experienced by the adult with chronic obstructive pulmonary disease has an effect upon his or her ability to cope with bodily changes brought about by the illness. During the stage of young adulthood (eighteen to forty-five years) intimacy with others is of importance (Erikson, 1963) both in friendship and in a mutually satisfying sexual relationship. If the individual feels his or her bodily appearance (barrel-chest, noisy respiration, or expectoration) is displeasing to others, he or she is likely to retreat into isolation. The female with COPD may be more concerned about her outward appearance as a result of her illness. The male is more likely to be concerned about how his respiratory function affects his ability to achieve.

The stage of adulthood (forty-five to sixty-five years) brings the need to establish and guide future generations in the hope of bettering society (Erikson, 1963). The adult suffering from COPD, however, may view the future bleakly. Instead of anticipating the contentment of older age and looking forward to guiding younger generations, he or she may consider himself or herself as an invalid undergoing economic ruin or even premature death (Paley and Luparello, 1973).

The stage of maturity (sixty-five years and over) brings frequent thoughts of death. The mature adult sees contemporaries dying and begins to contemplate his or her own death. It is a time in life when the individual may feel extreme loneliness and express his or her feelings by being cantankerous. Such behavior further estranges the individual from those to whom he or she looks for friendship and assistance. The result is increased loneliness. The mature adult with chronic obstructive pulmonary disease may find this developmental stage especially difficult since the individuals he or she tends to ostracize are the very ones relied upon for assistance in carrying out therapies and meeting needs.

The role of the nurse and other members of the health care team, when dealing with the somatic impact of COPD on an individual, is to encourage the individual to verbalize his or her feelings. Does the individual feel displeasing to look at, feel like an invalid, or feel lonely and isolated? When the individual with COPD openly ventilates these feelings, he or she may be able to identify, with the assistance of the family and health team members, ways of coping with the changes in his or her appearance. In addition, family members should be alerted to the fact that the individual with COPD may harbor concerns about his or her appearance and about how others view him or her. Since isolation can result from fears of rejection because of bodily appearance, family members may have to be encouraged to demonstrate signs of acceptance of their loved one. Including the individual in family decision making, touching the individual, and recognizing his or her presence are but a few ways of demonstrating acceptance.

The nurse can assist the individual with chronic obstructive pulmonary disease in dealing with the altered body image by pointing out that the appearance of the barrel chest, the excessive sputum production, the presence of noisy respirations, and the skin color changes are expected occurrences in the disease process. Simply realizing that his or her bodily appearance is not unusual for an individual with COPD may lessen the anxiety. In addition, encouraging the individual to carry out pulmonary hygiene routinely and whenever he or she expects or notes a buildup in respiratory secretions can aid in reducing noisy respirations and excessive sputum accumulation. The respiratory patient needs encouragement to carry out pulmonary hygiene in the privacy of the bathroom or in the bedroom. Thus, he or she avoids the concern and embarrassment of wondering how others will react to his or her appearance at that time.

Clothing can play an important role in how the individual with COPD appears to others. Encouraging the individual with a barrel chest to avoid wearing tapered and form-fitting clothing that accentuates the shape of the chest can prove beneficial. Also, clothing made of colors that accentuate ashen or pale skin color should be avoided. Since these colors depend upon natural skin tones, they may vary among individuals. Therefore, the person may have to experiment with clothing colors in order to determine which ones look best on him or her.

Since the individual with COPD often is concerned about how others interpret his or her body position while sitting, the nurse can point out that this assumed posture is necessary to facilitate respiratory function and to decrease the workload of breathing. In addition, the individual may find that by maintaining eye contact with others while communicating can decrease some of the concerns of appearing inattentive during social conversation.

Above all, the individual with COPD and the family need encouragement to discuss their feelings about bodily changes encountered by the respiratory patient and to identify ways in which they best can cope with these bodily alterations.

Sexual Impact

The respiratory system's ability to function can affect many aspects of human life and the ability to function sexually is no exception. The sex act involves an increase in energy expenditure, an elevated ventilatory rate, and an increase in oxygen consumption. Since the individual with chronic obstructive pulmonary disease has an inefficient respiratory system, he or she may encounter difficulties in supplying the air exchange needed to meet the metabolic demands of the increased energy expenditure created by the sex act. This does not mean that an individual with COPD cannot take part in sexual expression, but alterations in the manner of expression may be necessary.

Since chronic obstructive pulmonary disease is a chronic condition and physiologic changes tend to occur over a period of time, the individual involved may demonstrate a progressive decrease in the frequency of sexual encounters. Such a decrease may not be readily evident to the individual with COPD since it has occurred over the years. However, if openly approached about the frequency of coitus, the individual with chronic obstructive pulmonary disease usually will be able to identify the fact that his or her sexual activity has diminished with the progression of the disease process. Unless sexual function of the respiratory patient is openly dealt with, it can create difficulties in a sexual relationship. Humiliation may result when unsuccessful attempts to complete the sex act occur. The male may feel that he is less than a man and the female may believe that she has lost her powers of femininity.

In addition to feelings of humiliation, problems involving the sex partner may occur. For example, the sex partner unknowingly may become frustrated because of the respiratory patient's decreased ability to take part in the sex act. As a result, the sex partner may sabotage the sexual relationship by doing things just prior to coitus which increase anxiety in the environment of the respiratory patient. Two examples are using an aerosol product just prior to coitus, which elicits respiratory difficulties because of its irritating effects or alluding to the respiratory patient's incapacity because of the illness. The outcome is the creation of additional energy expenditure and oxygen consumption just prior to coitus. This further decreases the respiratory patient's already altered ability to tolerate the demands of the sex act. On the other hand, the sex partner may avoid sexual encounters with the respiratory patient if it is believed that such activity will create undue stress for the individual. The outcome may be increased frustrations and feelings of rejection for the individual with COPD which, in turn, can lead to an increased energy expenditure and oxygen consumption.

The members of the health team can assist the respiratory patient in dealing with the altered abilities to tolerate sexual activity by encouraging the patient to discuss the sex act openly with the sex partner. The primary goal is to encourage the individual with COPD and the sex partner to identify methods that are comfortable, tolerable, and satisfying for both of them. Some possible suggestions which the health care team can provide include the following:

1. Avoid activities prior to coitus which tend to create an increase in respiratory rate and shortness of breath.
2. Utilize rest periods just prior to coitus.
3. If pooling of respiratory secretions is a problem, avoid coitus in the morning just prior to rising. If pooling of respiratory secretions is

not a problem, morning coitus may prove most desirable since the individual with COPD may be well rested.

4. Avoid coital positions that place excessive pressure on the thorax and abdomen since these positions tend to decrease the thorax's ability to expand to its optimum. Some couples may find the "doggy-fashion" position most desirable.

5. Breathe slowly and rhythmically during the sex act. Purse the lips during expiration in order to prevent bronchiole constriction and subsequent respiratory distress.

6. Encourage the sex partner to avoid using scents, body powders, or aerosol products that might elicit sneezing or coughing.

If the individual with chronic obstructive pulmonary disease finds that he or she is unable to tolerate the additional demands placed upon the respiratory system by the sex act, the individual may find manual stimulation (masturbation) satisfying as a means of sexual expression. Difficulties may arise for couples who utilize oral-genital sex as a means of sexual expression since individuals with COPD often become mouth breathers. Again, manual stimulation may be a desirable alternate method.

In summary, sexual expression is a necessary component of human life. Since the individual with chronic obstructive pulmonary disease may not be able to tolerate the additional respiratory demands created by sexual expression, counseling may be in order. The primary goals of sexual counseling for the individual with COPD and the sex partner are to prevent undue anxiety brought on by unsatisfying sexual expression and to identify maneuvers of sexual expression that do not create excessive demands upon respiratory function.

Occupational Impact

One of the greatest impacts of chronic obstructive pulmonary disease is the change it imposes upon the individual's work role (Barstow, 1974). Emphysema, a condition contributing to the formation of COPD, tends to affect individuals in the fourth to fifth decades of life, a time when a working individual ordinarily is at the peak of his or her career. Family economic responsibilities are high at this time since offspring are often attending college, getting married, or being assisted in their careers. Since the physiologic consequences of COPD produce a decrease in energy level, the individual affected often is required to make alterations in occupational pursuits. These alterations may be minor or major and may cause a change in the individual's standard of living.

Minor alterations can occur in any job setting such as in an office, a factory, or on a farm. A minor alteration may be removing the individual from an environment that contains irritating airborne pollutants or sudden temperature changes and placing the individual in a setting that does not contain substances or temperature settings which are irritating to the respiratory tract. For example, placing the individual with COPD in an office with people who do not smoke can prove beneficial. The respiratory patient who is working in a factory assembly line that has irritating fumes can be moved to a different assembly line that does not have such fumes. The farmer with COPD may find it helpful to harvest on a tractor with an air-conditioned cab or to wear a scarf or mask of some type over the mouth and nose when going out into cold weather. Each of these alterations is minor in that the individual is still able to carry out the same job with only minimal alterations in work pattern.

Another minor alteration may include reorganizing the approach to the individual's job by simplifying and pacing activities. In simplifying activities, the individual with COPD needs to plan ahead in order to maximize economy of effort. For example, instead of carrying a heavy object (such as an electric typewriter) across the room, the individual should put it on a cart and roll it to its destination. This maneuver saves energy.

Pacing one's activities is another approach to economizing energy. To illustrate, the housewife can do a few household chores that require physical exertion and then sit down and rest while she mends clothes or writes letters. By planning activities for the conservation of energy, the individual with COPD can continue to perform many occupational responsibilities.

Major alterations in occupational pursuits may include totally changing one's job or being forced into early retirement. If the severity of the disease process (as in the case of acute episodes of asthma or bronchitis) causes frequent lost working days, the individual with COPD may find his or her job in jeopardy. The individual may be asked to resign or be discharged if the loss of work time cannot be resolved. The chance of obtaining another job may be slim since letters of recommendation sent from one employer to another generally would allude to the missed work days. As a result, the potential employer might consider the individual with chronic obstructive pulmonary disease an economic risk and refuse to hire him or her. In such a situation, the individual with COPD may find job retraining necessary.

The nurse's primary role in dealing with the occupational impact of chronic obstructive pulmonary disease is to assist the individual in identifying necessary alterations in the work pattern. Assisting the individual and the family in recognizing potential situations and problems in one's work that may contribute to respiratory difficulties is necessary. Since each individual is different and occupations are diverse, problems related to occupational respiratory hazards will vary. Encouraging both the patient and the family to describe the occupational environment and identify situations that they feel potentiate respiratory difficulties is a helpful beginning. In addition, approaching the employer, the industrial nurse, or company physician about alterations in the respiratory patient's work situation can prove beneficial since these individuals can be directly involved in initiating necessary changes.

Encouraging the respiratory patient and the family in an ongoing effort to identify ways of conserving energy is vital. For example, simply sitting down to iron can help in conserving energy. If, however, a major alteration in occupational pursuits is necessary, the nurse's role is to contact members of the health care team prepared in occupational rehabilitation. Such individuals may include the social worker, the occupational therapist, or the rehabilitation counselor.

Above all, the individual with COPD must be kept as active as his or her physical ability allows. The nurse must encourage the respiratory patient and the family to avoid overprotecting the patient and placing him or her in a state of dependence by not allowing the patient to engage in any form of physical activity or by continually assisting him or her with every physical movement.

The use of breathing retraining is necessary in increasing the individual's exercise tolerance. The individual with chronic obstructive pulmonary disease should be instructed how to allow for maximum descent of the diaphragm and to use the diaphragm and abdominal muscles to aid in emptying the lungs (Petty, Hudson, and Neff, 1973). The respiratory therapist is a valuable member of the health care team prepared in teaching the respiratory patient diaphragmatic strengthening exercises. The basic principle involved is relaxation during controlled coordinated respiration. The individual with COPD is instructed to use a period of short inspiration and to allow for maximum descent of the diaphragm. This maneuver is then followed by contraction of the abdomen during expiration and exhalation against pursed lips (Petty, Hudson, and Neff, 1973). This simple technique improves the efficiency of ventilation and gas transport (Mueller, Petty, and Filley, 1970).

Physical reconditioning is also important. Once the individual with COPD has established effective bronchial hygiene to promote the reduction of airway resistance and has learned breathing retraining, a graded exercise program should begin. For example, daily walks can be carried out, increasing the number of walks in a 24-hour period. Improving the individual's exercise capacity is possible despite the irreversible lung damage that is present as a result of the disease process.

If the respiratory patient is not kept active, he or she is likely to become immobilized both physically and emotionally. Both states of immobility can hasten the progression of the already chronic condition. Lack of physical activity leads to stasis of respiratory secretions and to subsequent respiratory infections and distress. Emotional immobility leads to boredom which, in turn leads to physical immobility and subsequent respiratory complications.

Social Impact

As the individual's disease process progresses, he or she curtails social activities and contacts. In fact, social and recreational activities are often the first noticeable major alteration in the individual's life-style. The individual with COPD finds that he or she does not have the energy to become involved with others emotionally or in activities requiring physical expenditures. Not only is it difficult to take part in physical activities, but even talking may prove too exhausting. As a result, the individual withdraws from others and may become an isolate.

Since the progression of COPD occurs over a period of years, the individual afflicted may not be aware of the progressive changes occurring in his or her social activities. The gradual withdrawal from others may go unnoticed. As the withdrawal from social contacts and involvement progresses, the individual also may become increasingly depressed. This depression may be the result of loneliness and boredom.

The individual with COPD must be encouraged to take part in social activities in order to prevent progressive withdrawal and subsequent depression. Alterations in activities pursued may, however, be necessary so that the individual's energy is conserved. For example, the individual with COPD can be advised to take part in activities in which energy expenditure is not excessive, such as attending the theater or watching a sports event. The kind of social event engaged in should be discussed by the respiratory patient and the family prior to attendance. Whether or not the activity is advisable for the individual should be determined ahead of time because some social activities may elicit emotional responses such as excessive laughter, excitement, or anger which can prove deleterious to respiratory function.

The individual with COPD may need encouragement to avoid social events with large crowds during peak periods of upper respiratory infections (early fall, midwinter, and early spring) and where excessive air pollutants exist (smoke-filled rooms). Avoiding these situations aids in decreasing the individual's exposure to respiratory infections and irritants. To aid in dealing with each of these situations, individuals with COPD are encouraged to obtain flu shots for the prevention of upper respiratory infections. Sitting in the no smoking sections of planes, buses, and trains assists in decreasing contacts with air pollutants. Traveling by car in metropolitan areas before morning and evening rush hour traffic also facilitates in decreasing avoidance of airborne irritants.

Preparing the individual prior to a social interaction proves beneficial. For example, carrying out good pulmonary hygiene to clear out the respiratory tract before going out for an evening of entertainment can aid in preventing the occurrence of accumulated respiratory secretions and subsequent respiratory difficulty during social interaction. Lying down for a period of rest prior to a social function also aids in preventing physical exhaustion and subsequent respiratory distress.

If the individual wishes to vacation, he or she should be alerted to the fact that visiting areas that have temperatures over 90° Fahrenheit can be harmful since high temperatures increase metabolism which lead to an increase in oxygen consumption. If such circumstances are unavoidable, arrangements should be made for the provision of an air conditioner. By the same token, exposure to very cold weather can be harmful and elicit respiratory distress since cold weather can irritate the respiratory tract and lead to bronchospasms. If these temperatures are unavoidable, covering the mouth and nose with a scarf to warm the air that enters the respiratory tract is helpful.

Allergies can produce respiratory difficulties for the individual with COPD. Therefore, potential allergens in the areas to be visited need to be identified. Ragweed, a common source of allergic reactions, is prevalent in the central and eastern parts of the United States, but it does not grow in the far west and south. Therefore, during the flowering season of ragweed, it would be ideal for the individual with COPD to take a trip to California or Southern Florida.

If traveling in areas of high altitudes presents problems because of the decreased prevalence of oxygen, the individual should check with his or her physician to determine which altitude is advisable. Travel in places such as Pikes Peak and some passes through the Rocky Mountains may prove hazardous to the individual with COPD.

The abstinence from or a decrease in smoking is generally advisable for individuals with COPD since smoke acts as an irritant to the respiratory tract. Since smoking is a habit often cultivated during social interaction, the individual with COPD may find it difficult not to smoke if everyone else is smoking.

If the individual has been smoking for a number of years, it may prove difficult to alter his or her smoking habit. To aid in altering these smoking habits, Fuhs (1976) has made the following suggestions:

1. Place cigarettes in an inconvenient location.
2. Hide ashtrays.
3. Buy one pack of cigarettes at a time.
4. Do not carry matches or a cigarette lighter.
5. If the urge to smoke occurs, wait a few minutes and then immediately change the activities or thoughts being pursued.

6. Try to go longer each day without a cigarette.
7. Slowly stop smoke-linked habits such as a cup of coffee and a cigarette, a meal and a cigarette, or a party and a cigarette.
8. Stop smoking while in bed with an illness.
9. Stop smoking during vacation or on a relaxing day if the habit of smoking is associated with stressful situations.
10. Have a friend stop smoking at the same time.

In addition to the above suggestions, the individual who is attempting to stop smoking may require a replacement for the oral gratification obtained from smoking. Individuals may use any number of methods, for example, chewing gum, chewing toothpicks, or sucking hard candy. Unfortunately, some individuals may increase their food consumption as a means of oral gratification replacement once they stop smoking with the results leading to weight gain.

If the individual is unable to stop smoking completely, he or she can decrease the number of cigarettes smoked. Some of the acts suggested by Fuhs (1976) to decrease the hazards of smoke inhalation are:

1. Select a cigarette with less tar and nicotine.
2. Smoke half the cigarette and discard the other half.
3. Take fewer and smaller puffs on each cigarette.
4. Cut down on inhaling.

Above all, encouragement from family, friends, and members of the health care team is necessary as the individual alters smoking habits. Encouragement to alter smoking habits and praise for progress made toward alterations in smoking habits are helpful. If possible family, friends, and members of the health care team should avoid smoking in the presence of the individual with COPD since the smoke is a respiratory irritant and having a smoker present may increase the individual's desire to smoke.

In summary, if appropriate precautions are carried out to avoid respiratory irritants and infections and if the conservation of energy is kept in mind, the individual with COPD can engage in a fulfilling and enjoyable social life.

SUMMARY

Respiration is a vital activity; therefore, alterations in respiratory function can affect man's ability to carry out the activities of daily living. The individuals with chronic obstructive pulmonary disease are continually aware of the effect that their disease process has upon their life-styles.

Chronic obstructive pulmonary disease (COPD) is a term applied to respiratory alterations that involve persistent obstruction of bronchial airflow. Bronchial asthma, chronic bronchitis, and pulmonary emphysema are the three conditions that most frequently give rise to COPD.

The exact cause(s) of COPD is not known. However, various etiologic factors are considered important in the development of the condition. Of all the etiologic factors, research has identified smoking to be of greatest importance in the development of the chronic illness.

Since one's respiratory function can have an effect upon the ability to carry out activities of daily living, the impact of this chronic condition can affect emotional stability, somatic identity, sexuality, occupational identity, and social role. Members of the health care team need to assist the individual with chronic obstructive pulmonary disease in identifying how the presence of this chronic respiratory illness affects the individual's everyday life and to aid him or her in dealing with each of these alterations.

Patient Situation

Mr. P. E. is a sixty-seven-year-old retired sawmill employee with a history of chronic obstructive pulmonary disease. He has been smoking 2½ packs of cigarettes a day for the past 30 years. He and his wife live with their divorced daughter and her three teenage children. Since neither Mr. P. E., Mrs. P. E., nor their daughter works, the family is supported by welfare assistance.

Mr. P. E. is currently being treated for an acute respiratory infection in the county welfare clinic on an outpatient basis. Mrs. P. E. and daughter bring Mr. P. E. to the clinic weekly for a checkup. During the assessment the clinical nurse was able to identify patient-centered problems related to Mr. P. E.'s emotional well-being, somatic identity, sexuality, occupational identity, and social role.

Below are Mr. P. E.'s nursing care plan and patient care cardex dealing with each of these areas of concern.

NURSING CARE PLAN

Problems	Objectives	Nursing Interventions	Principles/Rationale	Evaluations
Emotional Impact Expressed anger about teenage grandchildren occupying the bathroom for extended periods of time.	To decrease Mr. P. E.'s anger. To assist Mr. P. E. in appropriately expressing his anger.	Encourage Mr. P. E. to verbalize his anger to his family.	A family aware of situations that provoke emotional responses in the individual with chronic obstructive pulmonary disease is better prepared to identify ways of dealing with emotionally charged situations.	The nurse would observe for: Increased verbalization between Mr. P. E. and his family about situations that provoke an emotional response.
	To prevent respiratory distress caused by feelings of anger.	Encourage Mr. P. E.'s family to identify and discuss with Mr. P. E. ways in which they can alleviate the difficulties of shared bathroom usage (e.g., set up a time schedule for extended periods of bathroom use).	Actively involving the entire family in making a decision about a matter that affects each family member facilitates the likelihood that each member will adhere to the final decision.	Active decision making between Mr. P. E. and his family on how best to deal with the problem of shared bathroom use.
			Appropriately expressing emotional feelings instead of internalizing them aids in decreasing the likelihood of respiratory symptoms and physiological decompensation in the individual with COPD caused by an emotional reaction.	A lack of or a decrease in Mr. P. E.'s respiratory symptoms during episodes of anger.
Somatic Impact Verbalization that sputum production is disgusting and displeasing.	To assist Mr. P. E. in dealing with his altered body image.	Point out to Mr. P. E. that the presence of his excessive sputum production is an expected change related to chronic obstructive pulmonary disease.	Realizing that certain bodily changes tend to occur with COPD helps decrease anxiety related to an altered body image.	The nurse would observe for: Decreased expression by Mr. P. E. that his bodily appearance is disgusting.
		Encourage Mr. P. E. to carry out his pulmonary hygiene routinely and whenever he expects or notes a buildup in	Pulmonary hygiene aids in decreasing the accumulation of respiratory secretions and subsequent embarrassment as a	Mr. P. E.'s routine adherence to good pulmonary hygiene.

Problem	Goal	Nursing Intervention	Rationale	Evaluation
	out his pulmonary hygiene in the privacy of his room or in the bathroom.		hygiene helps decrease the concern and embarrassment of wondering how others will react to his bodily appearance at this time.	Open expression by Mr. P. E. about his self image, and likely methods for dealing with his altered bodily appearance.
		Encourage Mr. P. E. to verbalize how he feels about himself.	Open ventilation of feelings about bodily appearance can aid in the individual's ability to identify ways of coping with these changes.	
	To assist Mr. P. E. from isolating himself from others.	Point out to Mr. P. E. that Mr. P. E.'s family harbors concerns about his bodily appearance and requires expressions of acceptance.	Expressions of acceptance by family members toward the individual with COPD who is undergoing a change in body image assists in preventing him from isolating himself from others as a result of feelings of rejection.	A decrease in Mr. P. E.'s attempts to isolate himself from others.
Sexual Impact Expressed concern about a decreased tolerance of sexual activity because of shortness of breath.	To enhance Mr. P. E.'s feelings of masculinity.	Encourage Mr. P. E. to discuss openly with Mrs. P. E. his concerns about his sexual capabilities.	Unless sexual functions of the individual with COPD are openly dealt with, difficulties in a sexual relationship can result. By openly discussing their sexual activity, the individual with COPD and his sex partner are more likely to identify and prevent the occurrence of sexual sabotaging acts that may unknowingly be carried out prior to coitus.	The nurse would observe for: Mr. P. E.'s verbalization of an increased satisfaction in his sexual relationship with his wife.

NURSING CARE PLAN (cont.)

Problems	Objectives	Nursing Interventions	Principles/Rationale	Evaluations
Sexual Impact (cont.)	To facilitate a satisfying sexual relationship for both Mr. and Mrs. P. E.	Encourage Mr. P. E. to:		
		1. Avoid activities prior to coitus that tend to create an increase in respiratory rate and shortness of breath.	Preventing excessive demands upon the respiratory tract prior to coitus enhances the respiratory patient's ability to tolerate intercourse.	
		2. Utilize rest periods prior to coitus.		
		3. Avoid coitus in the morning just prior to rising if pooling of respiratory secretions is a problem. If pooling of respiratory secretions is not a problem, morning coitus may prove most desirable since Mr. P. E. would be most rested at this time.		
		4. Avoid coital positions that place excessive pressure on the thorax and abdomen.	Preventing pressure on the abdomen and rib cage enhances the thorax's ability to expand to its optimum, thereby decreasing the chances of respiratory distress.	
		5. Breathe slowly and rhythmically during the sex act. Purse lips during expiration.	Breathing maneuvers that enhance respiration prevent respiratory distress and assist in increasing the respiratory patient's ability to tolerate sexual activity.	
		6. Advise Mrs. P. E. not to use perfumes, body powders, or aerosol products that elicit sneezing or coughing epi-	Avoiding air pollutants prior to and during coitus aids in preventing the occurrence of respiratory difficulty caused by irrita-	

Expressed concern about the occurrence of fatigue and respiratory distress after carrying out odd jobs around the house.	To reduce the incidence of fatigue and respiratory distress after work.	Encourage Mr. P. E. to plan ahead in order to maximize economy of physical effort (e.g., instead of carrying a heavy object across the room placing it on a cart with wheels and rolling it to its destination). Encourage Mr. P. E. to pace his activities (e.g., work for 30 minutes and rest for 10 minutes).	Planning and spacing activities for the conservation of energy can prevent undue respiratory distress. Planning and spacing activities for the conservation of energy can enhance the individual's ability to continue to carry out many occupational responsibilities.	The nurse would observe for: Mr. P. E.'s verbalization that by properly carrying out acts of energy conservation his respiratory distress and fatigue are decreased.
	To maintain Mr. P. E.'s optimal level of physical performance.	Encourage Mr. P. E. to build up gradually his level of physical activity each day (e.g., increasing the distance walked by a few yards). Encourage Mr. P. E. to avoid completely stopping his physical activity.	Gradually increasing an individual's exercise capacity can decrease the chances of respiratory distress resulting from overexertion. Immobilization leads to stasis of respiratory secretions and subsequent respiratory infection and distress.	Mr. P. E.'s verbalization that he has gradually increased his physical activity with minimal resulting distress.
Social Impact Verbalized anxiety about inability to stop smoking.	To assist Mr. P. E. in decreasing his cigarette consumption.	Encourage Mr. P. E. to: 1. Place cigarettes in an inconvenient location. 2. Hide ashtrays. 3. Buy one pack of cigarettes at a time. Avoid carrying matches or a cigarette lighter. 4. Wait a few minutes and then immediately change the activities or thoughts being pursued if the urge to smoke occurs. 5. Try to go longer each day without a cigarette.	Increasing understanding about factors that contribute to smoking can enhance the desire to control smoking habits. Increasing the difficulty to smoke can decrease the desire to smoke. Decreasing the availability of smoking materials may decrease the frequency of smoking.	The nurse would observe for: Mr. P. E.'s verbalization about a decrease in the number of cigarettes that he is smoking.

NURSING CARE PLAN (cont.)

Problems	Objectives	Nursing Interventions	Principles Rationale	Evaluations
Social Impact (cont.)		6. Slowly stop smoke-linked habits such as a cigarette and a meal or a cigarette and a cup of coffee. 7. Stop smoking while in bed with an illness. 8. Stop smoking during vacation or on a relaxing day if the habit of smoking is associated with stressful situations. 9. Have a friend stop smoking at the same time.	Interacting with individuals attempting to alter a similar habit can provide emotional support and may facilitate the alteration of the habit.	
		10. Utilize a replacement for the oral gratification obtained from smoking, for example, chewing gum, chewing toothpicks, or sucking hard candy.	Developing adaptive responses to the oral need of smoking can facilitate in altering one's desire to smoke.	
		Encourage Mr. P. E.'s family to support him in his efforts to alter his smoking habits.	Support from significant others facilitates in the accomplishment of the alteration of a habit.	
		Encourage Mr. P. E.'s family to provide positive feedback for his attempts and accomplishments made in the alterations of his smoking habit.	Positive feedback for accomplishments facilitates feelings of self-worth.	

PATIENT CARE CARDEX

PATIENT'S NAME: ___Mr. P. E.___   DIAGNOSIS: ___Chronic obstructive pulmonary disease___

AGE: ___67 years___   SEX: ___Male___

MARITAL STATUS: ___Married___   OCCUPATION: ___Retired sawmill employee___

SIGNIFICANT OTHERS: Wife, daughter, and three teenage grandchildren

Problems	Nursing Approaches
Emotional: Expressed anger about grandchildren's occupying bathroom for extended periods of time.	1. Encourage verbalization of anger to family. 2. Encourage family and patient to identify and discuss ways of alleviating the bathroom difficulties.
Somatic: Verbalization that sputum production is disgusting and displeasing.	1. Point out that excessive sputum production is an expected change related to COPD. 2. Encourage use of pulmonary hygiene on a routine basis and whenever sputum buildups are expected. 3. Encourage to carry out pulmonary hygiene in the privacy of the bathroom or bedroom. 4. Encourage verbalization of feelings about self. 5. Point out to family that patient harbors concerns about bodily appearance and requires expression of their acceptance.
Sexual: Expressed concern about a decreased tolerance of sexual activity because of shortness of breath.	1. Encourage open discussion between patient and wife about patient's sexual capabilities. 2. Encourage: (a) Avoidance of activities prior to coitus that create an increase in respiratory rate and shortness of breath. (b) Utilization of rest periods prior to coitus. (c) Avoidance of coitus in morning if pooling of secretions is a problem. (d) Avoidance of coital positions that place excessive pressure on the thorax and abdomen. (e) Use of slow and rhythmical breathing using pursed-lip breathing during the sex act. (f) Avoidance of the use of perfumes, body powders, or aerosol-applied products by wife prior to coitus that elicit sneezing or coughing.

PATIENT CARE CARDEX (cont.)

Problems	Nursing Approaches
Occupational: Expressed concern about the occurrence of fatigue and respiratory distress after carrying out odd jobs around the house.	1. Encourage to plan ahead in order to maximize economy of physical effort. 2. Encourage to pace activities. 3. Encourage to gradually build up level of physical activity each day. 4. Encourage to avoid completely stopping physical activity.
Social: Verbalized anxiety about being unable to stop smoking.	1. Encourage to: 　(a) Place cigarettes in inconvenient place. 　(b) Hide ashtrays. 　(c) Buy one pack of cigarettes at a time. 　(d) Avoid carrying matches or a cigarette lighter. 　(e) Wait a few minutes and then change activity or thoughts being pursued when urge to smoke occurs. 　(f) Try to go longer each day without a cigarette. 　(g) Slowly stop smoke-linked habits (e.g., a cigarette and a cup of coffee). 　(h) Stop smoking while in bed with an illness. 　(i) Stop smoking during vacation or on a relaxing day if smoking tends to be associated with stressful situations. 　(j) Have a friend stop smoking at the same time. 　(k) Utilize a replacement for the oral gratification obtained from smoking (e.g., gum chewing). 2. Encourage family to be supportive during patient's efforts to alter smoking habits. 3. Encourage family to provide positive feedback for attempts and accomplishments made by the patient in alterations in smoking habit.

REFERENCES

American Lung Association. *Chronic obstructive pulmonary disease: a manual for physicians*. New York: American Lung Association, 1973a.

American Lung Association. *Facts about selected respiratory conditions in the United States*. National Center for Health Statistics, Rockville, Md.: Public Health Service, Series 10, No. 110, 1976a.

American Lung Association. *Facts about selected respiratory conditions in the United States*. National Health Survey, Rockville, Md.: Public Health Service, Series 10, No. 84, 1973b.

American Lung Association. *Facts about selected respiratory conditions in the United States*. Social Security Disability Applicant Statistics, Social Security Administration. Baltimore: Office of Research and Statistics (personal communication), 1976b.

Barstow, R. Coping with emphysema, *Nursing Clinics of North America.* 1974, *9* (1), 137-145.

Department of Health, Education, and Welfare, Public Health Service. *The health consequences of smoking*. Department of Health, Education, and Welfare Publications, No. 72-7516, Washington, D.C.: GPO, 1973, 3.

Dudley, D., Wermuth, C., and Hague, W. Psychological aspects of care of the chronic obstructive pulmonary disease patient, *Heart and Lung,* 1973, *2* (3), 389-393.

Erikson, E. *Childhood and society*. New York: W. W. Norton and Co., Inc., 1963.

Fuhs, M. Smoking and the heart patient. *Nursing Clinics of North America.* 1976, *11* (2), 361-369.

Fuhs, M., and Stein, A. Better ways to cope with COPD, *Nursing '76.* 1976, *6* (2), 28-38.

Mueller, R., Keble, D., Plummer, J., and Walker, S. The prevalence of chronic bronchitis, chronic airway obstruction, and respiratory symptoms in a Colorado city, *American Review of Respiratory Disease.* 1971, *103,* 209-228.

Mueller, R., Petty, T., and Filley, G. Ventilation and arterial blood gas changes induced by pursed lip breathing, *Journal of Applied Physiology.* 1970, *28* (6), 784-489.

Paley, A., and Luparello, T. Understanding the psychologic factors in asthma, *Geriatrics.* 1973, *28* (8), 54-62.

Petty, T., Hudson, L., and Neff, T. Methods of ambulatory care, *Medical Clinics of North America.* 1973, *57* (3), 751-761.

Spain, D., Siegel, H., and Bradess, V. Emphysema in apparently healthy adults, *Journal of the American Medical Association.* 1973, *224* (3), 322-325.

11

The Patient with an
ALTERATION
IN
METABOLIC FUNCTION

INTRODUCTION

Metabolic alterations, such as Addison's disease, hyperthyroidism, hypo-thyroidism, Cushing's syndrome, and diabetes mellitus, constitute some of the major health care problems in the United States today. Diabetes mellitus is probably the most commonly encountered metabolic disorder. Therefore, this chapter will deal exclusively with the impact created by diabetes mellitus upon the afflicted individual's well-being.

Diabetes mellitus is defined as a chronic metabolic alteration involving a disorder in carbohydrate metabolism which eventually leads to derangement of protein and fat metabolism. The exact cause of diabetes mellitus is un-known, but the condition inevitably develops as a result of persistent insulin deficiency. Not only is this a chronic condition requiring life-long therapy, but frequently it is associated with the major causes of death in the United States: ischemic heart disease, hypertension, and renal failure (Felig, 1976). Cer-tain individuals are identified as being especially susceptible to diabetes, for example, older people, obese people, women who have had many children, and people who have diabetic relatives (Luckmann and Sorensen, 1974).

It is estimated that between 4 million and 6 million individuals in the United States have diagnosed diabetes mellitus with an additional 2 million being undiagnosed (Felig, 1976). It is evident that an increasing number of people are diagnosed each year. No doubt this is because people live longer, a large proportion of older, more susceptible individuals are alive, diagnostic tests are being improved, and the public is becoming increasingly aware of the alteration.

CLASSIFICATION OF DIABETES MELLITUS

Juvenile diabetes and adult-onset diabetes are the two identifiable types of diabetes. In juvenile diabetes the condition generally appears before the age of fifteen years, manifests an absolute deficiency in insulin, and can be controlled by insulin injections along with a therapeutic diet and exercise program. By comparison, adult-onset diabetes usually occurs in obese individuals over forty years of age, manifests a partial insulin deficiency, and often is controlled by diet and oral hypoglycemic agents.

Although juvenile and adult-onset diabetes may differ in age of onset, etiology, and means of treatment, both tend to demonstrate the same four cardinal symptoms: polyuria, polydypsia, weight loss, and polyphagia. Polyuria (frequent urination) occurs as a result of decreased water reabsorption by the renal tubules due to osmotic activity of the increased blood glucose levels. Polydypsia (excessive thirst) results from polyuria which can create a state of dehydration and subsequent thirst. Weight loss may result since glucose is not available to the cells and since fat and protein stores are broken down and utilized for energy. Polyphagia (excessive hunger) occurs as a result of tissue breakdown and wasting which, in turn, creates a state of starvation compelling the individual to eat in excess.

Regardless of whether the adult sustained the diabetes during childhood or during adulthood, many of the ramifications of the impact of the illness are the same. Diabetes mellitus has an effect upon the stricken individual's emotional well-being, somatic identity, sexuality, occupational identity, and social role.

IMPACT OF DIABETES MELLITUS

Emotional Impact*

Exactly which behavioral manifestations set the diabetic apart from other individuals has been pursued by researchers. Several investigators have directed their attention toward the personality traits of individuals with diabetes mellitus. Their findings have identified behaviors such as passivity, dependency, immaturity, insecurity, indecisiveness, and masochism (Dunbar, Wolfe, and Rioch, 1936), but these behaviors are similar to those found in individuals with other chronic illnesses. Hence, many clinicians refute the association of any specific personality traits with diabetes mellitus and feel that behavioral manifestations exhibited by the diabetic are simply reactions to the condition itself (Kolff, 1974).

*It is advisable for the reader to have read Chapters 1 and 3 before continuing with this section.

How the newly diagnosed diabetic responds to the illness is of importance to all members of the health care team. As with any major stressful situation, the individual's response to the stress can be predicted somewhat by how he or she has dealt with stress in the past. Has the individual been able to deal with prior losses? What have been his or her responses to previous stressors? Farberow, Stein, Darbonne, and Hirsch (1970) have found that for some diabetics the presence of the illness serves as an outlet for feelings of frustration and inadequacy. Yet for others it may provide a fast means of reestablishing a nurturing relationship. When assessing the diabetic's response to illness, the nurse should be cognizant of the role diabetes mellitus plays for the individual affected.

Often the newly diagnosed diabetic may view the illness as a lifelong disability that negatively affects every aspect of his or her life. Such a response can create difficulties for the nurse when attempts are made to teach necessary health care therapies. If the meaning of food goes beyond that of meeting one's nutritional needs, it may be extremely difficult for the diabetic to make alterations in eating habits. Some adult insulin-dependent diabetics have been noted to manifest anxiety and depression related to fears for the future, worries about complications such as vascular disease, and concerns about severe hypoglycemia (Sanders, Mills, Martin, and Horne, 1975). Therefore, before initiating instructions on necessary therapies, such as dietary alterations and insulin injection, it is advisable for the nurse to assess the meaning that each therapy holds for the diabetic.

Once the meaning that the therapy holds for the diabetic has been identified, the nurse and the diabetic can proceed with the necessary health care instruction. However, as the therapies are carried out, the meaning which they hold must be incorporated into the diabetic's therapeutic program. For example, if dietary habits have religious or cultural ramifications, the patient, nutritionist, and nurse can plan the diet with these considerations in mind. Many clinicians have found that a more liberal approach to the diabetic diet is better because the diabetic is more likely to adhere to it than to a strictly regimented approach.

If the diabetic demonstrates passivity and dependency about injecting himself or herself, the nurse must structure the teaching plan accordingly. For example, on the first teaching encounter, the nurse can assume the total task of insulin administration. With each subsequent insulin injection, the diabetic should be encouraged to assume more responsibility for the drug administration. Each time the diabetic assumes more responsibility, positive feedback should be provided. This teaching approach should continue until the diabetic assumes total responsibility for self-administration of the insulin. It can be seen that in a situation such as this teaching insulin administration in the acute care setting should not be left until the day prior to discharge. As the diabetic is instructed about diet and drug therapy, family members also need to be included. They serve both as augmentors and backups for the diabetic's necessary health care therapies.

Denial, anger, depression, and negotiation may be responses exhibited by the newly diagnosed diabetic. It must be remembered that the diabetic is undergoing loss of wellness and, therefore, will experience the stages of loss. The reader is advised to consult Chapter 3 for further information about dealing with the stages of loss.

The effect that stress has upon the diabetic is of extreme importance in planning and dealing with his or her care. Stress may include experiences such as pregnancy, infection, surgery, trauma, or loss of a loved one. Stress, be it physiological or emotional, can evoke bodily reactions that are unfavorable to the control of diabetes. For example, the sympathetic nervous system is activated in time of stress and the result is an increased production of epinephrine. Epinephrine activates glycogenolysis and the result is an increase in blood glucose. During a stress, such as surgery, an acceleration of biologic forces opposing the peripheral tissue utilization of insulin occurs along with an increased release of hepatic glucose. The result again leads to an increased blood glucose (Shuman, 1975). These normal responses to stress can grossly upset the diabetic's precarious metabolic state. In fact, stressful situations have been the precipitating factors that have led to the diagnosis of diabetes mellitus in some individuals (Luckmann and Sorensen, 1974).

To assist the diabetic and the family in coping with stress, the nurse needs to encourage them to identify and discuss any situation that the diabetic finds stressful. To illustrate, if the diabetic finds certain food preparations repulsive, he or she and members of the family may wish to discuss how best to prepare the food to enhance its palatability for everyone. If frequent telephone calls from friends during mealtime produce stress for the diabetic, the nurse should encourage the family to ask friends not to call when the family generally eats. Regardless of which situations are stressful to the diabetic, they must be openly identified and dealt with by the diabetic and the family. If they are ignored, the diabetic's metabolic state is likely to be in a constant state of instability.

While initiating diabetic care and teaching, the nurse must consider the occurrence of behavioral responses to an alteration in glucose level. The nurse, the diabetic, and the family should assess behavioral changes such as nervousness, difficulty in concentrating, mood swings, irritability, shakiness, and drowziness which might occur prior to a metabolic upset. If any of these behavioral responses is identifiable the diabetic's physical state should be assessed. For example, has the diabetic taken the insulin or hypoglycemic agents? Has the diabetic eaten too much or not enough? Has the diabetic recently engaged in excessive exercise? Has a stressful situation recently been encountered by the diabetic? Once the answers to these questions and the diabetic's presenting signs and symptoms (e.g., hunger, sweating, thirst, headache) are evaluated, it can be determined whether a state of hyperglycemia or hypoglycemia is occurring. Once the metabolic state is identified, then the appropriate medical therapy can be instituted.

While assessing the diabetic's behavioral responses, the nurse needs to be aware of whether or not these behavioral responses are the diabetic's attempt to control others or his or her environment. In other words, is the diabetic using the illness as an excuse to manifest irritability or overt anxiety? The nurse, diabetic, and family members should discuss the diabetic's behavioral reactions in an attempt to identify if the illness is being used for secondary gains. If the diabetic is using the illness for secondary gains, this fact should be pointed out and the diabetic should be encouraged to discuss his or her feelings. If the manifestations of behavioral reactions for secondary gains are not dealt with openly, the diabetic is likely to increase turmoil within the family structure and hence increase the possibilities of stressful situations. In turn, these stressful situations upset the diabetic's already precarious metabolic state.

In summary, how the diabetic responds to the diabetes depends upon how he or she views the ramifications of the illness and how well he or she has coped with stress and loss in the past. How the diabetic interprets the illness and the necessary therapies will subsequently determine the nurse's approach to diabetic care.

Somatic Impact*

The effect that diabetes mellitus has upon one's body image can vary considerably. Somatic alterations caused by the illness may be so diverse as to range from no outward changes in bodily structure to bilateral amputations of the lower extremities.

When assessing the somatic impact of diabetes mellitus, the nurse first must assess the severity of the disease process and what health care therapies are required for control. The individual who is capable of controlling the illness by alterations in diet will undoubtedly feel differently about his or her body image caused by the diabetes from the individual who is required to control his or her diet, regulate exercise, and inject himself or herself every day with insulin. Once the variables that can affect the diabetic's body image are identified, the nurse can progress with planning and initiating appropriate health care teaching.

If the diabetic requires daily injections of insulin, the nurse needs to assess how the diabetic perceives the act of sticking himself or herself with a needle and placing medications into his or her body tissues. It must not be

---

*It is advisable for the reader to have read Chapter 2 before continuing with this section.

forgotten that injecting oneself with a needle is an invasion of body boundaries and the diabetic may view it as just that. In addition, although the act of injecting oneself with a needle is relatively painless, the diabetic may view the insulin injections as an assault upon his or her body structure and hence upon his or her body image.

To assist the diabetic in dealing with his or her thoughts about how the insulin therapy affects him or her somatically, the diabetic requires encouragement to verbalize his or her feelings to the health care team and family members. By verbalizing these thoughts, the diabetic not only may decrease his or her own anxieties, but these verbalizations also can provide additional data for the nurse to utilize in the planning of care. For example, knowing that the diabetic has uneasy feelings about invading his or her body boundaries and inflicting some discomfort, the nurse may find it helpful to reinforce proper injection techniques. Many clinicians have found that in trying to alleviate unnecessary fears, it is helpful to demonstrate the techniques of injection and to have the diabetic do a series of return demonstrations. Above all, providing the diabetic with positive reinforcement on the use of proper injection techniques is vital.

Teaching the diabetic to use proper wrist action when injecting aids in avoiding unnecessary discomfort caused by gradual entry of the needle into the skin. Encouraging the use of sharp needles is also helpful. Diabetics who use disposable needles, most likely, will not encounter so great a problem with dull needles as those who utilize reusable needles. In addition, it is of great importance to instruct the diabetic to inject the insulin deep into the subcutaneous tissue, not to use cold insulin, and to rotate injection sites in an attempt to avoid the development of lipodystrophy. Lipodystrophy can be an additional unwanted change in body image since it creates a noticeable thickening or dimpling of body tissue.

In addition to dealing with the diabetic's ability to administer the insulin, family members should be taught the techniques of insulin administration. If the diabetic is unable to administer the insulin, he or she still will be able to receive the required insulin therapy from a family member.

Some diabetics may experience the somatic impact of loss of sensation in peripheral body parts as a result of neuropathy. When this occurs an assault to one's body image results. No longer does the diabetic perceive his or her body boundaries as they once existed since a retraction in body boundaries is likely to occur. One of the greatest problems that develops with loss of sensation to body parts is the potential for injury. When the diabetic's body parts no longer have normal sensation, the diabetic is more likely to burn, cut, break, or injure himself or herself in some way. Therefore, the diabetic and the family require assistance in identifying and carrying out ways of preventing injury. For example, using a heating pad to warm the feet may prove hazardous and cause burns. Going barefoot is extremely dangerous for the diabetic since cuts in the skin may go unnoticed and serve as potential sites for infection. Since the diabetic's healing process is impaired, infection can have devastating effects.

Vascular changes are another bodily alteration that can occur as a result of diabetes mellitus. Because of the vascular changes, ulcerations of the lower extremities may result. The ulcerations may range from small to very large wound sites and the diabetic's reaction to these ulcerations will vary. Responses may include feelings of contamination, disgust, and anger at the thought of the unpleasant appearance of the ulceration.

To aid the diabetic in dealing with the somatic impact of ulceration, the diabetic should be informed that the occurrence of ulcers is not uncommon. Being aware that ulcer formation is not unique to the individual's diabetes may prove somewhat reassuring. Verbalizing feelings about his or her bodily appearance because of these ulcerations is vital. In addition to allowing for a mechanism to release anxieties, the diabetic may also identify ways in which to cope with feelings about the altered body image. In addition, providing encouragement about the improvement that results in the healing of the ulceration is beneficial. However, at no time should the diabetic receive false reassurance. When stating that improvement has occurred in the wound, it is best for the nurse to state the improvement in specific terms. For example, comments such as the following may prove beneficial: "The ulceration appears less inflamed." "The ulceration has more granulation tissue." or "The tissue surrounding the ulceration has a healthy color."

Appropriate wound care for the ulcerative site is necessary. Carrying out the wound care may be the responsibility of the diabetic or the family, especially if the diabetic is in the home setting. Demonstrating the care of the wound to the diabetic and the family and requiring a return demonstration prove most helpful. The nurse working in the community setting may find it necessary to make frequent home visits until the diabetic and the family feel comfortable in dealing with wound care. If the ulcerations require débridement (more likely to occur in the acute care setting), the purpose of the procedure requires explanation. Débridement can be uncomfortable and is a further assault upon one's body image. Again, verbalization of how the diabetic feels about his or her altered body image is helpful.

Unfortunately, some diabetics require amputations because there have been vascular changes. Such a procedure creates a major alteration in body boundaries and subsequent alterations in body image. The reader is advised to consult Chapter 4 for material related to the care of an individual undergoing an amputation.

Blindness is another complication resulting from changes in vascularity. Approximately 10 percent of blindness (in all age groups) is a result of diabetic retinopathy. For individuals between the ages of forty-five and seventy-four, 20 percent of all new cases of blindness are a result of diabetic retinopathy (Kahn and Moorhead, 1973). Thus, visual impairment is a major complication of diabetes. Undoubtedly, fear of losing one's sight as a result of diabetes is a common reaction in the diabetic. When blindness occurs, one's body image is altered since sensory reception is affected. To aid the diabetic in dealing with alteration in visual function, the reader is advised to consult Chapter 15 for appropriate material.

The diabetic's response to alterations in body image is affected by the diabetic's developmental stage at the time of the body change. If the diabetic is in the stage of young adulthood (eighteen to forty-five years), he or she may find such complications as ulceration, amputation, or blindness a hindrance to intimacy formation with others (Erikson, 1963). If these apparent bodily changes are not dealt with appropriately, they could cause the young adult diabetic to retreat into isolation. He or she may believe that the ulcerated or missing extremity or the visual impairment makes him or her less than perfect and, therefore, an undesirable companion in both friendship and in a sexually satisfying relationship. The female diabetic may find ulcerations more difficult to deal with since she tends to devote more attention to her body than does the male diabetic. On the other hand, the male diabetic may encounter more difficulty in coping with blindness since he is more likely to interpret such a change as an impediment to achievement.

The diabetic experiencing the stage of adulthood (forty-five to sixty-five years) may encounter difficulties in achieving the task of generativity (Erikson, 1963). Ulcerations, an amputation, or blindness may lead the diabetic to believe that he or she is ill-equipped to guide future generations with the hope of improving society. An ulcerated or missing limb or blindness may be interpreted as a prelude to premature old age, and as a result the diabetic may retreat into isolation and self-pity.

The stage of maturity (sixty-five years and older) brings with it the task of ego integrity (Erikson, 1963). If the mature adult has developed a strong sense of self-worth and is able to place value in past life experiences, he or she most likely will not develop a feeling of despair. But if the individual has not developed a strong sense of self-worth, he or she may view bodily changes, such as an amputation or blindness, as signs of premature death. Frequent thoughts of death are not uncommon for adults in the stage of maturity. The diabetic encountering complications of the illness may experience even more frequent thoughts of death. The mature adult diabetic may feel great despair and manifest it by demonstrations of disgust.

In summary, it is apparent that diabetics encounter many assaults upon their body image. Invasion of body boundaries occurs when insulin injections are required. Changes in body boundary limits take place as a result of ulceration and amputation. Sensory perception is altered when diabetic retinopathy causes blindness. Finally, how the individual deals with body image alterations can be affected by the individual's stage of development. To assist the diabetic in dealing with the somatic impact of diabetes, the nurse must be aware of how the diabetic views his or her bodily changes and be cognizant of what approaches to use in assisting the diabetic in coping with these somatic alterations.

Sexual Impact

Sexual dysfunction is a common complication of diabetes mellitus for both men and women. All too often this fact is overlooked by health care professionals as they plan and initiate diabetic health care therapies. Researchers have demonstrated that the most frequent sexual dysfunction in the male diabetic is impotence (Goldman, Schechter, and Eckerling, 1970; Abelson, 1975). Some investigators have reported an incidence of impotence among diabetics as high as 40 percent (Faerman, Glacer, Fox, Jadzinsky, and Rapaport, 1974). Other studies have noted a two to five times greater occurrence of impotence in diabetics than in the general population (Rubin and Babbott, 1958). Although the incidence of impotence tends to increase with age, there does not appear to be any relationship between the frequency of impotence and the duration of the diabetes (Kolodny, Kahn, Goldstein, and Barnett, 1974).

Extensive research has been conducted in an attempt to identify the mechanisms involved in the diabetic's impotence. Faerman and associates (1972 and 1974) noted that the diabetic male often has thickening and beading of the penile nerves. Abelson (1975) noted that the diabetic male has a decrease in penile blood pressure and blood flow. In addition, researchers have observed calcification of the male diabetic's scrotal vessels thought to be caused by the vascular degenerative complications of the illness (Wilson and Marks, 1951). At one time, the possibility of hormonal changes was a concern, but now there is no solid evidence that a diabetic's impotence can be attributed to a deficiency of testosterone (Faerman, Vilar, Rivarola, Rosner, Jadzinsky, Fox, Perez Lloret, Bernstein-Hahn, and Saraceni, 1972).

In addition to impotence, impaired sperm motility, normal to low ejaculate volume, and normal to high sperm counts have been demonstrated (Bartak, Josifko, and Horackova, 1975). However, impaired sperm motility appears to be the most consistent finding in the analysis of the ejaculate.

Ejaculation malfunction is another possible sexual disorder that can occur in the diabetic male. Premature ejaculation and retrograde ejaculation (ejaculation into the bladder) are the two ejaculatory difficulties that occur (Kolodny, Kahn, Goldstein, and Barnett, 1974). Premature ejaculation is felt to be caused by an emotional disturbance whereas retrograde ejaculation has an anatomical basis (Spellacy, 1976), a smooth muscle dysfunction caused by a nerve deficit (Kolodny, Kahn, Goldstein, and Barnett, 1974). The evidence of sexual dysfunction in male diabetics is well-known but few studies have been published documenting the incidence of such problems in diabetic females. Kolodny (1971) noted that orgasmic dysfunction was significantly more prevalent among diabetic women than among nondiabetic women. In addition, his findings demonstrated that the appearance of sexual dysfunction in diabetic women correlated with the duration of the illness. However, no association with age, insulin dose, or complication (e.g., nephropathy, neuropathy, or vaginitis) existed.

When identifying the presence of a sexual dysfunction, such as impotence, the possibility of psychogenic factors should be considered. Since there are no data that reflect the frequency of psychogenic versus organic impotence, psychogenic factors should be considered as a possible cause. If the sexual dysfunction is automatically ascribed as being organic without proper assessment and it is, in fact, psychogenic, a treatable symptom may go unmanaged.

Once the type of sexual dysfunction is identified (organic or psychogenic), then appropriate therapy may be initiated. In the case of organic impotence, most therapies have proven to be limited in their success, but this does not mean that the diabetic's problem simply should be dismissed. The problem is very real to the individual and one of the major functions of the nurse is to assist the diabetic in coping with his organic impotence. Encouraging the diabetic to verbalize his feelings to health care members and to the sex partner is vital. It is extremely important for the diabetic and the sex partner to discuss openly the diabetic's feelings about the sexual dysfunction. Does the individual see himself as less than a man? Does the diabetic think that he is imperfect? When the sex partner is aware of the diabetic's feelings about the sexual dysfunction, emotional support is more likely to be provided by the sex partner. In addition, the affected male diabetic requires reassurance that the occurrence of impotence is not unique to him, but tends to be present in a large percentage of diabetics. Simply realizing that he is not the only individual affected can aid in relieving some anxiety.

Whether the impotence is organic or psychogenic, the diabetic needs to be reassured that sexual activity can continue. Although caressing body parts may prove sexually satisfying for some individuals, using the "stuffing technique" (simply stuffing the penis into the vagina) may be desirable for other couples. The important part is for the diabetic and the sex partner to find a mutually satisfying means of sexual expression. Some couples may encounter difficulties in identifying ways of achieving sexual satisfaction and, as a result, require sex counseling. After sex consultation, the use of a collapsible Silastic penile implant that allows for erection by means of manual control (Kolff, 1974; Guthrie, and Guthrie, 1977) may be suggested.

A fear of being unable to produce children may be an expressed concern of the male diabetic with sexual dysfunction. If the diabetic's semen quality is adequate, fertilization is very possible. In cases of retrograde ejaculation, bladder washings to retrieve sperm for artificial insemination have proven successful (Bourne, Kretzchmar, and Esser, 1971). If, however, the diabetic male encounters fertility problems, he should be advised to seek fertility counseling. Above all, the diabetic male needs reassurance that the children conceived by diabetic fathers are not discernibly different from those of nondiabetic fathers (Babbott, Rubin, and Ginsburg, 1958).

Diabetic females may express concern about their ability to conceive children. Since stillbirths, abortions, and large birth-weight babies are more frequent among diabetic women than nondiabetic women, such facts must be shared with the diabetic female contemplating a family. If the diabetic female becomes pregnant, the necessity for close medical supervision should be stressed in order to maintain the health of both the expectant mother and child. In addition, genetic counseling is extremely important. Both diabetic men and diabetic women must be aware that diabetes can be genetically transmitted. Therefore, genetic counseling is necessary so that both partners recognize the problems of disease transmission.

Since the susceptibility toward infection is higher in the diabetic, the occurrence of vaginitis may be common in the female diabetic. The presence of such a condition not only can prove uncomfortable for the female, but because of this discomfort, it may also affect her desire to partake in coitus. Thus, the diabetic female should be taught the necessity of good feminine hygiene.

The presence of a neurogenic bladder also may affect the diabetic's sexual activity. If the individual is not adequately instructed on the crede's maneuver, which aids in emptying the bladder, the chances of overflow incontinence can occur. If overflow incontinence occurs during sexual activity, either partner may find the accident unappealing and hence refrain from sexual contact.

In summary, the diabetic's sexual activity can be affected by a number of factors. Such factors may include impotence, inadequate semen quality, ejaculation malfunction, vaginitis, and a neurogenic bladder. The nurse's role is to assist the diabetic in coping with existing difficulties that affect sexual activity and at guiding the diabetic to seek appropriate sexual, fertility, and genetic counseling. Above all, the diabetic should always be encouraged to maintain good diabetic control in an attempt to decrease the rapidity with which complications occur.

Occupational Impact

The impact that diabetes mellitus has upon the individual's work situation varies considerably from one person to another. Investigators have found that, in general, diabetics are not subject to undue discrimination in employment, since the majority of diabetics are of the adult-onset type (Tetrick and Colwell, 1971). How the diabetic is dealt with when he or she is seeking employment is affected by various factors. For example, if the diabetic's employment requires a physical examination prior to hiring, some companies may hesitate to employ the diabetic. This is especially true in the case of nonprofessional workers (Desimone, 1977). Instead of looking at the individual's abilities and motivation, the company considers its regulations and policies, which often include not hiring anyone with a physical ailment or disability.

The nonprofessional worker who is qualified for only a limited range of jobs will encounter additional problems in employment opportunities if the diabetes makes him or her unacceptable for those jobs for which he or she is trained. Jobs that are often considered ill-advised for the diabetic include those that involve heavy physical labor, rotating shifts, operation of dangerous machinery, military service, or periods of prolonged walking or standing.

In comparison to the nonprofessional worker, the professional worker encounters fewer difficulties in finding employment. The employer is more likely to be interested in the professional worker's credentials and past work achievement than in the diabetes (Desimone, 1977). Since professionals more often can control their work activities and environment, diabetes is not as threatening to job security and health safety. For example, a teacher generally can stop what he or she is doing in order to take required glucose or insulin, but the individual who is working on an assembly line in a factory cannot do this.

The most important factor for determining a diabetic's work placement is the status of diabetic control (Alexander, Tetrick, and Friedman, 1974). Undoubtedly, the status of control is affected by the severity of the illness, the adequacy of medical management, and the presence of complications (Alexander, Tetrich, and Friedman, 1974). Research has demonstrated that diabetics miss fewer work days than nondiabetics (Moore and Buschbom, 1974). Hence, some industries and companies are becoming more lenient and more understanding about placing diabetics in jobs. However, the diabetic who is poorly controlled and/or suffers from complications will encounter problems in securing and maintaining employment. To illustrate, the diabetic who is suffering from impaired vision caused by retinopathy may have difficulty maintaining a job if the job requires extensive reading. The presence of impaired sensation in the hands caused by diabetic neuropathy will create problems for the individual who works around objects, such as glass, which could cause injury. In such a case, trauma may occur but go unnoticed as a result of the impaired sensation.

Once a company decides to hire a diabetic, the jobs he or she may receive can be limited. For example, occupations which may enhance the occurrence of complications are best avoided (e.g., jobs with rotating shifts or jobs requiring prolonged standing). As a result, the diabetic may have to take a job that he or she finds unappealing or one that has a lower pay scale.

In addition to the problems of securing and maintaining employment, the diabetic may have to deal with the lifelong financial burden of diabetes. Insulin, syringes, and/or oral hypoglycemic agents are an additional expense. For diabetics who are on a low or fixed income, this financial burden can be overwhelming.

The nurse's responsibility in assisting the diabetic undergoing the occupational impact of the illness is to aid the diabetic in dealing with the impact and to help him or her prevent diabetic complications that may be provoked by the job situation. Since finding suitable employment may be difficult for some diabetics, the nurse needs to encourage the diabetic to express his or her feelings to health care members and family members about the job situation, for verbalizing these feelings can aid in decreasing some of the anxiety. In addition, family members are more likely to be supportive if they understand the frustrations experienced by the diabetic. If the financial situation becomes unmanageable, family members may find it necessary to supplement the income. Above all, the diabetic should never be encouraged to lie about the illness to employers. Not being truthful about the illness could be life threatening if ketoacidosis or hypoglycemia occur.

If the diabetic encounters extreme difficulties in finding employment, the nurse may encourage the individual to seek assistance from an occupational therapist or rehabilitation counselor. If the diabetic is prepared to perform only a limited number of skills and these skills are considered out of the question for the individual, he or she may need job training.

Assisting the diabetic in identifying job situations that can contribute to diabetic complications is vital. The occupational nurse is in an excellent position for this intervention. For example, if the diabetic's job responsibilities encompass prolonged standing or walking, proper foot care should be encouraged since plantar ulceration can be a major complication (Stokes, Faris, and Hutton, 1975). If the diabetic must stand for prolonged periods of time, he or she should be instructed to carry out isotonic exercises because they aid in facilitating venous return and hence decrease the possibility of ulcer formation. If the diabetic works around objects that can create injury, such as glass, the use of protective devices (e.g., gloves) should be encouraged, unless, of course, the devices increase the chances of injury, as in the case of certain machinery. Frequent examination of extremities for injury should be stressed. Periodically observing the hands for cuts throughout the day can aid in identifying possible sources of infection. If there is a cut, immediate treatment should be instituted.

In summary, the occupational impact of diabetes varies among diabetics. Research has indicated that the majority of diabetics do not encounter extreme difficulties since most of them are of the adult-onset type, but if the diabetic does encounter difficulties, he or she requires assistance in dealing with the impact of the difficult job situation and in preventing diabetic complications that can be provoked by the work environment. Above all, the diabetic needs continual encouragement and support to carry out proper diabetic control. Fortunately, some companies and industries are becoming more lenient and understanding about hiring diabetics.

Social Impact

The presence of diabetes mellitus can create an impact upon the adult diabetic's social role. Often newly diagnosed diabetics may feel that since dietary control is necessary, they will have to discontinue social dining both in restaurants and at the homes of friends. The diabetic needs to be assured that such a practice is not necessary. With the assistance of the dietician the diabetic can learn how to select appropriate foods from restaurant menus and from the hostess's dining table. If the diabetic attends a banquet where the meal is already served on the plate, he or she can learn to eat appropriate portions of necessary food to meet nutritional requirements.

Often diabetics express concern about attending cocktail parties where alcoholic beverages and fancy foods are readily available. Concerns are related to being tempted by the presence of many tasty foods and appearing unusual because others are drinking when they are not. Possible suggestions which the nurse may offer include advising the diabetic who is planning to attend a cocktail party to include in the daily nutritional requirements a fruit juice drink or a low-calorie drink. The fruit juice drink or the low-calorie drink can be garnished with orange slices and cherries just like any alcoholic drink. In dealing with the presence of many tempting foods, the diabetic can utilize maneuvers that decrease contact with foods, such as not standing close to the table containing the tempting culinary delights. The diabetic may want to use maneuvers often suggested for the obese individual who is attending a party. For further details on these maneuvers the reader is advised to consult Chapter 7.

Travel may present questions concerning health maintainence for some diabetics. The most frequent expressed concerns deal with the fear of loss of diabetic control and with how to transport insulin. To aid in preventing loss of control, the diabetic should maintain regularity in medication, diet, and exercise during travel. Simply carrying out the diabetic routine as usual will tend to prevent the occurrence of difficulties.

The transportation of insulin need not create undue difficulties for the traveling diabetic. Manufacturers of insulin (Lilly Research Laboratories, personal communication, 1975) state that insulin kept at room temperature will not undergo significant lowering of activity during the period of time that a single vial is in use. Of course, this is assuming that the vial will be exhausted within a few weeks, for insulin preparations are stable at room temperature for one to three months. Therefore, the vial being actively used by the diabetic may be stored at room temperature. In fact, it is better for the diabetic to administer room-temperature insulin because it reduces the chances of lipodystrophy (Luckmann and Sorensen, 1974).

The traveling diabetic is advised to carry an extra vial of insulin in case something should happen to the vial being actively used (e.g., breakage of the vial or appearance change of the insulin due to possible heat exposure). The extra vial may be kept at room temperature and then stored in a cool place, such as a refrigerator, once the diabetic reaches his or her travel destination. If the diabetic is camping for extended periods of time, keeping the extra vial of insulin in an ice chest or in an insulated bag proves workable. In addition, the traveling diabetic should obtain an extra written prescription from his or her physician as a safety precaution in case he or she needs additional insulin during the trip. This alleviates the problem of being without necessary medication.

The diabetic should carry and/or wear some kind of identification indicating that he or she is a diabetic and how he or she is maintained (e.g., insulin dosage and/or oral hypoglycemic agents). This is advisable for all diabetics, but especially for the traveling diabetic. Various forms of "medical alert" jewelry (e.g., necklaces or bracelets) are available which have the appropriate diabetic information inscribed. Some diabetics may express concern about wearing a bracelet with this information because the bracelet draws attention to their illness and, as a result, makes them feel uncomfortable. If the diabetic feels this way, the nurse might encourage him or her to wear a long-chained necklace with a medallion containing the necessary information. The necklace would not be very noticeable because it could be worn under clothing.

Complications such as ulcerations and failing vision can have social ramifications for the diabetic. If either one or both of these complications occur, the diabetic may withdraw from social interactions. He or she may feel that the ulcerations are unsightly and/or the poor vision is a hindrance to social interaction. Therefore, the nurse should encourage family members to be aware of the possibility of withdrawal if such complications occur and actively engage the diabetic in social contacts. Social interactions that draw attention to the diabetic's complications should be avoided (e.g., taking a diabetic with failing vision to a movie). For further information about dealing with individuals who have impaired vision, see Chapter 15.

In addition, encouraging the diabetic to verbalize feelings about the existence of the complications is necessary. If the diabetic continues to encounter difficulties in dealing with the diabetes and its related complications and maintains a state of isolation, group therapy may be in order. The nurse may need to send the diabetic to the psychiatric nurse clinician, to a psychologist, or to a psychiatrist.

In summary, although diabetes mellitus can have social ramifications, the diabetic, generally, should be able to carry out normal social functions with only minor alterations. The continuance of social interaction is as important for the diabetic as it is for any other individual.

SUMMARY

Diabetes mellitus, one of the most commonly encountered metabolic disorders, affects between 4 million and 6 million individuals in the United States. It is evident that this illness is increasing in prevalence. No doubt this is because people live longer, larger proportions of older, more susceptible persons are alive, diagnostic tests are being improved, and the public is becoming increasingly aware of the alteration.

An individual afflicted with diabetes mellitus is either of the juvenile-onset type or the adult-onset type. Regardless of the type of diabetes experienced by the individual, the illness creates multiple impacts upon life-style. When an individual is faced with diabetes, his or her emotional well-being, somatic identity, sexuality, occupational identity, and social role are affected. Therefore, to aid an individual in dealing with each of these areas of concern, the nurse must identify how the illness affects each component of the diabetic's life and then assist him or her in coping with each impact to the best of his or her ability.

Patient Situation

Mr. D. M., a fifty-four-year-old, married, lathe operator for a furniture company has been a diabetic for the past eight years. Over the past six months he has encountered difficulties with diabetic control while on a regulated diet and oral hypoglycemic agents. Therefore, one month ago Mr. D. M.'s family physician placed him on insulin and a regulated diet. Mrs. D. M. has been administering the insulin to her husband since it was prescribed.

Mr. D. M. is now in the furniture company's dispensary after having experienced a state of hypoglycemia during work. He is being treated for the hypoglycemia by the company's occupational health nurse. During the intervention the nurse notes that Mr. D. M. is encountering difficulties with his illness related to his emotional well-being, somatic identity, sexuality, occupational identity, and social role.

Following are Mr. D. M.'s nursing care plan and patient care cardex dealing with each of these areas of concern.

NURSING CARE PLAN

Problems	Objectives	Nursing Interventions	Principles/Rationale	Evaluations
Emotional Impact Expressed anxiety and fear about future bouts of hypoglycemia.	To decrease Mr. D. M.'s anxiety and fear.	Encourage Mr. D. M. to verbalize how he feels about his illness and the related therapies. Review with Mr. D. M. the aspects of proper diabetic control (e.g., relationship of dietary intake, insulin therapy, and exercise regime). Reassure Mr. D. M. that, with proper control, the chances of complications, such as hypoglycemia, are reduced.	Verbalization assists in decreasing one's anxieties and fears. Identifying how a diabetic feels about his illness and its related therapies assists in planning future approaches to nursing care. Increasing and reinforcing one's knowledge about one's illness and its related therapies can aid in decreasing anxiety related to fear of the unknown.	The nurse would observe for: Mr. D. M.'s verbalization about feeling secure with controlling his diabetes.
Somatic Impact Expressed feelings of uneasiness about injecting himself with insulin.	To decrease Mr. D. M.'s feelings of uneasiness about administering his own insulin.	Encourage Mr. D. M. to verbalize how he views his insulin injections.	Diabetics may view insulin injections as an assault upon their body structure and body image since the act of injecting insulin invades body boundaries. Verbalizing aids in decreasing one's anxieties. Knowing how the diabetic perceives insulin injections aids in developing an appropriate approach to teaching the	The nurse would observe for: Mr. D. M.'s verbalization of increased feelings of competence about injecting himself with insulin.

feelings of competence about administering his own insulin.	injection therapy (e.g., use of wrist action, use of sharp needles, deep subcutaneous injections).	about one's therapies can aid in decreasing anxiety related to fear of the unknown.	...balization about Mr. D. M.'s taking an active role in his insulin administration.
	Demonstrate the technique of insulin injection and have Mr. D. M. do a series of return demonstrations.	Having an individual demonstrate, under supervision, progressive abilities in carrying out insulin injections can aid in increasing a sense of security about medication self-administration.	
	Provide positive reinforcement on the use of proper injection technique.	Positive reinforcement for a job well done aids in enhancing one's feelings of self-worth.	
	Encourage Mrs. D. M. to urge her husband to carry out his own insulin injections.	Encouragement from significant others to do one's own insulin injections helps prevent the occurrence of secondary gains from the illness.	
	Encourage Mrs. D. M. to provide her husband with positive reinforcement on his administration of insulin and his use of proper injection technique.	Positive feedback from significant others aids in enhancing feelings of self-worth.	
Sexual Impact Expressed feelings of emasculation caused by impotence.			
To enhance Mr. D. M.'s feelings of manliness.	Encourage Mr. D. M. to verbalize his feelings to his wife.	A sex partner who is aware of a diabetic's feelings about sexual dysfunction is more likely to provide emotional support.	The nurse would observe for: Mr. D. M.'s verbalization that he has fewer feelings about being less than a man.
	Reassure Mr. D. M. that this problem is not unique to him but that it is present in a large percentage of diabetics.	Realizing that one is not the only individual afflicted with a problem can aid in relieving anxiety.	

NURSING CARE PLAN (cont.)

Problems	Objectives	Nursing Interventions	Principles/Rationale	Evaluations
Sexual Impact (cont.)		Encourage Mr. D. M. to see his physician so that the basis of his impotence can be identified (organic versus psychogenic).	In most cases of organic impotence caused by diabetes mellitus, past therapies have proven limited in their success. However, psychogenic impotence has proven to be a treatable symptom.	
		Encourage Mr. and Mrs. D. M. to identify means of achieving a mutually satisfying sexual experience (e.g., caressing of body parts, use of the stuffing technique). (If Mr. and Mrs. D. M. are unable to achieve sexual satisfaction, sex counseling may be suggested).	Satisfying sexual experiences can continue to exist in spite of the presence of impotence.	Mr. D. M.'s verbalization that he and his wife are achieving mutually satisfying sexual experiences.
Occupational Impact Expressed concern about being unable to maintain his position in the furniture company.	To decrease Mr. D. M.'s concerns about job security.	Encourage Mr. D. M. to carry out proper diabetic control (e.g., appropriate dietary regulation, insulin, and exercise).	Proper diabetic control can aid in decreasing the rapidity with which complications can occur.	The nurse would observe for: Mr. D. M.'s verbalization about job security.
	To facilitate Mr. D. M.'s ability to maintain his job as a lathe operator.	Encourage Mr. D. M. to recognize situations in his work environment that could provoke the incidence of diabetic complications and to carry out appropriate preventive measures (e.g., wearing gloves when handling splintered pieces of wood and wearing steel-toed shoes to prevent foot injury in case he drops a piece of wood	Carrying out maneuvers for identifying work situations that could provoke diabetic complications aids in decreasing the possible incidence of these complications. A diabetic who suffers from diabetic complications is more likely to encounter difficulties in maintaining employment.	Mr. D. M.'s identification of work situations that could provoke diabetic complications and the institution of appropriate protective maneuvers.

Social Impact				
Verbalized feelings of discomfort about attending parties that serve alcoholic beverages and fancy foods.	To increase Mr. D. M.'s feelings of comfort while attending parties that have food and alcoholic drink.	Encourage Mr. D. M. to check his hands frequently for cuts and puncture wounds and to seek attention in the dispensary immediately if he is injured.	Identifying and treating a potential source of diabetic complications aids in decreasing the incidence and severity of that complication.	The nurse would observe for: Mr. D. M.'s verbalization about increased comfort when attending social engagements where food and alcoholic drink are to be served.
		Advise Mr. D. M. that when he plans to attend a party where alcoholic drinks will be served he should include in his daily nutritional planning the allowance for a fruit juice drink or a low-caloric drink for party consumption.	Feelings of awkwardness provoked by not engaging in social drinking are decreased when the diabetic makes dietary allowances for the consumption of an allowed beverage for the social engagement.	
		Encourage Mr. D. M. to utilize maneuvers that decrease his contact with the fancy foods (e.g., not standing close to the serving table).	Decreasing the availability of tempting foods aids in preventing their consumption.	
	To prevent Mr. D. M. from withdrawing from social interaction.	Encourage Mr. D. M. to take part in social interactions.	Withdrawing from social interactions can lead to isolation which can lead to depression.	Mr. D. M.'s continuing to take part in social interaction.

PATIENT CARE CARDEX

PATIENT'S NAME:	Mr. D. M.	DIAGNOSIS:	Diabetes mellitus (insulin dependent)
AGE:	54 years	SEX:	Male
MARITAL STATUS:	Married	OCCUPATION:	Lathe operator
SIGNIFICANT OTHERS:	Wife		

Problems	Nursing Approaches
Emotional: Expressed anxiety and fear about future bouts of hypoglycemia.	1. Encourage verbalization of feelings about illness and related therapies. 2. Review aspects of proper diabetic control (relationship of dietary intake, insulin therapy, and exercise regime). 3. Point out that with proper control chances of complications are reduced.
Somatic: Expressed feelings of uneasiness about injecting self with insulin.	1. Encourage verbalization about feelings concerning insulin injections. 2. Review proper injection therapy. 3. Demonstrate injection technique and have patient do a series of return demonstrations. 4. Provide positive reinforcement on the use of proper injection technique. 5. Encourage wife to urge husband to carry out own insulin administration and to provide positive reinforcement when he does.
Sexual: Expressed feelings of emasculation caused by impotence.	1. Encourage verbalization of feelings to wife. 2. Point out that impotence is not unique to him but that it is present in a large percentage of diabetics. 3. Encourage to see physician about the basis of impotence (organic versus psychogenic). 4. Encourage patient and wife to identify means of achieving a mutually satisfying sexual experience (use of caressing and stuffing technique). (Sex counseling may be in order.)
Occupational: Expressed concern about being unable to maintain position in furniture company.	1. Encourage to carry out proper diabetic control. 2. Encourage to recognize situations in work environment that could provoke incidence of diabetic complications and to carry out appropriate preventive measures. 3. Encourage frequent checks of hands for puncture wounds and cuts and to seek appropriate

... attending parties that serve alcoholic beverages and fancy foods.

... include in his daily nutritional planning the allowance for a fruit juice drink or a low-caloric drink for party consumption.
2. Encourage to utilize maneuvers that decrease contact with fancy foods (e.g., not standing close to serving table).
3. Encourage to take part in social interactions so that he will not become an isolate.

REFERENCES

Abelson, D. Diagnostic value of the penile pulse and blood pressure: a Doppler study of impotence in diabetics, *Journal of Urology,* 1975, *113* (5), 636-639.

Alexander, R., Tetrick, L., and Friedman, G. Physicians' guidelines for the diabetic in industry, *Journal of Occupational Medicine,* 1974, *16* (12), 802-803.

Babbott, D., Rubin, A., and Ginsburg, S. The reproductive characteristics of diabetic men, *Diabetes,* 1958, *7* (1), 33-35.

Bartak, V., Josifko, M., and Horackova, M. Juvenile diabetes and human sperm quality, *International Journal of Fertility,* 1975, *20* (1), 30-32.

Bourne, R., Kretzschmar, W., and Esser, J. Successful artificial insemination in a diabetic with retrograde ejaculation, *Fertility and Sterility,* 1971, *22* (4), 275-277.

Desimone, B. Psychosocial implications of diabetes. In D. Guthrie and R. Guthrie (Eds.), *Nursing management of diabetes mellitus.* St. Louis: C. V. Mosby Co., 1977.

Dunbar, H., Wolfe, T., and Rioch, J. Psychiatric aspects of medical problems: the psychic component of the disease process (including convalescence in cardiac, diabetic, and fracture patients), *American Journal of Psychiatry,* 1936, *93,* 649-679.

Erikson, E. *Childhood and society.* New York: W. W. Norton and Co., Inc., 1963.

Faerman, I., Glacer, L., Fox, D., Jadzinsky, M., and Rapaport, M. Impotence and diabetes—histological studies of the autonomic nervous fibers of the corpora cavernosa in impotent diabetic males, *Diabetes,* 1974, *23* (12), 971-976.

Faerman, I., Vilar, O., Rivarola, M., Rosner, J., Jadzinsky, M., Fox, D., Perez Lloret, A., Berstein-Hahn, L., and Saraceni, D. Impotence and diabetes: studies of androgenic function in diabetic impotent males, *Diabetes,* 1972, *21* (1), 23-30.

Farberow, N., Stein, K., Darbonne, A., and Hirsch, S. Self-destructive behavior of uncooperative diabetes, *Psychological Reports,* 1970, *27* (3), 935-946.

Felig, P. Managing diabetes, *Postgraduate Medicine,* 1976, *59* (1), 113-122.

Goldman, J., Schechter, A., and Eckerling, B. Carbohydrate metabolism in infertile and impotent males, *Fertility and Sterility,* 1970, *21* (5), 397-401.

Guthrie, D., and Guthrie, R. The adult. In D. Guthrie and R. Guthrie (Eds.), *Nursing management of diabetes mellitus.* St. Louis: C. V. Mosby, Co., 1977.

Kahn, H., and Moorhead, H. *Statistics on blindness in the model reporting area, 1969-1970.* Washington, D.C.: U.S. Department of Health, Education and Welfare, Public Health Service, Publication No. (NIH) 73-427, 1973.

Kolff, W. Discussion: psychosocial problems, *Kidney International Supplement No. 1,* 1974, S159-S162.

Kolodny, R. Sexual dysfunction in diabetic females, *Diabetes,* 1971, *20* (8), 557-559.

Kolodny, R., Kahn, C., Goldstein, H., and Barnett, D. Sexual dysfunction in diabetic men, *Diabetes,* 1974, *23* (4), 306-309.

Lilly Research Laboratories, personal communication. Division of Eli Lilly and Co., Indianapolis, Ind., 1975.

Luckmann, J., and Sorensen, K. *Medical-surgical nursing: a psychophysiologic approach.* Philadelphia: W. B. Saunders, 1974.

Moore, R., and Buschbom, R. Work absenteeism in diabetics, *Diabetes,* 1974, *23* (12), 957-961.

Rubin, A., and Babbott, D. Impotence and diabetes mellitus, *Journal of the American Medical Association,* 1958, *168* (5), 498-500.

Sanders, K., Mills, J., Martin, F., and Horne, D. Emotional attitudes in adult insulin-dependent diabetes, *Journal of Psychosomatic Research,* 1975, *19,* 241-246.

Shuman, C. The diabetic during surgery. In J. Kryston and R. Shaw (Eds.), *Endocrinology and diabetes.* Philadelphia: Grune & Stratton, 1975.

Spellacy, W. Carbohydrate metabolism in male infertility and female fertility-control patient, *Fertility and Sterility,* 1976, *27* (10), 1132-1141.

Stokes, I., Faris, I., and Hutton, W. The neuropathic ulcer and loads on the foot in diabetic patients, *Acta Orthopaedica Scandinavica,* 1975, *46,* 839-847.

Tetrick, L., and Colwell, J. Employment of the diabetic subject, *Journal of Occupational Medicine,* 1971, *13* (8), 380-383.

Wilson, J., and Marks, J. Calcification of the vas deferens: its relation to diabetes mellitus and arteriosclerosis, *New England Journal of Medicine,* 1951, *245,* 321-325.

12

The Patient with an

ALTERATION IN GASTROINTESTINAL FUNCTION

INTRODUCTION

The prevalance of alterations in gastrointestinal function is well recognized by members of the health care system. The occurrence of gastrointestinal malfunctions, either independently or secondarily to other disease processes, is voluminous. Even the presence of diarrhea, as a result of stress, is not an uncommon occurrence for many individuals. Regardless of what G.I. malfunction occurs, its presence can have an impact on daily living.

Two relatively common gastrointestinal malfunctions that have long-term significance are peptic ulcers and ulcerative colitis. They affect different anatomical structures within the G.I. tract, but the impact that each has upon one's emotional well-being, somatic identity, sexuality, occupational identity, and social role is very similar.

ALTERATIONS IN GASTROINTESTINAL FUNCTION

Peptic ulcers are sites of ulceration formed in the mucosa, submucosa, or muscle layers of the distal esophagus, stomach, upper duodenum, or jejunum (following a gastroenterostomy). Ulcers can occur at any age, but duodenal ulcers tend to appear most often in individuals between the ages of thirty and fifty years while gastric ulcers are most prevalent in the forty to sixty age category (Isenberg, 1975). Approximately 10 percent of the population in the United States suffers from peptic ulcers (Isenberg, 1975) with men being afflicted more often than women. Research has noted that the ratio of men to women suffering from gastric ulcers is two to one, whereas the ratio of duodenal ulcers is seven to one (Morgan, 1972).

The exact cause of peptic ulcers is unknown, but various factors have been identified as contributing to the development of the ulcerations. These factors include a source of irritation in the gastrointestinal tract, such as an increase in acid secretion with a decrease in alkaline mucous production, a breakdown in local tissue resistance, and the effects of heredity, hormones, personality, and environment. Even aspirin, cola beverages, coffee, and cigarettes have been found to increase the risk of peptic ulcer formation (Grossman, Guth, Isenberg, Passaro, Roth, Sturdevant, and Walsh, 1976).

The classic symptom of an uncomplicated peptic ulcer is gnawing, burning pain in the upper abdominal or epigastric region (Brandborg, 1975). The pain characteristically occurs one to two hours after meals and not infrequently awakens the individual at night. This gnawing, burning pain is usually relieved by food or antacids.

Ulcerative colitis is an inflammatory disease involving mainly the mucosa and submucosa of the colon. Bloody diarrhea is the primary clinical manifestation. Estimates of the number of individuals afflicted by this disease process vary widely since it generally tends to be an unreported condition in children when the symptoms are mild. However, it is believed that approximately 300,000 individuals suffer from this disease in the United States (Sachar and Janowitz, 1974).

The majority of individuals suffering from ulcerative colitis have the initial onset between fifteen and forty-nine years of age (Jackson, 1973), with the peak age range of onset being sixteen to twenty years (Rogers, Clark, and Kirsner, 1971). Males and females tend to be equally afflicted by this gastrointestinal malfunction (Roger, Clark, and Kirsner, 1971). A two to four times greater incidence of ulcerative colitis occurs in those of Jewish ancestry with a distinctly lower frequency of occurrence among the blacks and members of the Spanish-American population (Sachar and Janowitz, 1974; Hertz and Rosenbaum, 1977).

Numerous theories concerning the etiology of ulcerative colitis exist. Although some of these theories have emphasized allergic, psychosomatic, vascular, genetic, immunologic, and microbiologic factors, no research has convincingly identified a specific factor as the etiological basis of this disease.

Thus, it can be seen that a large population of individuals in the United States suffers from one of two major gastrointestinal malfunctions. Peptic ulcers affect the esophagus, stomach, duodenum, and, possibly, the jejunum. They manifest themselves clinically by a gnawing, burning pain in the epigastric region. Ulcerative colitis affects the colon and presents a clinical picture of bloody diarrhea. Numerous research studies have been conducted on both disease entities, but many questions remain unanswered.

Regardless of which G.I. alteration the individual demonstrates, the impact of the illness upon the person can be overwhelming.

IMPACT OF GASTROINTESTINAL ALTERATIONS

Emotional Impact*

Most of us are well aware of the gastrointestinal reactions resulting from emotional upset. Simply traveling can place some persons into an acute state of constipation while others deal with bouts of diarrhea. Therefore, it is no wonder that for some time researchers have asked what relationship exists between the two disease entities, peptic ulcer and ulcerative colitis, and the individual's emotional state.

Investigators have identified that persons suffering from peptic ulcers demonstrate a high degree of anxiety which possibly is related to their diffi- culty in expressing feelings of hostility or aggression (Weiner, Thaler, Reiser, and Mirsky, 1957; Cohen, Silverman, Waddell, and Zwidema, 1961). Ulcer sufferers often tend to have a great deal of initiative and drive (Lewis and Lewis, 1972). They are the compulsive go-getters who are usually successful in their occupations. Their occupational fields of endeavor often are demanding and require quick decision and the constant need to resolve problems (Lewis and Lewis, 1972). In addition, researchers have noted that persons who suffer from neurotic illnesses, especially neurotic depres- sion, appear to be more prone to peptic ulcers (Wretmark, 1953; Gosling, 1958). However, Gosling (1958) believes that the neurosis in ulcer patients may well be brought about by the ulcer itself.

Since the ulcer victim tends to be a compulsive go-getter who is success- ful in his or her occupation, the occupational situation often has been iden- tified as the sole contributor to the formation of the disease process. This is not necessarily true. Rather, the sufferer often is undergoing a conflict re- lated to his or her dependency-independency status. The majority of indi- viduals suffering from ulcers have an intense need to be independent (Lewis and Lewis, 1972). Emotionally, the individual has developed a superego that forbids the expression of the need for dependence (Evans, 1971). As a result, the adult tends to overcompensate by being overzealous in giving the impression of being self-sufficient, ambitious, competent, aggressive, and independent (Evans, 1971; Lewis and Lewis, 1972). The individual may refuse to accept assistance from others and may burden himself or herself with excessive responsibilities. These excessive responsibilities and the con- tinual struggle to deal with them only reinforce the desire for a dependent

*It is advisable for the reader to have read Chapters 1 and 3 before continuing with this section.

relationship. Beneath the façade of self-confidence lies an individual with strong dependency needs.

Unfortunately, one of the most devastating consequences of peptic ulcers is the widely held misconception that the gastrointestinal alteration is brought about exclusively by psychic stress. Members of the health care team who adhere to this belief are prone to blame the individual for creating the illness. This view is disastrous for the ulcer-prone person who must disguise his or her dependency needs as he or she copes with the illness (Engel, 1971). The outcome is likely to be administration of ineffective therapy on the part of the health team member, feelings of guilt on the part of the ulcer victim, and additional unneeded stress in the environment.

Regardless of whether the dependency-independency conflict brought about the ulcer or the ulcer created the dependency-independency conflict, the presence of the conflict exists. In either situation, a vicious cycle ensues since one state tends to feed into the other. Unless this vicious cycle is broken by appropriate intervention, the peptic ulcer sufferer's acute illness can result in a state of chronic illness.

Individuals suffering from ulcerative colitis are similar to persons afflicted with peptic ulcers in that they too tend to manifest certain behavioral responses. Investigators have identified the primary response to be the existence of conflict between rebellion and compliance (Castelnuovo-Tedesco, 1962; Prugh, 1950). In other words, the individual desires to be loved and accepted, but the individual identifies in himself or herself unacceptable feelings of anger and resentment toward the very ones from whom he or she requires love and acceptance. Some researchers believe that these conflicting feelings are brought about by an unresolved loss. Such a loss could be a disruptive relationship with a mother, father, family member, or any other key person (Castelnuovo-Tedesco, Schwertfeger, and Janowsky, 1970).

Because of the individual's inability to deal with the conflicts of rebellion versus complicance, anger and resentment are not adequately expressed. As a result, the mucous membranes of the colon respond to these suppressed emotions (Lewis and Lewis, 1972) and become inflamed and ulcerated. The typical victim often manifests immaturity, dependency, rigidity, perfectionism, and wariness of others (MacLean, 1976). The symptoms of the disease process tend to appear when the individual is confronted with a situation that appears uncontrollable to him or her (Lewis and Lewis, 1972). Along with the conflict between rebellion and compliance, the person afflicted with ulcerative colitis often manifests feelings of hopelessness and despair (Lewis and Lewis, 1972). The individual feels that his or her life situation has no chance of resolving itself.

Whether or not these behavioral manifestations occur prior to the disease process or after the illness has resulted remains a debate among clinicians and investigators. Emotional problems do occur in individuals with severe ulcerative colitis, but are these changes the consequence of the impact of the illness or the cause of the illness (Shields, 1972)? Who would not be worn down both physically and emotionally by passing 10 to 15 bloodstained bowel movements each day?

In summary, individuals demonstrating peptic ulcers and persons afflicted with ulcerative colitis manifest conflict in their emotional structure. The ramifications of the conflict, whether it be independence versus dependence or rebellion versus complicance, are physical illness and a need to rely upon someone else for support. Whether the conflict leads to the physical illness or the physical illness leads to the conflict need not be the major source of concern to the nurse. Instead, the major concern should be how the health provider can help the person afflicted with either one of these disease entities cope with the illness and how the individual can be assisted in dealing with his or her precarious emotional state.

The nurse's primary role in assisting the individual to deal with the gastrointestinal illness is to encourage and allow verbalization. The person with a peptic ulcer needs encouragement to express his or her feelings of dependence. While the individual is verbalizing how he or she feels the nurse or other members of the health team should at no time make judgmental responses about the individual's need to be dependent. To illustrate, suppose that the ulcer victim says, "I really like to have my wife lay out my clothes the night before I am to wear them." The nurse should not respond with a judgmental statement, such as, "Why, because you're lazy!"

In addition, the ulcer patient may require encouragement to express the reasons for having to push so vigorously. For example, why does the patient feel that he or she must obtain a job promotion within the next six months? As the patient explains the rationale for the need to create the impression of self-sufficiency, assertion, and independence, it may prove helpful to have him or her examine his or her goals. Encourage the patient to evaluate whether or not these goals are realistic. This forces the patient to contend with the vicious cycle of dependency versus independency.

When dealing with the individual afflicted with ulcerative colitis, the need to verbalize is also extremely important and this verbalization may have to be channeled in the direction of expressing feelings of rebellion. Since the person afflicted with ulcerative colitis often encounters difficulty in opposing others in thoughts and actions, he or she may require encouragement to express an opposing view. The individual should be told that it is all right to disagree with others and the individual should not be reprimanded when he or she does disagree. As the person with ulcerative colitis expresses this rebellion, he or she should receive positive feedback about the increasing ability to verbalize opposing viewpoints. In addition to difficulties in expressing disagreement, feelings of frustration often mount when the individual with ulcerative colitis encounters severe bouts of diarrhea. The frequent trips to the bathroom may be overwhelming and depressing. Verbalization is vital and the person requires encouragement to express his or her frustration about this devastating situation.

Family members of individuals suffering from gastrointestinal alterations play a vital role in the health care of their loved one. Family members often require information about the importance of encouraging the individual with G.I. alterations to verbalize feelings. The ulcer patient's need to express feelings of dependency and the ulcerative colitis patient's need to verbalize feelings of rebellion must be stressed to family members. Also, family members must be discouraged from reprimanding the individual with G.I. alterations as he or she expresses feelings of dependence or feelings of rebellion.

As the individual with gastrointestinal alterations verbalizes these feelings, family members may encounter difficulties in dealing with them. Therefore, family members may require assistance from health team members on how to deal and to cope with their own feelings. Again, ventilation of feelings is vital even for family members. As the family members verbalize their feelings, they may require guidance to see why they might encounter difficulties in dealing with their loved one's expressed feelings. They should be encouraged to examine their own feelings about the illness. For example, do they see the individual as weak, do they feel that the illness places a stigma upon them, or do they feel responsible for the illness? Above all, they require information on the disease process and its consequences.

Once the individual with G.I. alterations has verbalized his or her feelings and the rationale for demonstrating independence and/or compliance, encouraging the individual to look realistically at his or her behavior is helpful. The individual may require guidance in evaluating the reality of his or her life-style and the reality of the behavior that feeds into the fulmination of the illness. Helping the person identify goals that are achievable can prove beneficial. For example, the young executive who is driving himself to become vice-president of the company in order to please his parents may find, with assistance from health team members, that achieving the position of supervisor or assistant vice-president is more realistic. As the individual with gastrointestinal alterations reestablishes his or her goals in a more realistic light, positive feedback is valuable since it provides the individual with a sense of achievement.

In times of stress the individual with gastrointestinal alterations often undergoes an acute crisis in the disease process. Symptoms such as gnawing burning abdominal pain or an increased frequency of bloody diarrhea may appear. Therefore, both the patient and the family should be encouraged to identify those situations which they believe, or know, to be stressful for the patient. For example, if taking part in a golf tournament exacerbates the symptoms, it may be advisable to avoid taking part in these tournaments. If the patient and the family are cognizant of how stress can increase the chances of symptom exacerbation, they are more likely to avoid such circumstances. However, it must be realized that not all stressful situations can be avoided.

The person with alterations in G.I. function, such as peptic ulcers and ulcerative colitis, often requires guidance in carrying out maneuvers to enhance relaxation. Both the afflicted individual and the family need to identify the maneuvers that the patient finds relaxing. What one person finds relaxing another individual may find stress producing; therefore, personalized identification of such maneuvers is necessary. For example, some people find fishing, golfing, and hiking relaxing while others enjoy sauna baths, movies, and reading.

Once relaxing maneuvers have been identified, the individual must be encouraged by the family and health team members to carry them out. Family members play a vital role here because they are most aware of the patient's reactions to tension and stress and of the need to take part in relaxing activities.

Since the need to rest is an important component of the health care of the patient with G.I. alterations, it is no wonder that bed rest may be ordered when the individual is admitted to an acute care facility during an acute attack of the disease process. Placing a patient who is in an acute crisis in the hospital setting encourages physical rest and often is an attempt to enforce mental relaxation. The nurse, however, needs to be aware of the patient's activities during hospitalization since mental relaxation may not be occurring. For example, how restful is the business person who has his or her secretary visit all day in order to continue to carry out business affairs from a hospital bed? In such a case, limit setting may be necessary. The limits should not be rigid since rigidity may add to the person's already stressful state. Instead of refusing the secretary admission into the patient's room, it is better to discuss with the patient the advisability of the secretary's visiting for only a few hours each day. This sets the limits for rest and work.

When an individual with gastrointestinal alterations is admitted to an acute care setting, dependency needs may be increased. The desire to be waited on and cared for may be manifested both by the person with a peptic ulcer and the individual with ulcerative colitis. During the stage of repudiation and/or when the illness is in an acute state, dependency needs will have to be met. During these periods the individual expends energy in denying and/or coping with the impact of the physical state. It is advisable to reassure the person that during this time it is acceptable to express dependency.

As the patient moves out of the stage of repudiation and/or progresses toward a more stable state of physical health, limits may have to be provided to decrease the patient's dependency. What is expected of him or her should be carefully described and health team members must be consistent in carrying out the requirements of these expectations. For example, if a patient with ulcerative colitis avoids going for scheduled laboratory tests so that hospitalization and hence dependency are prolonged, limits must be provided. It may be advisable to encourage the individual to discuss with the nurse why he or she is avoiding the laboratory tests and how he or she might cope with the feelings of dependency. Limits, however, should not be extremely rigid. Rigidity often increases stress which can, in turn, lead to exacerbation of the symptoms. One of the difficulties in working with patients who have gastrointestinal alterations is identifying that fine line between adequately set limits and rigidity, dependency and overdependency, and rebellion and compliance.

In summary, the emotional well-being of both the individual with a peptic ulcer and the individual with ulcerative colitis may be unstable. Regardless of whether the emotional difficulties occurred prior to or after the physical disease process is not the major concern of the nurse. Instead, the nurse's role is to deal with the existing emotional upheaval by assisting the afflicted person to cope with the physical illness and to resolve the emotional difficulties.

Somatic Impact*

The impact that gastrointestinal alterations have upon an individual's somatic identity may not always be readily obvious to others. From all outward appearances no problem exists. Only when complaints of burning abdominal pain are made or frequent trips to the bathroom are observed does the bystander recognize the existence of a problem.

The individual afflicted with a peptic ulcer projects his or her somatic focal point toward the gastrointestinal tract. The presence of a gnawing, burning, abdominal pain becomes uppermost in the individual's mind as he or she attempts to carry out his or her usual activities. Since the pain often is rhythmic in character, occurring one to two hours after eating, daily activities may become controlled by the usual time of the presence of pain. Life literally becomes controlled by "gut reactions" as the digestive tract works away at digesting itself.

Once the individual with a peptic ulcer encounters bleeding of the G.I. tract, he or she may tend to focus attention on the appearance of his or her stools. Ritualistic observations for black, tarry-appearing bowel movements may be carried out by the individual. Again, the somatic focus is on the function of the gastrointestinal tract.

*It is advisable for the reader to have read Chapter 2 before continuing with this section.

Unfortunately, some individuals believe that the ulcer victim's demise is solely the results of his or her own doing. Thus, when comments such as, "You don't look like the type of person who should have an ulcer!" are made, feelings of guilt may be elicited, for example, guilt about inflicting this somatic alteration upon himself or herself and guilt about not being able to control the reaction of the gastrointestinal tract. More severe reactions of guilt may occur when the ulcer victim's life situations become out of control and result in an exacerbation of symptoms.

The individual with ulcerative colitis also has the somatic focal point directed toward the gastrointestinal tract. The individual's existence during acute attacks of the disease process revolves around the frequent excretion of waste. The individual is constantly afraid that he or she may soil his or her clothing and that the accident will become obvious to others. The individual is continually concerned about emitting a stool odor as a result of improper cleansing after a bowel movement or as a result of a diarrhea accident.

In addition to the fear of being obvious about frequent stools, the individual with ulcerative colitis may harbor feelings of regression and feel that he or she has regressed to the toddler stage (when toilet training has not yet been accomplished). This may be common when the individual has encountered frequent soiling episodes. Thus, the person with ulcerative colitis is controlled by the reactions of the gastrointestinal tract.

How the person with a gastrointestinal alteration responds to the somatic impact of the illness can be affected by the developmental stage being experienced at the time of the illness. During the stage of young adulthood (eighteen to forty-five years) the incidence of both peptic ulcer and ulcerative colitis is common. Peptic ulcers tend to occur more often in the last half of young adulthood, while the peak age of onset of ulcerative colitis tends to occur in the early years of young adulthood. It is during this developmental stage that the task of establishing a meaningful relationship with others, both in friendship and in a mutually satisfying sexual relationship, becomes important (Erikson, 1963). The individual sustaining alterations in gastrointestinal function may encounter difficulties in accomplishing a state of intimacy and may retreat into isolation. This is especially true when the person afflicted with a gastrointestinal malfunction finds his or her body image displeasing.

The female in young adulthood who is undergoing a G.I. alteration may not encounter as much difficulty in dealing with her body image and its relationship to her disease process as the male. The female has more clearly defined body boundaries (a high-barrier person) and is more atuned to devoting attention to the appearance of her body (Fisher, 1964).

The male in young adulthood has a less defined body boundary (a low-barrier person) and tends to devote his attention to the ability to achieve rather than to the appearance of his body structure (Fisher, 1964). Fisher (1964) points out that low-barrier individuals are more likely to experience internal physiologic responses (peptic ulcers and ulcerative colitis) when under stress. Since the presence of abdominal pain and/or frequent diarrhea stools would tend to decrease the afflicted individual's ability to perform, the male may encounter difficulties in coping with his altered body image because of this G.I. malfunction.

The individual in the age category of forty-five to sixty-five years is experiencing the developmental stage of adulthood in which the primary task is generativity. During this time interests outside the home become important and the adult strives to establish and guide future generations (Erikson, 1963). If the individual in adulthood is afflicted with a gastrointestinal alteration, a sense of stagnation may result. The physiologic changes occurring as the result of the altered G.I. function (pain or diarrhea) may be interpreted as premature old age. As a result, the afflicted person may retire to a rocking chair before his or her time and become self-absorbed.

The person sixty-five years and over is in the stage of maturity. It is during this time that the adult withdraws body boundaries to more internal sites (Fisher and Cleveland, 1968) and may become fixated upon his or her gastrointestinal function. The presence of G.I. alterations, such as peptic ulcers or ulcerative colitis, may intensify the withdrawal of these body boundaries. Since frequent thoughts of death are common during this developmental stage, the existence of a gastrointestinal malfunction may intensify the frequency of these thoughts and, as a result, the person may enter a state of despair.

The nurse's role in dealing with the somatic impact of a gastrointestinal alteration is to assist the afflicted individual to cope with the altered body image. Verbalization about how he or she feels that the disease entity affects the body image is essential. If the individual feels guilty about the existence of the G.I. malfunction, he or she should be encouraged to look at the reality of these guilt feelings. Does the individual, in fact, feel totally responsible for the illness? As the individual examines these guilt feelings, he or she may require additional assistance in talking through why he or she feels responsible. In some situations, individuals afflicted with G.I. alterations who encounter difficulty in coping with their illness may require appropriate psychiatric intervention.

In order to deal with an altered body image, the person with a G.I. alteration should be educated about the basis of the disease process. He or she needs to know what the illness entails and what factors contribute to its existence. If the individual has a peptic ulcer, the importance of taking antacids or food on time in order to prevent the occurrence of abdominal pain should be stressed. It has been demonstrated that the kind of food consumed is of little importance as long as the individual can tolerate the food eaten (Menguy, Nelson, Nyhus, Samloff, Schafer, and Snodgrass, 1973). This should be pointed out to the person with a peptic ulcer, since the likelihood of eating regularly to avoid pain is increased when the person does not always have to adhere to a bland food diet.

Instructing the individual with a peptic ulcer to identify stressful situations that tend to elicit pain can be beneficial. Once these situations are identified, the individual should attempt to avoid them whenever possible.

Stool observation may be a common ritual for the person with a peptic ulcer. To aid in relieving anxiety, the individual should be reassured that it is all right to carry out this procedure since it aids in identifying the presence of gastrointestinal bleeding, but the person should be informed about drugs and foods that may darken the color of stools (i.e., iron, bismuth, and beets).

Assisting the individual with ulcerative colitis to deal with the altered body image is mainly focused on coping with diarrhea stools. Using a sitz bath, washing the perineal and rectal area after each stool can help to decrease the occurrence of odors. In addition, using soft, high-quality toilet tissue for cleansing and applying a lubricant, such as A & D ointment or Vaseline, to the rectal area can facilitate in decreasing skin irritation. Also encouraging the individual to identify stressful situations and foods that tend to bring on bouts of diarrhea can be helpful. Then, if possible, such situations and foods should be avoided.

If the person with ulcerative colitis expresses concern about soiling himself or herself, plastic-covered underwear or a perineal pad may be beneficial, but before suggesting such a maneuver, it is well advised for the nurse to encourage the afflicted person to express his or her feelings about wearing such devices. Plastic underwear can intensify feelings of regression and a perineal pad can be emasculating to the male patient.

In summary, the presence of a gastrointestinal alteration creates an impact upon the afflicted person's somatic identity. Assisting the individual to cope with his or her altered body image is the nurse's primary role in dealing with the somatic impact of G.I. malfunction. Verbalization and patient education constitute the two major nursing interventions for coping with an altered body image caused by an altered gastrointestinal function.

Sexual Impact

The impact that gastrointestinal alterations have upon one's sexuality may not always be obvious. Therefore, members of the health care team must be particularly observant for indications that one's sexual being is affected by the G.I. malfunction.

The individual with a peptic ulcer may encounter difficulty achieving a satisfying sexual experience if he or she is suffering from a gnawing, burning pain during the sexual experience. Not only is the pain uncomfortable, but it also can be distracting. The presence of pain may decrease libido and even postpone or completely eliminate the sexual experience. If the individual encounters a stressful situation prior to the sexual experience or considers the sexual experience stressful, the likelihood of pain is greater. For example, if the person is engaging in an illicit sexual experience or feels the pressure of having to perform adequately during the sexual experience, chances of abdominal pain may increase.

In addition to a gnawing, burning abdominal pain, the presence of burping may create additional problems during the sexual experience. The ulcer victim may not feel sexually desirable if he or she has to burp during the sexual encounter. The sex partner also may find eructation annoying and distracting if it occurs during the sex act and, therefore, may not achieve a satisfying sexual experience.

Limited research has been conducted on the sexual ramifications of gastrointestinal malfunction. It would be of value to note whether the ulcer victim or the sex partner tends to be the aggressor during the sexual experience. Since the ulcer victim often has a strong drive to appear independent and self-sufficient in an attempt to conceal his or her need for dependency (Lewis and Lewis, 1972), it would seem reasonable to predict that he or she may be the aggressor in the relationship. Recognizing this can be beneficial when carrying out sex counseling.

Research conducted on individuals with gastrointestinal malfunction has related to the fertility of individuals with ulcers. Kubickova and Vesely (1974) noted that ulcer victims had a 25 percent reduction in fertility compared to non-ulcer controls. It was felt that this lower fertility was a result of a higher incidence of childless marriages and a smaller number of children per family. Since ulcer victims have often been identified as having a high drive to achieve, the presence of children may very possibly be seen as a deterrent to reaching their goals.

The nurse's responsibility in dealing with the sexual impact on the individual with a peptic ulcer is to assist him or her in decreasing the circumstances that hinder a satisfying sexual experience. Since abdominal pain and burping tend to occur when the stomach is empty, encouraging the consumption of antacids or food prior to engaging in a sexual experience can aid in preventing pain and eructation during the sexual encounter. Encouraging the sex partner not to stress the importance of performance during coitus can aid in decreasing the ulcer victim's anxiety about the need to perform during the sex act. Also, it may be advisable to point out to the ulcer victim that stressful situations prior to the sexual experience can contribute to the occurrence of pain during the encounter. If the ulcer victim is aware that stress prior to a sexual experience can create difficulties during the experience, he or she is more likely to avoid stressful circumstances prior to a sexual encounter. If the ulcer victim finds the sexual experience stressful, the individual should be advised to discuss this openly with the sex partner. In some situations, however, the stress produced by a sexual experience may not be easily solved and sex counseling may be in order.

The sexual impact of ulcerative colitis is similar to that of peptic ulcers in that the difficulties encountered generally are related to symptoms of the disease process. Undoubtedly, one of the greatest concerns of the individual with ulcerative colitis is the fear of emitting a fecal odor or encountering a bout of diarrhea during the sexual experience. If either of these situations occurs, embarrassment and humiliation may result. Future sexual encounters may be avoided by both the ulcerative colitis victim and the sex partner for fear of a similar accident occurring; thus, a great deal of strain is placed upon the sexual relationship.

If anal sex is practiced by the afflicted individual and the sex partner, this practice may have to cease or at least decrease during acute attacks of the illness. Since anal stimulation may lead to a bout of diarrhea, this practice would be ill-advised for the ulcerative colitis victim. During acute states of diarrhea the ulcerative colitis victim probably will not engage in sexual activity because he or she fears soiling himself or herself and the sex partner and because he or she usually is physically exhausted from the acute state of illness.

Research on the sexual ramifications of ulcerative colitis has been minimal. It would be of value to note whether the ulcerative colitis victim or the sex partner is the aggressor during the sexual encounter, especially since the ulcerative colitis victim has been found to suffer from a conflict between rebellion and compliance (Castelnuovo-Tedesco, 1962). It seems reasonable to predict that most of the time the ulcerative colitis victim is not the aggressor in the sexual encounter. Knowing the role of the ulcerative colitis victim in a sexual encounter can be of value when sex counseling is being planned and implemented.

One of the nurse's roles is to assist the individual with ulcerative colitis to cope with the sexual impact of the illness. Encouraging verbalization between the ulcerative colitis victim and the sex partner about fears of diarrhea and/or fecal odor during the sexual encounter is beneficial. During verbalization both individuals may require guidance on how best to handle the presence of diarrhea or a fecal odor during a sexual experience. For example, if the sex partner can remain very matter-of-fact about a diarrhea accident, a great deal of the ulcerative colitis victim's embarrassment and humiliation can be decreased. Placing an absorbent towel or pad on the bed in the buttocks region of the sexual partners can be helpful in decreasing a messy situation if diarrhea does occur. Readily available tissues or washcloths can help decrease chaotic commotion if a diarrhea accident results. In addition, burning incense or using an air deodorizer in the bedroom can aid in decreasing the awareness of fecal odor.

The ulcerative colitis victim should be encouraged to identify stressful situations that could elicit bouts of diarrhea and, if possible, he or she should be encouraged to avoid these circumstances prior to a sexual experience. In some relationships, spontaneity of a sexual encounter may be advisable since spontaneity tends to decrease anxiety brought on by preparing for the sexual activity. In some cases, sex counseling may be the only answer for dealing with the sexual impact of ulcerative colitis.

In summary, people afflicted with alterations of the gastrointestinal tract can encounter an impact on their sexuality. The nurse's major role in assisting these victims to cope is directed toward preventing, decreasing, and dealing with those symptoms of the disease process that can prevent a satisfying sexual experience.

Occupational Impact

The existence of gastrointestinal disorders creates an economic impact, not only upon the individual afflicted, but also upon society in general. Palmer (1970) notes that the presence of peptic ulcers leads to manpower waste in all occupational activities that rely upon man's ability to perform. He has identified five ways in which ulcer disease affects manpower:

1. Rejection from employment due to a code of physical standards for job applicant.
2. Time lost from work due to hospitalization, doctor's appointments, illness-time spent at home, diagnostic tests, and convalescent periods.
3. Substandard performance due to decreased productivity on the part of some ulcer victims.
4. Termination of occupation due to ulcer disability.
5. Draining of company funds due to compensation claims by ulcer victims.

Although no research and no publications have made reference to the incidence of similar economic difficulties existing for the person afflicted with ulcerative colitis, it would seem reasonable that this gastrointestinal alteration would create a similar impact upon occupational stability. For example, the presence of diarrhea may make one incapable of doing shift work because of the frequent changes in the work schedule. The ulcerative colitis victim may note a regularity to his or her diarrhea stools, but inconsistent working hours may disrupt any attempt made at working around the occurrence of the diarrhea stools. Another problem that may result for the individual with ulcerative colitis is working in an occupational situation that demands an aseptic environment, such as a bacteriology laboratory or an operating room. If the ulcerative colitis victim were to encounter several diarrhea accidents while on duty, he or she might be asked to change jobs or to leave the job since he or she would be frequently contaminating the environment.

In addition to Palmer's (1970) five factors that contribute to the occupational impact of peptic ulcers, it must not be forgotten that certain occupations contribute to the incidence of gastrointestinal alterations. For example, the individual in an occupation in which important and/or costly decisions are required may suffer from a higher incidence of gastrointestinal disorders. Research has found that air traffic controllers demonstrate an exceptionally high risk of developing peptic ulcers because of the stresses of the job (Cobb and Rose, 1973).

In addition to the pressures of the occupation itself, the position held by the individual may have an effect upon the incidence of the gastrointestinal disorder. Often when a person holds a high status job positive feedback on a job well done is not forthcoming. He or she is so far up the occupational hierarchy that there is no one above to provide positive feedback on high quality performance. Thus, frustration and stress can be produced as a result of the lack of praise.

In dealing with the occupational impact of gastrointestinal alterations, the nurse's role centers around encouraging the afflicted person to verbalize how he or she feels about the job. Very possibly the occupation is extremely stressful and the individual is encountering difficulty coping with this stress. Through verbalization this can be made apparent to the nurse, to the individual, and to the family. In some situations, the nurse may have to encourage the individual to alter or change his or her job in an attempt to decrease this excessive stress. In addition, regularity in the work schedule is advisable. Continually changing shifts makes it difficult for the person with a peptic ulcer to eat and take antacids regularly in an attempt to decrease the incidence of abdominal pain. The ulcerative colitis victim has difficulty regulating his or her work schedule around diarrhea stools if the working hours constantly fluctuate. Also, the continual change in working hours is a stress to which some individuals may encounter difficulties adapting.

The family members of the peptic ulcer victim and of the ulcerative colitis victim should be encouraged to allow the individual afflicted with the gastrointestinal alteration to ventilate about his or her job situation. Simply ventilating about job related problems can aid in decreasing anxiety. Once the anxiety is out in the open, the chances for the gastrointestinal tract to react to the stressful situation may be decreased. If the occupation is stressful or if the demands of the job are incompatible with the gastrointestinal illness, the afflicted individual requires support from the family to alter his or her occupational pursuits. For some individuals job retraining may be in order.

In summary, the presence of gastrointestinal alterations can create an impact upon occupational stability both for the afflicted person and society in general. The afflicted person may be rejected from employment, lose time from work, perform in a substandard manner, be terminated from employment and/or consume large amounts of a company's compensation fund. The work situation itself may be a contributing factor in the formation of the gastrointestinal alteration. The nurse's role in dealing with the occupational impact of gastrointestinal alterations is to assist the afflicted individual and the family in dealing with this impact to the best of their ability.

Social Impact

The effect that gastrointestinal alterations have upon one's social well-being varies considerably among individuals since social encounters are as divergent as the persons afflicted. Therefore, some of the more common social encounters that may present problems for the individual with G.I. alterations will be presented.

For both the peptic ulcer victim and the ulcerative colitis victim, anxiety provoked by the social encounter can be a problem. Although social encounters are generally considered a form of relaxation, they can be stressful. To illustrate, the individual with gastrointestinal alterations may feel discomfort or extreme excitement about engaging in a particular social affair. In either case, anxiety is elicited and the individual suffers the consequences.

For the individual afflicted with a peptic ulcer, the presence of the illness creates a social impact related to the activities confronted in a social situation. For example, since alcohol consumption is not advisable for the individual with an ulcer because of the potentiation of the secretion of gastric acid, social functions that serve alcoholic beverages may prove uncomfortable for the afflicted person. The ulcer patient may wish to be a part of the social activity involving social drink and, therefore, feel awkward if he or she is not drinking something along with everyone else at the social affair. In addition to drinking alcoholic beverages, many people smoke at social encounters. Smoking is ill-advised for the ulcer patient since it tends to increase gastric motility. Thus, the ulcer victim's difficulties in a social situation often revolve around contending with activities that are not advisable for him or her.

The social impact of ulcerative colitis tends to be related to the consequences of the symptoms of the disease process. The afflicted individual's major social concerns are the fear of odor and excrement associated with the illness and the ways in which the illness restricts the use of his or her time for social purposes (Jackson, 1973). For example, managing the frequent diarrhea stools and the presence of odor can be difficult, especially if bathroom facilities are not readily available. In addition, the ulcerative colitis victim's time for activities is limited and his or her schedule and planning are very variable since any plans may be subject to last minute changes because of bouts of diarrhea.

The nurse's role in dealing with the social impact of gastrointestinal alterations is to assist the individual and the family in identifying and carrying out ways of dealing with social interactions. If alcoholic beverages are present at social engagements, the nurse should encourage the peptic ulcer victim to drink juice or soft drinks. Both generally are available when alcoholic beverages are served. The drink can be disguised with garnishes of cherries or fruit slices. If other people's smoking tempts the individual with a peptic ulcer to smoke a cigarette, the individual can be instructed how to decrease smoking. The reader is advised to consult Chapter 10 for a discussion of preventive tactics.

To assist the individual with ulcerative colitis to cope with the social impact of the illness, the nurse should aid the individual in identifying preventive strategies. For example, the afflicted person can carefully map his or her route for social engagements according to the accessibility of bathrooms. If the individual encounters a strange or new environment, he or she should identify the location of the toilets. Also engaging in activities, such as long car rides, which prolong the inaccessibility of bathroom facilities should be avoided.

Unless the individual with ulcerative colitis is in an acute state of illness, he or she should be encouraged to maintain social interactions. Having family and friends act as interactional allies (Jackson, 1973) is helpful. In other words, family and friends can aid by explaining or justifying the ulcerative colitis victim's unconventional behavior as he or she attempts to maintain activities despite frequent and abrupt exits. The afflicted person can learn to excuse himself or herself graciously from the company of others, quickly change clothing if needed, and rapidly repair a soiled environment. If the afflicted individual can remain calm about the situation, others are more likely to retain their composure following the accident. In addition, if family members and friends can remain matter-of-fact about a diarrhea accident, less tension is created.

In dealing with the anxiety brought about by a social encounter, the nurse should encourage the individual with a gastrointestinal alteration to ventilate feelings about social engagements. Verbalizing aids in decreasing anxiety and it also makes others aware of the afflicted individual's feelings about a social circumstance. If the social circumstance provokes anxiety, the afflicted person and the family may wish to identify alternate means of social interaction.

It must not be forgotten that family members may experience anxiety about attending a social function with a loved one afflicted with a gastrointestinal alteration. The frequent need to consume food or antacids or the frequent exits to the bathroom may elicit feelings of discomfort or disgust on the part of the family member. To deal with the family member's reaction to the social impact of the loved one's G.I. alteration, the nurse should encourage the family member to verbalize his or her feelings. In addition, the family member may need encouragement to discuss his or her feelings with the afflicted individual. Once the afflicted person is aware of the family member's feelings about the social impact of the illness, attempts to deal with these feelings need to be made.

Encouraging the identification of and involvement in social affairs that are equally enjoyable for both the family member and the afflicted person can prove helpful. To illustrate, a family member may find attending a lecture series on art with the individual with G.I. alterations unpleasant since the individual's movements can be very obvious to others. Instead of attending an art lecture series, visiting an art museum may be less uncomfortable for both the family member and the afflicted person since the individual with G.I. alterations can consume antacids in the privacy of the bathroom or unobtrusively use the toilet. Thus, it is best when the social affair selected is a joint decision between the afflicted person and the family.

In summary, although gastrointestinal alterations can create an impact upon an individual's social well-being, the afflicted person should be encouraged to take part in social interaction. The maintenance of social interaction is the desired goal as the afflicted person and the family develop strategies for involvement in social affairs. Alterations in activities, however, may have to be made and the afflicted person and the family may need to identify various ways of contending with each social function.

SUMMARY

Gastrointestinal alterations are well-recognized health care problems. Two of the more common G.I. alterations affecting the adult are peptic ulcers and ulcerative colitis. Peptic ulcers are sites of ulceration occurring in the mucosa, submucosa, or muscle layers of the distal esophagus, stomach, upper duodenum, or jejunum. The classic symptom of a peptic ulcer is gnawing, burning, epigastric pain often occurring one to two hours after eating. Ulcerative colitis is an inflammatory disease involving, mainly, the mucosa and submucosa of the colon. The classic symptom of this condition is bloody diarrhea.

Regardless of which gastrointestinal alteration affects an individual, impacts are created upon the individual's emotional well-being, somatic identity, sexuality, occupational identity, and social role. To aid the afflicted person in dealing with either one of these gastrointestinal malfunctions, the nurse needs to identify how the illness is affecting each component of the individual's life and then assist him or her in dealing with each impact to the best of his or her ability.

Patient Situation

Mr. D. U. is a forty-five-year-old single, investigative newspaper reporter who is very active in his work and often attends job-related cocktail parties. When at these parties he drinks alcoholic beverages and smokes from one to two packs of cigarettes. Mr. D. U. has experienced persistent gnawing, burning pain in the epigastric region over the past three months. His pain tends to occur one to two hours after eating. Because of persistent discomfort, Mr. D. U.'s male sex partner encouraged him to see his physician about the problem. As a result, Mr. D. U. was admitted to the hospital for a gastrointestinal work-up.

It is now three days postadmission and Mr. D. U.'s diagnostic tests indicate the presence of a duodenal ulcer. During the nursing assessment the nurse in charge of Mr. D. U.'s care identified patient-centered problems related to his emotional well-being, somatic identity, sexuality, occupational identity, and social role.

Following are Mr. D. U.'s nursing care plan and patient care cardex dealing with each of these areas of concern.

NURSING CARE PLAN

Problems	Objectives	Nursing Interventions	Principles/Rationale	Evaluations
Emotional Impact Refusal to carry out health care therapies without frequent encouragement and approval from the nursing staff.	To decrease Mr. D. U.'s need to be dependent.	Encourage and allow Mr. D. U. to express his feelings of dependency.	Verbalization of feelings of dependency can aid in the development of insight into one's behavior.	The nurse would observe for: Open communication between Mr. D. U. and the nursing staff about his feelings of dependency.
	To increase Mr. D. U.'s self-esteem.	Avoid judgmental responses when Mr. D. U. expresses his need to be dependent.	Judgmental responses are barriers to communications.	
		Encourage Mr. D. U. to verbalize his feelings of dependency to his male sex partner.	Significant others who are aware of an individual's feelings are more likely to be supportive.	Open communication between Mr. D. U. and his male sex partner about Mr. D. U.'s feelings of dependency.
		Encourage Mr. D. U.'s male sex partner not to reprimand Mr. D. U. as he expresses his feelings of dependency.	Judgmental responses are barriers to communication.	
		Encourage Mr. D. U.'s male sex partner to verbalize his feelings about Mr. D. U.'s expressions of dependency.	Being aware of significant other's feelings aids members of the health care team in assisting the significant other to deal and cope with his feelings.	Mr. D. U.'s sex partner's open communication to the nursing staff about his feelings about Mr. D. U.'s feelings of dependency.
		Provide Mr. D. U. with realistic limits (e.g., explain to Mr. D. U. what health care therapies he is expected to carry out).	Setting limits aids in decreasing an individual's dependency.	A decrease in Mr. D. U.'s dependent behavior.
		Avoid rigidity in limit setting (e.g. do not enforce the consumption of antacids/milk exactly on the hour or half-hour).	Rigidity often increases stress which can lead to an exacerbation of symptoms.	

NURSING CARE PLAN (cont.)

Problems	Objectives	Nursing Interventions	Principles/Rationale	Evaluations
Somatic Impact Expressed feelings that body is completely controlled by the presence of the duodenal ulcer.	To assist Mr. D. U. in coping with his altered body image.	Encourage Mr. D. U. to verbalize how he feels his disease entity affects his body image.	Open ventilation of feelings about body image can aid in the individual's ability to identify ways of coping with bodily changes.	The nurse would observe for: Open expression by Mr. D. U. regarding how he feels his disease entity affects his body image with possible solutions of how to deal with his altered body image.
		Provide Mr. D. U. with sound education about the basis of his disease process (e.g., what the illness entails and what factors contribute to its existence).	Realizing that certain bodily changes tend to occur with peptic ulcer can help in decreasing one's anxiety about an altered body image.	
		Instruct Mr. D. U. on the importance of food/antacid consumption on a regular basis to prevent occurrence of epigastric pain.	Realizing that regular consumption of food/antacids aids in decreasing the incidence of epigastric pain can aid in the ulcer victim's likelihood of adhering to this health care therapy.	Mr. D. U.'s regular consumption of food/antacids.
		Aid Mr. D. U. in identifying and avoiding, if possible, situations that produce stress for him.	Avoidance of stressful situations can aid in decreasing the incidence of ulcer symptoms (e.g., epigastric pain).	Mr. D. U.'s identification and avoidance of stressful situations.
Sexual Impact Expressed concern about decreased libido during and after	To decrease the incidence of circumstances that hinder a satisfying	Encourage Mr. D. U. to remember to consume antacids or food prior to engaging in a	Having food or antacids prior to a sexual experience can aid in decreasing the incidence of pain	The nurse would observe for: Mr. D. U.'s verbalization that he is experiencing satisfying

		and avoid stressful situations prior to a sexual encounter.	perience can contribute to the occurrence of epigastric pain during the sexual encounter.	The nurse would observe for: Mr. D. U.'s verbalization of job situations that may contribute to his epigastric discomfort.
Occupational Impact States that epigastric distress often occurs while at work.	To assist Mr. D. U. in identifying situations in the work environment that may potentiate his epigastric discomfort.	Encourage Mr. D. U. to verbalize to members of the health care team and to his male sex partner how he feels about his job.	Verbalization about a job aids in assisting the individual to identify the possible stresses of the job.	
		Encourage Mr. D. U. to avoid shift work, if possible.	Changing shifts makes it difficult for an ulcer victim to consume foods and antacid regularly in an attempt to decrease the incidence of abdominal pain.	
Social Impact* States that epigastric distress tends to occur while attending cocktail parties.	To inform Mr. D. U. of social activities that can increase the incidence of epigastric distress.	Encourage Mr. D. U. to avoid alcohol consumption and smoking.	Alcohol consumption and smoking are both ill-advised activities for the ulcer victim since they can potentiate epigastric discomfort.	The nurse would observe for: Mr. D. U.'s verbalization of how alcohol, smoking, and stress can affect his peptic ulcer.
		Encourage Mr. D. U. to drink fruit juices or soft drinks garnished with cherries and fruit slices at cocktail parties.	Drinking soft drinks while others are drinking alcoholic beverages can aid in decreasing the ulcer victim's feelings of awkwardness at a cocktail party.	
		Suggest the use of tactics that attempt to decrease the incidence of smoking. (Refer to Chapter 10 for details.)	Smokers are more likely to smoke when in the presence of other smokers.	
		Encourage Mr. D. U. to verbalize how he feels about attending cocktail parties.	Verbalizing feelings about social engagements aids in decreasing one's anxiety.	

*Social activities are generally considered a form of relaxation, but they can be stressful.

PATIENT CARE CARDEX

PATIENT'S NAME:	Mr. D. U.	DIAGNOSIS:	Peptic ulcer—duodenal
AGE:	45 years	SEX:	Male
MARITAL STATUS:	Single	OCCUPATION:	Investigative newspaper reporter
SIGNIFICANT OTHERS:	Male sex partner		

Problems	Nursing Approaches
Emotional: Refusal to carry out health care therapies without frequent encouragement and approval from the nursing staff.	1. Encourage verbalization of feelings about dependency. 2. Avoid judgmental responses to expressions of dependency. 3. Encourage verbalization of feelings of dependency to male sex partner. 4. Encourage male sex partner not to reprimand partner's expression of dependency. 5. Encourage male sex partner to express feelings about partner's expression of dependency. 6. Provide with limits (e.g., describe expected behavior in regards to health care therapies). 7. Avoid rigidity in limit setting (e.g., do not force consumption of antacids/milk exactly on the hour).
Somatic: Expressed feelings that body is completely controlled by the presence of the duodenal ulcer.	1. Encourage verbalization about how disease entity affects body image. 2. Provide with sound education about basis of disease process (e.g., what illness entails and what factors contribute to its existence). 3. Instruct on importance of regular food/antacid consumption. 4. Aid in identifying and avoiding stressful situations.
Sexual: Expressed concern about decreased libido during and after gnawing, burning, epigastric pain.	1. Encourage regular consumption of antacids or food prior to engaging in sexual experience. 2. Encourage the identification and avoidance of stressful situations prior to a sexual encounter.
Occupational: States that epigastric distress often occurs while at work.	1. Encourage to verbalize how he feels about his job. 2. Encourage to avoid shift work, if possible.
Social: States that epigastric distress tends to occur while attending cocktail parties.	1. Encourage the avoidance of alcohol consumption and smoking. 2. Encourage to drink fruit juices or soft drinks garnished with cherries and fruit slices when at cocktail parties. 3. Suggest the use of tactics that attempt to decrease the incidence of smoking. 4. Encourage to verbalize feelings about attending cocktail parties.

REFERENCES

Brandborg, L. Peptic ulcer disease, *Primary Care,* 1975, *2* (1), 109-119.

Castelnuovo-Tedesco, P. Ulcerative colitis in an adolescent boy subjected to a homosexual assault, *Psychosomatic Medicine,* 1962, *24* (2), 148-156.

Castelnuovo-Tedesco, P., Schwertfeger, H., and Janowsky, D. Psychological characteristics of patients with ulcerative colitis and patients with peptic ulcer: a comparison, *Psychiatry in Medicine,* 1970, *1* (1), 59-75.

Cobb, S., and Rose, R. Hypertension, peptic ulcer, and diabetes in air traffic controllers, *Journal of the American Medical Association,* 1973, *224* (4), 489-492.

Cohen, S., Silverman, A., Waddell, W., and Zwidema, G. Urinary catechol amine levels, gastric secretion, and specific psychological factors in ulcer and non-ulcer patients, *Journal of Psychosomatic Research,* 1961, *5* (2), 90-115.

Engel, G. The psychosomatic approach as a prophylactic measure in the care of patients with peptic ulcer, *Advances in Psychosomatic Medicine,* 1971, *6,* 186-189.

Erikson, E. *Childhood and society.* New York: W. W. Norton and Co., 1963.

Evans, F. *Psychosocial nursing: theory and practice in hospital and community mental health.* New York: The Macmillan Company, 1971.

Fisher, S. Sex differences in body perception, *Psychological Monographs,* 1964, *78,* 1-22.

Fisher, S., and Cleveland, S. *Body image and personality.* New York: Dover Publications Inc., 1968.

Gosling, R. Peptic ulcer and mental disorder—II, *Journal of Psychosomatic Research,* 1958, *2* (4), 284-301.

Grossman, M., Guth, P., Isenberg, J., Passaro, E., Roth, B., Sturdevant, R., and Walsh, J. A new look at peptic ulcer, *Annals of International Medicine,* 1976, *84,* 57-67.

Hertz, D., and Rosenbaum, M. Gastrointestinal disorders. In E. Wittkower and H. Warnes (Eds.), *Psychosomatic medicine: its clinical applications.* New York: Harper & Row Publishers, 1977.

Isenberg, J. Peptic ulcer disease, *Postgraduate Medicine,* 1975, *57* (1), 163-169.

Jackson, B. Ulcerative colitis from an etiological perspective, *American Journal of Nursing,* 1973, *73* (2), 258-264.

Kubickova, Z., and Vesely, K. Fertility and reproduction in patients with duodenal ulcers, *Journal of Reproduction and Fertility,* 1974, *36* (2), 311-317.

Lewis, H., and Lewis, M. *Psychosomatics: how your emotions can damage your health.* New York: The Viking Press, 1972.

MacLean, G. An approach to the treatment of an adolescent with ulcerative colitis, *Canadian Psychiatric Association Journal,* 1976, *21* (5), 287-293.

Menguy, R., Nelson, R., Nyhus, L., Samloff, I., Schafer, D., and Snodgrass, W. Which routine for "routine" ulcer? *Patient Care,* 1973, *7* (18), 88-100.

Morgan, D. Psychosomatic aspects of peptic ulcer disease, *Psychosomatic Medicine,* 1972, *209* (7), 114-120.

Palmer, E. Military experience with ulcer disease: a review, *Military Medicine,* 1970, *135* (10), 871-877.

Prugh, D. Variations in attitudes, behavior, and feeling states as exhibited in the play of children during modifications in the course of ulcerative colitis, *Association for Research in Nervous and Mental Disease, Proceedings,* 1950, *29,* 692-705.

Rogers, B., Clark, L., and Kirsner, J. The epidemiologic and demographic characteristics of inflammatory bowel disease: an analysis of a computerized file on 1400 patients, *Journal of Chronic Diseases,* 1971, *24* (12), 743-773.

Sacher, D., and Janowitz, H. Inflammatory bowel disease, *Disease-A-Month,* 1974, (July), 1-44.

Shields, R. Psychosomatic aspects of ulcerative colitis, *The Practitioner,* 1972, *209* (12), 851-858.

Weiner, H., Thaler, M., Reiser, M., and Mirsky, I. Etiology of duodenal ulcer. I— Relation of specific psychological characteristics to rate of gastric secretion (serum pepsinogen), *Psychosomatic Medicine,* 1957, *19* (1), 1-10.

Wretmark, G. The peptic ulcer individual: a study in heredity physique, and personality, *Acta Psychiatrica ef Neurologica Scandinavica,* 1953, 84 (supplement), 1-183.

13

The Patient with an
ALTERATION
IN
NEUROLOGICAL
FUNCTION

INTRODUCTION

Among the most devastating health care problems affecting humans are those involving neurological function. When a neurological malfunction is present, an individual's ability to move about freely and safely often is affected. The afflicted individual may become dependent upon others for assistance in carrying out his or her daily activities. There are numerous conditions affecting the neurological system, but only two of the more common alterations, cerebrovascular accidents and spinal cord injuries, will be dealt with in this chapter. Members of the health care team, however, will find that the health care concepts in this chapter may also be applied to persons afflicted with other neurological alterations.

PATIENT PROFILE

Approximately 500,000 persons suffer from cerebrovascular accidents (CVAs) each year (Schultz, 1973; McDowell, 1976) with almost 200,000 dying annually (Luckmann and Sorensen, 1974). Modern and effective rehabilitation has made it possible for 75 to 85 percent of the individuals suffering from a CVA to care effectively for themselves (Riehl and Chambers, 1976).

By definition, a cerebrovascular accident is a condition brought about by an acute vascular lesion in the brain. The lay term frequently used for a CVA is stroke. The three most common causes of a CVA are thrombosis, embolism, and hemorrhage. Thrombosis is the most common (Luckmann and Sorensen, 1974). A CVA may produce an almost limitless variety of neurological symptoms, but hemiplegia, aphasia, and sensory alterations are some of the more common.

Both men and women can be afflicted with a cerebrovascular accident, with the greatest incidence occurring after forty years of age. The onset of the disease process may be mild with the afflicted person experiencing transient symptoms such as slight disturbances in speech or mild mental confusion. Or the onset of the illness may be violent with the afflicted individual falling to the floor in a comatose state, breathing stertorously, and demonstrating paralysis on one side of the body.

Approximately 11,500 individuals sustain a spinal cord injury annually in the United States (Kraus, Franti, Riggins, Richards, and Borhani, 1975). Almost 56 percent of all spinal cord injuries can be attributed to motor vehicle accidents (Kraus, Franti, Riggins, Richards, and Borhani, 1975). Diving accidents and gunshot wounds also are contributing causes of cord injury.

Four out of five cord injuries are experienced by men (Cole, 1975), with the male age group of fifteen to thirty-five years of age accounting for the single largest category of afflicted persons (Kraus, Franti, Riggins, Richards, and Borhani, 1975). Age-adjusted incidence rates are highest for black males and lowest for males of Asian origin. In addition, single, divorced, or separated individuals have been reported to encounter a higher risk of spinal cord injuries than married persons (Kraus, Franti, Riggins, Richards, and Borhani, 1975). The increased incidence of spinal cord injuries among nonmarried persons may be due to a greater probability of risk-taking.

The symptoms manifested by a spinal cord injury vary greatly since they depend upon the level, severity, and extent of the injury. The spinal cord may be completely severed or only partially destroyed. Damage of the cord may cause paralysis of the body parts innervated by nerves leaving the cord below the level of injury. However, the most frequent type of impairment among hospitalized persons with a spinal cord injury is quadriparesis, slight or incomplete paralysis of all four extremities (Kraus, Franti, Riggins, Richards, and Borhani, 1975).

A CVA or a spinal cord injury can inflict alterations upon an individual's motor and sensory status. The degree of alteration depends upon the severity and extent of the illness. For the person afflicted with a CVA or the individual who has sustained a spinal cord injury, an impact has been imposed upon his or her emotional well-being, somatic identity, sexuality, social identity, and occupational role. The remainder of this chapter will discuss how both illnesses affect these areas of concern and how the nurse and other members of the health care team can assist the afflicted individual in coping with the resulting impact.

IMPACT OF NEUROLOGICAL ALTERATIONS

Emotional Impact*

When an individual is afflicted with a cerebrovascular accident, the emotional response to the illness encompasses the individual's basic personality characteristics, the personality disturbances accompanying cerebrovascular disease prior to the CVA, and the mental symptoms resulting from the cerebral damage and physical disability of the CVA (Schwab, 1972). It is not uncommon for the afflicted individual, prior to a CVA, to display affective and intellectual disturbances due to cerebrovascular disease. According to Goldstein (1959), impairment of the abstract thought process is the most characteristic feature of brain damage. With a loss of the abstract thought process, the afflicted individual becomes more stimulus-bound and, as a result, encounters difficulty with attention and judgment. The individual tends to react to stress in a patterned way. Irritability, inability to withstand stress at home or at work, emotional liability demonstrated by sudden tears or jocularity, and increased anxiety or depression are early expressions of cerebrovascular disease. Such expressions, according to Goldstein (1959), are the individual's attempts to come to terms with his or her world.

Once the person sustains a CVA, additional emotional responses occur. The sense of powerlessness tends to be one of the cardinal emotional reactions immediately following the illness. This powerlessness is intensified by the loss of function in the affected body parts. The individual may find that he or she is unable to move, is incontinent of urine and feces, and is incapable of verbal communication in an understandable form. This sense of powerlessness often is compounded by the victim's fantasy that his or her body parts and body functions similarly will be crippled and by fears that death may be near. His or her self-image has sustained a major blow and the individual questions his or her self-worth. Two questions often asked by the CVA victim are: "What will become of me?" "What will others think of me now?"

The individual afflicted with a CVA undergoes two additional emotional reactions: anxiety and depression. The anxiety tends to be associated with an awareness of the presence of diminished cerebral function in addition to physical incapacitation. The victim may find that he or she is encountering difficulties in thinking clearly and is disoriented as to time, place, and person. Attempts to communicate may be futile since others are unable to comprehend what he or she is attempting to say. As a result, the CVA victim's anxiety heightens and his or her attempts to communicate become increasingly incomprehensible. A vicious cycle is created.

*It is advisable for the reader to have read Chapters 1 and 3 before continuing with this section.

Since both physical and mental processes are altered, the afflicted person experiences threats to both his or her physical and psychosocial security. If the CVA victim was the supporter of the family, he or she may feel incapable of carrying out this family role. For example, a housewife may question whether she will be able to function in an independent manner within the family structure.

As the CVA victim undergoes anxiety, it must not be forgotten that he or she also must contend with loss. The individual goes through the stages of loss* (repudiation, recognition, and reconciliation) as he or she grieves over the loss of various motor and sensory functions.

The family also may undergo anxiety which often is characterized by apprehension and uncertainty about the future integrity of the family unit (Schwartzman, 1976). The family members may demonstrate anger at the CVA victim because of their own feelings of helplessness and powerlessness about the illness. Since a cerebrovascular accident creates many impacts upon the afflicted person's daily activities, the individual and the family may encounter difficulties coping with these alterations in life-style. The curtailment of the CVA victim's way of life has to be dealt with by every member of the family unit.

To aid the CVA victim and the family in dealing with the sense of powerlessness and the feelings of anxiety, the nurse needs to assess and identify the coping mechanisms used by both the individual afflicted with the CVA and the family. Since every person goes through life developing various means of coping and adapting to stressful situations, the nurse and other members of the health care team must become cognizant of these mechanisms. In other words, "How did this individual deal with previous stresses, such as illness?" "What are the individual's physical and mental strengths?" "What are the family's strengths?" The nurse needs to identify the premorbid personality of the CVA victim and the premorbid personality of each family member. Once the coping mechanisms and strengths of the CVA victim and the family have been identified, the nurse can assist them in utilizing these behaviors to deal with the illness. For example, if the CVA victim or the family members have found crying a means of relieving anxiety, then such a maneuver should be encouraged as a means of coping with stress. Possibly the counsel of a clergyman has been effective for the afflicted person or the family when crisis situations have occurred. If so, they should be encouraged to seek counsel from such a person as they attempt to cope with the impact of a cerebrovascular accident. In addition, as the afflicted person and the family confront the stages of loss, the nurse needs to utilize the techniques and approaches outlined in Chapter 3.

Depression, a second emotional reaction to a CVA, is generally a behavior manifested in those persons who have encountered little intellectual

*Refer to Chapter 3.

impairment (Schwab, 1972). Therefore, once the acute stage of the stroke has passed and the afflicted person's behavior patterns have stabilized, the nurse and other health team members must determine which behaviors are a result of brain damage and which are not. For example, when the CVA victim bursts into tears, is the behavior the result of "organic crying," the result of motor discharge, or the result of thinking sad thoughts?

The afflicted person's feelings of depression may be brought about by numerous situations. For example, the CVA victim may feel depressed at the thought of being unable to carry out his or her daily activities. No longer can the individual take for granted walking, feeding, bathing, or dressing himself or herself. The CVA victim now is dependent upon others for assistance. The CVA victim's concerns about the family's welfare, finances, and job security may precipitate feelings of depression. As the afflicted person looks at his or her situation, he or she may feel completely overpowered by the ramifications of the illness.

To assist the CVA victim and family members in dealing with depression, members of the health care team must reassure them that they will not be abandoned by them. Constant reassurance about the presence of both physical and emotional assistance is in order. In addition, the afflicted individual must regularly receive positive feedback on all progress made. For example, the nurse should point out to the CVA victim that he or she assumed more responsibility in feeding himself or herself today than he or she did three days ago and praise the individual when he or she demonstrates increasing independence in getting from the bed into the chair. It also proves beneficial to reassure the individual that as he or she physically progresses, these feelings of depression tend to subside.

Above all, encouraging the expression of feelings of depression is vital. Depression may be expressed verbally or nonverbally. The afflicted person *never* should be reprimanded for expressing feelings. Often family members become embarrassed if their afflicted loved one suddenly bursts into tears. In such a circumstance, it should be explained to the family that the CVA victim often encounters difficulties in controlling emotions and that he or she always should be allowed to express these feelings openly. If family members continue to encounter difficulty in dealing with their loved one's expression of feelings, they may require encouragement to verbalize their own feelings to members of the health care team. Simply expressing their feelings can aid in decreasing their frustration about their loved one's demonstration of depression.

The emotional impact of a spinal cord injury often is very intense since the afflicted individuals are most commonly young adults who have sustained a traumatic accident. Immediately following the injury, the afflicted person enters the first stage of loss, repudiation. The initial reaction is one of shock. Thought processes are slowed down and the person appears confused and numb. The spinal cord injury victim appears unresponsive and rather remote when questioned about the accident. Feelings often are flat and rather vague since the afflicted person fails to comprehend the total impact of what has happened to him or her. The primary concern at this time is survival.

Following a reaction of shock, the spinal cord injury victim begins to deny the total impact of the illness. He or she finds it difficult to believe or accept that sensory and/or motor alterations are present. The inability to move around freely seems totally incomprehensible. The individual does not want to talk or think about the injury. False hopes often pass through the victim's mind as he or she has fantasies of moving around freely and safely on his or her own. A statement such as, "I'm going to walk out of this hospital come hell or high water!" is a demonstration of the afflicted person's denial.

To aid the spinal cord injury victim during the stage of repudiation, it is best to allow him or her to deny, but by no means should the nurse join the individual in denial. To remove denial suddenly would be disastrous since it is his or her only means of coping at this time. Instead, the spinal cord injury victim should be provided with truthful information about the illness, but the information should not be so extensive that it intensifies the use of further denial. For example, if the individual asks if he or she will walk again, a simple statement such as, "It is very unlikely" can suffice. Giving the individual a five-minute explanation about the neurological reasons why he or she will not walk again will only overwhelm the individual's already taxed emotional state. Eventually the spinal cord injury victim's denial breaks down because he or she begins to discover that he or she will not be able to walk and that his or her wishful thinking is not coming true.

Following demonstrations of denial, the spinal cord injury victim enters the second stage of loss, recognition. It is during this stage of loss that the individual begins to face the reality of the permanent disability. This stage of loss is marked by anxiety, hostility, guilt, and depression (Peter, 1975). It is not uncommon for the spinal cord victim to believe that he or she is being punished by God for real or imagined sins. The individual may feel that the fate that has befallen him or her is his or her own fault. The afflicted person may withdraw and be uncommunicative. The individual may lie quietly in bed with the sheets drawn over his or her head to hide weeping. The spinal cord injury victim says things like, "I would be better off dead" or "I would like to die."

Suicide in nonspecific terms may be contemplated. If the suicidal idea-tion takes on a specific plan, such as how, when, and where the act will be carried out, immediate psychiatric intervention is mandatory (Beck, Resnick, and Lettieri, 1974). It is a grave mistake to believe that because an individ-ual is disabled that disability mechanically precludes his or her ability to commit suicide. Suicide is a significant cause of death in this population (Nyquist and Bors, 1967).

Since the spinal cord injury victim may blame others for the loss, expressions of hostility may be manifested during the stage of recognition. Members of the health care team and family members often are the target of the individual's hostility. The afflicted person's language may become abusive and he or she is likely to be physically and verbally assaultive. The individual's behavior becomes demanding, intolerant, and impatient (Hohmann, 1975). Although the spinal cord injury victim may demonstrate thoroughly disagreeable behavior during the stage of recognition, it is a most opportune time to make rapid gains in the rehabilitative process.

To utilize the spinal cord injury victim's negative behavior during the stage of recognition, the nurse needs to channel the behavior into constructive endeavors. The afflicted person needs to be provided with support and reassurance. He or she should be encouraged to ventilate feelings, and these expressed feelings should be accepted. In addition, the afflicted individual should be encouraged to share his or her thoughts with family members. It is not uncommon for the victim of a spinal cord injury to attempt to dissociate himself or herself from the family since he or she believes it is the only decent thing to do. In the case of the afflicted married male, suggestion of and insistence on divorce are not infrequent (Hohmann, 1975).

During periods of hostile and aggressive behavior the spinal cord injury victim needs to be provided with activities that appropriately and constructively channel his or her energies. For example, if the individual is physically capable, he or she should be provided with a punching bag to hit, materials for leather tooling, or materials for rug hooking. All of these activities require physical expenditure of energy and at the same time aid in building muscles in the upper extremities. The individual also should be encouraged to express his or her hostility verbally, but the individual needs to be reminded that he or she must make an effort to control and direct these feelings appropriately.

It is also helpful to point out to the afflicted individual his or her positive attributes during the stage of recognition. Making a point of referring to what the patient can do for himself or herself both physically and mentally (Pepper, 1977) and what plans exist for his or her rehabilitation is most beneficial. These maneuvers are a direct attempt to help rebuild the spinal cord victim's self-concept.

Family members may encounter difficulties in dealing with their loved one's expressed feelings during the stage of recognition. Therefore, family members should be encouraged to ventilate their feelings of helplessness and frustration to members of the health care team. Ways in which they can help in channeling the afflicted person's energies into constructive endeavors should be suggested. For example, bringing in the spinal cord injury victim's dumbbells for lifting or bringing in the person's T.V. so that he or she can expend energy while watching a boxing match or a competitive skiing event are but two possible suggestions. If the family continues to encounter difficulty in coping with the spinal cord victim's feelings during the stage of recognition, counseling may be in order and the nurse must refer the family accordingly.

The spinal cord injury victim enters the third stage of loss, resolution, when he or she comes to accept himself or herself as a disabled person. During resolution the individual begins to obtain satisfaction from his or her new positive experiences, such as learning to drive a car with hand controls or transferring himself or herself from a wheelchair to a car.

These positive experiences enable the afflicted individual to feel good as a person. As a result, the individual begins to view himself or herself as someone who has the ability to be independent, to make decisions, and to realistically become a responsible individual. It is during resolution that the person with a spinal cord injury demonstrates a capability for organizing and planning his or her life in such a manner that he or she will be able to move on to a more mature level of function.

The nurse's responsibility does not end when the individual with a spinal cord injury reaches the stage of resolution. It is during this period that the nurse must be ever aware of the individual's need for honesty, support, and reassurance. It should be remembered that although the spinal cord victim may have reached the stage of resolution, underlying feelings of helplessness and anxiety are always present. These feelings may have to be dealt with periodically throughout the lifetime of the spinal cord injury.

In summary, the emotional impact both of a CVA and of a spinal cord injury can be overwhelming to the person afflicted and to the family. Anxiety, depression, hostility, and powerlessness are all emotional reactions encountered by either the individual stricken with a CVA or the person afflicted with a spinal cord injury. Both conditions can produce a lifelong disability that hampers the ability to move about independently. As a result, both the life-style of the afflicted person and the life-style of the family are affected. Therefore, it is the nurse's responsibility to aid the afflicted individual and the family in dealing with their reactions to the emotional impact of either one of these neurological conditions.

Somatic Impact*

The somatic impact of a cerebrovascular accident or a spinal cord injury can be devastating. The extensiveness of the cerebrovascular accident or the spinal cord injury will determine the type of bodily dysfunction occurring

*It is advisable for the reader to have read Chapter 2 before continuing with this section.

as a result of either illness. Certain bodily dysfunctions, however, tend to occur commonly in both of these illnesses. Therefore, these alterations and the impact they create upon one's body image will be presented in this section.

An individual afflicted with a CVA undergoes numerous assaults to his or her body image. Some of the more common assaults include an alteration in bladder and bowel function, a loss of motor and sensory function on one side of the body, and an alteration in verbal communication. Each of these alterations creates difficulties for the afflicted person as he or she attempts to redefine and deal with the post-CVA body image.

Urinary incontinence is a rather common problem for the person afflicted with a CVA (Jacobansky, 1972). Micturation is both voluntary and involuntary in control. The voluntary component is controlled by the cerebrum and the involuntary component is controlled by the reflex arc of the spinal nerves. Since the person afflicted with a CVA has undergone an alteration in cerebral function, the bladder may empty when intrabladder pressure stimulates the spinal nerve reflex. For the individual afflicted with a CVA, the awareness of the need to void tends to occur almost simultaneously with the automatic reflex act. If voluntary emptying of the bladder does not take place when the urge to void occurs, involuntary emptying of the bladder will result. The consequences are incontinence and embarrassment.

Constipation, unlike bowel incontinence, is a problem for the person afflicted with a CVA. The passage of fecal material slows down in the colon of the afflicted person, but water absorption from the fecal mass continues as long as the fecal mass is in the colon. The results are constipation and ultimately impaction if the problem is not dealt with appropriately.

Since bladder and bowel control are bodily habits dealt with early in childhood, their dysfunction during adult life can create difficulties for the afflicted person. Feelings of humiliation and thoughts of regression are not uncommon when the adult afflicted with a CVA soils himself or herself. Therefore, the role of the nurse is to aid the afflicted person in dealing with this somatic impact of illness by attempting to regulate bowel and bladder function in order to prevent soiling.

In the early course of recovery the use of external catheters for male patients and indwelling catheters for female patients may be necessary to prevent urinary incontinence and subsequent skin breakdown. However, once the acute crisis of illness is over, it is advisable to set up a routine schedule for bladder retraining. In other words, regularly and consistently placing the individual on a bedpan or a commode for voiding aids in establishing the patient's voiding patterns and cuts down on the risks of catheterization. For bowel dysfunction, placing the afflicted individual on stool softeners or on laxatives, regularly or as needed, aids in alleviating constipation. Routinely checking the afflicted person for an impaction also cuts down on the accumulation of hardened stool in the rectum. For some patients it may be necessary to use enemas or suppositories to establish a bowel pattern. When the afflicted person's usual time for defecation is identified, he or she should be placed on a bedpan or a commode, in privacy, to facilitate the passage of feces and to prevent soiling. If the individual afflicted with a CVA soils himself or herself with either urine or feces, the individual requires reassurance from the nurse that he or she no longer has preillness control over elimination habits. The individual should be cleaned up quickly and in a matter-of-fact fashion. The individual never should be reprimanded for the accident. Instead, the individual needs to release his or her feelings of humiliation and embarrassment about the loss of the elimination function. In addition, family members may require information about the afflicted person's inability to control waste products in the usual manner. They need reassurance that bowel and bladder retraining may be slow, but that with time most afflicted persons can be kept free of elimination accidents. They too must be encouraged to avoid reprimanding the afflicted person when an accident occurs.

Loss of motor and sensory function on one side of the body is another impact upon the CVA victim's body image. As a result of the altered sensory and motor function, the afflicted individual may manifest, on the affected side, hemianopia, a decrease or loss of sensory input, and a decrease or loss of motor control.

Hemianopia or blindness in one-half of one or both eyes often occurs in the CVA victim. The type of hemianopia the person has must be determined so that appropriate measures can be taken to facilitate visual stimulation. For example, if the afflicted person has homonymous hemianopia (blindness of the nasal half of one eye and the temporal half of the other eye), he or she should always be approached on the nonaffected side. The food tray should be positioned so that the individual can visualize all of the food on it. To aid in dressing, the CVA victim with homonymous hemianopia needs to be reminded to turn the head toward the affected side so that he or she can see the body part to be dressed. During personal contacts the afflicted person's nonaffected side should be placed toward the other person to enable visualization of the other individual and subsequently enhance communication (Schultz, 1973).

Decreased or absent sensation in the affected side creates an image of one-half a body for the CVA victim. When asked to describe how he or she sees himself or herself, the CVA victim often says that he or she views himself or herself as only half a person. The individual may describe the affected side as useless, no good, and nonexistent. The CVA victim may actually verbalize a desire to rid himself or herself of part or all of the affected side.

Since the afflicted individual fails to perceive normal sensations from the affected side, the chances of accidental injury to that side are great. Accidental burning or cutting of the skin on the affected side may go unnoticed since painful stimuli are not perceived. Therefore, the nurse and other members of the health care team need to point this out to the afflicted person and the family. Use of heating pads, hot bath water, and constricting shoes and clothing, staying in one position for a long period of time, and going barefoot should be discouraged. Each of these activities can be a source of injury to the affected side. Both the CVA victim and the family should be encouraged to examine daily the affected side for possible cuts, burns, or pressure areas. If any of these injuries is noted, appropriate care must be initiated. (The reader is advised to consult a textbook of medical-surgical nursing for physical care of the individual with a CVA.)

The decrease or loss of motor control on the affected side results in alterations in mobility, facial appearance, and ability to feed oneself. As a result, the CVA victim may find that he or she will have to undergo rehabilitative processes in order to learn to walk and to feed himself or herself again. The individual may require the assistance of a custom-built fork, a cane, a walker, or a sling. Since ambulatory aids and feeding devices are necessary for mobility and independence, they eventually become an integral part of the person's body image. The CVA victim sees these aides and devices as an extension of himself or herself since without them he or she cannot function independently.

As a result of sensory and motor loss, facial drooping on the affected side is common. When viewing himself or herself in the mirror the CVA victim may feel uneasy about his or her facial appearance since every time he or she smiles only one-half of the face demonstrates an expression of pleasure. The affected side demonstrates an unhappy or drooping appearance as a result of the loss of muscle function. The afflicted individual needs to be encouraged to verbalize both to the members of the health care team and to the family how he or she feels about the facial appearance. In addition, expressions of acceptance by health team members and family members are vital. For example, including the afflicted person in decision making, directly looking at him or her during communication, and making body contact are but a few maneuvers to use to express acceptance. Above all, health team members and family members must avoid making comments or derogatory remarks about the CVA victim's facial expression.

Because of the facial drooping, the CVA victim may drool and be unable to remove food in the cheek of the affected side. To aid in decreasing the obviousness of these two problems, the afflicted person should be encouraged to carry tissues (these can be tucked inside the arm sling) to wipe up secretions and to check the cheek for residual food after eating. The CVA victim should be instructed to turn away from other individuals while carrying out these maneuvers so that he or she will avoid attracting attention.

A decreased ability to use body language also exists for the CVA victim since he or she suffers from altered motor control. No longer can the individual freely move the affected arm and leg to express himself or herself nonverbally. As a result, the CVA victim's use of body language initially may diminish. The individual may feel hindered in expressing himself or herself nonverbally since he or she is unable to utilize freely one-half of the body. But as the CVA victim's recovery and rehabilitative process progresses, there will, no doubt, be a more conscious use of the unaffected side for nonverbal expression. Hence, the afflicted individual needs reassurance that as independence and mobility increase, spontaneous body language will also increase.

Another impact upon the CVA victim's body image is an alteration in verbal communication, aphasia. Aphasia is a defect in the utilization and interpretation of the symbols of language brought about by a dysfunction in the cerebral cortex (Luckmann and Sorensen, 1974). Aphasia may be sensory in nature (receptive aphasia) in that the afflicted individual encounters difficulties comprehending speech. Aphasia may be motor in nature (expressive aphasia) and the ability to produce speech is affected.

Some CVA victims afflicted with receptive aphasia may be able to follow simple verbal commands with relative ease, others may be able to follow verbal commands accompanied by gestures, and some may be unable to follow even one-word and one-gesture commands. CVA victims with expressive aphasia vary from being able to say one word over and over to being unable to utter a sound. These individuals often point, nod, shake their heads, and use pantomime in an attempt to express themselves. Since a major human need is to communicate effectively with others, the presence of either receptive or expressive aphasia can be overwhelming.

To facilitate communication, the nurse and the CVA victim's family members need to keep the following basic techniques in mind when they communicate with the aphasic individual:

1. Provide the aphasic individual with a variety of auditory and visual stimuli.

2. Speak directly to the aphasic person.

3. Encourage the aphasic individual to look directly at the speaker.

4. Use simple one-word commands and gestures.

5. Speak in a normal tone of voice and at a slower than usual pace.

6. Keep sentence structure brief and simple.

7. Allow the aphasic person time to respond if a response is expected.

8. Provide the aphasic individual with paper and pencil, if he is able to write, so he or she can draw a picture of the object wanted.

9. Provide the aphasic person with a book containing pictures of all the items he or she may request. The individual can point to the picture of the item as he or she needs it.

10. Be patient as the aphasic person attempts to comprehend communication and/or express himself or herself.

For some CVA victims, speech therapy may be necessary. In such a case, the nurse should contact the health team member who is qualified to carry out the necessary therapy.

In summary, the presence of a CVA can create multiple impacts upon the afflicted person's body image. Sight, speech, bowel and bladder function, and motor abilities are but a few possible body image alterations the person may face after suffering a CVA. The nurse's role is to assist the afflicted individual and the family as they attempt to cope with the somatic impact of this illness.

The somatic impact of a spinal cord injury is similar, in some respects, to the somatic impact of a cerebrovascular accident. The individual who has sustained a spinal cord injury also views his or her body as being half of its original size. With the spinal cord injury victim, however, the missing body parts extend either from the waist down (paraplegia) or extend from the neck down (quadriplegia). The spinal cord injury victim who has become a quadriplegic, as a result of the injury, may describe his or her body image as nothing more than a head and a chest.

To aid the afflicted person in coping with his or her altered body image, the individual needs encouragement to verbalize to the nurse and to family members how he or she feels about not being able to move one-half or three-quarters of the body. Does the individual consider himself or herself dependent upon others? Does he or she think that he or she is less than an adult? These are but two questions that may enter the afflicted individual's mind. In addition, the spinal cord injury victim requires reassurance that through rehabilitation he or she will be able to become more independent and mobile with the aid of ambulatory aids. As the individual develops skills of mobility and self-care, some of the feelings about being only one-half or three-quarters of a person may subside.

To facilitate mobility, the spinal cord injury victim learns to utilize ambulatory aids such as a walker or a wheelchair. Since ambulatory aids are essential for independence and mobility, the spinal cord injury victim sees these aids as a direct extension of himself or herself.

One body image alteration that the spinal cord injury victim sustains, if he or she uses a wheelchair, that the CVA victim may not sustain, unless he or she uses a wheelchair, is a shortening in stature. Since the spinal cord injury victim spends a large portion of the time sitting in a wheelchair, his or her plane of communication is altered. Instead of communicating face to face with others, the individual communicates face to chest or face to waist. The spinal cord injury victim literally is looked down upon during communication just as the young child often is looked down upon by the adult. This alteration in body image may seem demeaning and even, for the male spinal cord injury victim, emasculating.

To aid the spinal cord injury victim in coping with this feeling of being talked down to, the individual should be encouraged to request others to pull up a chair and sit down next to him or her if a conversation is to extend for any length of time. Members of the health care team and family members also need to remember to carry out this maneuver. In addition, the spinal cord injury victim should be encouraged to express how he or she feels about the shortened stature to both health team members and to family members. Verbalization not only aids in relieving some of the anxiety, but it also assists others in understanding how the spinal cord victim feels about himself or herself.

In the paraplegic, changes in the size of the muscle mass of the upper extremities can be an additional body image alteration. The spinal cord injury victim learns to use the upper extremities for moving the paralyzed body from one location to another. As a result, muscles become strengthened and enlarged. Generally, this alteration does not create problems unless the afflicted individual considers this increased muscle mass grotesque. The male spinal cord injury victim often believes that an increased muscle mass is a mark of masculinity. The female spinal cord injury victim, however, is more likely to view this change in an unpleasant light. Therefore, explaining to the afflicted female the value and reason for the increased muscle mass and encouraging her to wear clothing that loosely covers the arms and chest to aid in concealing the enlarged muscle mass can prove beneficial.

Changes in bladder and bowel function are alterations to the body image of the spinal cord injury victim. Unlike the CVA victim, the spinal cord injury victim often is unable to control micturation. The person becomes dependent upon a catheter and a leg bag for the remainder of his or her life. Initially, the individual may feel as though he or she has regressed in the ability to control elimination habits. However, he or she soon realizes that having to use a catheter is much better than being incontinent of urine. Reassuring the afflicted person that the catheter and leg bag can be worn under clothing in an unobvious manner is helpful. In addition it is beneficial to advise the avoidance of wearing tight trousers and pants in an attempt to decrease the noticeable protrusion that the leg bag can create.

Bowel alterations for the spinal cord injury victim are related to a decrease in gastrointestinal motility. Because of constipation an impaction can be common if not adequately treated. The approaches for dealing with this problem are the same as the approaches used for the CVA victim with altered bowel function (see pages 285-286).

In summary, the spinal cord injury victim sustains alterations in his body image related to sensory and motor function, body build and stature, and bowel and bladder function. The nurse's role revolves around assisting the afflicted person and the family in coping with these somatic alterations as the spinal cord injury victim learns to reconstruct his or her body image and self-concept.

The developmental stage being experienced by the CVA victim and the spinal cord injury victim at the time of illness has an effect upon the ability to cope with an altered body image. If the individual is in the stage of young adulthood (eighteen to forty-five years), energies are centered around sharing himself or herself with others both in friendship and in a mutually satisfying sexual relationship (Erikson, 1963). If a CVA or a spinal cord injury occurs during this developmental stage and if the afflicted person encounters problems dealing with the illness, a sense of isolation is likely to develop. The sense of isolation may be brought about by the afflicted person's inability to see his or her body as useful and/or attractive. The acceptance of one's body image plays a vital role in being able to relate successfully to others. For the female afflicted with a CVA or a spinal cord injury, her body image centers around the appearance that she believes her body presents. If she sees herself as unattractive, she is likely to retreat from others. The male, on the other hand, is more likely to define his body image in terms of achievement rather than bodily attributes. If the afflicted male believes that, because of his altered body image, he cannot achieve, he too may retreat from others and fail to establish either a meaningful friendship or a mutually satisfying sexual relationship.

The person in the stage of adulthood (forty-five to sixty-five years) directs his or her energies toward establishing and guiding future generations with the hope of bettering society (Erikson, 1963). The presence of a CVA or a spinal cord injury may lead the afflicted person to believe that he or she is incapable of carrying out this task. Instead of attempting to guide others, he or she may withdraw and feel that he or she has little to offer. Chronic defeatism and depression result as the afflicted person retreats into isolation and self-pity.

The final stage of life, maturity (sixty-five years and over), brings with it frequent thoughts of death. The presence of an altered body image as the result of a CVA or spinal cord injury may intensify the frequency of these thoughts. The afflicted person may view the illness as the final prelude to terminating his or her existence and, as a result, enters into a state of despair. The individual may question his or her self-worth and wonder if he or she is of value to anyone.

To aid the afflicted person regardless of whether he or she is in the stage of young adulthood, adulthood, or maturity, the person must be made to feel that he or she has something positive to offer others. Pointing out the person's assets and what he or she can do for himself or herself and others through rehabilitation can help to prevent isolation, stagnation, and despair. For example, if the afflicted person was an avid and critical reader, he or she may find that he or she can proofread rough draft manuscripts. If the individual was an outstanding cook, putting recipes into written form for others to use is another example of utilizing one's positive assets. Thus, the nurse and other members of the health care team must be creative in aiding the afflicted person in recognizing his or her attributes and utilizing them to their fullest.

In summary, the presence of a neurological alteration creates an impact upon the afflicted person's somatic identity. The nurse's role centers around assisting the afflicted individual and the family in dealing with each alteration through rehabilitation. In addition, the individual sustaining a body image alteration caused by neurological malfunction needs to be made aware that he or she has something positive to offer others and that these positive attributes are of value. Identifying and aiding the afflicted individual in using his or her assets to their greatest potential provide limitless opportunities for creativity for members of the health care team.

Sexual Impact

Sexuality neither begins nor ends in the bedroom; it involves more than just coitus and is therefore an ever present part of life. Therefore, just because an individual has sustained a neurological alteration by no means should he or she be considered void of sexuality and/or sexual expression.

The impact of a neurological alteration upon one's sexuality will vary depending upon the location, extent, and nature of the alteration. Therefore, the first task in dealing with the sexual impact of a neurological condition, such as a CVA or a spinal cord injury, is to assess and identify with the aid of the afflicted individual and his or her sex partner what changes in sexual behavior have occurred or will occur as a result of the illness.

The sexual impact of a CVA often demonstrates itself by a lack of interest in sexual activity or the development of new sexual inhibitions. It is not uncommon for the sex partner of the afflicted person to make the following comments: "My lover just is not interested in sex anymore." "We use to have such a fulfilling sex life!" The lack of interest or development of new inhibitions often is related to the afflicted person's fear of being unable to perform sexually and the fear of being sexually undesirable. The fear of being unable to perform sexually tends to be more prevalent in the male afflicted with a CVA than in the female. This is so because men more often perceive their bodies as means of achieving and as a result take on the aggressive role during the sex act. The fear of lacking sexual desirability may prove to be more prevalent in the female CVA victim than in the male since women place more value on their appearance.

Since one side of the body has undergone altered sensory/motor function as a result of the CVA, the afflicted person suffers from a loss in the ability to feel body contact and a loss in the ability to support body weight on the affected side. As a result, it is difficult, if not impossible, to derive pleasure from sexual tactile experiences on the affected side or to support the body weight on the affected side. Nevertheless, members of the health care team must not write off the afflicted individual's ability to take part in and derive satisfaction from a sexual experience.

The nurse's role in dealing with the sexual impact of a CVA is to identify and discuss the potential difficulties related to the sexual experience with the afflicted person and his or her sex partner. This must be done prior to the afflicted person's discharge from the acute care setting. One of the most frustrating things for the sex partner is not being aware of the possible difficulties related to the afflicted person's sexuality.

Encouraging both partners to ventilate feelings with each other about the sex act is important. Encouraging them to identify and discuss with each other sexual experiences which each finds pleasurable is vital. For example, since the CVA victim has altered sensory and motor function on one side of the body, the sex partner may find it desirable to direct caresses toward the unaffected side. Using the side-lying position for the sex act may prove more comfortable for both partners since the CVA victim may encounter difficulties supporting his or her body weight if he or she assumes the superior position. Both partners need to be encouraged to experiment with various positions and maneuvers so that they can identify what acts are most pleasurable for them. Above all, the sex partner should be encouraged to reassure the CVA victim of his or her sexual desirability. Complimenting the CVA victim on his or her attractive appearance or simply saying how nice it is to be with the individual are but two such examples. In addition, the sex partner should be encouraged to avoid referring to the afflicted person's ability to perform sexually. Comments to this effect only add to intensifying existing fears of sexual inadequacy. If the sexual impact of the CVA becomes overwhelming and seems unresolvable for the couple, the nurse may have to encourage sex counseling by a prepared therapist.

The sexual impact of a spinal cord injury depends upon the location and extent of the lesion since the level and type of lesion greatly influence the component of the sexual experience. Bors and Comarr (1960) did a survey of individuals with spinal cord injuries and found that three possible problems occur for the male spinal cord injury victim: the absence of an erection, the absence of ejaculation, and the absence of orgasm.

Bors and Comarr (1960) state that in males afflicted with a complete upper motor neuron lesion, erection (reflexogenic* only) is possible in 93 percent of the victims, ejaculation is rare, and orgasm is absent. In males

Reflexogenic: in response to local stimulation

afflicted with an incomplete upper motor neuron lesion erection is possible in 99 percent of the victims (reflexogenic in 80 percent and reflexogenic and psychogenic* in 19 percent), ejaculation is infrequent, and orgasm is present if ejaculation occurs. In males afflicted with a spinal cord injury with a complete lower motor neuron lesion erection is infrequent, ejaculation is infrequent, and orgasm is present if ejaculation occurs. Finally, in males with an incomplete lower motor neuron lesion erection (psychogenic and reflexogenic) is possible in 90 percent of the victims, ejaculation is frequent, and orgasm is present if ejaculation occurs. Comarr (1971) also found that generally the afflicted person will know within six months of the injury how much sexual function will return. Thus, it can be seen that the sexual capabilities of the afflicted person are based upon the extent and location of the cord injury.

To assess sexual potential, the victim requires a complete neurological examination. Once sexual potential has been determined, sex counseling should be carried out. Lack of information on the victim's sexual potential could lead to the dissemination of erroneous explanations and inappropriate counseling.

The nurse's role in assisting the spinal cord injury victim deal with the sexual impact of the illness is to aid him or her and the sex partner in maximizing their sexual experiences based upon the spinal cord injury victim's sexual potentials. Manual stimulation of the penis generally is an effective method for promoting erection when psychogenic stimulation is ineffective. The use of a condom stretched around the base of the penis and held in place with stretchable tape may be used to maintain engorgement and prevent detumescence before intromission (Jackson, 1972). However, the spinal cord injury victim should be encouraged not to position the condom too tightly or to leave it in place for more than a half-hour (Woods, 1975) since an alteration in blood supply to the penis could occur. Caressing the inner surfaces of the thighs and the lower abdomen also can lead to an erection (reflex) and can prove beneficial for some couples during their sexual experiences. In addition, the male victim should be cautioned against the use of drugs or alcohol prior to intercourse since they act as central nervous system depressants and, as a result, may act to eradicate an erection (Romano and Lassiter, 1972).

Alternate means to sexual stimulation may need to be suggested to the spinal cord injury victim and his or her sex partner. For example, oral-genital contact may be desirable for some couples. Manual stimulation of the clitoris and the "stuffing-technique" may serve as substitutes for intromission for the male incapable of an erection (Woods, 1975). Some men may prefer to use prosthetic devices, vibrators, or fantasy material as aids to sexual arousal. Whatever means of sexual expression is suggested, the

Psychogenic: in response to psychic stimulation

afflicted person and the sex partner must decide which forms of expression are most desirable for them. In addition, the frequency of their sexual activity also is individual and depends upon their sexual appetites.

Another component of the spinal cord injury victim's sexuality is the ability to have children since the greatest percentage of afflicted persons are adults of childbearing age. A spinal cord injury does not necessarily preclude having children, but the afflicted person's chances may be decreased. If the male spinal cord injury victim is unable to ejaculate successfully, there is little chance of impregnating the sex partner. In such cases, it may be advisable to recommend semen analysis for the purpose of artificial insemination. Spermatazoa for artificial insemination have been retrieved from some men who cannot ejaculate. However, live births have been rare (Guttman and Walsh, 1971). If artificial insemination is inadvisable, adoption or donor insemination may be recommended as alternative approaches.

Positioning during coitus may be a concern of the spinal cord injury victim. If the victim is a quadriplegic, a supine position with the sex partner on top and providing the activity may prove most successful. With the paraplegic male, the use of top, bottom, or side-lying positions are possible (Jackson, 1972). The amount of activity engaged in by the spinal cord injury victim, of course, depends upon the level of injury.

The presence of a urethral catheter is a matter with which the male spinal cord injury victim may have to contend. Some males may find it desirable to leave the catheter in place by bending it over the end of the penis and stripping a condom over the penis and the catheter. Others may find this experience difficult since traction is placed on the catheter and subsequent aggravation of a urinary tract infection can occur (Jackson, 1972). If the male uses an external catheter, it should be removed prior to coitus and replaced afterward.

Both the male spinal cord injury victim and the sex partner must be made aware that during coitus excessive activity may lead to urination into the vagina. To aid in avoiding urination during intercourse, individuals who remove their internal and external catheters or who utilize intermittent catheterization should be advised to empty their bladders prior to coitus (Comarr and Gunderson, 1975). Since in most situations the urge to urinate is indicated by spasms, the spinal cord injury victim usually is able to withdraw in time to avoid such an experience (Jackson, 1972). To aid in dealing with the possible presence of urination during coitus, it is advisable for the couple to place a heavy absorbent towel under the buttocks.

Since many male spinal cord injury victims have chronic bladder infections, the continual potential for infecting the sex partner is present. Therefore, it is essential to instruct the male in good perineal care. Careful cleansing of the penis is a must. If the male is not circumcised, retracting the foreskin for cleansing is necessary in maintaining good hygiene.

Unfortunately, since limited research has been done on females sustaining spinal cord injuries, many questions on sexual function remain unanswered. It is known, however, that in complete lesions of the spinal cord the female does not experience vaginal sensations (Jackson, 1972). Although she may experience emotional satisfaction from intercourse, she experiences little in the way of physical satisfaction. According to Jackson (1972), few such women experience orgasm and it remains doubtful whether a true physiological orgasm can occur in the female with a complete spinal cord lesion. Faking an orgasm is not an uncommon practice and this, no doubt, is because the female wishes to please her sex partner.

It should not be assumed that females who have undergone a spinal cord injury will have fewer fears and concerns about their feminine sexual identity than their male counterparts. Researchers have demonstrated that women appear to be less disturbed than men about maintaining their sexuality with the opposite sex (Weiss and Diamond, 1966; Long, 1965). This probably can be attributed to the fact that women, in general, tend to assume a more passive role during coitus. However, at no time should members of the health team negate the existence of fears and concerns about sexuality in the female spinal cord injury victim.

For the female spinal cord injury victim, the existence of an internal catheter may raise questions about what to do with it during coitus. Since the catheter is positioned in an orifice separate from the orifice used for intercourse, it need not be removed. If the female wishes to remove the catheter or if she is on intermittent catherizations, she should be encouraged to empty her bladder prior to coitus in order to prevent urination during intercourse.

Positioning for the female during intercourse generally is supine. However, other positions are not out of the question and the afflicted individual and her sex partner may desire to experiment with various positions in order to find the ones most desirable for their particular sexual experiences.

As part of the sexual experience the ability to bear children may be a question raised by the female spinal cord injury victim. The female who is still menstruating can, of course, conceive and give birth to children (Guttman, 1964; Comarr, 1966). In this respect the female's sexual function is unchanged after injury. She must be informed, however, that her normal menstrual cycle *may* be disrupted for approximately a period of six months following the injury. If she is in or near menopause, she probably will not menstruate after the injury (Comarr, 1966). Most women should be able to deliver children vaginally and a Caesarean section generally is not necessary unless anatomical or physiological problems intervene (Robertson and Guttman, 1963).

For both the male and female spinal cord injury victims, communication between the victim and the sex partner is vital. It is essential for both to discuss with each other their fears, feelings, and desires. For example, if the spinal cord injury victim desires an oral-genital experience and the sex partner finds this unpleasant, they should discuss this matter. During this discussion they may identify an alternate means of sexual expression which is desirable for both of them. It is through communication that the sharing of activities which are most pleasurable takes place. Open and honest communication is the key to a healthy relationship (Bregman and Hadley, 1976). To illustrate, the female spinal cord injury victim may find that placing pillows under her thighs to support her legs is not only comfortable, but that it also increases the enjoyment of her sex partner's sexual experience. What spinal cord injury victims and their sex partners need to realize is what they together find enjoyable is what is important.

The impact that the spinal cord injury has upon the stability of the relationship between the victim and spouse may be a concern of the afflicted person. If the relationship was unstable at the time of the injury, the chances of a separation or a divorce may be greater. The divorce and separation rate has been found to be significantly higher in those afflicted individuals who had been married more than once at the time of the injury and who were once employed but are not currently (Ghatit, 1975). Most divorces tend to occur within a five-year period following the injury (Ghatit, 1975). Research has indicated that the divorce rate for the spinal cord injury victim does not differ from the divorce rate throughout the United States (Ghatit and Hanson, 1976). The separation rate, however, appears to be lower (Deyoe, 1972) among spinal cord injury victims than among the general population.

In summary, the sexual impact of a neurological condition, such as a CVA or a spinal cord injury, can be overwhelming. The effects may include difficulty and/or inability to perceive sensations in certain erotic areas of the body, difficulty and/or inability to move vital body parts, and disruption of erection, ejaculation, and orgasm. The total effect the neurological condition has upon the person's sexuality depends upon the location and extent of the alteration. Members of the health care team must be cognizant of this before proceeding with interventions aimed at dealing with the sexual impact of the illness. The nurse's role centers around assisting the afflicted individual and his or her sex partner to identify and discuss alternate means they can use for the sole purpose of achieving a mutually satisfying sexual experience. If the couple encounters difficulties in coping with the sexual impact of the neurological condition, the nurse should not hesitate to direct the couple to a therapist for sex counseling.

Occupational Impact

The occupational impact of a neurological condition can be devastating. As with all other impacts created by a neurological condition, the extent of the deficit greatly affects what impact the illness will have upon the afflicted person's ability to function in an occupational role.

Since CVAs often afflict the individual in adulthood or mature adulthood, an economic disaster can be created. The individual stricken with a CVA often is ready to enter retirement or may already be in retirement. If the afflicted individual is employed at the time of the CVA, he or she stands a chance of being forced out of his or her job because he or she is unable to move about freely and independently. If the individual is retired and has managed to save money to have a reasonably comfortable and independent old age, medical expenses are likely to deplete his or her savings. Generally, the afflicted individual's job-related health insurance ends when he or she retires, and, as a result, the individual has limited resources to use for adequate payment of health care or rehabilitation. Even with Medicare, the retired person may become a recipient of public welfare assistance following a CVA.

If the CVA victim is not close to retirement age, the occupational impact of the illness can also be overwhelming. In assessing the impact that the illness has upon the occupation, the nurse needs to know whether or not the afflicted person must have full use of two arms and two legs to carry out occupational endeavors. For example, a college professor, most likely, will have less difficulty in maintaining his or her occupational position than the individual who is a heavy equipment operator.

The nurse's role in dealing with the occupational impact of the CVA centers around assisting the afflicted person and the family in identifying what alterations in the work situation will be necessary so that the CVA victim can continue to pursue his or her occupation prior to the illness. On the other hand, the presence of the illness may make the afflicted person totally incapable of continuing his or her preillness occupational endeavor. When the afflicted person and the family begin to identify the impact the CVA will have upon occupational endeavors, the nurse's responsibility should be directed toward contacting members of the health care team qualified in assisting the CVA victim to deal with the occupational impact of the illness. Such health team members may include the social worker, the rehabilitation counselor, or the occupational therapist. These health team members can contact the CVA victim's employer and, with the employer, identify what alterations, if any, can be made in the work situation to accommodate the CVA victim. If accommodations cannot be made, job retraining may be in order.

The individual afflicted with a spinal cord injury generally is a young adult. He or she often is at the beginning of his or her occupational endeavors. As a result, the impact of a spinal cord injury may demand alterations in occupational goals. For example, if the afflicted person was a professional football player, he may find it necessary to change his pursuits to coaching. However, since the spinal cord injury victim, namely, the paraplegic, has functional use of the upper extremities, he or she retains the ability to carry out many different jobs. The nurse should encourage the afflicted person and the family to identify what alterations, if any, may have to be made so that the spinal cord injury victim can continue his or her occupational endeavors. Occupations requiring four workable limbs obviously would be out of the question. However, a limitless number of jobs require only the use of the upper extremities. As with the CVA victim, if alterations in the work situation are not feasible, then job retraining is in order.

For both the CVA victim and the spinal cord injury victim, encouragement to reenter the work force as soon as possible is necessary. The nurse and other health team members must inform the afflicted person and the family of the importance of the afflicted individual's resuming gainful employment. Not only does gainful employment provide much needed economic support, but it also aids in building feelings of self-worth.

Alterations in family roles may occur as a result of a CVA or a spinal cord injury. Prior to the illness the afflicted person may have assumed total control over the family's financial matters. Following the illness other family members may have to assume part or all of this responsibility. If this happens, the afflicted person may feel that his or her self-worth is being threatened. Thus, the nurse should encourage the afflicted person and the family to discuss what means can be used to maintain realistic roles within the family. To exclude totally the afflicted individual from the role he or she lead within the family before the illness is not advisable, since it may create feelings of low self-worth. Open and honest verbalization among family members about each individual's contribution to the family structure and the allowance for each member's carrying out these contributions is vital for family stability.

In summary, the CVA victim or the spinal cord injury victim is likely to undergo alterations in occupational role. However, many victims with a CVA or a spinal cord injury are capable of assuming their jobs when minor alterations are made in the work environment (e.g., ramps instead of stairs). It is vital for the afflicted person to assume occupational endeavors as soon as possible and if job retraining is necessary to meet this goal, he or she should enter a job retraining program.

Social Impact

The effect a neurological alteration, such as a CVA or a spinal cord injury, has on an individual's social identity depends upon the degree of neurological deficit and the amount of social encounter engaged in by the specific individual. If little neurological deficit exists, the afflicted person probably will not have to alter social activities in any way, but when sensory and motor deficits cause the individual to be immobile, the afflicted individual may find it necessary to make alterations in social endeavors.

The person afflicted with a CVA often is an individual who has reached or is on the edge of retirement. As a result, social encounters may have either decreased or increased markedly because of the extra available time for activities. When the nurse is assessing the social impact of the afflicted person's illness it is advisable to be aware of the person's social life before the illness. The nurse's major goal is to assist the afflicted person in attaining and maintaining his or her social state before the illness.

One of the most common reactions to the social impact of a CVA is the fear of not being a desirable participant in social encounters. Since the afflicted person may have difficulty with or alterations in mobility, he or she may feel a burden to the enjoyment of others. As a result, he or she may withdraw from social encounters and retreat into isolation. The person afflicted with a CVA may find that in order to engage in the social activities he or she once enjoyed, alteration in the activities is necessary. For example, if he or she was an avid square dancer or an active cross-country skier, these activities may have to be altered or dispensed with entirely. Instead of square dancing, the afflicted person may find slow ballroom dancing more desirable or may even enjoy sitting along the sidelines conversing while watching others dance. If cross-country skiing was a sport enjoyed by the afflicted person, he or she may find bird watching an enjoyable substitute since this activity places the individual in the out-of-doors, just as skiing did. If the afflicted individual took part in more sedentary activities prior to the illness, then card playing, stamp collecting, or coin collecting may be feasible social activities.

In dealing with the social impact of a CVA, the nurse must alert the afflicted person and the family to the possibility of the CVA victim's withdrawing from social contacts. The nurse and other members of the health care team should assist the afflicted person and the family to identify forms of social endeavors in which the CVA victim can partake. The family must be made aware of the importance of constantly encouraging the CVA victim to take part in social activities. As the type of activities are being identified, certain environmental considerations must be made. For example, does the environment housing the social activity have numerous steps for the CVA victim to climb and, if so, is a ramp available? Do the bathroom facilities provide one commode with handrails and an elevated commode seat to facilitate getting on and off the commode? Once the environment of the social function is examined, then the CVA victim and the family more reasonably can decide on the feasibility of taking part in the social event.

The presence of ambulatory aids may create difficulties for some individuals in the social setting. To illustrate, some CVA victims may find that their walkers are a hindrance in setting up a comfortable social distance. In such cases, the nurse can encourage the CVA victim to sit down and place the walker to one side when engaging in social conversation. By so doing, the ambulatory aid does not block the potential for personal body contact. If the CVA victim feels that the arm sling is a distraction, he or she can be encouraged to wear colorful or decorative arm slings. How colorful and decorative the afflicted person desires to be is strictly up to the individual. The possibilities for creativity in decorating an arm sling are limitless.

In addition to wearing colorful and attractive arm slings, the CVA victim should be encouraged to buy clothing that is both becoming and easy to put on and take off. Often one of the greatest deterrents to taking part in social functions is the concern about how he or she looks to others. Clothing that is both becoming and comfortable for the individual and easy to get in and out of (e.g., clothes that button and zip in the front) is more likely to be worn. In turn, if the person feels attractive to others, he or she is more likely to engage in social events.

The CVA victim and the family need to express to each other how they feel about taking part in social activities in which a handicapped individual is included. For example, if the CVA victim feels like a burden in some social encounters, he or she should be encouraged to say so. If young grandchildren feel that their grandparent is an unpleasant addition at certain social functions, they need to express these feelings. Once these feelings are out in the open, the afflicted person and the family are more capable of appropriately selecting, together, social activities that can be enjoyed by all. In some situations, however, the CVA victim and the family may find it advisable to attend certain social functions separately, but it is better if this is a joint decision made within the family structure.

Often social events where there are large crowds can create difficulties for the CVA victim. Crowding may cause the afflicted person to feel unstable on his or her feet and, as a result, may fear falling. One suggestion that the nurse can make to the afflicted individual and the family is that they plan to arrive at the social function early in an attempt to avoid the pushing and shoving encountered in large crowds. When it is time to leave the function, the CVA victim may find it helpful to wait until almost everyone else has left before leaving. These maneuvers are attempts to avoid feelings of instability on the part of the CVA victim.

In addition, the nurse may find it beneficial to encourage the CVA victim to take part in a stroke club. Such an organization can provide educational assistance and aid in offering a supportive milieu that helps the afflicted person to resocialize (Falknor and Harris, 1973). In addition to stroke clubs, senior citizen clubs, church groups, and retirement centers are other possible resources for socialization.

Unlike the CVA victim, the person afflicted with a spinal cord injury often is a young adult and probably engaged in a variety of social activities. However, just how important each social activity is to the afflicted individual varies. Therefore, it is advisable for the nurse to be aware of the spinal cord injury victim's social state before the illness before planning interventions related to the social impact of the illness.

Since the spinal cord injury victim's independent mobility generally is disrupted, one of the most common social impacts of the illness is how to contend with the presence of the much needed ambulatory aid, the wheelchair. Since the individual is dependent upon the wheelchair for mobility, the spinal cord injury victim will find it necessary to assess his or her social endeavors prior to the illness in order to identify whether the wheelchair will in any way hinder his or her carrying out a specific social activity. For example, can he or she maneuver the wheelchair into the building that houses the social activity (e.g., are ramps available?). Can he or she use the bathroom facilities in the building or are the doors to the commode too small for a wheelchair to enter? If the doors to the bathroom and the commode are large enough to allow the entry of the wheelchair, does the commode area allow for maneuverability of the wheelchair? Finally, are the commode areas equipped with handrails for use in transferring to and from the wheelchair?

Because of the wheelchair, the spinal cord injury victim may be required to alter a social activity. But, it should be pointed out to the victim and the family that many social and sports events need not be eliminated because of the wheelchair. For example, the spinal cord injury victim (i.e., paraplegic) confined to a wheelchair can continue to bowl, take part in archery, play cards, and even play baseball and basketball. In fact, there are sports tournaments for those confined to wheelchairs. These tournaments range from discus throwing to swimming competition (Guttmann, 1975). Swimming is an excellent sport for the paraplegic since the lower extremities are bouyant (Bleasdale, 1975).

With a little imagination and ingenuity, the wheelchair-bound spinal cord injury victim can carry out an almost limitless number of social and sports activities. The nurse and other members of the health care team should encourage the afflicted person and the family to use their imaginations so that the spinal cord injury victim can continue to enjoy many of his or her social and sports endeavors.

The presence of a wheelchair during social events may create concern for the spinal cord injury victim. He or she may fear that its presence is a deterrent to social interactions and that it draws attention to the individual's disability. To aid in dealing with these feelings, the nurse can suggest that the spinal cord injury victim transfer from the wheelchair to a couch or chair at social gatherings. If the individual attends a concert or the theater, transferring from the wheelchair to an aisle seat and putting the collapsed wheelchair out of the way aid in decreasing the noticeability of the ambulatory aid during social encounters.

In addition to the presence of the wheelchair, what to wear when confined to the wheelchair may be a concern of the afflicted person. Females can be advised to wear slacks or pantsuits because they prevent unnecessary exposure during transfer to and from the wheelchair. If the woman does not like slacks or pantsuits, then long dresses or dresses with full skirts are an alternative means of avoiding unnecessary exposure during transfer. Coats can create difficulties in a wheelchair since their length can be a nuisance when assuming a sitting position. Since short jackets and ponchos are much more manageable than coats, the female confined to the wheelchair will undoubtedly find them more comfortable.

Clothing does not usually create problems for the male spinal cord injury victim who uses a wheelchair. Men, however, are advised to wear jackets instead of long overcoats since they are more manageable and hence more comfortable.

Both men and women spinal cord injury victims using wheelchairs are advised to wear attractive clothing that accentuates the torso (Bregman and Hadley, 1976). If the afflicted person feels attractive to others, he or she is less likely to avoid social contacts. To add to one's attractiveness, the nurse can suggest to the spinal cord victim the selection of an attractive wheelchair (e.g., a patterned design or a favorite color).

Finally, verbalization about the engagement in social events is important for the spinal cord injury victim. He or she and the family should be encouraged to express to each other their feelings about taking part in social events. As with the CVA victim, situations identified as uncomfortable for either the afflicted person or the family should be discussed. Together they must decide what is the most appropriate way to handle a specific social activity. Above all, the afflicted person and the family require encouragement from the nurse not to allow themselves to withdraw from social involvement and retreat into isolation.

In summary, social activities need not be eliminated for an individual suffering from a neurological deficit. Alterations in the manner in which the social activity is carried out may have to be made. The CVA victim and the spinal cord injury victim may find that with a little creativity and ingenuity many of the social activities they engaged in before the illness can be maintained. The nurse's role includes assisting the afflicted person and the family in identifying and carrying out needed alterations in social encounters so that the individual with a neurological deficit can maintain a healthy and enjoyable social life.

SUMMARY

Alterations in neurological function can produce devastating impacts upon an individual's life-style. Two of the more common neurological disorders are cerebrovascular accident and spinal cord injury. Approximately 500,000 persons are afflicted yearly with a CVA and 11,500 persons yearly sustain an injury to the spinal cord. A cerebrovascular accident is a condition brought about by an acute lesion in the brain. Both men and women can be afflicted by this illness, with the greatest incidence of occurrence being after forty years of age. A spinal cord injury is generally brought about by trauma. Both men and women can be afflicted with a spinal cord injury, but four out of five spinal cord injuries are experienced by men. Individuals sustaining a spinal cord injury often are in the age group of fifteen to thirty-five years. Both conditions can produce a variety of neurological symptoms depending upon the location and extent of the cerebral or spinal cord involvement.

Regardless of whether an individual sustains a cerebrovascular accident or a spinal cord injury, the neurological deficits created by the illness place an impact upon the afflicted person's emotional well-being, somatic identity, sexuality, occupational identity, and social role. The nurse's role revolves around assisting the afflicted person and the family to identify what impact the illness has upon each component of the individual's life and to aid him or her in dealing with each resulting impact.

Patient Situation

Mr. C. A. is a fifty-seven-year-old art museum curator. He is married and the father of five children. Two of his children still reside at home with him and his wife. In conjunction with his job, Mr. C. A. is involved in many social activities including fund raising events for the art museum.

Eight days ago Mr. C. A. suffered a CVA while at work. He is now in an acute care center and plans are being made for his rehabilitation and discharge to home. The nurse in charge of Mr. C. A.'s discharge planning has identified problems related to Mr. C. A.'s emotional well-being, somatic identity, sexuality, occupational identity, and social role.

Following are Mr. C. A.'s nursing care plan and patient care cardex dealing with each of these areas of concern.

NURSING CARE PLAN

Problems	Objectives	Nursing Interventions	Principles/Rationale	Evaluations
Emotional Impact Expressed feelings about a sense of powerlessness.	To enhance Mr. C. A.'s feelings of self-worth.	Identify Mr. C. A.'s premorbid personality by asking his family to describe the behavior he manifested prior to his CVA.	Knowing what the CVA victim's personality was like prior to his illness provides the nurse with a data base from which to plan nursing interventions dealing with his emotional reactions toward his CVA.	The nurse would observe for: Mr. C. A.'s increased verbalization about his self-worth (e.g., his positive attributes).
		Encourage Mr. C. A. and his family to identify coping mechanisms used by Mr. C. A. in the past (e.g., how did he deal with previous stressors, such as an illness?).	Every person goes through life developing various means of coping with stressful situations.	
		Encourage Mr. C. A. to utilize coping mechanisms used in the past for dealing with stressful situations (e.g., crying or counsel of a religious leader).	Using coping mechanisms utilized in past stressful situations can aid the afflicted individual in coping with his present stress, a CVA.	
Somatic Impact Difficulty in expressing self.	To facilitate Mr. C. A.'s ability to communicate.	Encourage members of the health care team and family to carry out the following techniques:		The nurse would observe for: Mr. C. A.'s increased ability to communicate effectively.
	To decrease Mr. C. A.'s anxiety as he attempts to express himself.	1. Provide Mr. C. A. with a variety of auditory and visual stimuli.	A variety of auditory and visual stimuli prevent monotony which, in turn, enhances the likelihood of an increased comprehension of the stimuli.	Mr. C. A.'s decreased anxiety during his attempts to communicate.
		2. Speak directly to Mr. C. A. 3. Encourage Mr. C. A. to look directly at the speaker.	Speaking directly to the CVA victim decreases the chances of misinterpretation of the spoken word.	

NURSING CARE PLAN (cont.)

Problems	Objectives	Nursing Interventions	Principles/Rationale	Evaluations
Somatic Impact (cont.)		4. Use simple one-word commands and gestures. 5. Speak in a normal tone of voice and at a slower than usual pace. 6. Keep sentence structure brief and simple. 7. Allow time for Mr. C. A. to respond. 8. Provide Mr. C. A. with paper and pencil so that he can draw a picture of the object he wants. 9. Provide Mr. C. A. with a book containing pictures of all the items he could possibly request so that he can point to the pictures of the items he needs. 10. Be patient with Mr. C. A. as he attempts to express himself.	Uncomplicated communication is easier to comprehend. Normal voice tones and a slow speaking pace increase the likelihood of the CVA victim's comprehension of the spoken message. Simple sentence structure is easier to comprehend. Providing adequate time for the CVA victim to respond aids in decreasing his anxiety during his attempts to communicate. Providing the CVA victim with a variety of ways to communicate aids in enhancing his ability to communicate effectively. Providing alternate means of communication aids in decreasing the CVA victim's anxiety when one means of communication proves ineffective. Impatience demonstrated on the part of the health team members and family members when the CVA victim is attempting to communicate tends to increase the afflicted individ-	

Assessment	Goal	Nursing Intervention	Rationale	Evaluation
Expressed lack of interest in sexual activity.	To decrease Mr. C. A.'s fear about being unable to perform sexually.	Encourage Mr. and Mrs. C. A. to ventilate openly their feelings with each other about the sex act.	Open ventilation between the CVA victim and his sex partner aids in decreasing the afflicted person's anxiety about the sex act.	The nurse would observe for: Mr. C. A.'s verbalization about a more active interest in sexual activity with his wife.
		Encourage Mr. and Mrs. C. A. to identify and discuss with each other sexual experiences which each finds pleasurable (e.g., caressing Mr. C. A.'s unaffected side since sensory deficits exist on the affected side or using the side-lying position since Mr. C. A. may find it awkward to support his body weight in a superior position).	Identifying sexual experiences which both partners find enjoyable enhances the likelihood of a mutually satisfying sexual experience.	
		Encourage Mr. and Mrs. C. A. to experiment with various coital positions and sexual maneuvers.	Experimenting with various coital positions and sexual maneuvers can aid in identifying situations that enhance a mutually satisfying sexual experience.	
	To enhance Mr. C. A.'s feelings of sexual desirability.	Encourage Mrs. C. A. to reassure Mr. C. A. that he is sexually desirable (e.g., tell him how nice it is to be alone with him once again).	Reassuring a CVA victim of his sexual desirability helps enhance feelings of self-worth.	
		Encourage Mrs. C. A. to avoid referring to Mr. C. A.'s ability to perform sexually.	Comments about a CVA victim's abilities to perform sexually can add to existing fears of sexual inadequacy.	

NURSING CARE PLAN (cont.)

Problems	Objectives	Nursing Interventions	Principles/Rationale	Evaluations
Occupational Impact Verbalized concern about being able to maintain job.	To facilitate Mr. C. A.'s ability to look realistically at the possibility of having to make alterations in his job situation.	Encourage Mr. C. A. and his family to identify what alterations in the work situation will be necessary in order for Mr. C. A. to continue his job as museum curator.	CVA victims often are able to continue in their pre-illness occupational pursuits with only minor changes having to be made in the job environment.	The nurse would observe for: Mr. C. A.'s verbalization of how his illness may alter his occupational role.
		Contact members of the health care team qualified in assisting Mr. C. A. to deal with the occupational impact of his illness (e.g., social worker, occupational therapist, or rehabilitation counselor).	Health team members such as the social worker, occupational therapist, or rehabilitation counselor are in an excellent position to contact the CVA victim's employer and with his help identify what alterations, if any, can be made in the work situation to accommodate the afflicted employee.	
Social Impact Expressed concern about how he will appear to others during social engagements.	To prevent Mr. C. A.'s withdrawal from social interactions.	Encourage Mr. C. A. to verbalize to his family how he feels about attending social engagements.	Verbalization between the CVA victim and his family about attending social engagements aids in decreasing the afflicted person's anxiety about attending social functions.	The nurse would observe for: Mr. C. A.'s verbalized feelings of being less anxious about engaging in social activities.
		Inform Mr. C. A.'s family about the importance of encouraging Mr. C. A. to take part in social activities.	Difficulty or alterations in mobility may cause the CVA victim to feel like a burden during social engagements and, as a result, cause him to with-	

comfort when attending social events.	family to assess the social environment for features that facilitate the CVA victim's independence (e.g., ramps instead of stairs and elevated commode seats).	vironments that facilitate the CVA victim's independence are more likely to be attended by the afflicted person.
	Encourage Mr. C. A. to purchase clothes that are becoming and easy to put on and take off.	Clothing that is becoming and easy to put on and take off is more likely to be worn. In turn, if the CVA victim feels he is attractive to others, he is more likely to engage in social encounters.
	When Mr. C. A. attends events where there are large crowds, encourage him to arrive early and to wait until the majority of the crowd has left before leaving.	Maneuvers that aid the CVA victim to avoid the pushing and shoving of large crowds help the afflicted person avoid feeling unstable on his feet.
	Suggest to Mr. C. A. the possibility of attending a stroke club.	Organizations, such as a stroke club, can provide a supportive milieu that aids in the CVA victim's resocialization.

PATIENT CARE CARDEX

PATIENT'S NAME: _____ Mr. C. A. _____ DIAGNOSIS: _____ CVA

AGE: _____ 57 years _____ SEX: _____ Male

MARITAL STATUS: _____ Married _____ OCCUPATION: _____ Museum curator

SIGNIFICANT OTHERS: _____ Wife and five children (two living at home)

Problems	Nursing Approaches
Emotional: Expressed feelings about a sense of powerlessness.	1. Identify premorbid personality by conferring with family members.
	2. Encourage identification of coping mechanisms used in past stressful situations.
	3. Encourage utilization of coping mechanisms used in past stressful situations.
Somatic: Difficulty in expressing self.	1. Utilize the following techniques when communicating:
	(a) Provide with a variety of visual and auditory stimuli.
	(b) Speak to directly.
	(c) Encourage to look directly at the speaker.
	(d) Use simple one-word commands and gestures.
	(e) Speak in a normal tone of voice and at a slower than usual pace.
	(f) Keep sentence structure brief and simple.
	(g) Allow time for a response.
	(h) Provide paper and pencil for drawing a picture of items requested.
	(i) Provide a book containing pictures of all items possibly needed. Have patient point at items needed.
	(j) Be patient during attempts to express self.
Sexual: Expressed lack of interest in sexual activity.	1. Encourage to verbalize feelings to wife regarding the sex act.
	2. Encourage to identify with wife sexual experiences each find pleasurable (e.g., caressing unaffected side of body or using side-lying position).
	3. Encourage husband and wife to experiment with various coital positions and sexual maneuvers.
	4. Encourage wife to reassure husband that he is sexually desirable

able to maintain job.

to facilitate job as museum curator.

2. Contact members of the health care team qualified in dealing with the occupational impact of a CVA (e.g., social worker, occupational therapist, or rehabilitation counselor).

Social: Expressed concern about how he will appear to others during social engagements.

1. Encourage to verbalize to family how he feels about attending social engagements.
2. Inform family of importance of encouraging afflicted individual to take part in social activities.
3. Encourage, along with family, to assess social environments for features that facilitate a CVA victim's independence (e.g., ramps and elevated commode seats).
4. Encourage to buy clothes that are both becoming and easy to put on and take off.
5. Encourage when attending events where there are large crowds to arrive early and leave after most of the crowd has left.
6. Suggest involvement in a stroke club.

REFERENCES

Beck. A., Resnik, H., and Lettieri, D. *The prediction of suicide.* Bowie, Maryland: The Charles Press Publishers, Inc., 1974.

Bleasdale, N. Swimming and the paraplegic, *Paraplegia,* 1975, *13* (2), 124-127.

Bors, E., and Comarr, A. Neurological disturbances of sexual function with special reference to 529 patients with spinal cord injury, *Urological Survey,* 1960, *10,* 191-221.

Bregman, S., and Hadley, R. Sexual adjustment and feminine attractiveness among spinal cord injured women, *Archives of Physical Medicine and Rehabilitation,* 1976, *57* (9), 448-450.

Cole, T. Sexuality and physical disabilities, *Archives of Sexual Behavior,* 1975, 4 (4), 389-403.

Comarr, A. Observations on menstruation and pregnancy among female spinal cord injury patients, *Paraplegia,* 1966, *3* (4), 263-272.

Comarr. A. Sexual concepts in traumatic cord and equina lesions, *Journal of Urology,* 1971, *106,* 375-378.

Comarr, A., and Gunderson, B. Sexual function in traumatic paraplegia and quadriplegia, *American Journal of Nursing,* 1975, *75* (2), 250-255.

Deyoe, F. Marriage and family patterns with long-term spinal cord injury, *Paraplegia,* 1972, *10* (3), 219-224.

Erikson, E. *Childhood and society.* New York: W. W. Norton and Co., 1963.

Falknor, H., and Harris, B. Resocializing through a stroke club, *Nursing Outlook,* 1973, *21* (12), 778-780.

Ghatit, A. Outcome of marriages existing at the time of a male's spinal cord injury, *Journal of Chronic Diseases,* 1975, *28,* 383-388.

Ghatit, A., and Hanson, R. Marriages and divorce after spinal cord injury, *Archives of Physical Medicine and Rehabilitation,* 1976, *57* (10), 470-472.

Goldstein, K. Functional disturbances in brain damage. In S. Arieti (Ed.), *American Handbook of Psychiatry.* New York: Basic Books, Inc., 1959.

Guttman, L. The married life of paraplegics and tetraplegics, *Paraplegia,* 1964, *2* (2), 182-188.

Guttman, L. Sports and the spinal cord sufferer, *Nursing Mirror,* 1975, *141* (19), 64-65.

Guttman, L., and Walsh, J. J. Prostigmin assessment test of fertility in spinal man, *Paraplegia,* 1971, *9* (5), 39-51.

Hohmann, G. Psychological aspects of treatment and rehabilitation of the spinal cord injured person, *Clinical Orthopaedics and Related Research,* 1975, *112,* 81-88.

Jackson, R. Sexual rehabilitation after cord injury, *Paraplegia,* 1972, *10* (1), 50-55.

Jacobansky, A. Stroke, *American Journal of Nursing,* 1972, *72* (7), 1260-1263.

Kraus, J., Franti, C., Riggins, R., Richards, D., and Borhani, N. Incidence of traumatic spinal cord lesions, *Journal of Chronic Disease,* 1975, *28,* 471-492.

Long, C. Congenital and traumatic lesions of the spinal cord. In F. Krusen and P. Ellwood (Eds.), *Handbook of physical medicine and rehabilitation.* Philadelphia: W. B. Saunders Co., 1965.

Luckmann, J., and Sorensen, K. *Medical-surgical nursing: a psychophysiologic approach.* Philadelphia: W. B. Saunders Co., 1974.

McDowell, F. Evaluation and management of stroke, *Postgraduate Medicine,* 1976, *59* (3), 105.

Nyquist, R., and Bors, E. Mortality and survival in traumatic myelopathy during 19 years from 1946-1965, *Paraplegia,* 1967, *5* (5), 22-48.

Pepper, G. The person with a spinal cord injury: psychological care, *American Journal of Nursing,* 1977, *77* (8), 1330-1336.

Peter, A. Psychosocial aspects of spinal cord injury, *Maryland State Medical Journal,* 1975, *24* (2), 65-69.

Riehl, J., and Chambers, J. Better salvage for the stroke victim, *Nursing '76,* 1976, *6* (7), 24-31.

Robertson, D., and Guttman, L. The paraplegic patient in pregnancy and labour, *Proceedings of the Royal Society of Medicine,* 1963, *56,* 381-387.

Romano, M., and Lassiter, R. Sexual counseling with the spinal-cord injured, *Archives of Physical Medicine and Rehabilitation,* 1972, *53* (12), 568-572.

Schultz, L. Nursing care of the stroke patient, *Nursing Clinics of North America,* 1973, *8* (4), 633-642.

Schwab, J. In stroke, *New York State Journal of Medicine,* 1972, *72* (23), 2877-2880.

Schwartzman, S. Anxiety and depression in the stroke patient: a nursing challenge, *Journal of Psychiatric Nursing and Mental Health Services,* 1976, *14* (7), 13-17.

Weiss, A., and Diamond, M. Sexual adjustment, identification, and attitudes of patients with myelopathy, *Archives of Physical Medicine and Rehabilitation,* 1966, *47* (4), 245-250.

Woods, N. *Human sexuality in health and illness.* St. Louis: The C. V. Mosby Co., 1975.

14

The Patient with an
ALTERATION
IN
RENAL FUNCTION

INTRODUCTION

Historically, the concept of dialysis is not new to the world of health care. In the early 1900's attempts were made to devise the first prototype of the hemodialyzer (Abel, Rawntree, and Turner, 1913), but it has been just within the past three decades that hemodialysis has become a well-established form of therapy for individuals afflicted with renal failure or irreversible kidney damage (Kolff and Watchinger, 1965; Kiil, 1960). There are approximately 25,000 Americans maintained on hemodialysis, one-quarter of whom utilize home hemodialysis (Briefel, Hutchisson, Galonsky, Hessert, and Friedman, 1975). Thus, the professional nurse is responsible for working with individuals who are totally dependent upon the functioning of a machine for sustaining life.

Dialysis is the passage of particles from an area of high concentration to an area of low concentration across a semipermeable membrane. There are actually two forms of dialysis: peritoneal dialysis and hemodialysis. This chapter will deal exclusively with individuals undergoing hemodialysis.

The basic goals of hemodialysis are: (1) to remove from the blood end products of protein metabolism (urea and creatinine), (2) to maintain a safe concentration of serum electrolytes, (3) to correct acidosis and replenish the blood's bicarbonate system, and (4) to remove excess fluid from the blood (Luckmann and Sorensen, 1974).

Hemodialysis involves having the individual's blood flow from his or her body into a membrane package (the dialysis machine) and then having the blood return from the machine to his or her body. While the afflicted person's blood is in the dialysis machine diffusion takes place between the individual's blood and the dialysate solution across the semipermeable membrane of the dialysis machine. Either an external arteriovenous shunt is inserted or an internal arteriovenous fistula is made in order to make an access to the patient's blood supply for the dialysis procedure.

One of the greatest limitations imposed upon the person undergoing hemodialysis is the time involved in the therapy. The individual must spend approximately four to ten hours two to three times a week on the dialysis machine. Thus, it can be seen that depending upon hemodialysis for sustaining life has an impact upon the afflicted person's emotional well-being, somatic identity, sexuality, occupational identity, and social role. The remainder of this chapter will discuss how hemodialysis can affect each of these areas of concern.

IMPACT OF HEMODIALYSIS

Emotional Impact*

An individual afflicted with renal failure or irreversible kidney damage is faced with a life-threatening situation. Something must be done about the condition or the individual will die. Hemodialysis has saved many lives and continues to save many lives, but the emotional impact of severe kidney malfunction does not end when the afflicted individual is selected for and begins hemodialysis. When an individual undergoes hemodialysis, he or she literally becomes a marginal person (Landsman, 1975). The individual is neither ill nor well. He or she is forced to face one of the greatest losses of freedom that anyone can possibly sustain. The individual cannot live or function without total commitment to the dialysis machine.

Because of this total commitment to the dialysis machine, most individuals maintained on hemodialysis demonstrate three stages of adaptation. These stages, according to Reichsman and Levy (1972), are called the "honeymoon" period, the period of disenchantment and discouragement, and the period of long-term adaptation. The "honeymoon" period, Reichsman and Levy (1972) found, occurs one to three weeks after the individual's first hemodialysis treatment and lasts from six weeks to six months. It is during this stage of adaptation that the individual on hemodialysis demonstrates a marked improvement both physically and emotionally. The individual manifests confidence, hope, and a relative lack of perception of his or her own limitations and of the hardships that accompany this form of therapy (Levy, 1973b).

During the "honeymoon" period most afflicted persons readily accept their intense dependence upon the dialysis machine, the dialysis procedure, and the professional staff. Individuals who dislike being dependent initially

*It is advisable for the reader to have read Chapters 1 and 3 before continuing with this section.

may encounter more difficulties in coping with the "honeymoon" period than individuals who enjoy a state of dependence.

Reichsman and Levy (1972) noted that few individuals experience basic displeasure during this adaptive stage. Nevertheless, this period of adaptation is not free of problems. Many afflicted persons experience repetitive, intense periods of anxiety and fear. When questioned about their feelings, they tend to refer to a mechanical failure at the shunt site, to running out of shunt sites, to machine failure, to life expectancy, and to the ability to return to work (Jennrich, 1975; Reichsman and Levy, 1972). Even though there are expressed anxieties and fears during this period of adaptation, the "honeymoon" period is dominated by feelings of contentment, confidence, and hope (Reichsman and Levy, 1972). As a result, the afflicted person basically repudiates his or her loss of wellness.

The nurse's role in assisting the individual undergoing hemodialysis to cope with the "honeymoon" period involves encouraging ventilation of feelings. The afflicted person needs to be encouraged to express his or her fears and anxieties. As the individual expresses concern about the dialysis therapy (e.g., shunt failure or machine failure), he or she requires reassurance that competent health team members are always available to prevent and to deal with such problems. As the person expresses concerns about his or her job and his or her life expectancy, the nurse needs to be a good listener. At no time should the patient be cut off while verbalizing his or her feelings. In addition, the afflicted individual requires reassurance that these feelings of confidence, hope, and contentment are expected and accepted reactions.

When the "honeymoon" period ends, the second stage of adaptation to hemodialysis, the period of disenchantment and discouragement, begins (Reichsman and Levy, 1972). Disenchantment and discouragement last approximately 3 to 12 months. This stage of adaptation can be noted by a distinct change in the individual's affective behavior. The onset of this period of adaptation may be very abrupt or it may be gradual. Reichsman and Levy (1972) noted that the onset of the stage of disenchantment or discouragement tended to occur in relation to a specific stressful event. For example, the specific stressful event may be the individual's planning or actual resumption of employment or household duties. Feelings of contentment, confidence, and hope markedly decrease and/or disappear. In their place the afflicted person manifests feelings of helplessness and sadness. Thus, the afflicted person begins to recognize his or her loss of wellness.

During the stage of disenchantment and discouragement the afflicted person manifests an increase in dependency behavior. For example, the individual may refuse to make decisions, may be demanding of others, may verbally abuse family and health team members, and may basically regress in his or her emotional reactions. De-Nour (1972) believes that the demonstration of noncompliance with medical regime is attributable to the individual's striving for independence. The major difficulty at this time lies in the individual's dependency upon the dialysis machine for survival (Anderson, 1975). He or she needs the machine to survive but encounters difficulties in accepting the therapy's stringent restrictions. Not only are diet and fluid intake critically controlled, but also free time is limited since dialysis therapy can consume as much as 20 to 30 hours a week. Thus, the afflicted person undergoes a dependency-independency conflict.

In addition to the dependency-independency conflict, depression can result during the stage of disenchantment and discouragement. The afflicted person questions the value of his or her existence and the quality of his or her life. When these feelings of depression are not transient, health team members must be aware of the potential existence of suicidal ideations. Surveys have indicated that the incidence of suicide in hemodialysis patients is more than 100 times that of the general population (Abram, Moore, and Westerfelt, 1971).

The nurse's role during the period of disenchantment and discouragement is to assist the afflicted person in coping with his or her feelings. Since dependency is undoubtedly the major behavioral manifestation demonstrated during this period of adaptation, the nurse will find it necessary to aid the hemodialysis patient in dealing with the dependency-independency conflict. It must be pointed out to the dialysis patient that the reality of the illness requires dependence upon the dialysis machine. Just as insulin-dependent diabetics require medication for survival, the dialysis patient requires a dialysis machine for survival. In addition to being dependent upon the dialysis machine, the afflicted individual must be dependent upon health team members and/or family members to carry out the dialysis treatment. The afflicted individual must be reassured that these two forms of dependence are necessary and acceptable.

Regressive behavior, verbal abuse toward others, and demanding behavior are neither necessary nor acceptable forms of dependency. The overly dependent dialysis patient may need encouragement to look at his or her behavior when he or she uses these unacceptable manifestations of dependence. When the patient lashes out at family or health team members, he or she needs to be reminded that this behavior is not acceptable, but he or she requires reassurance that *he* or *she* is acceptable. For example, if a husband who is undergoing home dialysis therapy verbally strikes out at his wife, she may find it helpful to respond with, "Honey, I love you very much, but sometimes what you say to me is very upsetting!"

The individual undergoing hemodialysis should actively participate in the therapies. He or she should be encouraged to plan and to carry out diet and fluid restrictions. Each time the individual demonstrates more independence, positive feedback from others should be forthcoming. Above all, demonstrations of excessive dependence should be discouraged. For example, while receiving hemodialysis, whether in the acute care setting or at home, the afflicted person should remain in street clothes and rest comfortably in a reclining chair. Avoiding the use of night clothes and a bed aids in preventing the mechanical placement of the dialysant in the dependent role of illness.

Verbalization on the part of the dialysis patient is vital. Both the afflicted person and the family must ventilate their feelings. As the dialysis patient expresses his or her needs for dependence, the nurse should reinforce acceptable expressions of dependence (e.g., dependence upon the dialysis machine and others to carry out the necessary therapy) and discourage unacceptable expressions of dependence.

When depression is manifested by the person undergoing hemodialysis, the nurse and other members of the health care team must realize that these demonstrations of depression may be demonstrations of anger. The dialysis patient may be angry about what has happened, angry about being too dependent upon others, and angry about his or her lack of freedom. To help the individual deal with these feelings, the nurse should get the afflicted person involved in activities. Card playing, leather tooling, conversation, reading, and watching television are but a few possibilities. To allow the depressed hemodialysis patient to retreat into his or her own world only adds to feelings of depression.

Involvement is especially important during dialysis therapy because all too often the individual may want to retreat into sleep during therapy. One of the few times that sleep during the entire process would be advisable is when the treatment is set up during sleeping hours with the sole purpose of allowing for sleep and therapy simultaneously. Such an arrangement may be necessary when attempts are being made to meet the time demands of a work schedule. However, many dialysis patients find it difficult to sleep through the entire therapy process because they are anxious about the successful completion of the therapy.

Again, verbalization is vital. The afflicted person must ventilate his or her feelings. Ventilation aids in releasing feelings of anger and in decreasing anxieties. Above all, the nurse must be aware of the possible presence of suicidal ideations so that appropriate therapeutic intervention can be taken. For example, it may be necessary to make a contract with the individual to approach a member of the health care team whenever the individual feels like harming himself. In addition, appropriate members of the health care team (e.g., clinical specialist in psychiatric nursing and/or psychiatrist) should be notified and should therapeutically intervene.

The third and final stage of adaptation to hemodialysis, the period of long-term adaptation, is characterized by the afflicted person's manifestation of some degree of acceptance of the limitations, shortcomings, and complications of maintenance hemodialysis (Reichsman and Levy, 1972). Generally, the transition between the stage of disenchantment and discouragement and the stage of adaptation is gradual. The stage of long-term adaptation is marked by fluctuations in the afflicted person's sense of emotional and physical well-being (Reichsman and Levy, 1972). In other words, the individual may experience periods of contentment alternating with periods of depression of varying duration.

During both the states of contentment and depression, according to Reichsman and Levy (1972), the afflicted person's primary defense mechanism is denial. Denial used by these individuals tends to be more extensive than the denial used by patients with other physical illnesses. Denial in the hemodialysis patient appears to serve an effective adaptive function. During periods of depression it protects the individual from experiencing even more intense feelings of helplessness; during episodes of contentment denial aids in preserving a sense of well-being (Reichsman and Levy, 1972).

During the stage of long-term adaptation anger may be manifested. Aggressive feelings may take the form of verbal expression or the form of noncompliance to medical therapies (e.g., not following dietary restrictions and not taking proper care of the shunt site). However, despite the use of denial and the expression of anger, the hemodialysis patient in the stage of long-term adaptation generally is able to adapt to his or her new way of life. This adaptation often is partly attributable to the beginning and the continuance of meaningful work or to settling down to do little or no work (Reichsman and Levy, 1972).

Although during the stage of long-term adaptation the hemodialysis patient has come to some terms of acceptance of the illness and its related therapies, he or she continues to require professional nursing intervention. The nurse's role in dealing with this stage of adaptation is to assist the afflicted person in dealing with the behavioral manifestations of denial and anger. Since denial and anger both serve a purpose for the hemodialysis patient, the nurse should avoid attempting to remove either one of these protective behavioral mechanisms, but the individual's denial and anger should not be supported by the nurse, by the family, or by any member of the health care team. Instead, the afflicted individual requires assistance in looking at his or her behavior and rechanneling his or her form of expression. For example, when the individual demonstrated noncompliance with medical therapies, the nurse must encourage the dialysant to recognize how he or she is feeling both physically and emotionally. As the individual describes his or her feelings, the nurse will find it helpful to point out that feelings of both physical and emotional ill health can be directly related to noncompliance with medical therapies. To aid the dialysant in dealing with aggressive feelings, the nurse may find it helpful to encourage him or her to channel aggressive feelings into a form of constructive release. For example, if the home dialysis patient feels angry, he or she should be encouraged to become involved in such activities as dusting, vacuuming, typing, or painting instead of lashing out at others. In the hospital setting such activities as watching an active sports event or doing handcrafts can aid in releasing pent-up feelings of aggression. In addition, family members, the nurse, and other members of the health care team need to be available and willing to listen to the hemodialysis patient verbalize his or her feelings. Even though the afflicted individual may have reached the point of resolving the loss of wellness, he or she continues to require emotional support from others in the form of patience and understanding.

The individual undergoing hemodialysis is not the only person who suffers from the emotional impact of this demanding therapy. The family of the afflicted individual also must contend with the emotional assaults created by hemodialysis. One of the major family changes that occurs when an individual undergoes hemodialysis is alteration in family structure. When the afflicted person is being maintained on hemodialysis in the acute care setting, other family members may be required to assume some of the responsibilities that have been carried out in the past by the dialysis patient. For example, if the dialysis patient is a married woman, her husband and children may have to assume more responsibility in keeping the home clean, shopping for groceries, and washing the family clothing. If the dialysis patient is a married man, his wife and children may find it necessary to do such jobs as mowing the lawn, taking the car in for repairs, and contacting a carpenter for necessary household repairs. The jobs assumed by family members, of course, will depend upon which tasks each family member assumed prior to the afflicted individual's illness.

If the afflicted person is maintained on hemodialysis in the home setting, in addition to assuming some of the family responsibilities previously carried out by the dialysis patient, family members will find it necessary to carry out the actual dialysis procedure. Clinicians have noted that in the case of the married dialysis patient the role of the spouse plays a major part in the success or failure of home dialysis therapy. Successful home dialysis tends to be at risk if the spouse is naturally dependent upon the patient-partner (Streltzer, Finkelstein, Feigenbaum, Kitsen, and Cohn, 1976). Although home dialysis offers advantages such as greater flexibility in scheduling time, increased mobility, and a sense of control over the illness, it also places additional demands upon the spouse or family member responsible for carrying out the therapy.

The nurse's role, therefore, revolves around assisting the family members to deal with the alterations in family structure that occur as a result of dialysis therapy. Involving the family and the dialysis patient in group and/or family therapy proves beneficial. The major purpose of the therapy sessions is to allow the family members to verbalize their feelings about alterations in their family structure as a result of hemodialysis. In addition, therapy sessions allow for the opportunity to explore, together with others with similar problems, ways to cope with family structure alterations.

In the case of home dialysis, it is advisable to involve as many family members as possible in assisting with the dialysis treatment. Young children can assist by running errands for the parent involved in carrying out the dialysis treatment or by visiting with the parent on the dialysis machine. Older children can be taught the dialysis treatment so that the responsibilities and demands of the therapy are not placed solely upon one family member. However, when involving family members, guilt can be elicited if the family member feels responsible for the dialysant's progressive deterioration in health status. This is particularly significant in regards to children. Regardless of the circumstances, the dialysis patient should be informed of the reason for sharing responsibilities so that he or she does not interpret this action as rejection by the spouse or by any other family member. Although major alterations in family structure do occur as a result of hemodialysis, these problems can be dealt with successfully.

In summary, hemodialysis creates an emotional impact upon both the afflicted person and the family. While adjusting to dialysis therapy, the afflicted person progresses through three adaptive stages: the "honeymoon" period, the period of disenchantment and discouragement, and the period of long-term adaptation. As the individual progresses through each one of the stages of adaptation, the nurse needs to assist the afflicted person in dealing with the behavioral reactions manifested. Since family members also sustain an emotional impact to hemodialysis, the nurse needs to aid them in dealing with their reactions to this demanding therapy. Although hemodialysis can create an overwhelming emotional impact upon the afflicted person and the family, with appropriate nursing intervention the involved individuals can be helped to cope.

Somatic Impact*

The individual undergoing hemodialysis suffers several impacts to his or her body image. These somatic impacts include skin discoloration, hair loss, fluctuations in weight, the presence of an arteriovenous shunt or an arterio-

*It is advisable for the reader to have read Chapter 2 before continuing with this section.

venous fistula, and the incorporation of the dialysis machine as part of one's self. Unless these alterations are dealt with appropriately, difficulties can arise.

Because of the kidney malfunction, individuals who undergo hemodialysis manifest a characteristic change in skin color. The nailbeds and mucous membranes become pale as a result of the anemia, which generally is present. The skin of white people takes on a sallow, yellow-brown cast and the skin of blacks becomes darker in color. Both of these alterations are caused by the combination of anemia and of melanin deposits (Harrington and Brener, 1973). The color changes are most evident in the exposed areas of the face and hands since light tends to accentuate its presence.

To assist the afflicted person in dealing with the characteristic alterations in skin color, it is beneficial to point out that this somatic alteration is part of the disease process. The individual becomes aware that skin color changes are expected and occur in other individuals afflicted with the same alterations in kidney function. In addition, as the afflicted person expresses feelings about this alteration in skin color, the family and health team members should not divert or impede his or her verbalization. The individual has a need to express how he or she feels about his or her appearance and the individual should be allowed to do so.

As the individual shares his or her concerns about skin color changes, the nurse can take this opportunity to point out how clothing of certain colors and hues can accentuate skin color alterations. The afflicted person may find that he or she needs to experiment wearing different colors of clothing. For example, light-skinned individuals may find that certain shades of yellow and green will accentuate their sallow, yellow-brown cast. The black-skinned individual may find that dark colors such as navy blue, brown, or black draw attention to the darkened color.

Hair loss, another alteration in body image, can affect the hemodialysis patient. The amount and distribution of hair loss will vary among individuals. Therefore, the approach used to deal with hair loss will depend upon the location of loss. Whether the hair loss is on the head or on the rest of the body, the afflicted individual requires reassurance that the hair will grow back. Some dialysis patients have been known to lose and regrow hair several times over a five-year period.

If the hair loss occurs predominantly on the head, the nurse may find it beneficial to suggest a restyling of the hair in an attempt to cover areas of little or no growth. The advice of a hair stylist may also prove helpful. If the hair loss is extensive, the use of a wig may be necessary. Females may be more concerned about the loss of head hair than males, but this is not always so. Therefore, before suggesting the use of a wig the nurse needs to be aware of how the afflicted person feels about his or her altered hair growth.

If the hair loss occurs predominantly on the arms, legs, and chest, the nurse's approach should be governed by the afflicted individual's response to such a loss. For example, the female may actually view hair loss on the legs as an advantage. The male, however, may view hair loss on the chest as a visible loss of masculinity. As a result, he may be more comfortable wearing shirts that button up to the collar.

A third alteration in body image, fluctuation in weight, often occurs as a result of the interplay between the afflicted person's disease process and the dialysis therapy. Fluid tends to accumulate in the body between dialysis treatments. This accumulation is the result of electrolyte and waste product retention. As the person undergoes hemodialysis, fluid is removed along with the excess electrolytes and waste products. The outcome is a weight loss. The nurse may find it helpful to explain the reasons for weight gain between treatments and weight loss resulting from dialysis. It is not uncommon for dialysis patients to see their weight loss as a positive secondary gain. In fact, some dialysants have been known to be concerned only with how much weight they have lost as a result of hemodialysis.

In order to carry out hemodialysis, adequate access to the bloodstream is essential; thus, an imposed alteration in body image occurs. The two methods of access used are the arteriovenous shunt and the subcutaneous arteriovenous fistula. Since both methods have advantages and disadvantages, the method utilized will depend upon the individual patient situation.

The arteriovenous shunt is the method in which the arterial system and the venous system are connected by a cannula. The cannula is placed in the nondominant limb so that the cannulated limb can be favored by the individual. If the afflicted individual's work calls for the use of both arms, the nondominant leg is utilized. If, however, the hemodialysis patient uses his or her legs extensively, an arm site may be preferred. The home dialysis patient generally has the shunt site in the leg so that both arms are free for carrying out his or her own dialysis procedure.

The presence of an arteriovenous shunt necessitates an external cannula and a bulky dressing. As a result, the shunt site requires daily cleansing and the application of a sterile dressing that must be kept on at all times. Since the most frequent complication of the cannula is wound infection, this daily procedure is imperative. However, the presence of the visible cannula and dressing can cause the afflicted person to feel uncomfortable about his or her appearance. He or she may feel that it draws attention to the presence of the illness and the existence of the therapy.

To deal with these feelings, the nurse will find it beneficial to encourage verbalization. Having the hemodialysis patient express his or her feelings aids in decreasing anxiety. In addition, the afflicted person can be encouraged to wear loose-fitting clothing over the cannula. For example, women with cannulas in the lower extremity might be encouraged to wear pantsuits.

Above all, the dialysis patient should be reminded of the necessity to inspect the shunt site routinely and to carry out daily dressing changes.

The second method of access to the bloodstream, the subcutaneous arteriovenous (A-V) fistula, is a surgically created connection between the arterial system and the venous system. An anastomosis of the cephalic vein and the radial or branchial artery is made (Harrington and Brener, 1973). The advantage of the A-V fistula is that since a cannula is not used, there is no need for daily cleansing and bulky dressings. However, the disadvantage is that venipunctures are necessary for each dialysis treatment.

The role of the nurse in dealing with the presence of the A-V fistula involves assisting the afflicted person to cope with discomfort each time a venipuncture is performed. Encouraging verbalization about the discomfort of a needle puncture and reassuring the individual that the discomfort will soon subside prove to be beneficial interactions in decreasing the individual's anxiety related to the pain.

The incorporation of the dialysis machine as part of one's self is probably the greatest assault that hemodialysis has upon the afflicted person's body image. Since the afflicted individual is dependent for life upon the machine, he or she may verbalize the existence of umbilical fantasies (Abram, 1969). For example, the individual may describe his or her dependency upon the machine as a "fetal-placenta" one. Or the afflicted person may allude to believing that the machine controls and makes him or her into an "android" or a "zombie." Apart from feeling controlled by the machine, some dialysis patients have alluded to the machine as part of their body. They may ascribe human qualities to the dialysis machine and actually speak to the machine as if it would make a response.

To deal with the hemodialysis patient's altered body image, as a result of the controlling and lifelike factors attributed to the dialysis machine, the individual needs to be encouraged to verbalize. In other words, the afflicted person needs to express how he or she feels about the dialysis machine. As the patient relays feelings about the machine, the nurse needs to point out the reality of the situation. The individual is dependent for life upon the machine and it is an ever present part of his or her existence. In addition, the nurse should stress to the afflicted person that reactions toward the dialysis machine are not unusual. Many dialysants express feelings about the machine whether they be "monster-like feelings" or "human-like feelings." Finally, it is beneficial for members of the health care team to assist the dialysis patient in exploring how he or she can cope with these feelings toward the machine. Often verbalization to family and health team members is sufficient. Some individuals find sharing feelings with other dialysants is most beneficial. If the afflicted person is unable to contend with his or her feelings about the dialysis machine, appropriate psychiatric intervention may be in order.

In addition to the somatic impacts created by hemodialysis, how the afflicted person copes with each of these impacts is greatly affected by the developmental stage the person is experiencing at the time of dialysis. The hemodialysis patient who is between eighteen and forty-five years of age is in the stage of young adulthood. It is during this time that an individual begins to share himself or herself with others, both in friendship and in a mutually satisfying relationship (Erikson, 1963). Because of the dialysis therapy, the afflicted person may encounter difficulties merging his or her identity with others and, as a result, may develop a sense of isolation. The dialysant may believe that he or she is unattractive because of the hair loss and skin color changes and withdraw from the company of friends and relatives. The dialysant may also view the illness as a deterrent to achievement. Because of the extensive time required for dialysis therapy, the individual may feel incapable of demonstrating an acceptable image and believe that he or she is unable to achieve his or her goals. Unless the dialysant can be made to feel that he or she has something to offer others in friendship and in a mutually satisfying sexual relationship, intimacy will not be attained.

Between the ages of forty-five and sixty-five years of age the individual enters the stage of adulthood. This stage spans the middle years of life. It is during this time that one focuses interest on establishing and guiding future generations (Erikson, 1963). The occurrence of renal alterations and subsequent hemodialysis may lead the afflicted individual to believe that he or she is incapable of guiding and directing future generations. Chronic defeatism and depression may result and the dialysant may retreat into isolation and self-pity. The individual may view the ramifications of the affliction (e.g., skin color changes, hair loss, and time-consuming therapy) as premature old age. As a result, the individual may stagnate and retire to the rocking chair prematurely. Therefore, the dialysant in the stage of adulthood requires assistance in identifying how he or she can be generative.

The final stage of life, the stage of maturity, occurs from sixty-five years of age and over. During this period frequent thoughts of death occur. The individual's satisfaction in life comes from the acceptance of his or her past triumphs and disappointments (Erikson, 1963). The adult's view of himself or herself is affected by how he or she feels that others see him or her. With the occurrence of kidney malfunction and subsequent hemodialysis, the afflicted adult may question his or her value. Thoughts of death may become more prevalent because of the presence of illness and the resulting therapy. The outcome may lead to feelings of despair. Therefore, the adult in the stage of maturity undergoing hemodialysis requires assistance in identifying his or her self-worth.

In summary, hemodialysis therapy creates several somatic impacts upon the adult. How the person deals with these alterations in body image will be affected by the developmental stage he or she is experiencing at the time of dialysis. Some of the more common body image alterations occurring as a result of the disease process and hemodialysis include skin discoloration, hair loss, fluctuations in weight, the presence of an arteriovenous shunt or an arteriovenous fistula, and the incorporation of the dialysis machine as part of one's self. The nurse's role in dealing with the somatic impact of hemodialysis centers around assisting the dialysant in identifying how he or she best can deal with each of these somatic impacts.

Sexual Impact

Kidney alterations that require hemodialysis create an impact upon the afflicted person's sexuality. A national survey conducted by Levy (1973a) demonstrated that hemodialysis patients of both sexes (but especially males) undergo substantial deterioration in sexual functioning. For males, the major sexual alterations are impotence and a decreased libido (Jennrich, 1975). The male on hemodialysis often feels emasculated because of his total dependence upon the dialysis machine. Since his wife often becomes the main source of economic support, additional losses in the male dialysant's self-esteem and masculinity occur (Harari, Munitz, Wijsenbeek, Levi, Steiner, and Rosenbaum, 1971).

Research has indicated that sexual activity is greatly affected by the afflicted individual's illness. Male dialysants have reported as much as a 50 percent decrease in intercourse between the onset of their disease process and the adjustment of maintenance hemodialysis (Bommer, Tschope, Ritz, and Andrassy, 1976). Levy (1973a) noted that, as a group, males maintained on hemodialysis fail to resolve their sexual dysfunction problems. In fact, a large percentage of them experienced worsening of sexual functioning. It is likely that both physical and emotional factors play a major part in the cause of sexual dysfunction among male dialysants.

Unfortunately, little research has been conducted on the sexual dysfunction of the female dialysant. Amenorrhea and decrease in the frequency of intercourse and orgasm, however, have been noted (Schreiner, 1965; Levy, 1973a). Although some female dialysants have been known to experience an improvement in sexual function while being maintained on hemodialysis, the majority encountered a worsening in sexual functioning (Levy, 1973a). Thus, it can be seen that both male and female dialysants sustain a severe impact to their sexuality as a result of alterations in kidney function and subsequent dialysis therapy.

The nurse's role in dealing with the sexual impact of hemodialysis is to assist the dialysant and sex partner in coping with sexual alterations. One of the most important nursing interventions for dealing with the sexual impact of hemodialysis is to inform the dialysant's sex partner about the possible alterations in sexual function that the dialysant may undergo. Nothing tends to be more devastating to the sexual life of a couple than the lack of information about sexual functioning on the part of one of the partners. In addition, the dialysant and sex partner should be informed about the factors that can contribute to the sexual alteration. For example, extreme tiredness, as a result of therapy, the large blocks of time the therapy consumes, feelings of emasculation caused by the dependence upon both the dialysis machine and the spouse, fears of loss of sexual desirability because of hair loss and skin color changes, and fears of dislodgment of the arteriovenous shunt during coitus are but a few possible contributing factors.

To assist the couple in dealing with possible factors contributing to the dialysant's alteration in sexual functioning, the nurse needs to encourage the couple to identify and discuss ways in which they can facilitate the achievement of a mutually satisfying sexual relationship (Hickman, 1977). To illustrate, if physical tiredness following therapy or the amount of time the therapy takes is a problem, the couple may find setting aside a specific time for sexual activity a helpful measure. Although spontaneity may be lost, complete or massive reduction in sexual activity may be prevented. If the male dialysant feels emasculated because of his dependence upon both the dialysis machine and his spouse, efforts should be made to reassure him of his masculinity. For example, encouraging the resumption of employment, maintaining joint decision making within the family structure, and avoiding the mechanical placement of the dialysant in the sick role (e.g., use of night clothes and a bed during dialysis treatment) are but a few possible suggestions. If the female dialysant encounters a decrease in feelings of sexual desirability because of the hair loss and skin color changes, attempts should be made to reassure her of her sexual desirability. Complimenting her on her personal appearance or having her routinely visit a hairdresser are two possible interventions that can facilitate feelings of femininity. If fear of dislodging the arteriovenous shunt during coitus creates difficulties for the couple, the nurse should encourage the dialysant to check cannula connections and dressing secureness prior to engaging in sexual activity. It is advisable to encourage the avoidance of excessive use or pressure on the cannulated extremity. The dialysant also may find it helpful to avoid coital positions that place the cannulated extremity in a dependent position or that allow the sex partner to lie on the arm or leg.

In summary, although kidney alterations and subsequent hemodialysis create a decided impact upon the sexual functioning of the dialysant, the afflicted individual and sex partner can be assisted in dealing with sexual alterations. The nurse can play a vital role in keeping the dialysant and sex partner informed about the possible nature of sexual alterations that occur and in guiding the couple in ways of dealing with sexual dysfunctions.

Occupational Impact

Hemodialysis is an expensive form of therapy. The treatment involves sophisticated equipment, the possible use of an acute care setting, and the utilization of specially prepared personnel. The financial burden of the therapy, formerly imposed upon the afflicted person and the family, has been eliminated as a result of Public Law 92-603, Section 2991, which amended the Social Security Act in 1972. This amendment provides for Medicare coverage for eligible individuals requiring hemodialysis (U.S. Department of Health, Education and Welfare, 1976). In addition to Public Law 92-603, Section 2991, other means of medical assistance include health care insurance, state funding, and CHAMPUS (Civilian Health and Medical Program of the Uniformed Services). Nevertheless, an alteration in the standard of living may occur for the dialysant and the family as a result of the economic impact imposed by hemodialysis. If the dialysant is the breadwinner and is incapable of maintaining full-time employment, other members of the family may find it necessary to seek jobs to supplement the family income. Often jobs secured by other family members do not provide adequate salaries to meet the financial deficit created by the dialysant's decrease or loss of income. The result may be a drop in the family's standard of living.

The impact that hemodialysis has upon the afflicted person's occupational pursuits will vary. A great deal depends upon the afflicted person's adjustment to dialysis, the accessibility of home dialysis, and the dialysant's occupation. According to Goldberg (1974), between 50 and 83 percent of chronic hemodialysis patients are able to maintain employment. How well the dialysant has adjusted to the therapy is a primary factor affecting employability. The dialysant who has made an adjustment to the emotional and physical demands of dialysis is more likely to maintain a higher level of employment than the dialysant who is poorly adjusted to the therapy. If the afflicted person has learned to plan activities around the demands of the treatment, there will be fewer difficulties in maintaining employment. In turn, maintaining employment aids in increasing the dialysant's feelings of self-worth and fosters his or her adaptation to long-term therapy.

Research has indicated that individuals maintained on home hemodialysis report the highest rates of employment (Blagg, Hickman, Eschbach, and Scribner, 1970; Pendras and Pollard, 1970). Thus, the second factor affecting the dialysant's employment rate is the accessibility of home hemodialysis. Since this form of dialysis is carried out in the privacy of one's home, there is conservation of time because the afflicted person does not have to spend time going to and from the acute care center for therapy. In addition, the dialysant can carry out any number of tasks and/or occupational pursuits while on dialysis in the privacy of the home.

The dialysant's occupation is a third factor affecting the occupational impact of hemodialysis. For example, Katz (1970) noted that employment was higher for the professional person than for the manual laborer. This finding can be attributed to several factors. Manual labor often requires extensive use of the extremities. If the dialysant requires a cannula for carrying out the therapy, the dangers of traumatizing the cannulated extremity could be greater for the dialysant who is a manual laborer than for the dialysant who is a professional person. The use of an arteriovenous fistula for dialysis, of course, should not present the same problems. In addition, being extremely tired following dialysis is not uncommon. Often the total physical demands on the manual laborer are greater than the total physical demands on a professional person. The result is a decrease in the manual laborer's occupational productivity.

To aid the dialysant in coping with the occupational impact of the therapy, the nurse should assist him or her in dealing with the three major factors that affect employability: adjustment to dialysis, accessibility of home hemodialysis, and the dialysant's occupation. Since the dialysant's adjustment to the therapy plays a vital role in maintaining occupational pursuits, the nurse needs to assist the individual in working through his or her feelings about the therapy. To avoid repetition here, the reader is advised to consult the sections on the emotional, the somatic, and the sexual impact of hemodialysis in this chapter for specific nursing interventions.

The accessibility of home hemodialysis, the second factor affecting the occupational impact of hemodialysis, may be a factor over which the nurse has little control. However, the professional nurse can play a major role in aiding both the dialysant and the family in adjusting to home hemodialysis. If the dialysant or the family encounters grave difficulties in dealing with this form of therapy, the dialysant may be forced to resume hemodialysis in the acute care setting. This move could decrease some of the possibilities for his or her maintenance of employment. To avoid repetition here, the reader is advised to consult the sections on emotional, somatic, and sexual impact in this chapter for specific nursing interventions dealing with the adjustment to home hemodialysis.

The nurse can assume an active part in aiding the dialysant to deal with the third factor affecting employability, the dialysant's occupation. The nurse's function involves assisting the dialysant in identifying and carrying out maneuvers that aid in maintaining his or her employability. Since the presence of a cannula (for some dialysants) and excessive fatigue often create problems, the nurse may find it helpful to contact the rehabilitation counselor, social worker, or occupational therapist for assistance. These specially prepared health team members can contact the dialysant's employer to see if necessary alterations in the work setting or in the dialysant's job responsibilities can be made. For example, jobs that lead to continual contamination of the cannula dressing (e.g., wet environments) often can be altered. Responsibilities that do not demand excessive use of the extremities (if the dialysant requires a cannula) or require excessive physical exertion also might be arranged.

In addition, the nurse will find it beneficial to discuss with the dialysis patient ways to prevent contamination of the cannula dressing and ways to conserve energy. To illustrate, covering the cannula dressing with a piece of plastic that is well sealed around the edges can aid in decreasing contamination in some settings. Arranging one's schedule and job responsibilities in order to avoid unnecessary trips to and from other locations within the work environment can be accomplished. Avoiding heavy lifting also conserves energy. Instead of carrying heavy stacks of papers or pieces of equipment, these items can be placed on a cart and rolled to and from the designated area. By having the dialysant identify energy consuming work situations and ways of dealing with each of these situations, the likelihood of the individual's becoming unnecessarily fatigued will be decreased.

If the dialysant is unable to meet the demands of the job, even after initiating the above suggested maneuvers, a change in occupation may be required. Some dialysants have found working from their homes a feasible means of maintaining economic support. In this way rest and home hemodialysis are easily carried out. Examples of jobs that might be performed in the home setting include repairing electronic equipment (i.e., televisions, radios, stereos), tailoring, maintaining professional office hours, or operating a small business attached to the house. In this case, the dialysant may find it necessary to engage family members in assisting with these forms of employment in order to avoid excessive strain and fatigue. When the means of employment is in the home, it often is easier to involve other family members than if the job were outside the home. Some dialysants, however, may have to undergo retraining in order to maintain a feasible means of employment. And still other dialysants may have to give up work completely.

In summary, although hemodialysis often creates an impact upon the dialysant's occupational stability, it is an impact that usually can be dealt with successfully. The primary goal, if feasible, is to assist the dialysant in maintaining some form of employment. To do this, alterations in the work setting or in job responsibilities may be necessary.

Social Impact

One of the most devastating social impacts created by hemodialysis is the restriction placed upon oral intake. The dialysis patient is continually asked to restrict the consumption of certain foods and fluids. Unlike many other individuals, the dialysis patient cannot eat what he or she likes when he or she wants to. Eating and drinking, mechanisms often used in response to stress, are no longer sensible for the person maintained on dialysis. Social interactions that totally revolve around eating and drinking may require restriction or some alteration. As a result, dealing with diet and fluid restrictions of the dialysis patient tends to be one of the major problems with which the nurse must contend.

To assist the dialysis patient in dealing with dietary and fluid restrictions, the nurse needs to encourage the afflicted individual to verbalize. He or she needs to express his or her feelings about the required alterations in food and fluid consumption. As the dialysant relates these feelings, the nurse will find it helpful to encourage the dialysant to identify ways in which he or she can deal with the imposed alteration in oral gratification. To illustrate, some dialysants find that sucking ice cubes instead of drinking water aids in decreasing the sensation of thirst and in decreasing the frustrations of fluid restriction. Of course, the dialysant must account for the amount of water in the ice cubes when he or she computes the total daily fluid intake. The dialysant may find that serving his or her food in an attractive way aids in palatability which, in turn, helps decrease the anxiety resulting from food restrictions.

If the dialysant plans to attend social functions involving food and drink, he or she can be instructed by the dietician to select food and drink from a menu or a hostess' table that are within the diet restrictions. In planning and spacing the total 24-hour intake, the dialysant should be advised to include the amount of fluid he or she wishes to allot for the social function. Above all, the nurse and the family need to be understanding and supportive of the dialysant as he or she attempts to carry out these food and fluid restrictions. Positive reinforcement should be forthcoming when the dialysant maintains these food and fluid restrictions.

Since the dialysant's mobility is greatly decreased because of the need to be close to a dialysis machine, travel often is restricted. To deal with such a problem, some patients have been known to travel in groups to other dialysis centers within and outside the United States. These trips are organized by organizations such as the National Association of Patients on Hemodialysis and Transplants. Nevertheless, medical problems and scheduling difficulties often impede free travel on the part of the dialysis patient. Dialysis units in the United States may be filled to capacity and unable to accept guest patients. Overseas dialysis centers may be extremely expensive or closed to visitors. As a result, some dialysants have resorted to a compact, travel hemodialysis system (Briefel, Hutchisson, Galonsky, Hessert, and Friedman, 1975). This self-dialysis unit can easily be carried by the patient to a hotel or motel room.

Although travel may be restricted for some dialysants, these individuals need encouragement to avoid withdrawing from others by ceasing their social interaction. Lack of social contact often leads to feelings of frustration and depression which, in turn, impede the dialysant's adjustment to the necessary long-term therapy. Thus, the nurse needs to encourage the dialysant and the family to take part in social functions that are realistic for the dialysant. For example, planning social activities that are not exhausting and that do not occur immediately after therapy (since this often is a time of extreme fatigue) is advisable. The kind of social activity, however, will vary among dialysants since each afflicted person's activity tolerance varies.

In summary, although the dialysant may find it necessary to make alterations in his or her social activities, the dialysant should not totally discontinue socializing with others. The nurse's role involves assisting the family and the dialysant in identifying ways of altering social activities so that the dialysant can continue to carry out an active social life.

SUMMARY

As a result of the malfunction of their kidneys, approximately 25,000 Americans are maintained on hemodialysis, one-quarter of whom are dialyzed in their homes. Dialysis is the passage of particles from an area of high concentration to an area of low concentration across a semipermeable membrane. The basic goals of hemodialysis are to remove from the blood end products of protein metabolism, to maintain a safe concentration of serum electrolytes, to correct acidosis and replenish the blood's bicarbonate system, and to remove excess fluid from the blood.

As a result of the afflicted person's dependence for life upon the dialysis machine, impacts are created upon his or her emotional well-being, somatic identity, sexuality, occupational identity, and social role. Thus, the nurse must assist the individual undergoing hemodialysis to deal, to the best of his or her ability, with each of these impacts.

Patient Situation

Dr. H. D., a thirty-seven-year-old white college professor, who is married and the mother of two children, ages fourteen years and ten years, has been undergoing hemodialysis for the past six months. The D.'s have decided that in the family's best interest it would be advisable for Dr. H. D. to be maintained on home hemodialysis. As a result, the D's are undergoing a home hemodialysis orientation program. During the orientation program the nurse in charge identified problems related to Dr. H. D.'s emotional well-being, somatic identity, sexuality, occupational identity, and social role.

Following are Dr. H. D.'s nursing care plan and patient care cardex dealing with each of these areas of concern.

NURSING CARE PLAN

Problems	Objectives	Nursing Interventions	Principles/Rationale	Evaluations
Emotional Impact Expects husband and children to wait on her.	To assist Dr. H. D. in dealing with her dependency-independency conflict.	Point out to Dr. H. D. that the reality of her illness requires dependence upon the dialysis machine and family members for carrying out the dialysis therapy. Point out behaviors that are unacceptable manifestations of dependence (e.g., demanding behavior and verbal abuse).	Informing the dialysant of acceptable and unacceptable forms of dependence regarding dialysis therapy can aid in decreasing unacceptable demonstrations of dependence.	The nurse would observe for: Dr. H. D.'s decreased manifestation of unacceptable forms of dependence.
		Encourage Dr. H. D. to look at her behavior when she utilizes unacceptable manifestations of dependence (e.g., demanding behavior).	Having the dialysant examine her behavior aids in the development of insight.	
	To foster independence in Dr. H. D.	Encourage Dr. H. D. to take an active part in her therapy (e.g., planning diet and fluid restrictions).	Active participation in one's own care aids in fostering independence.	Dr. H. D.'s increased demonstration of independence.
		Encourage Dr. H. D.'s family to provide positive feedback to Dr. H. D. each time she assumes more independence.	Positive feedback regarding improved behavior aids in building the dialysant's self-esteem.	
		Encourage Dr. H. D. to wear street clothes and to sit in a comfortable recliner when carrying out dialysis therapy.	Avoiding the use of night clothes and a bed during dialysis therapy aids in preventing the mechanical placement of the dialysant in the dependent role of illness.	

NURSING CARE PLAN (cont.)

Problems	Objectives	Nursing Interventions	Principles/Rationale	Evaluations
Emotional Impact (cont.)		Encourage Dr. H. D. to express her feelings about her dependency needs.	Verbalization helps decrease anxiety and aids the dialysant in developing insight.	
		Encourage Dr. H. D.'s family to verbalize their feelings about her manifestations of dependence.	Verbalization aids in decreasing anxiety and aids family members in identifying possible ways of coping with their loved one's dependency needs.	
		Encourage Dr. H. D. to become involved in activities during her dialysis therapy (e.g., reading, grading papers, preparing lectures).	Activity during dialysis therapy aids in fostering independence.	
Somatic Impact Expressed concern about personal appearance because of her sallow, yellow-brown skin and the presence of a cannula in her leg.	To assist Dr. H. D. to cope with her altered body image.	Point out to Dr. H. D. that her skin color changes are a part of the disease process.	Realizing that certain alterations in body image are expected as a result of the disease process aids in decreasing anxiety related to their occurrence.	The nurse would observe for: Dr. H. D.'s verbalization about how she views herself and how she plans to deal with her altered bodily appearance.
	To enhance Dr. H. D.'s feelings of self-worth.	Encourage Dr. H. D. to select clothing colors that do not accentuate her skin color changes (e.g., avoid certain shades of yellow and green).	Feeling attractive to one's self and to others facilitates feelings of self-worth.	Dr. H. D.'s verbalization of how she will alter her clothing style and colors to avoid accentuating her altered body image.
		Encourage Dr. H. D. to express how she feels about the alterations in her skin color and the presence of the cannula in her	Verbalization about one's feelings aids in decreased anxiety and in identifying ways of dealing with one's feelings	

Sexual Impact Expressed concern about her decreased libido.	To facilitate a healthy and mutually satisfying sexual relationship between the D.'s.	Encourage Dr. H. D. to inspect routinely the shunt site and carry out daily dressing changes.	Maintaining good care of the shunt site aids in preventing further alterations in body image caused by the breakdown of the shunt site.	The nurse would observe for: Dr. H. D.'s verbalization of an increased satisfaction in her sexual relationship with her husband.
		Inform Mr. D. that a decrease in libido is not an uncommon occurrence for individuals maintained on hemodialysis.	Spouses aware of the possible existence of sexual alterations occurring in their partners are more likely to be understanding of their partner's problem and are likely to feel less frustrated with the situation.	
		Inform the D.'s of the possible factors that can contribute to the sexual alteration (e.g., tiredness, time consumed by the dialysis therapy, and fears of loss of sexual desirability as a result of skin color changes and the presence of the arteriovenous shunt).	Being aware of factors that can contribute to a sexual alteration aids in assisting the couple in identifying possible ways of coping with the alteration.	
		Encourage the D.'s to discuss and identify ways in which they can facilitate the achievement of a mutually satisfying sexual relationship (e.g., setting aside a specific time for sexual activity, having Mr. D. reassure Dr. H. D. of her sexual desirability, and carrying out maneuvers that aid in preventing dislodgment or pressure on the cannula).	Couples who work together to identify ways to improve their sex life are more likely to achieve mutual satisfaction.	

NURSING CARE PLAN (cont.)

Problems	Objectives	Nursing Interventions	Principles/Rationale	Evaluations
Occupational Impact Expressed concern about being able to maintain teaching responsibilities.	To decrease Dr. H. D.'s concern about being incapacitated as a result of her hemodialysis.	Point out to Dr. H. D. that dialysants on home hemodialysis tend to report a higher rate of employment than dialysants maintained on acute care setting dialysis. Point out that between 50 and 83 percent of chronic hemodialysis patients are able to maintain employment.	Knowing the incidence of employability among dialysants aids in decreasing the afflicted individual's anxiety about job maintainence.	The nurse would observe for: Dr. H. D.'s verbalization about possible ways to alter her work situation so that she can maintain her teaching responsibilities.
		Encourage Dr. H. D. to plan job-related activities around her therapy and to carry out certain job responsibilities while on dialysis (e.g., reading, computing grades, and writing student evaluations).	Dialysants who learn to plan their life's activities around the demands of their therapy encounter fewer difficulties in maintaining employment.	Dr. H. D.'s verbalization that with alterations she feels she will be able to maintain her teaching activities.
		Consult with the rehabilitation counselor, social worker, or occupational therapist.	Health team members specially prepared to deal with the occupational impacts of dialysis are in a position to contact the dialysant's employer to see if necessary alterations in the work setting or in the dialysant's job responsibilities can be made.	
Social Impact Expressed concern about being unable to entertain colleagues and business associates in her home.	To decrease Dr. H. D.'s concern about being unable to socialize. To prevent Dr. H. D.'s withdrawal from social contact.	Encourage Dr. H. D. to think of ways to incorporate her daily food and fluid restrictions into a home social function.	Actually involving the dialysant in planning social activities aids in decreasing the chances of her withdrawal from social contacts.	The nurse would observe for: Dr. H. D.'s verbalization about how she plans to carry out social entertaining in her home and at the same time incorporate her food and

her food and drink in an attractive way. Encourage Dr. H. D.'s family to be supportive of her as she attempts to carry out her food and fluid restrictions when in a social setting.	drink aid in palatibility and, in turn, decrease anxiety resulting from food and fluid restrictions. Positive reinforcement for a job well done in the social setting aids in increasing the dialysant's feelings of self-worth and aids in preventing the individual from withdrawing from social interactions.

PATIENT CARE CARDEX

PATIENT'S NAME: Dr. H. D.

DIAGNOSIS: Chronic renal failure

AGE: 37 years

SEX: Female

MARITAL STATUS: Married

OCCUPATION: College professor

SIGNIFICANT OTHERS: Husband and two children (14 years and 10 years)

Problems	Nursing Approaches
Emotional: Expects husband and children to wait on her.	1. Point out that the reality of the illness requires dependence upon the dialysis machine and family members for carrying out the therapy. 2. Point out behavior that is an unacceptable manifestation of dependence (e.g., demanding behavior). 3. Encourage to look at behavior when utilizing unacceptable manifestations of dependence. 4. Encourage family members to provide positive feedback each time more independence is assumed. 5. Encourage to wear street clothes and to sit in a comfortable recliner when carrying out dialysis therapy. 6. Encourage to express feelings about dependency needs. 7. Encourage family members to verbalize their feelings about their loved one's manifestations of dependence.
Somatic: Expressed concern about personal appearance (sallow, yellow-brown skin and the presence of a cannula in leg).	1. Point out that skin color changes are a part of the disease process. 2. Encourage to select clothing colors that do not accentuate skin color changes (e.g., avoid certain shades of yellow and green). 3. Encourage the expression of feelings about alterations in skin color and the presence of the cannula in her leg. 4. Encourage to wear less fitting clothing over the cannula

libido.

2. Inform both partners of the possible factors that can contribute to sexual alterations (e.g., tiredness or fears of loss of sexual desirability).

3. Encourage both partners to discuss and identify with each other ways in which they can facilitate the achievement of a mutually satisfying sexual relationship (e.g., setting aside a specific time for sexual activity).

Occupational: Expressed concern about being able to maintain teaching responsibilities.

1. Point out that dialysants on home dialysis tend to maintain a higher rate of employment than dialysants maintained on acute care dialysis.

2. Point out that between 50 and 83 percent of chronic dialysants are able to maintain employment.

3. Encourage to plan job-related activities around therapy and to carry out job-related activities during therapy.

4. Consult with the rehabilitation counselor, social worker, or occupational therapist.

Social: Expressed concern about being unable to entertain colleagues and business associates in home.

1. Encourage to think of ways to incorporate daily food and fluid restrictions into the home social function.

2. Encourage to serve food and drink in an attractive way.

3. Encourage family to be supportive during attempts to carry out fluid and food restrictions when in a social setting.

REFERENCES

Abel, J., Rawntree, L., and Turner, B. The removal of diffusible substances from the circulating blood by means of dialysis, *Transactions of the Association of American Physicians.* 1913, *28,* 51-54.

Abram, H. The psychiatrist, the treatment of chronic renal failure, and the prolongation of life: II, *American Journal of Psychiatry,* 1969, *126* (2), 157-167.

Abram, H., Moore, G., and Westerfelt, F. Suicidal behavior in chronic dialysis patients, *American Journal of Psychiatry,* 1971, *127* (9), 1199-1204.

Anderson, K. The psychological aspects of chronic hemodialysis, *Canadian Psychiatric Association Journal,* 1975, *20* (5), 385-391.

Blagg, C., Hickman, R., Eschbach, J., and Scribner, B. Home hemodialysis: six years' experience, *New England Journal of Medicine,* 1970, *283* (21), 1126-1131.

Bommer, J., Tschope, W., Ritz, E., and Andrassy, K. Sexual behavior of hemodialyzed patients, *Clinical Nephrology,* 1976, *6* (1), 315-318.

Briefel, G., Hutchisson, J., Galonsky, R., Hessert, R., and Friedman, E. Compact, travel hemodialysis system, *Proceedings of the Clinical Dialysis Transplant Forum,* 1975, *5* (11), 61-64.

De-Nour, A. Personality factors in chronic hemodialysis patients causing noncompliance with medical regimen, *Psychosomatic Medicine,* 1972, *34* (4), 333-344.

Erikson, E. *Childhood and society.* New York: W. W. Norton and Co., 1963.

Goldberg, R. Vocational rehabilitation of patients on long-term hemodialysis, *Archives of Physical Medicine and Rehabilitation,* 1974, *55* (2), 60-65.

Harari, A., Munitz, H., Wijsenbeek, H., Levi, J., Steiner, M., and Rosenbaum, M. Psychological aspects of chronic haemodialysis, *Psychiatria, Neurologia, Neurochirurgia,* 1971, *74,* 219-223.

Harrington, J., and Brener, E. *Patient care in renal failure.* Philadelphia: W. B. Saunders, Co., 1973.

Hickman, B. All about sex despite dialysis, *American Journal of Nursing,* 1977, *77* (4), 606-607.

Jennrich, J. Some aspects of the nursing care for patients on hemodialysis, *Heart and Lung,* 1975, *4* (6), 885-889.

Katz, A. Patients on chronic hemodialysis in the U.S.: preliminary survey, *Social Science and Medicine,* 1970, *3* (4), 669-677.

Kiil, F. Development of a parallel flow artificial kidney in plastics, *Acta Chirurgica Scandinavica Supplement,* 1960, *253,* 142-150.

Kolff, W., and Watchinger, B. Further developments of a coil kidney: a disposable artificial kidney, *Journal of Laboratory and Clinical Medicine,* 1965, *47* (6), 969-977.

Landsman, M. The patient with chronic renal failure: a marginal man, *Annals of Internal Medicine,* 1975, *82* (2), 268-270.

Levy, N. Sexual adjustment to maintenance hemodialysis and renal transplantation: national survey by questionnaire: preliminary report, *Transactions of the American Society for Artificial Internal Organs,* 1973a, *19,* 138-143.

Levy, N. The psychology and care of the maintenance hemodialysis patient, *Heart and Lung,* 1973b, *2* (3), 400-405.

Luckmann, J., and Sorensen, K. *Medical-surgical nursing: a psychophysiologic approach.* Philadelphia: W. B. Saunders, 1974.

Pendras, J., and Pollard, T. Eight years' experience with community dialysis center: the northwest kidney center, *Transactions of the American Society for Artificial Internal Organs,* 1970, *16,* 77-84.

Reichsman, F., and Levy, N. Problems in adaptation to maintenance hemodialysis, *Archives of Internal Medicine,* 1972, *130* (12), 859-865.

Schreiner, G. Hemodialysis for chronic renal failure, part 3 (medical, moral, and ethical, and socio-economical problems), *Annals of Internal Medicine,* 1965, *62* (3), 551-557.

Streltzer, J., Finkelstein, F., Feigenbaum, H., Kitsen, J., and Cohn, G. The spouses' role in home hemodialysis, *Archives of General Psychiatry,* 1976, *33* (1), 55-58.

U.S. Department of Health, Education and Welfare. *Living with end-stage renal disease.* Washington, D.C.: Public Health Service, Health Services Administration, Bureau of Quality Assurance, U.S. Government Printing Office, 1976.

15

The Patient with an

ALTERATION IN SENSORY EXPERIENCE

INTRODUCTION

Humans are continually exposed to sensory experiences. The types of sensory experiences constantly change. For example, sleep exposes an individual's senses to a low degree of activity, but attending an active sports event exposes an individual's sense to a high degree of activity.

How one interprets and deals with each specific sensory experience also varies among individuals. A sensory experience described as pleasant by one individual may be described as unpleasant by another. To illustrate, a rock concert may be pleasant to the young adult but unpleasant to the elderly individual. Regardless of whether a sensory experience is pleasant or unpleasant, it must be remembered that sensory experiences are necessary in order for humans to function.

The professional nurse often is required to deal with persons who are undergoing alterations in sensory experience. Patients in protective isolation, individuals with visual impairments, people with progressively decreasing hearing ability, patients in pain, and individuals with altered smell and/or taste because of the common cold are but a few examples of individuals undergoing an alteration in a sensory experience. How an afflicted individual deals with an altered sensory experience varies, but an altered sensory experience, regardless of its type, is likely to create an impact upon the afflicted person's emotional well-being, somatic identity, sexuality, occupational identity, and social role.

SENSORY PROCESS

In order for the nurse and other health care professionals to deal effectively with alterations in a sensory experience, they must be cognizant of the sensory process. The sensory process comprises two components: (1) the ability to *receive* mental impressions by way of the body organs and (2) the ability to *perceive* or organize the stimuli received (Chodil and Williams, 1970). Reception is the biological component of the sensory process and includes such functions as hearing, seeing, smelling, and touching. Perception is the psychological component of the sensory process and involves the individual's ability to select and organize the impressions received by the body organs. Without selection and organization of the mental impressions received, the stimuli remain meaningless to the individual involved.

The selection of an impression received is affected by certain characteristics of the stimulus, which include (1) intensity, (2) size, (3) change, and (4) repetition (Chodil and Williams, 1970). For example, the more intense the sound, the more likely it is to be heard. The larger the visual stimuli, the more likely they are to attract attention. A change in stimuli, such as a pink dot in a field of black dots, demands attention because there is a break in the monotony. Finally, frequently repeated stimuli are more likely to be remembered than are infrequently repeated stimuli. It must be remembered, however, that there is a limit to the effectiveness of repetition and, with time, change may become more effective than repetition.

By the same token, the organization of mental experiences received is influenced by certain factors. These factors include past experiences, knowledge, and attitudes. To illustrate, if an individual has encountered a prior experience with a stimulus, how the individual has dealt with the stimulus in the past will have an effect upon the way in which the individual will deal with it now. Knowledge about the stimulus influences how the person will assimilate his or her interpretation of the stimulus into his or her cognitive process. Finally, attitudes about the stimulus will effect the individual's acceptance or rejection of his or her interpretation of the stimulus. If the individual likes the stimulus, no doubt he or she will accept it. If the individual finds the stimulus displeasing, he or she probably will reject it. Thus, it can be seen that the receptive component of the sensory process is an involved experience that depends upon many environmental and personal factors.

SENSORY RESTRICTION VERSUS SENSORY OVERLOAD

Humans rely upon sensory experiences in order to survive. To be totally deprived of sensory experiences results in sensory deprivation and eventual death. Thus, one's experiences can be viewed as a continuum. The individual's sensory balance lies in the middle of the continuum with sensory deprivation and sensory overload lying on opposite ends (see Figure 1).

An individual finds himself or herself somewhere on this sensory experience continuum every moment of his or her life. Since sensory experiences are constantly changing, an individual will be in a constant state of flux on this sensory experience continuum. To illustrate, when an individual is confronted with a decrease in sensory balance, he or she falls in the area of sensory restriction, that is, to the left of the sensory experience continuum. When a person is bombarded and becomes overtaxed with a sensory experience, he or she falls in the area of sensory overload, that is, to the right of the sensory experience continuum.

Health team members are frequently confronted with situations in which sensory restriction or sensory overload occurs. For example, sensory restriction can occur with the eye-patched cataract patient, with the individual who is in isolation because of a contagious disease, with the individual who is suffering from loss of sight because of glaucoma, with the person who is losing his or her sense of hearing because he or she is aging, and even with the individual who is living in an isolated region of the country. By comparison, sensory overload is not uncommon for the individual requiring care in the intensive care unit, for the newly diagnosed diabetic being taught all of his or her necessary health care measures, for the individual admitted to an acute care setting for the first time, or for the recently discharged patient returning home to curious and inquisitive relatives and neighbors.

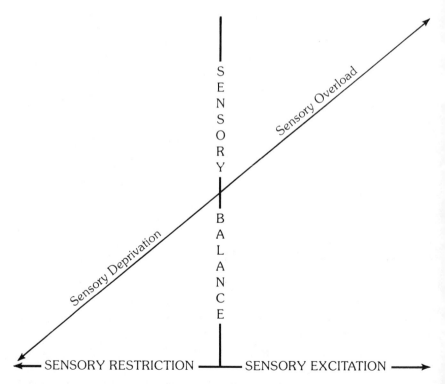

Figure 1   Man's sensory experience continuum

How an individual deals with each sensory experience makes him or her unique. Therefore, the professional nurse and other health team members must be cognizant of the individuality of each person as health care related to his or her sensory experiences is being planned.

IMPACT OF SENSORY ALTERATIONS

Emotional Impact*

Since humans rely upon sensory experiences in order to function, it is no wonder that when alterations in sensory experiences occur the afflicted person manifests certain emotional responses. Research shows that persons subjected both to sensory restriction and sensory overload manifest boredom, impaired concentration and lack of coherent thinking, anxiety, fear, depression, rapid mood changes, and even the extreme of auditory and visual hallucinations (Lindsley, 1961; Bolin, 1974; Chodil and Williams, 1970). The intensity of these emotional responses is very individual and may range from mild to severe.

The primary responsibility of the nurse when dealing with alterations in sensory experiences revolves around preventing their occurrence. The nurse must be continually observant and cognizant of situations that can contribute to the development of alterations in sensory experiences. Once the nurse or other members of the health team have identified potential and existing situations leading to altered sensory experiences, intervention must occur. The environment has to be manipulated in an attempt to prevent and/or decrease the occurrence of emotional responses that result from sensory alterations. For example, when the nurse has identified that a patient will be required to wear eye patches after cataract surgery, alternate sensory experiences will have to be provided for the patient. When a patient enters an intensive care unit, the nurse needs to be aware that many individuals have difficulty dealing with the bombardment and overtaxing sensory stimulation in such a setting. As a result, alterations in the environment may have to be provided (e.g., periodic dimming of the lights), as well as constant feedback to the afflicted person that the feelings he or she is experiencing are not unusual in such a situation.

In order to plan appropriate health care for an individual who is subjected to alterations in sensory experiences, it is essential for the nurse to obtain a data base from both the individual and the family about past activities in which the afflicted person has taken part. This prepares the nurse to identify activities and situations that will provide meaning for the individual's

---

*It is advisable for the reader to have read Chapters 1 and 3 before continuing with this section.

sensory experiences. Boredom, one of the emotional responses to an altered sensory experience, can best be dealt with by providing the afflicted person with a variety of ways to explore his or her environment. For example, the individual in protective isolation can be given puzzles to put together, books to read, television to watch, a radio to listen to, or handicrafts with which to work. But before providing any of these activities, it is best for the nurse to discuss with the patient his or her interests and then determine the feasibility of each activity. By involving the afflicted person in selecting activities, provisions are made to provide for activities that are personally meaningful.

In the case of the individual suffering from alterations in visual function or alterations in auditory function, the remaining senses need to be activated in an attempt to compensate for the altered sense. To illustrate, the eye-patched individual may require more sensory input by way of verbal and/or nonverbal communication. For example, it is important to announce one's presence to the afflicted individual and to describe what is occurring in the environment. In addition, human touch can provide a great deal of sensory input for the visually impaired person. Touch provides not only comfort, but it is also a means of nonverbal communication. To encourage the individual experiencing a visual deficit to explore the environment, the nurse should encourage the individual to listen to a radio, attend a concert, and verbally interact with others.

For the individual afflicted with a hearing deficit, enhancing the remaining senses is valuable. For example, utilizing communication through sight, as in the written form, is beneficial. To prevent or deal with boredom, providing reading material and handicrafts with which to work or planning visits to museums are a few possible and feasible activities. Again, the nurse must never underestimate the value of human touch. Simply holding an individual's hand transmits the feeling of caring and the existence of another's presence. Above all, it is valuable to identify with the afflicted person and the family activities that possibly may stimulate him or her. Such an act can lead to a variety of creative and meaningful activities.

The emotional responses of impaired concentration and lack of coherent thinking can best be dealt with by engaging the sensory afflicted person in conversation on topics that he or she finds meaningful and by providing him or her with time orientation. For example, if the nurse or other members of the health team have identified an individual's interest as sports, involving the person in conversation about sports can be beneficial. In addition, if the nurse identifies others who share a similar interest, encouraging interaction between them can prove most helpful in preventing impaired concentration and incoherent thinking. If an individual afflicted with a hearing impairment has a problem with conversation, written communication or sign language may have to be utilized. Clocks and calendars prove very helpful in providing time orientation. Verbally orienting the person to date and time can also be beneficial. The following statements are a means of providing time orientation: "This certainly is a cold October morning!" "Mr. J., how are you this fine Thursday afternoon?"

To deal with the emotional responses of anxiety, fear, and depression, the nurse will find it helpful to provide the individual suffering from sensory alterations with meaningful reference points that indicate progress toward a goal. This can be achieved by pointing out the person's improvements in health status. For example, the nurse will find it beneficial to point out to the newly diagnosed diabetic who is experiencing sensory overload while learning necessary health care therapies what he or she is doing for himself or herself (i.e., planning his or her own diet) that he or she had not done in the past. Another example is indicating to the individual with an auditory deficit how he or she has improved his or her observation skills. By providing the sensory afflicted person with reference points that show progress, a sense of security can be created. As a result, anxiety, fear, and depression are likely to be decreased.

A sudden change in mood constitutes another possible emotional response suffered by the individual afflicted with an alteration in sensory experience. But before the nurse concludes that an individual's mood change is a result of an altered sensory experience, it is necessary for a complete physical and psychosocial assessment to be made. Since there are many physical conditions and psychosocial situations that can contribute to sudden mood changes, it is best that these contributing factors be ruled out. Once an alteration in sensory experience has been identified as the contributing factor in the person's sudden mood change, then the nurse must determine whether the alteration in sensory experiences is a result of sensory restriction or sensory overload. After this has been determined, appropriate nursing intervention can proceed.

If sensory restriction is a problem, measures should be instituted to increase appropriate sensory stimulation. If sensory overload is the difficulty, alterations in the environment to decrease sensory stimulation are needed. Nursing interventions discussed earlier in this chapter are applicable for dealing with this particular response to an alteration in sensory experiences. In addition, it is advisable for the nurse and other members of the health care team to explore with the afflicted individual his or her sudden change in mood. In other words, the nurse must find out if the patient has any insight into his or her behavior and if the patient can identify ways of altering this behavior. With the assistance of health team members many individuals with alterations in sensory experiences are able to identify creative ways of dealing with their responses to sensory restriction or sensory overload.

The final emotional response to altered sensory experiences, hallucinations (auditory or visual), is without a doubt the most devastating response. To deal with such an emotional response, the nurse needs to provide the afflicted individual with reality validation so that the individual does not have to read nonexistent stimuli into the environment. In other words, the nurse must not feed into or challenge the individual's hallucinatory experiences. For example, if the afflicted person says that he or she hears the androids calling him or her, an appropriate response from the nurse would be, "I'm sure the androids seem real to you, but I do not hear them. It must be very frightening for you to have these experiences." Patience and an understanding of why the afflicted person is responding in such a manner are a must. Psychotherapy and psychotropic medications may be in order for the hallucinating individual.

In summary, emotional responses to alterations in sensory experiences can occur. These responses may include boredom, diminished concentration, lack of coherent thinking, anxiety, fear, depression, sudden mood changes, and hallucinations. The severity of these emotional responses will vary among individuals. When something happens that causes an alteration in a sensory experience, the nurse must try to deal with it appropriately.

Somatic Impact*

The impact that an alteration in sensory experience has upon a person's body image varies among individuals. Both the specific sensory alteration and how the afflicted person reacts to that alteration play vital roles in the resulting changes in body image. For example, a visual impairment may be viewed by the afflicted person as impinging upon his or her ability to communicate effectively since he or she cannot see the eye movements or facial expressions of others. An auditory alteration often is thought of as a "nonvisible" handicap. Unfortunately, people with hearing deficits often are labeled slow or dull because their inability to hear what is going on causes their responses to be delayed. Since others cannot see the auditory deficit, understanding often is lacking. Therefore, the nurse needs to be aware of how the sensory alteration itself has affected the person and in what way the afflicted person perceives himself or herself.

The person afflicted with an alteration in sight will have to rely upon his or her other senses to a greater degree in order to obtain data about himself or herself and the environment. Often touch becomes an alternate and vital means of obtaining personal and environmental data. Since the afflicted individual cannot see his or her body parts and must rely solely upon touch, there may be distortions in the interpretations of the body image. For example, if there is a lesion on the leg of a visually impaired person, he or she may misinterpret the size and condition of the lesion because he or she relies solely upon touch to obtain data about the lesion. If an auditory impaired individual is not able, by alternate means, to understand what others

---

*It is advisable for the reader to have read Chapter 2 before continuing with this section.

are saying about his or her personal and environmental well-being, he or she may become suspicious of others. By the same token, the individual placed in protective isolation may view his or her body image as dirty and undesirable since everyone coming near him or her wears protective clothing.

The stage of development being experienced by the individual with an altered sensory experience also has an effect upon the afflicted person's adaptation to the sensory alteration. The afflicted person in the stage of young adulthood (eighteen to forty-five years) may encounter difficulties in sharing himself or herself with others both in friendship and in a mutually satisfying relationship. It is during this developmental stage that the young adult is ready and willing to merge his or her identity with that of others (Erikson, 1963). Since the individual is suffering from an alteration in a sensory experience, the individual may view his or her body as less than perfect or desirable to himself or herself and to others. The results may be withdrawal from others and isolation.

The stage of adulthood (forty-five to sixty-five years) is the period in one's life when a vital interest outside the home is founded. The major focus for the adult during this time is to establish and guide future generations with the hope of bettering society (Erikson, 1963). If an individual in the stage of adulthood encounters an alteration in a sensory experience, he or she may feel ill-equipped to guide future generations. The individual may view his or her altered sensory experience as a premature sign of old age and, as a result, become engulfed in personal needs and self-comforts and enter into a state of self-absorption and stagnation.

The final stage of life, the stage of maturity (sixty-five years and over), brings with it frequent thoughts of death. The mature adult tends to derive strength from satisfaction in his or her life's experiences and accomplishments (Erikson, 1963). When an alteration in a sensory experience occurs, the mature adult may develop feelings of despair that are manifested by disgust.

The nurse's role in dealing with an individual who has sustained an alteration in sensory experiences revolves around assisting the afflicted person in coping with these alterations. To accomplish this, the nurse will find it advisable to encourage the afflicted person to verbalize how he or she feels about himself or herself. For example, does the individual feel less than perfect because he or she cannot see? Does the individual feel that others think him or her dull or slow because he or she cannot hear? Does the individual think that he or she is repulsive to others because he or she requires protective isolation? Finally, does the individual feel insane because he or she finds it impossible to tolerate the noises in the intensive care unit? These are but a few thoughts that may enter the mind of the person encountering an altered sensory experience. As the individual discloses these feelings about himself or herself, the nurse will find it beneficial to aid the individual in exploring ways of dealing with these feelings.

To illustrate, if the auditory impaired person feels ostracized by others during conversation, he or she needs to be encouraged to verbalize to others ways to include him or her in the conversation (i.e., use of sign language, written communication, or measures to facilitate lip reading). If the person is suffering from an overload of sensory experiences, the nurse needs to encourage the person to aid others in helping him or her identify those environmental factors which are overwhelming (e.g., the presence of constant, bright lights or the continual beeping of the cardiac monitor). Once overwhelming stimuli are identified, such maneuvers as dimming the lights or providing soft relaxing radio music through earphones can be provided.

Above all, the person afflicted with an alteration in a sensory experience must be provided with correct data about himself or herself and the environment. To illustrate, since a visually impaired person cannot see the intricacies of body lesions he or she may have, the nurse must make a concerted effort to describe the appearance of these body lesions. If this is not done, misinterpretation and distortion about the individual's body image may result. If the auditory impaired person cannot communicate with others, feelings of isolation may result. The auditory impaired individual may interpret his or her feelings of isolation to be the result of a less than perfect body. Adequate alternate means of communication must be provided. Finally, the individual placed in protective isolation may feel that others find him or her disgusting and, therefore, avoid him or her. Thus, the nurse must make an effort to provide appropriate sensory experiences for the individual. Simply stopping in to visit with the person in protective isolation and making body contact, by touching, are two basic and helpful measures that can prevent misinterpretation of the environment as a result of altered sensory experiences.

In summary, the individual afflicted with an alteration in sensory experiences can also sustain an altered body image. This alteration is often the result of misinterpreting the environment and one's personal well-being. It is the responsibility of the nurse and other health team members to provide the person afflicted with an alteration in a sensory experience with adequate and appropriate data about himself or herself and the environment through his or her intact and functioning senses.

Sexual Impact

The specific impact that an alteration in a sensory experience may have upon one's sexuality often depends upon the sensory alteration itself. Feelings of inadequacy or feelings of being sexually undesirable may result in the person afflicted with an alteration in a sensory experience. If the afflicted person feels less than perfect, he or she may believe that others see him or her that way too. Therefore, it is necessary for the nurse and other health team members to recognize the effect that a specific alteration in a sensory experience may have upon an individual. For example, the individual suffering from visual impairment cannot rely upon sight for sexual stimulation. He or she is unable to become sexually aroused by looking at the sex partner. The individual cannot see the sex partner's response to his or her sexual advances. During the sex act the visually impaired person must rely solely upon touch and sound to determine the effectiveness of his or her role during sex play and coitus.

The individual who has sustained an auditory impairment is unable to hear what the sex partner is saying during sexual activities. Whether or not the sex partner is enjoying the maneuvers of sex play will have to be determined by the auditory impaired person by means other than sound. Erotic thoughts cannot be aroused in the afflicted person by means of verbal communication or relaxing music. As a result, the other senses need to be utilized for producing sexual excitement. If the sense of touch or smell is impaired, the afflicted person will be unable to utilize these senses for enhancing erotic feelings. In the case of touch, body areas that have sustained alterations in sensation should be avoided during the act of caressing. Caressing sensory impaired body areas may fail to arouse erotic feelings and thus lead to feelings of frustrations for both the afflicted person and the sex partner. If the sense of smell is impaired, the use of colognes or powders that enhance erotic feelings may prove unsuccessful for the afflicted person. In such a case, the person afflicted with an alteration in a sensory experience will need to identify alternate sensory experiences that will aid in providing the fulfillment of a sexual relationship for both the afflicted person and the sex partner.

The individual placed in protective isolation may find many of his or her sensory experiences altered. It is not uncommon for this person to act out inappropriate sexual behavior (i.e., a male patient's patting a female nurse's buttocks). Since the isolated victim cannot fulfill his or her sexual needs in a physical manner because of his or her physical removal from others, he or she may attempt to meet sexual needs through delusional mechanisms (i.e., dreaming about sexual fulfillment or imagining the effect his or her sexual prowess has upon members of the opposite sex). As a result, the isolated person may be faced with having to provide his or her own sexual fulfillment.

In the case of the individual suffering from an overload of sensory stimulation, sexual satisfaction also may create a problem. Coping with a constant bombardment of stimuli from the environment may render the afflicted person totally incapable of dealing with his or her sexual needs. For example, since part of one's sexuality is psychic, the sensory overloaded person may be unable to relax enough to enjoy a sexual experience. This overloaded sensorium results in an intrapsychic sexual conflict. Thus, it can be seen that whether a person is suffering from a restriction or an overload in a sensory experience, an impact upon sexuality can result.

The nurse's role in dealing with the sexual impact of an alteration in a sensory experience revolves around assisting the afflicted person and the sex partner to identify and utilize alternate sensory experiences that can enhance a fulfilling sexual relationship. To accomplish this goal, the nurse needs to encourage the afflicted person and the sex partner to verbalize their feelings to each other about the effect the altered sensory experience has upon their sexual relationship. By sharing their feelings, the couple can more easily identify possible and existing areas of concern. For example, the sex partner may be caressing a sensory-deprived body part of the afflicted person and then become totally frustrated because no sexual arousal results. A problem such as this hopefully can be identified and resolved by verbally sharing feelings.

Once areas of concern are identified, ways to deal with each of the areas of concern need to be developed. To illustrate, if an individual suffers from auditory impairment, the sex partner and afflicted person may have to develop some means of communicating during their sexual experience. For example, to communicate to the auditory impaired individual that certain sexual activities are displeasurable, the sex partner could gently tap the impaired individual's arm in order to transmit the message. A gentle stroke on the arm of the auditory impaired person could be used to transmit the message of pleasure.

For the person placed in protective isolation, the nurse may find it advisable to encourage uninterrupted sessions for the afflicted person and the sex partner. Such sessions can allow for private conversation and caressing. Often their own beliefs about human sexuality prevent members of the health care team from encouraging sexual relations between a patient and his or her sex partner in an acute care setting.

In the case of sensory overload, the afflicted person and sex partner may have to be encouraged to discuss and identify ways of assisting the afflicted person to relax so that he or she can have a fulfilling sexual experience. Taking warm baths or showers, listening to relaxing music, or discussing pleasant topics prior to sexual activity are but a few possible maneuvers to use in aiding relaxation. The important factor is for the sensory overloaded individual and the sex partner to find maneuvers that are relaxing and sexually satisfying for both.

Whether the afflicted person suffers from sensory restriction or sensory overload, the nurse needs to encourage the individual to maintain a high standard of personal appearance. An appealing appearance not only increases one's feelings of self-worth, but it also makes one appealing to others.

In summary, the person afflicted with an alteration in a sensory experience may sustain an alteration in sexuality, but with the assistance of the nurse and other members of the health care team, alternate sensory experiences can be identified and utilized that can aid in the sexual fulfillment of both the afflicted person and the sex partner.

Occupational Impact

The impact that an altered sensory experience has upon one's occupational pursuits depends upon the specific requirements of the job. Exactly which capabilities are necessary for the job will determine whether or not the person's altered sensory experience will hinder his or her occupational endeavors. For example, if excellent vision is an important factor for a specific job, such as piloting a commercial airplane, then a person afflicted with any kind of visual impairment may encounter difficulties with this job. In addition, both the degree of the altered sensory experience and the kind of altered sensory experience have an effect upon one's occupation. For example, moderate difficulties in visual acuity, color blindness, and total blindness are all visual alterations, but each one imposes a different impact upon the person's occupational situation. Therefore, before an individual can be labeled as ill-suited for an occupation, the precise effect that the altered sensory experience imposes upon the work situation must be identified.

Alterations in visual experiences can impose a variety of problems for an afflicted person. To illustrate, if the job entails reading fine print, visual acuity is essential. If one's visual acuity is less than desirable, but if it can be improved by corrective lenses, a problem no longer may exist. If, however, wearing corrective lenses in an attempt to deal with an impairment in visual acuity becomes a hazard in the work situation, the individual may find it necessary to make alterations in his or her job. Color blindness, another altered visual experience, can create difficulties in a work situation. For example, an individual afflicted with color blindness may find it difficult to obtain jobs in which identifying colors is essential, as in the case of an air traffic controller. Even certain professionals in the health care system, for example, medical technologists, rely upon their ability to detect changes in color (e.g., color changes that occur during testing glucose in the urine).

Alterations in hearing can create problems for the afflicted person while in the work situation. The person afflicted with severe hearing deficits may find it difficult to carry out a job that involves identifying and recording various sounds. Occupations involving use of the telephone, such as that of a receptionist, might be out of the question for the auditory impaired person. If, however, the hearing deficit is manageable by amplification of the sound, as with a hearing aid or by using a printout of the spoken word, jobs involving phone usage would be feasible. In some occupations being able to identify sounds may not be crucial, but the hearing impairment itself may be a safety hazard for the afflicted person. For example, a heavy machine operator may not need excellent hearing to operate the machine, but he or she must be able to hear verbal commands from others to stop or start the machine. If he or she cannot hear these commands, the safety of others may be at stake. Here an alteration in job responsibilities may prove essential.

Alterations in smell, in taste, and in touch can create an impact upon one's occupational pursuits. For example, someone who is involved in the culinary arts may find it difficult to judge the quality of fine foods and drink if taste and/or smell are hindered. By the same token, an altered sense of touch may greatly impede the individual who relies upon sensitive hands and fingers to carry out his or her occupational endeavors. An altered sense of touch in the hands or fingers could create an occupational hazard for someone who works with very hot and very cold items.

The nurse must not forget that sensory overload is just as likely as sensory restriction to have an impact upon one's occupational pursuits. Undoubtedly, the greatest occupational impacts created by sensory overload deal with safety and high-quality performance in the work setting. The person encountering sensory overload is less likely to focus his or her total attention on his or her work. If the individual is bombarded by sensory experiences, most likely chances for an accident will increase and the quality of his or her work will decrease. For example, the bookkeeper afflicted with sensory overload is more likely to make errors than the bookkeeper not afflicted with sensory overload. The assembly line worker suffering from sensory overload is more likely to be involved in an accident caused by lack of attention than is the nonsensory overloaded worker. Thus, it is evident that both sensory restriction and sensory overload have an impact upon one's occupation.

The nurse's responsibility related to the occupational impact of alterations in sensory experiences revolves around identifying whether the altered sensory experience will affect the afflicted person's ability to perform his or her job responsibilities. If the altered sensory experience creates difficulties in the occupational setting, the nurse and other health team members need to identify ways in which changes can be made in the work environment to deal with the afflicted person's altered sensory experience. For example, if an individual suffers from auditory alterations and his or her job involves using the telephone, possibly this responsibility could be delegated to someone else in the job setting. If visual impairment is present and the afflicted person's job relies upon the ability to identify an object by sight, possibly a job relying upon his or her other senses, such as hearing and touch, could be arranged. If sensory overload creates problems in the work environment, an alteration of the stimulus or its removal from the environment should be considered. If it is impossible to make the necessary adjustments in the environment, the afflicted person may have to consider job retraining. The nurse will find it helpful and beneficial to call upon the expertise of the social worker, the occupational therapist, or the rehabilitation counselor for assistance in identifying and dealing with the occupational impact created by an altered sensory experience.

In summary, alterations in sensory experiences can create problems for the afflicted person who is working. Before a judgment is made on whether the afflicted person's altered sensory experience will affect his or her ability to carry out the job responsibilities, the specific occupational impact that the alteration imposes must be identified. The nurse's role in dealing with the occupational impact of an altered sensory experience involves identifying which alterations in the work situation, if any, have to be made and then dealing with these needed changes.

Social Impact

The social impact created by an altered sensory experience will depend upon the specific sensory experience that has undergone change. For example, in cases of sensory restriction, such as auditory, visual, olfactory, and gustatory impairment, the effect that each change imposes will depend upon the specific social encounter.

Social events that deal exclusively with visual interaction may not be enjoyable for the visually impaired person. For example, movies are enjoyable only when they do not depend greatly on visual detail for their impact. The afflicted person may find it beneficial to have another person along to describe what is occurring visually. Unfortunately, this can create difficulties because it may annoy other people in the theater. Concerts and lectures may be desirable alternatives to attending movies. In addition, many visually impaired people find enjoyment in touring historical sections of cities or walking through arboretums and gardens where braille signs and recorded speeches describe the location and the foliage. The fragrances in the gardens can be an additional pleasant feature.

Social engagements that focus largely on conversation may be enjoyable for the visually impaired, since he or she is able to hear the conversation of others and to take part in the discussion. One possible inconvenience lies in the inability of the visually impaired person to rely upon nonverbal indicators, such as facial expressions and body language, to understand what is going on. As a result, important clues in nonverbal communication may be missed by the afflicted person. For example, if one of the members of a small group at a social gathering walks away, his or her absence may not be detected by the visually impaired person.

Another difficulty that the visually impaired person may encounter is transportation to and from social events. In large cities the afflicted individual may feel vulnerable to attackers and muggers if he or she rides public transportation. In rural areas lack of sufficient transportation may hinder his or her ability to attend a social event. In either case, the visually impaired person may prefer to be transported by car with a friend or family member if it is at all possible. If this kind of transportation is not available, the visually impaired person may have to rely upon public transportation.

The person afflicted with an auditory impairment is faced with social setting problems of a different nature. For example, at social gatherings where conversation is the primary source of entertainment, the person with an auditory impairment may feel isolated if he or she cannot read lips or communicate with others by sign language or the written word. Even if the person with an auditory impairment can read lips if fluorescent lights are used, which can be a strain on the eyes, or if the lighting creates shadows on the faces of the individual who is speaking, lip reading may become difficult. In addition, it is very tiring for an auditory impaired person to read lips in order to keep up with the conversation. Activities that an auditory impaired person might find enjoyable include T.V., observing a sports event, such as a basketball game, or attending a movie that has subtitles. Television, however, can be frustrating if the afflicted person has difficulty lip reading. Because of this difficulty, some television programs have an individual communicate their verbal messages in sign language for those who are auditorily impaired. Additional forms of entertainment for the afflicted person may include visiting museums or art centers.

Most social occasions can be enjoyed by the individual afflicted with an alteration in smell and/or taste except those involving food and drink. If the afflicted person has alterations in olfaction and gustation, he or she may not find it enjoyable to spend money on a lavish meal or on tasty drinks. Thus, it would be advisable for the individual to engage in entertainment that does not focus mainly on the consumption of culinary delights.

Individuals afflicted with sensory overload also encounter difficulties in the social setting. If a person is overwhelmed by sensory stimuli, he or she may find it difficult to enjoy himself or herself at a social engagement. To illustrate, the person from a rural area who has come to a metropolitan area for the sole purpose of entertainment may feel overwhelmed by the large number of people and the congested traffic. As a result, he or she may find it difficult to direct his or her attention to the social function he or she came to enjoy. The individual's inability to relax and enjoy the social encounter because of his or her overloaded sensorium may make him or her unpleasant company.

The nurse's role in dealing with the social impact of altered sensory experiences involves identifying social encounters that are enjoyable for the afflicted person and making necessary adaptations in the social setting to facilitate the afflicted person's comfort. For example, if the visually impaired person enjoys movies or plays but is uncomfortable in public when he or she has to have someone verbalize the visual data of the production, an alternative may be to enjoy T.V. at home or attend drive-in movies with family or friends who augment the auditory component of the program by verbalizing the visual data. If a visually impaired person enjoys playing cards, braille playing cards can be used so that the afflicted person can play both with sighted and nonsighted friends. Reading braille or being read to, either by way of a recorded message or with the assistance of a reader are other forms of entertainment that the visually impaired individual may enjoy.

If sensory overload is a problem in the social setting, the nurse needs to aid the person in identifying those social settings that may add to the sensory overload. For example, a sports event in a large arena where there is a large crowd may overwhelm the individual who comes from a small, noncongested community. Placing this person in such a social setting will undoubtedly decrease the chances for enjoying the event. Thus, it may be advisable for the nurse to encourage the selection of a social event that is not so crowded. When a person from a large metropolitan area moves to an isolated rural town, sensory restriction may result. Here the nurse will find it necessary to identify events and activities that the person can attend for a stimulating sensory experience.

In summary, social encounters are vital for the person afflicted with an altered sensory experience, and with the assistance of health team members, family, and friends, enjoyable and appropriate social activities can be identified for and attended by the person with an altered sensory experience.

SUMMARY

Humans are continually exposed to a variety of sensory experiences. How each person deals with each sensory experience makes him or her unique. An experience seen as pleasant by one individual may be seen as unpleasant by another.

The nurse often is required to deal with individuals who are undergoing alterations in a sensory experience. These alterations may include a restriction in the sensory experience or an overload in the sensory experience. Whether the person is afflicted with a restriction or an overload in a sensory experience, the individual's altered sensory experience is likely to create an impact upon his or her emotional well-being, somatic identity, sexuality, occupational identity, and social role.

Patient Situation

Miss S. A. is a forty-nine-year-old, single, American Sioux Indian who is suffering from progressive loss of vision due to glaucoma. For the past twenty-five years she has been living in a small housing project on an Indian reservation. For economic support, Miss S. A. beads Indian jewelry which she sends to jewelry stores in surrounding cities.

Miss S. A. is currently being treated for glaucoma at the health clinic on the reservation. During her last clinic visit the nurse in charge of her care identified problems related to Miss S. A.'s emotional well-being, somatic identity, sexuality, occupational identity, and social role.

Following are Miss S. A.'s nursing care plan and patient care cardex dealing with each of these areas of concern.

NURSING CARE PLAN

Problems	Objectives	Nursing Interventions	Principles/Rationale	Evaluations
Emotional Impact Expressed anxiety about the presence of visual impairment.	To decrease Miss S. A.'s anxiety.	Provide Miss S. A. with meaningful reference points indicating progress toward a goal (e.g., explain and point out to Miss S. A. that by adhering to her prescribed therapies, the incidence of her progressive visual impairment will be greatly reduced).	Having a meaningful reference point with which to relate aids in decreasing anxiety.	The nurse would observe for: Miss S. A.'s verbalization about how her anxiety concerning her visual impairment has decreased.
	To prevent further progression of Miss S. A.'s anxiety.	Encourage Miss S. A. to verbalize her anxiety.	Verbalization aids in decreasing anxiety and assists the individual in identifying ways of dealing with anxiety.	Miss S. A.'s verbalization about her feelings.
Somatic Impact Expressed fear of looking distorted.	To decrease Miss S. A.'s misconception about her body image. To provide Miss S. A. with correct data about her body image.	Provide Miss S. A. with accurate verbal data about her personal appearance (e.g., describe to her how she appears).	Visually impaired individuals must rely upon touch to obtain data about their body image. As a result, distortions in their interpretation of their body image may occur. Providing a visually impaired person with verbal feedback about the actual appearance of her body can aid in decreasing her misconceptions about her body image.	The nurse would observe for: Miss S. A.'s accurate description of her body image.
		Encourage Miss S. A. to verbalize how she feels about herself (e.g., does she view her body as less than perfect since she has a visual impairment?).	Verbalization of feelings aids the individual in exploring ways of dealing with her feelings.	

Problems	Objectives	Nursing Interventions	Principles/Rationale	Evaluations
Sexual Impact Verbalized fear of appearing unfeminine.	To enhance Miss S. A.'s feelings of self-worth.	Encourage Miss S. A. to maintain an appealing personal appearance (e.g., dress neatly, keep hair clean and arranged in an orderly fashion, and wear garments that are becoming to her).	Maintaining a high standard of personal appearance aids in increasing one's feelings of self-worth and makes one appealing to others.	The nurse would observe for: Miss S. A.'s verbalization about feeling attractive to herself and others.
Occupational Impact Expressed fear of not being able to continue beading Indian jewelry.	To enhance Miss S. A.'s ability to maintain her occupational pursuits.	Encourage Miss S. A. to use visual aids (e.g., her prescribed glasses and/or a magnifying glass).	Providing appropriate alterations in the work environment can facilitate the visually impaired individual's chances of maintaining her occupational endeavors.	The nurse would observe for: Miss S. A.'s verbalization that she is able to carry out her Indian beading.
		Encourage Miss S. A. to use good lighting when she works with her beads.	Lighting that does not cause shadows or eyestrain facilitates the individual's ability to carry out activities that involve vision.	
		Encourage Miss S. A. to take periodic breaks during her beading sessions.	Resting the eyes periodically aids in preventing eyestrain and, in turn, facilitates the ability to carry out activities that involve vision.	
Social Impact Withdrawal from social events that take place on the reservation.	To prevent Miss S. A. from becoming socially isolated.	Encourage Miss S. A. to attend social activities on the reservation.	Engaging in social activities prevents withdrawal and social isolation.	The nurse would observe for: Miss S. A.'s increased involvement in social activities.
	To involve Miss S. A. in social activities.	Encourage Miss S. A. to contact friends for transportation to and from the social activities	Lack of public transportation in rural areas may hinder the visually impaired person's	

PATIENT CARE CARDEX

PATIENT'S NAME: Miss S. A.	DIAGNOSIS: Glaucoma and progressive visual impairment
AGE: 49 years	SEX: Female
MARITAL STATUS: Single	OCCUPATION: Beader of Indian jewelry
SIGNIFICANT OTHERS: Fellow tribal members	

Problems	Nursing Approaches
Emotional: Expressed anxiety about the presence of visual impairment.	1. Provide meaningful reference points indicating progress toward a goal (e.g., explain and point out how adherence to prescribed therapies will reduce the incidence of progressive visual impairment). 2. Encourage verbalization of anxiety.
Somatic: Expressed fear of looking distorted.	1. Provide accurate verbal data about her personal appearance (e.g., describe to her how she appears). 2. Encourage verbalization of how she feels about herself. (Does she view her body as less than perfect because she has a visual impairment?)
Sexual: Verbalized fear of appearing unfeminine.	1. Encourage maintenance of an appealing personal appearance (dress neatly, keep hair clean, and wear becoming clothing).
Occupational: Expressed fear of not being able to continue beading Indian jewelry.	1. Encourage use of visual aids (e.g., prescribed glasses and/or a magnifying glass). 2. Encourage use of good lighting when working with beads. 3. Encourage taking periodic breaks during beading sessions.
Social: Withdrawal from social events on the reservation.	1. Encourage to attend social activities on the reservation. 2. Encourage contacting friends for transportation to and from social activities.

REFERENCES

Bolin, R. Sensory deprivation: an overview, *Nursing Forum*, 1974, *13* (3), 241-258.

Chodil, J., and Williams, B. The concept of sensory deprivation, *Nursing Clinics of North America*, 1970, *5* (3), 453-465.

Erikson, E. *Childhood and society*. New York: W. W. Norton and Co., 1963.

Lindsley, D. Common factors in sensory deprivation, sensory distortion, and sensory overload. In P. Solomon, P. Kutzansky, P. Leiderman, J. Mandelson, R. Trumbull, and D. Wexler (Eds.), *Sensory deprivation*. Cambridge, Mass.: Harvard University Press, 1961.

INDEX